LEARNING COMMERCIAL LAW: CORE CONCEPTS

SECOND EDITION

• • •

Wayne Barnes

Texas A&M University School of Law

Paula A. Franzese

Peter W. Rodino Professor of Law,
Seton Hall University School of Law

Kevin V. Tu

University of Maryland
Francis King Carey School of Law

David G. Epstein

George E. Allen Chair,
University of Richmond School of Law

LEARNING SERIES

WEST
ACADEMIC
PUBLISHING

© 2018 LEG, Inc. d/b/a West Academic
© 2022 LEG, Inc. d/b/a West Academic

444 Cedar Street, Suite 700
St. Paul, MN 55101
1-877-888-1330

West, West Academic Publishing, and West Academic are trademarks of West Publishing Corporation, used under license.

Printed in the United States of America

ISBN: 978-1-64708-756-2

For my wife Kristi, without whom none of this would be possible. —WB

To Michael Luigi, Nina Paula, and my students—
past, present, and future. —PAF

For my wife, Carly, and my parents, Ai and Thao. —KVT

For Soia Mentschikoff and Ellen Peters and Marjorie Girth and . . . , without
whom there would not be Professor Paula Franzese and
Professor Elizabeth Warren and . . . . —DGE

WITH SPECIAL GRATITUDE

The Authors are indebted to Prof. Samuel W. Calhoun for his review and comments on earlier drafts, and Stephanie J. Beach, Esq., for her invaluable research and editorial assistance.

FIRST WORD TO STUDENTS

The Uniform Commercial Code (UCC or Code) was a joint project of the American Law Institute and the National Conference of Commissioners on Uniform State Laws. It was drafted in the 1940s and 1950s. There have been, of course, later amendments to the UCC but, in the main, the UCC is a 60+ year-old statute. At times, its provisions will seem antiquated. Still, the legislatures of every state other than Louisiana have adopted the UCC, albeit with some minor variation from state to state.[1] Indeed, the UCC is the first place that lawyers working on matters within its scope look to for answers.

The UCC is not limited to commercial transactions. Many of the UCC questions on the bar exam and in practice involve consumer transactions such as Paula buying David's computer or Kevin writing a check to Wayne to repay a loan.

Further, the UCC is not a true "code." It is a statute. A true code preempts its field, supplanting the common law and equity. By contrast, the UCC is expressly supplemented by common law and equity. Indeed, UCC section 1–103(b) provides in pertinent part: "Unless displaced by the particular provisions of the Uniform Commercial Code, the principles of law and equity supplement its provisions." At its core, the practice of commercial law is about transactions, not litigation. An effective transactional lawyer uses core commercial concepts to minimize any possibility of later litigation. Of course, if things go bad (as they sometimes do), then an effective litigator will use core commercial concepts to win the case for her client. But, the goal from the outset should be to get the transaction right.

Accordingly, this book does not include any reported cases. Instead, it contains edited UCC sections ("reading the code"), original text that explores and explains those UCC sections and problems that require the application of those UCC provisions ("applying the code"). The most important parts of the book are the edited UCC provisions that permeate the book. Carefully read those provisions.

This book is divided into three parts. Part I, drafted by Prof. Franzese, examines the law of sales and Article 2 of the UCC. Part II, drafted by Prof. Barnes, covers the law of secured transactions and Article 9 of the UCC. Part III, drafted by Prof. Tu, explores the law of negotiable instruments and Articles 3 and 4 of the UCC.

---

[1]   For a mere $2,076 a year you can subscribe to a service that keeps you informed about the various state legislatures' variations to the UCC. http://legalsolutions.thomsonreuters.com/law-products/Case-Law/Uniform-Commercial-Code-State-Variations-and-Fees/p/100027475

Understanding the core concepts of the UCC will serve you well in practice and in life. We are all buyers and sellers and debtors and creditors.

Set forth below is a short list of ten core commercial concepts.

Article 2

1. Lack of legal formalism in contract formation

2. Merchants held to higher standards

3. Resolve open questions as similarly situated parties would had they bargained over the matter

Article 9

4. Security interest as a present, non-possessory property right

5. Floating liens are enforceable

6. Notice filing is the ethos for perfection

7. Purchase-money security interests are given special treatment

Articles 3 and 4

8. Holder in due course of a negotiable instrument takes free from personal defenses and claims and subject to real defenses

9. Relationship of bank and customer and the properly payable rule

10. Legal rights and responsibilities of people who transfer negotiable instruments

You will need to understand those concepts to pass the bar, to effectively represent clients who buy and sell consumer goods, equipment, inventory, and businesses, and to effectively represent clients engaged in credit transactions as lenders or borrowers.

TABLE OF CONTENTS

DETAILED TABLE OF CONTENTS

TABLE OF UNIFORM CODES

LEARNING COMMERCIAL LAW: CORE CONCEPTS

SECOND EDITION

PART I

Contracts for the
Sale of Goods: Article 2

1

Getting Started

An Introduction to Article 2, the Law of Sales, and an
Overview of Article 1, Organizing Principles

Key Concepts

- The scope of Article 2 of the UCC for the sale of goods
- "Goods" as defined under Article 2
- "Sale" as defined under Article 2
- Transactions outside Article 2's scope
- The continued applicability of law and equity
- The relevance of course of performance, course of dealing, and usage of trade

---

The law of sales is contained in Article 2 of the UCC. The brainchild of legal realist Karl Llewellyn,[1] the UCC emerged as the most successful statutory achievement of the twentieth century. Its provisions on sales, or contracts for the sale of goods, aim to clarify, simplify and modernize what previously was known as "the law merchant," or the way things are done in the marketplace of mercantile exchange.

Article 2 applies to both commercial and consumer transactions, and to merchants as well as non-merchants. It applies to contracts for the sale of goods and so-called "hybrid" or "mixed deal" transactions that involve the provision of both goods and services.

---

1   Karl Llewellyn, one of the most influential scholars of the 20th Century, was a primary drafter of the UCC. His approach to legal realism is summarized in his iconic book written for law students, The Bramble Bush: On Our Law and Its Study (1930).

Article 2 is best approached in accordance with the statute's own internal symmetry. Consistent with that very organized approach, our scope of coverage is divided into five sections: **Formation of the Article 2 Contract, Content of the Article 2 Contract, Performance of the Article 2 Contract, Breach of the Article 2 Contract and Remedies for Breach of the Article 2 Contract.**

Since the law of sales is the product of a statute, our analysis will be quite statute-specific, mindful that an assimilation of the subject matter is best achieved by reading and deconstructing Article 2's most important sections.[2] Cases are secondary to the goal of mastery here. Whether on your final exam or in practice, when presented with a question within the scope of Article 2, your first task will be to discern which of the UCC provisions potentially applies to the dispute's resolution. It is only thereafter, armed with those potentially relevant statutory provisions, that you will be equipped to delve into the applicable jurisdiction's case law on point.

A. Getting Started: A Quick Review of Article 2's Scope and Governing Principles

Article 2 does not apply to all contracts. It applies only to contracts for the sale of goods. In determining whether the given transaction is within Article 2's scope, you must ask two questions. First, is the subject matter of the deal a "good" as defined by section 2–105 and second, does the transaction qualify as a "sale" of that good as defined by section 2–106?

READING THE CODE

■ DCC SECTION 2–105: Definitions: "Goods"

"Goods" means all things (including specially manufactured goods) which are movable at the time of identification to the contract for sale other than the money in which the price is to be paid, investment securities (Article 8) and things in action. "Goods" also includes the unborn young of animals and growing crops and other identified things attached to realty as described in the section on goods to be severed from realty (section 2–107).

---

2   Articles 1 and 2 for purposes of the chapters on Sales are from the Delaware UCC, abbreviated here as "DCC." (Title 6, Subtitle 1, Uniform Commercial Code, sections 1–101 et seq).

To qualify as a "good," the subject matter of the transaction must possess "tangible movability." Thus, a blender is a good. A copyright is not a good. Do you see why? A car is a good. Real property is not within Article 2's scope, but the sale of a mobile home is. Why?

READING THE CODE

> ### ◼ DCC SECTION 2–106: Definitions: "Sale"
>
> A "sale" consists in the passing of title from the seller to the buyer for a price.

To qualify as a sale, the transaction must involve the passing of title in exchange for a price. What is title? How might it be distinguishable from other forms of possession? What sorts of transactions might involve the transfer of goods without payment?

B. Hybrid Transactions: Exchanges Involving Both the Sale of Goods and the Provision of Services

Many commercial exchanges involve both the provision of goods and services, or perhaps the provision of goods and real estate. For example, a landscaper charges for his services as well as for the shrubs he plants, just as the fee for a plumber's services might include the costs of the faucet installed. Article 2 does not apply to pure services contracts (such as a contract for a wedding singer), but it does apply to contracts that involve both the provision of goods and services when the sale of goods represents the predominant part of the transaction. Some courts deem the sale of goods the predominant part of the deal when their value exceeds fifty percent of the transaction's total cost. Other courts assess whether similarly situated parties would reasonably expect the contract to be primarily for goods as opposed to services. Also, some courts apply an "all-or-nothing" approach to whether Article 2 applies in a mixed purpose transaction, while other courts will apply Article 2 to the goods portion and another law to the non-goods portion.

APPLYING THE CODE

Problem 1-1: Understanding Article 2's Scope

A)   David brought his shirts to Paula's dry cleaner for cleaning. When he returned to retrieve the shirts, he remitted $40 in payment. Thereafter, he discovered that the shirts had been burned and stained, presumably during the cleaning process. Is this transaction within the scope of Article 2? Why or why not?

B)   Wayne bought Thirsty's Bar. The assets purchased included the furnishings, equipment and the building. Does Article 2 apply? Why or why not?

C)   Kevin adopted a shih-tzu from Furry Friends and paid an "adoption fee" of $200. The fee included i) neutering, ii) vaccinations and iii) grooming. Is the transaction within Article 2's scope? Why or why not?

D)   Paula contracts with David to custom-design the wedding cake for her daughter's wedding. Does Article 2 apply? Would it apply to the contract for the wedding photographer? Why or why not?

C. An Overview of Article 1: The UCC's Glossary and Organizing Principles

An introduction to Article 2 would be remiss if it did not include a brief overview of Article 1 of the UCC. Article 1 sets forth a glossary of relevant terms and governing policies for each article of the UCC, including the law of sales. Many students and practitioners overlook Article 1 when they study and assimilate the law of sales. Do not make that mistake. Article 1 is a gold mine of salient information relevant to the law of sales. Here are the Article 1 sections to pay particular attention to.

DCC section 1–103 is the most important of the UCC's general provisions.

READING THE CODE

> ### ■ DCC SECTION 1–103: Construction of [Uniform Commercial Code] to Promote Its Purposes and Policies; Applicability of Supplemental Principles of Law
>
> **(a)** The Uniform Commercial Code must be liberally construed and applied to promote its underlying purposes and policies which are:
>
> **(1)** to simplify, clarify, and modernize the law governing commercial transactions;
>
> **(2)** to permit the continued expansion of commercial practices through custom, usage, and agreement of the parties; and
>
> **(3)** to make uniform the law among the various jurisdictions.
>
> **(b)** Unless displaced by the particular provisions of the Uniform Commercial Code, the principles of law and equity, including the law merchant and the law relative to capacity to contract, principal and agent, estoppel, fraud, misrepresentation, duress, coercion, mistake, bankruptcy, and other validating or invalidating cause supplement its provisions.

DCC section 1–103 embraces two essential precepts.

1. First, it provides that the Code should be liberally construed in order to advance its overarching policies, which are to simplify and clarify the law governing commercial transactions. No matter that the UCC is sometimes obtuse, it is intended to keep things simple and clear. Hence, as a practice pointer, if your adversary someday puts forth a strained or unduly complicated interpretation of governing Code doctrine, be the voice of reason and remind him or her of the section 1–103 imperative, apropos of Albert Einstein's quite salient observation that "everything should be kept as simple as possible. Never simpler than that, but still as simple as possible."

2. Second, section 1–103 makes plain that unless displaced, the principles of law and equity, such as fraud, duress, detrimental reliance, unjust enrichment or promissory estoppel, continue to apply. In practice, and on an exam, this reminder can be of immeasurable assistance. Sometimes, the Code will fail to address a particular issue that should be within its

scope. In that case, use section 1–103 to supplement the Code with the principles of law and equity. For that matter, sometimes resolution of a controversy by resort solely to the four corners of the statute yields an unjust or patently unfair result. In those instances too, use section 1–103 to endeavor to finesse a result that is more in accord with equity.

DCC section 1–201 is the UCC dictionary. Count on it as your glossary, and turn to it when you encounter an unfamiliar term in the text of Article 2. In particular, note the following definitions.

1. **Agreement:** Section 1–201(b)(3) defines agreement as the bargain of the parties in fact (meaning, what the parties actually bargained for), as determined on the basis of: i) their words, ii) any prior course of performance between them, iii) any prior course of dealing between them and iv) any relevant custom or usage of trade in their industry.

    Not all agreements are legally enforceable. When the parties' agreement comports with certain requirements that are addressed in our chapter on contract formation, it will enjoy the force of law and thereby be worthy of the designation of "contract."

2. **Contract:** Section 1–201(b)(12) defines the parties' contract as the total legal obligation that results from their agreement. That legal obligation is set forth in the whole of Article 2, as supplemented by pertinent provisions of law and equity.

    What is the practical difference between an agreement and a contract? The legal difference?

3. **Good faith:** Section 1–201(b)(20) imposes a two-pronged test for gauging a party's good faith. First, good faith requires honesty in fact. This is a subjective test that asks whether or not the given buyer or seller actually believed that he or she was acting honestly at the particular point in question. Second, good faith requires the "observance of reasonable commercial standards of fair dealing."

    Why not determine the given actor's good faith on the basis of a purely subjective standard? What are the advantages of gauging good faith on the basis of both subjective and objective criteria? The disadvantages?

READING THE CODE

▪ DCC SECTION 1–303: Course of Performance; Course of Dealing; and Usage of Trade (the Triplets)

(a) A "course of performance" is a sequence of conduct between the parties to a particular transaction that exists if:

    (1) The agreement of the parties with respect to the transaction involves repeated occasions for performance by a party; and

    (2) The other party, with knowledge of the nature of the performance and opportunity for objection to it, accepts the performance or acquiesces in it without objection.

(b) A "course of dealing" is a sequence of conduct concerning previous transactions between the parties to a particular transaction that is fairly to be regarded as establishing a common basis of understanding for interpreting their expressions and other conduct.

(c) A "usage of trade" is any practice or method of dealing having such regularity of observance in a place, vocation, or trade as to justify an expectation that it will be observed with respect to the transaction in question. The existence and scope of such a usage must be proved as facts. If it is established that such a usage is embodied in a trade code or similar record, the interpretation of the record is a question of law.

(d) A course of performance or course of dealing between the parties or usage of trade in the vocation or trade in which they are engaged or of which they are or should be aware is relevant in ascertaining the meaning of the parties' agreement, may give particular meaning to specific terms of the agreement, and may supplement or qualify the terms of the agreement. A usage of trade applicable in the place in which part of the performance under the agreement is to occur may be so utilized as to that part of the performance.

(e) Except as otherwise provided in subsection (f), the express terms of an agreement and any applicable course of performance, course of dealing, or usage of trade must be construed whenever reasonable as consistent with each other. If such a construction is unreasonable:

    (1) Express terms prevail over course of performance, course of dealing, and usage of trade;

    (2) Course of performance prevails over course of dealing and usage of trade; and

> **(3)** Course of dealing prevails over usage of trade.
>
> **(f)** Subject to section 2–209, a course of performance is relevant to show a waiver or modification of any term inconsistent with the course of performance.
>
> **(g)** Evidence of a relevant usage of trade offered by one party is not admissible unless that party has given the other party notice that the court finds sufficient to prevent unfair surprise to the other party.

An Article 2 contract must not be divorced from its commercial context. Thus, the parties' course of performance, course of dealing and relevant trade usage (in that order) are important when determining the nature of the bargain struck. We will refer to those three important predictors of the parties' conduct and expectations as "the triplets." Let's examine each of the three terms.

1. **Course of performance** is defined as the "sequence of conduct between the parties to a particular transaction that exists if the agreement of the parties with respect to the transaction involves repeated occasions for performance by a party." Look for the parties' course of performance whenever your contract calls for successive performances.

   For example, course of performance is relevant in an installment sales contract, where seller is to deliver in separate installments, or in an open-ended requirements or output contract, where regular deliveries are made with quantity determined on the basis of seller's output or buyer's needs. What the parties did without objection on those previous performance occasions, all within the confines of this particular contract, becomes germane to an understanding of what they can expect moving forward. Course of performance is closest to the parties' immediate expectations, and therefore is the most dispositive of the triplets.

   What are some other examples of course of performance? Is it wise to allow those prior performances to ordain enforceable future expectations? What are the advantages and drawbacks of such an approach?

2. **Course of dealing** is the "sequence of conduct concerning previous transactions between the parties to a particular transaction that is fairly to be regarded as establishing a common basis of understanding for interpreting their expressions and other conduct."

While course of performance asks, *what did the parties do previously in the context of performing this very deal?*, course of dealing asks, *what did the parties do previously in the context of other past contracts between them?* Course of dealing does not glean the parties' expectations from what the parties did or did not do while performing this contract, but instead looks to what they did in earlier contracts that they may have entered into with each other.

Course of dealing, which by definition is more remote in time, is relevant but of lesser moment than course of performance, and of greater moment than trade usage. Do you see why? Is there a basis for quibbling with that approach?

3. **Trade usage** is "any practice or method of dealing having such regularity of observance in a place, vocation or trade as to justify an expectation that it will be observed with respect to the transaction in question."

    The business norms and customs of the trade in question always provide a relevant backdrop against which the parties' deal will be interpreted. Think about likely examples of trade usage in, for example, the fresh produce industry, the poultry trade, and the clothing industry. What might those be?

APPLYING THE CODE

Problem 1-2: Applying Article 1

Paula is the sales manager for Sprintly Shoes, a manufacturer of athletic shoes. David, formerly an architect, recently opened a local sneaker shop called Just for Kicks, LLC. He contracted with Paula for the purchase of 12 dozen Sprintex sneakers, delivery Oct. 1. Paula delivered the sneakers on Oct. 20. David refused to accept them.

A) Paula argued that in the athletic apparel industry delivery dates are mere forecasts. Will that argument succeed? Why or why not? Which additional facts would you need to learn?

B) Suppose now that in previous contracts between Paula and David, Paula delivered on time. Would that matter? Why?

C)   What if in previous contracts between those parties, Paula delivered on time but that in this contract, which called for delivery in two installments with the first delivery to take place on May 1st and the second on Oct. 1st, Paula delivered the first installment on May 15. David accepts that delivery. When Paula delivers the second installment on Oct. 20, David refused to accept the goods, arguing that Paula breached the contract. What result?

Test Your Knowledge

To assess your understanding of the material in this chapter, click here to take a quiz.

2

Foundations of the Law of Sales

Four Guideposts of Article 2 Construction

Key Concepts

- Article 2's commitment to legal realism
- Article 2's goal of honoring reasonable consumer expectations
- The heightened standards that merchants are held to in an Article 2 contract
- The role of the unconscionability doctrine in gauging abuses during the formation stage of an Article 2 contract
- The court's options in dealing with a contract or clause that is deemed unconscionable
- The role of good faith standards in gauging abuses during the performance stage of an Article 2 contract

We now begin building the Article 2 house of learning. Its foundation rests on four essential guideposts. They form the bedrock on which the law of sales is based. Apply them throughout your study of Article 2 to be sure that your resolution of a dispute within its scope vindicates not only the form but also the spirit of the statute. Moreover, use them to inform your resolution of those Article 2 questions that fall between the cracks of the various statutory mandates. While Karl Llewellyn and his protégés, the Code's principal architects, did a masterful job of drafting Article 2, they could not anticipate every case or controversy. Hence, particularly when in doubt, allow the following guideposts to inform and become the foundation for your understanding of the law of sales.

A. Guidepost One: Never Divorce the Article 2 Contract from Its Commercial Setting

The Code's drafters were legal realists, meaning that they aimed to codify the law merchant, or the way commercial transactions and business exchanges were actually conducted in the context of the given industry or trade. Hence, the drafters did not seek to reinvent the wheel. They sought instead to replicate, in a streamlined and cohesive fashion, the customary and reasonable norms of mercantile exchange. The result that the Code reaches with respect to any particular controversy should not stray from those reasonable norms. What are the advantages of that approach? The disadvantages?

Practice Pointer: Since the Code could not anticipate every issue likely to arise in the course of contract formation and performance, sometimes a gap or gray area will come up. Particularly then, always ask, *How would similarly situated parties have resolved this matter had they explicitly bargained over it?*

Article 2's commitment to legal realism means that the statute endeavors to honor business people's reasonable and commonly held expectations. Those expectations are derived from the parties' words (what they promised to do), their actions or conduct (what they actually did), and, when applicable, their prior course of performance, course of dealing and relevant trade usage. (*See* the discussion of the triplets in Chapter 1.) A contract for the sale of goods should never be divorced from its commercial setting.

The Code favors the practical over the formalistic. Common law doctrines that are unduly rigid or exalt form to the detriment of substance are either disfavored or discarded outright.

APPLYING THE CODE

Problem 2-1: Deemphasizing Formalities

Wayne orders casebooks from Kevin Academic Press over the phone. Do you think that seller's assent must be manifested by phone? Would the fact that Wayne's order is not in writing render it unenforceable? Would the fact that the assent does not exactly match the order's terms prevent the formation of the contract?

B. Guidepost Two: Merchants Are Held to Higher Standards

Article 2 applies to commercial and consumer transactions and to merchants as well as non-merchants. Merchants, who by definition have expertise with respect to the goods in question, as well as the norms of commercial exchange, are held to more exacting standards than non-merchants.

READING THE CODE

> ### ■ DCC SECTION 2–104: Definitions: "Merchants"
>
> "Merchant" means a person who deals in goods of the kind or otherwise by his or her occupation holds himself or herself out as having knowledge or skill peculiar to the practices or goods involved in the transaction or to whom such knowledge or skill may be attributed by his or her employment of an agent or broker or other intermediary who by his occupation holds himself or herself out as having such knowledge or skill.

Notice that the definition of "merchant" sets forth two categories of actors: those who deal in goods that are the subject matter of the given transaction and those who hold themselves out as having knowledge or skill peculiar to the practices or goods involved in the transaction. What are examples of those in the first category and, by contrast, those in the second category? Is a plumber who sells his car a merchant? Is the clerk behind the counter of a department store a merchant and, if so, of what? What about a university purchasing boxes of copy paper for its library copy machines?

C. Guidepost Three: Abuses During the Formation Stage of an Article 2 Contract Are Proscribed by the Unconscionability Doctrine, Which Is Set Forth in Section 2–302

READING THE CODE

> ### ■ DCC SECTION 2–302: Unconscionable Contract or Clause
>
> (1) If the court as a matter of law finds the contract or any clause of the contract to have been unconscionable at the time it was made the court may refuse to enforce the contract, or it may enforce the

remainder of the contract without the unconscionable clause, or it may so limit the application of any unconscionable clause as to avoid any unconscionable result.

(2) When it is claimed or appears to the court that the contract or any clause thereof may be unconscionable the parties shall be afforded a reasonable opportunity to present evidence as to its commercial setting, purpose and effect to aid the court in making the determination.

1. **Unconscionability defined.** Section 2–302 does not define the term. Hence, to give meaning to unconscionability we turn to the supplemental principles of the common law, as section 1–103 would have us do. The case law tells us that unconscionability is rooted in disparity in bargaining power coupled with a contract term or terms that unreasonably favor the party with superior bargaining power. A term is unconscionable if it is the product of "undue oppression" born of another's bargaining advantage. *See* Official Comment 1 ("The basic test is whether, in the light of the general commercial background and the commercial needs of the particular trade or case, the clauses involved are so one-sided as to be unconscionable under the circumstances existing at the time of the making of the contract. The principle is one of the prevention of oppression and unfair surprise.")

2. **Never divorce the question of what is or is not unconscionable from the contract's commercial setting.** Section 2–302(2) makes plain that the contract's commercial context is important when gauging whether or not a term or terms are unconscionable. Why do you think that is?

3. **Unconscionability is determined on the basis of the facts in existence at the time of the contract's formation.** Hindsight is irrelevant. Indeed, the parties must be given the opportunity to brief the question of commercial setting at the time of the deal's formation when asserting or defending a claim of unconscionability. Since context is everything, when a court refuses to give this opportunity, it has committed reversible error.

4. **Unconscionability is a determination of law, and therefore freely appealable.** What are the advantages of that approach?

5. **If the court deems the contract or any clause contained therein to be unconscionable, it has three options:**

a) Nullify the offensive term and enforce the remainder of the contract

b) Limit the application of the offensive clause to avoid any unconscionable result

c) Void the entire contract

Some critics have asserted that section 2–302 gives courts too much discretion. What is the basis for that critique? What is the best response to the criticism?

APPLYING THE CODE

Problem 2-2: Unconscionability Doctrine

Several months ago, David, chief purchasing agent for Silkline Textiles, ordered 10,000 yards of silk fabric from Paula, a manufacturer. Ordinarily, the fabric is sold for approximately $4 per yard. When David placed his order, significant labor unrest and a global silkworm shortage drove the cost of the fabric up to $10 per yard. The parties agreed on a price of $10/yard. Paula delivered the fabric on time. Now, David refuses to remit payment. Paula has sued for the price, and in response, David has asserted that the contracted-for price of $10 per yard is unconscionable. He adds that in fact the present-day market price for the very same fabric is $4.25 per yard.

You are the law clerk to the judge. Brief the judge on the questions presented, the options available to the court and the best way, in your estimation, to resolve this dispute.

[handwritten margin notes: Valid claim? Did Paula Any breach?]

Problem 2-3: Unconscionability Doctrine

David, a small independent farmer, bought cabbage seed from Kevin Seed Co., a large national producer and distributor of seed. The contract provided that David's only remedy for breach is return of the purchase price. Earlier that year, Kevin Seed Co. had discontinued its practice of "hot water" decontamination, a process that eradicates "black leg," a seed-borne fungus that causes affected plants to rot before maturing. Kevin Seed Co. did not disclose that fact to David. Later, when David notified Kevin Seed

Co. that most of his cabbage crop was worthless because it had been infected by black leg fungus, Kevin Seed Co. replied that it would return David's purchase price, but nothing more. Is David bound by the limitation of remedy clause in the contract?

D. Guidepost Four: Abuses During the Performance Stage of an Article 2 Contract Are Regulated by the Good Faith Doctrine, Which Is Set Forth in Section 1–201(b)(20)

READING THE CODE

> **DCC SECTION 1–201(b)(20): General Definitions: "Good Faith"**
>
> "Good faith," except as otherwise provided in Article 5, means honesty in fact and the observance of reasonable commercial standards of fair dealing.

APPLYING THE CODE

Problem 2-4: Applying Good Faith Standards

Wayne runs a law school bookstore. He orders Contracts casebooks from Kevin Academic Press, for delivery on August 15, just in time for the busy start of the fall semester. On August 14, Kevin Academic Press calls to tell Wayne that it can only get the needed books to Wayne on time if Wayne agrees to remit an additional hefty surcharge. Will Kevin Academic Press succeed with that demand? Which additional facts would you need to learn?

3

Formation of an Article 2 Contract

Key Concepts

- The definition of an offer for the sale of goods
- The definition of a merchant's firm offer under Article 2
- The manners by which to demonstrate acceptance of goods
- The role of the battle of the forms provision when the terms of an offer and assent conflict
- The admission of variant terms of a contract if a party is a merchant or a non-merchant
- The applicability of the statute of frauds for contracts for the sale of goods for $500 or more
- The five exceptions to the writing requirement of the statute of frauds
- The scope of the parol evidence rule in admitting contradictory or supplementary terms
- The difference between fully integrated and partially integrated writings
- The admission of post-contract modifications after a deal has been finalized

Article 2 contains an internal symmetry that is organized around the stages of a contract. It begins with the statutory sections relevant to the contract's formation. Those sections are contained in the 2–200s. Once you have determined that the contract for the sale of goods comports with the Code's provisions on valid contract formation, you would move on to the Code provisions relevant to the contract's content (the 2–300s), then its performance (the 2–500s and 2–600s) and then, if there is a breach of one or both parties' performance obligations, the remedies for breach (the 2–700s).

In this chapter, we are concerned with the elements of contract formation. Set forth below is a checklist of the questions and Article 2 sections relevant to an assessment of whether a binding contract for the sale of goods has been formed:

- **Has an offer for the purchase or sale of goods been made?** "Offer" is not defined in Article 2. Use the Restatement (2d) of Contracts definition, contained in section 24 ("An offer is the manifestation of willingness to enter into a bargain, so made as to justify another person in understanding that his assent to that bargain is invited and will conclude it.").

- **Has a firm offer been made by a merchant?** "Firm offer" is defined in section 2–205 and applies only to merchants who promise in a signed writing to keep an offer to buy or sell goods open or firm, typically for a stated period of time, when that offer is unsupported by consideration.

- **Has the offer been properly accepted?** "Acceptance" is defined in section 2–206. It may be demonstrated in any manner reasonable under the circumstances unless the offer clearly indicates precisely how assent must be made.

- **Do the terms of the offer and the terms of the assent conflict? Turn to section 2–207, the battle of the forms provision.** For purposes of determining whether variant terms in the assent become part of the contract, section 2–207 distinguishes deals involving non-merchants from deals between merchants. In either case, as long as the assent is definite and not made conditional on the offeror's agreement to its variant terms, it is a valid acceptance and not a counteroffer. But if one of the parties is a non-merchant, the variant terms from the assent drop out unless expressly assented to by the offeror. In contrast, when the deal is between merchants, the variant terms are automatically included unless the offer limited assent to its terms, the variant terms work a material alteration, or the variant terms are objected to within a reasonable time.

- **Does the agreement have to be in writing to be enforceable? Article 2's statute of frauds is contained in section 2–201.** Contracts for the sale of goods for $500 or more must be in writing to be enforceable unless one of five exceptions applies. The writing must evidence that a contract for the sale of goods was formed, contain a quantity term and be signed by the party against whom enforcement is sought. If a deal was struck but is not evidenced by an appropriate writing, see if any of the five exceptions to the writing requirement applies (reply doctrine or merchant's confirmation, specially manufactured goods, admission, partial payment, and partial acceptance).

- **Is a party to the contract seeking to contradict or supplement its terms by evidence of some prior or contemporaneous oral or written agreement?** Invoke the parol evidence rule of section 2–202. It applies only to final writings, which cannot be contradicted but can be explained or supplemented unless so carefully crafted as to be "final, complete and exclusive." Course of performance, course of dealing, and trade usage are always admissible to explain or supplement even final contracts.

- **Has there been a post-formation change to the contract?** Post-contract modifications are governed by section 2–209. Post-contract changes do not require independent consideration but must be in writing if the contract, as modified, is within the statute of frauds.

A. The Offer

Every contract for the sale of goods begins with an offer. Article 2 does not define offer, thereby inviting consultation with supplemental sources (*see* section 1–103 and the accompanying discussion in chapter one). The most often-invoked source is the Restatement (2d) of Contracts, section 24, which defines the offer as "the manifestation of willingness to enter into a bargain, so made as to justify another person in understanding that his assent to that bargain is invited and will conclude it."

B. The Firm Offer: DCC Section 2–205

Article 2 does define firm offer in section 2–205.

READING THE CODE

> **DCC SECTION 2–205: Firm Offer**
>
> An offer by a merchant to buy or sell goods in a signed writing which by its terms gives assurance that it will be held open is not revocable, for lack of consideration, during the time stated or if no time is stated for a reason-

able time, but in no event may such period of irrevocability exceed three months; but any such term of assurance on a form supplied by the offeree must be separately signed by the offeror.

It is important to note that section 2–205 applies only to offerors who are merchants. Why do you think that is? (*See* section 2–104 and the discussion of merchants in chapter 2).

At common law, firm offers unsupported by consideration were unenforceable. Article 2 modifies that result by rendering a merchant's firm offer enforceable no matter that it is unsupported by consideration. Why would the statute dispense with the need for consideration here?

A merchant's firm offer rendered in a signed writing but without some consideration in return is enforceable for the time stated, or, if no time is stated, for a reasonable time, but in no event for longer than three months. By contrast, if that merchant's firm offer rendered in a signed writing is supported by consideration, it lasts for the time stated unconstrained by the three-month cap.

Use the following three-step analysis for assessing section 2–205:

> **Step one:** Is this a merchant offeror? *See* section 2–104 for the definition of merchant. If so, proceed to step two.

> **Step two:** Has that merchant offeror promised, in a signed writing, to keep its offer to buy or sell goods open or firm? If so, proceed to step three.

> **Step three:** Is that firm offer made by the merchant in a signed writing supported by consideration? If so, it endures for the time stated, and if no time is stated, it is binding for a reasonable time. If the firm offer is unsupported by consideration, it endures for the time stated, and if no time is stated, it is binding for a reasonable time, but in no event may the period of irrevocability exceed three months.

APPLYING THE CODE

Problem 3-1: The Firm Offer

David's Lumber, Inc., a supplier of lumber, offers to sell hardwood to Kevin, who is overseeing renovations to his family's home, at $9 per square foot. Kevin knows this is a good price and at least 20% less than the best price that his research turned up. Still, he is not sure if he will be using hardwood for the renovations. He asks David's Lumber to keep the offer firm, or fixed, for the next six months, at which point Kevin will know if he needs the goods. In a signed writing, David's Lumber agrees to do so, in exchange for Kevin remitting $75 to keep the offer open. The receipt that David's Lumber gives to Kevin indicates that half of that sum would be applied to Kevin's order but is nonrefundable in the event that no order is placed. Four months later, Kevin calls David's Lumber to indicate that he would like to place an order for the hardwood at the promised $9 per square foot. David's Lumber responds that the quoted price "was too low" and that the price is $12 per square foot. Is David's Lumber bound by the terms of its original promise? Why or why not? Would your answer change if Kevin had not remitted the $75?

C. Acceptance

READING THE CODE

DCC SECTION 2–206: Offer and Acceptance in Formation of Contract

(1) Unless otherwise unambiguously indicated by the language or circumstances

  (a) an offer to make a contract shall be construed as inviting acceptance in any manner and by any medium reasonable in the circumstances;

  (b) an order or other offer to buy goods for prompt or current shipment shall be construed as inviting acceptance either by a

> prompt promise to ship or by the prompt or current shipment of conforming or non-conforming goods, but such a shipment of non-conforming goods does not constitute an acceptance if the seller seasonally notifies the buyer that the shipment is offered only as an accommodation to the buyer.
>
> **(2)** Where the beginning of a requested performance is a reasonable mode of acceptance an offeror who is not notified of acceptance within a reasonable time may treat the offer as having lapsed before acceptance.

There are three essential takeaways from section 2–206:

1. **Unless the offer clearly indicates otherwise, whether by its express terms or surrounding circumstances, it may be accepted by any reasonable means and manner.** This is significant. Consistent with the Code's efforts to replace formalism with pragmatism, section 2–206 rejects the common law's "mirror image" rule. That formulaic rule insisted that a given assent, to succeed in locking in a contract, had to mirror the offer's terms and prescribed procedure for acceptance in the offer. The mirror image rule often frustrated the parties' intent or, worse, allowed a bad faith player to worm its way out of what should have been a binding contract by finding some betrayal, however slight, of the offer's terms. Section 2–206 instead permits acceptance through any means and by any manner appropriate in view of the deal's commercial setting, unless the offeror unambiguously indicates otherwise.

2. **The offeror can still be the so-called "master of the offer" by clearly indicating in the offer precisely how acceptance is to be manifested in order to close the deal.** Section 2–206(1) permits the offeror to "unambiguously indicate" how, when and by what means acceptance must be communicated to conclude the transaction.

3. **Unless it clearly states otherwise, an offer or order to buy goods for immediate or prompt shipment can be accepted in one of two ways: i) by prompt promise to ship or ii) by prompt shipment.** Significantly, in this context, even the shipment of non-conforming goods qualifies as an acceptance (and not a counteroffer) and locks in a contract on the buyer's terms. Hence, a seller who promptly ships non-conforming goods in response to a buyer's order or offer to buy goods for immediate

or quick shipment makes and breaches a contract at the same time unless the seller makes plain that the shipment is merely an accommodation (in which case it is a counteroffer).

Orders or offers to purchase goods for quick or immediate shipment typically are fraught with a sense of urgency or exigent circumstances. In those instances, at common law, an unscrupulous seller could take advantage of the buyer's vulnerability by shipping even substandard or otherwise non-conforming goods without risk. Because of the mirror image rule, that shipment would qualify not as an acceptance but instead as a counteroffer that the buyer could take or leave without risk to the seller. In the best case, the desperate buyer might accept the goods, locking in a contract on the seller's terms and thereby relieving the seller of liability for breach of contract. If the buyer declines to accept, the seller would face no legal consequences for its non-conforming tender. Section 2–206 endeavors to close the door to that tactic. Hence, the seller's prompt tender even of non-conforming goods in response to a buyer's offer to buy for prompt shipment qualifies as an acceptance of the buyer's offer, thereby locking in a contract and simultaneously breaching that contract.

APPLYING THE CODE

Problem 3-2: Acceptance

A) Paula, owner of Paula's Appliances, LLC, a local appliance store, leaves a voicemail with Wayne, her local Maytag representative, ordering one Maytag dryer, Model X4300, at the manufacturer's list price. Wayne emails Paula his reply: "*Thank you for your message. We will ship that out to you by the end of the week.*" Has a valid contract been locked in?

B) Suppose now that Paula's voicemail includes the following: "*Wayne, give me a call before 5pm this evening to let me know.*" Instead, the next day Wayne emails his reply: "*Thank you for your message. We will ship that out to you by the end of the week.*" Not hearing from Wayne the day before, Paula placed the order with another supplier. Is she obliged to take the Maytag dryer?

C) Kevin, Vice-President of Apex Oil, is in charge of regional sales in the volatile and changing gasoline market, where prices often fluctuated by the hour. He faxes an offer to Hillcrest Exxon that states, *"Our best offer: 100 barrels of regular gasoline at 95 cents per gallon."* If Hillcrest Exxon phones Kevin the next day to accept, will a valid contract have been formed?

D) Paula, owner of a local appliance store, faxes an order to Wayne, her Maytag representative, which states: *"Please ship within 24 hours 2 Model G-350 washers at list price."* Within 24 hours Wayne ships 2 Model H-425 washers, a more expensive model. Has a contract been formed?

E) Suppose that in the above problem Wayne had included with the non-conforming shipment a note that said, *"This is the best we could do on such short notice."* What result?

D. The Battle of the Forms: DCC Section 2–207

READING THE CODE

■ DCC SECTION 2–207: Additional Terms in Acceptance or Confirmation

(1) A definite and seasonable expression of acceptance or a written confirmation which is sent within a reasonable time operates as an acceptance even though it states terms additional to or different from those offered or agreed upon, unless acceptance is expressly made conditional on assent to the additional or different terms.

(2) The additional terms are to be construed as proposals for addition to the contract. Between merchants such terms become part of the contract unless:

(a) the offer expressly limits acceptance to the terms of the offer;

(b) they materially alter it; or

(c) notification of objection to them has already been given or is given within a reasonable time after notice of them is received.

(3) Conduct by both parties which recognizes the existence of a contract is sufficient to establish a contract for sale although the writings of the

> parties do not otherwise establish a contract. In such case the terms of the particular contract consist of those terms on which the writings of the parties agree, together with any supplementary terms incorporated under this subtitle.

Sometimes the terms of the offer and the terms of what seems to be an assent do not match up. Section 2–207 addresses that problem, commonly referred to as the "battle of the forms" because the seller's acknowledgment form contains additional or different terms from those contained in the buyer's order form (or purchase order).

APPLYING THE CODE

Problem 3-3: Understanding Section 2–207's Context

Paula submits an order to David's Custom Tees, Inc., ordering eight dozen custom t-shirts for her Commercial Law class. The order form states that the shirts must be delivered by Oct. 1, price $10 per shirt, free shipping. David's Custom Tees sends back its acknowledgment form, which states that it will provide eight dozen custom t-shirts, delivery by Oct. 1, price $10 per shirt, free shipping. That form also states, *"Seller disclaims all warranties. As a new customer, buyer must pay a one-time $100 design and typesetting fee."* Has a valid contract been locked in? On whose terms?

When the terms of a seeming assent and the terms of the offer do not match up, use the following three-step approach to determine whether a contract has been formed, and if a contract has been locked in, which terms are included within its scope.

First, has a contract been formed no matter that the terms of the seeming assent deviate from the terms contained in the offer? To answer, apply section 2–207(1).

At common law, because of the mirror image rule, an expression of acceptance that contained variant terms was not an acceptance but instead a counteroffer. Article 2 discards the mirror image rule. Instead, section 2–207(1) provides that an unequivocal and timely expression of acceptance is indeed an acceptance and not a mere counteroffer, no matter that it contains terms additional to or different from those contained in the offer, unless that acceptance is conditioned on the offeror's assent to its variant terms (in which case it would be deemed a counteroffer).

Second, if the assent does qualify as an acceptance, thereby locking in a deal, what becomes of the assent's variant terms? To answer, turn to section 2–207(2).

1. **If one or both parties are non-merchants:** If one or both parties are non-merchants, the variant terms should be treated as mere proposals for addition to the contract. They will drop out if not explicitly assented to.

2. **If both parties are merchants:** Recall that merchants are held to higher standards. If the contract is between merchants, section 2–207(2) applies the so-called "automatic inclusion rule," meaning that the variant terms will automatically become part of the contract unless the offer limits assent to the offer's terms, the offeror objects to the variant term(s) within a reasonable time or the variant term(s) materially alters the contract.

   Note that the exceptions to the automatic inclusion rule essentially subsume the rule. The rule automatically includes only the most inoffensive and trivial of variant terms. Do you see why? First, an offer that expressly limits assent to only the offer's terms is exempted from the specter of automatic inclusion. Second, even if the offer did not limit assent only to its terms, all that the offeror need do to preclude automatic inclusion of any variant terms contained in the assent is object to those terms within a reasonable time after notice of them is received. Third, even if the offer did not limit assent only to its terms and the offeror failed to object within in a reasonable time to any variant terms contained in the assent, those variant terms will drop out if they materially alter the contract. Official Comment 4 indicates that a term would materially alter the contract if its incorporation without express awareness by the other party would result in surprise or hardship. For example, a clause negating otherwise applicable warranties, limiting remedies or departing from trade usage would work a material alteration.

Third, if the parties' writings do not establish a contract but their conduct does, turn to section 2–207(3).

Sometimes the terms of the offer and the terms of a seeming assent are at an impossible impasse. Merchants have learned to track Article 2's statutory language to include as a matter of standard form boilerplate a clause in the purchase order that states, "This offer expressly limits acceptance to the terms of the offer." Standard form acknowledgments often include a clause that makes acceptance "conditional on assent to its terms." In those situations, apply section 2–207(3). A contract for sale will arise when the parties' conduct recognizes the existence of a contract no matter that their respective forms are at odds. In such instances, the terms of the contract are those on which the writings agree, together with any supplementary terms incorporated by the parties' course of performance, course of dealing, trade usage or Code gap-fillers (taken up in Chapter 4).

APPLYING THE CODE

Problem 3-4: The Battle of the Forms

A) Kevin, owner and operator of Little Falls Plumbing, faxed a purchase order for 12 Keeler faucets, model G-420, to Wayne, his Keeler agent. Wayne faxed back an acknowledgment, confirming receipt of the order. The acknowledgment limited buyer's remedies to repair or replacement. The faucets arrived, and Kevin installed two of them, only to find that they were defective, causing a major pipe breakage and significant damage. Kevin wishes to proceed against Keeler for that damage. What result?

B) After negotiations, Paula, purchasing agent for Prado Fashions, Inc., sent a purchase order to David's Textiles Equipment, Inc., for a trim press, a piece of equipment used in dress manufacturing. The purchase order contained a clause that stated, "*This order expressly limits acceptance to its terms.*" David's Textiles Equipment, Inc., agent sent back its standard acknowledgment form, marked "ACKNOWLEDGMENT" with a space labeled "accepted by," which was signed by David's Textiles Equipment, Inc. The acknowledgment contained a provision that stated, "*Purchaser agrees to indemnify and hold David's Textiles Equipment, Inc., harmless from all actions, claims, or demands arising out of use of the trim press*" and another that stated, "*Unless you advise us within seven days of receipt of this acknowledgment of objection to any of its terms, we are proceeding with the construction of the equipment as per the specifications and terms contained herein."* David's Textiles Equipment, Inc., completed manufacture of the trim press and shipped it to Prado Fashions, Inc. Thereafter, one of Prado Fashions, Inc.'s employees suffered injuries while operating the trim press and sued Prado Fashions, Inc. Prado Fashions, Inc., in turn sued David's Textiles Equipment, Inc., for the settlement that Prado Fashions, Inc., had to pay to its employee. What result?

E. The Statute of Frauds: DCC Section 2–201

READING THE CODE

DCC SECTION 2–201: Formal Requirements; Statute of Frauds

(1) Except as otherwise provided in this section a contract for the sale of goods for the price of $500 or more is not enforceable by way of action or defense unless there is some writing sufficient to indicate that a contract for sale has been made between the parties and signed by the party against whom enforcement is sought or by his or her authorized agent or broker. A writing is not insufficient because it omits or incorrectly states a term agreed upon but the contract is not enforceable under this paragraph beyond the quantity of goods shown in such writing.

(2) Between merchants if within a reasonable time a writing in confirmation of the contract and sufficient against the sender is received and the party receiving it has reason to know its contents, it satisfies the requirements of subsection (1) against such party unless written notice of objection to its contents is given within ten days after it is received.

(3) A contract which does not satisfy the requirements of subsection (1) but which is valid in other respects is enforceable

    (a) if the goods are to be specially manufactured for the buyer and are not suitable for sale to others in the ordinary course of the seller's business and the seller, before notice of repudiation is received and under circumstances which reasonably indicate that the goods are for the buyer, has made either a substantial

> beginning of their manufacture or commitments for their procurement; or
>
> **(b)** if the party against whom enforcement is sought admits in his or her pleading, testimony or otherwise in court that a contract for sale was made, but the contract is not enforceable under this provision beyond the quantity of goods admitted; or
>
> **(c)** with respect to goods for which payment has been made and accepted or which have been received and accepted (section 2–606).

Unless one of five exceptions applies, a contract for the sale of goods for the price of $500 or more is not enforceable unless authenticated by an appropriate writing. The purpose of the statute of frauds is to prevent fabrication of contracts that were never entered into. It is not intended to bar the enforcement of contracts actually formed.

Use the following three-step approach when applying the statute of frauds:

First, is this a contract for the sale of goods for $500 or more? If so, go to section 2–201 and proceed to step two.

Second, is there a writing or writings to **authenticate the facts of the contract that is sufficient to satisfy the elements of section 2–201(1)?** Specifically, the writing or composite of writings must indicate that a contract for the sale of goods was made, it must contain a quantity term, and it must be signed by the party against whom enforcement is sought (the defendant). The Code drafters deemed quantity the term most susceptible to fabrication or fraud. Hence, to qualify as a valid writing, the contract must reference quantity. Other terms, including price, can be supplied by the parties' course of performance, course of dealing or trade usage (the Code's gap-filler provisions). If the writing or writings do not meet the three invariable requirements of section 2–201(1), proceed to step 3.

Third, does one of the following five exceptions to the writing requirement set forth in section 2–201(2) and (3) apply?

The Reply Doctrine, or Merchant's Confirmation Rule (DCC section 2–201(2)). Prior to Article 2, the only type of writing to satisfy the statute of frauds was one signed by the party against whom enforcement was sought. Thus, a party who wrote a letter of confirmation of a given deal would be bound, but the recipient of that confirmation, who never signed, would not be bound. An unscrupulous recipient of such a confirmatory memo could simply wait for the time of performance to come due to decide whether to perform or not, knowing that the deal was enforceable only against the sender. The Code's reply doctrine changes that inequitable result and deems a letter of confirmation or confirmatory memo a reliable method of satisfying the statute of frauds.

To successfully invoke the reply doctrine, four requirements must be met: 1) the contract must be between merchants (another example of how merchants are held to higher standards), 2) a letter of confirmation or confirmatory memo must be received within a reasonable time and the party receiving it must have reason to know of its contents, 3) the confirmation must meet the three invariable components of a binding writing so that it would bind its sender (the writing must contain a quantity term, it must evidence a contract for the sale of goods and it must be signed by its sender) and 4) the party receiving the confirmation must not object to its contents in writing within ten days after it is received.

APPLYING THE CODE

Problem 3-5: The Reply Doctrine

Wayne owns and operates Luxe Goods, Inc., a luxury brand chain of boutiques. On Oct. 1, he phoned Kevin, the Northeast sales director for Chaneile, Inc., to order one dozen "Urban Campers," a high-end Chaneile, Inc., backpack, purchase price $600 per unit. When Kevin indicated that the backpack was in stock, Wayne said, "Great! How soon can it ship?" Kevin promised to ship by the end of the week. That same afternoon, Kevin faxed Wayne a signed confirmation that stated, "*Thank you for your business. The one dozen Urban Campers will ship by the end of the week.*" Wayne saw the fax but did not pay much attention to it. When the shipment arrived on Oct. 12, he refused to sign for it, returning it to sender. When Kevin followed up, Wayne replied, "I never signed anything. Sue me." What result?

Admissions (DCC section 2–201(3)(b)). The party against whom enforcement is sought cannot admit in court pleadings the existence of the contract and simultaneously claim the benefit of the statute of frauds. Recall that the purpose of the statute of frauds is to prevent fraud, not serve as a formalistic impediment to the enforcement of a contract actually formed (albeit orally). Hence, one who admits in pleadings, testimony or otherwise in court that a contract was made is bound by that admission, up to the quantity of goods admitted.

APPLYING THE CODE

Problem 3-6: The Admission Exception

Paula Soyso, Inc., buys and sells soybeans. Last month, David Grower, LLP, and Paula Soyso, Inc., spoke by phone, wherein David Grower agreed to sell 4,000 bushels of yellow soybeans for $60 per bushel, delivery within ten days. Following that conversation, Paula Soyso, Inc., e-mailed a quick note to its office manager, stating: *"This confirms agreement by David Grower, LLP, to provide yellow soybeans at $60 per bushel, delivery in ten days."* The market shifted in favor of seller and the soybeans were never delivered. David Grower's position is that any alleged deal between it and Paula Soyso is not enforceable because "there's no written contract." At the ensuing lawsuit, David Grower was deposed and asked by Paula Soyso's counsel, *"Didn't you agree to sell these beans to Paula Soyso, Inc., over the phone for a certain price?"* You are counsel to David Grower. You ask for a ten-minute break to speak with your client. What does that conversation sound like?

Specially manufactured goods (DCC section 2–201(3)(a)). Contracts for the sale of specially manufactured goods are exempted from the writing requirement if four criteria are met: 1) the goods were specially manufactured for the buyer, 2) they are not suitable for sale to others, 3) the circumstances reasonably indicate that the goods are for the buyer and 4) before repudiation the seller has made a substantial beginning in their manufacture.

APPLYING THE CODE

Problem 3-7: Specially Manufactured Goods

Paula stopped into the Custom Athlete Shop and ordered four dozen gym bags for her Commercial Law class at a price of $20 per bag, monogrammed with the phrase "Code Connoisseur." Paula does not recall signing anything but she did receive a receipt from the shop confirming the quantity, price and monogram. One day later, she phoned the shop to tell them that she had changed her mind and no longer wanted the bags. The shop's manager said, "*Too late. We already set up the press for the monogram.*" How should Paula proceed? Which additional facts would you need to learn?

Partial payment (DCC section 2–201(3)(c)). Absent a writing, an otherwise valid contract is enforceable to the extent to which payment has been made and accepted.

APPLYING THE CODE

Problem 3-8: Partial Payment

Suppose that in problem 7 Paula had remitted to the Custom Athlete Shop a down payment of $100 for the bags. What result?

Partial delivery (DCC section 2–201(3)(c)). Absent a writing, an otherwise valid contract is enforceable with respect to goods that have been received and accepted.

APPLYING THE CODE

Problem 3-9: Partial Delivery

Suppose in problem 7 that Custom Athlete Shop tenders delivery of the gym bags. Paula opens the box and exclaims, "*Oh no! I told them that I didn't want the bags.*" What result? On what basis do you render that conclusion?

F. The Parol Evidence Rule: DCC Section 2–202

READING THE CODE

> ### DCC SECTION 2–202: Final Written Expression: Parol or Extrinsic Evidence
>
> Terms with respect to which the confirmatory memoranda of the parties agree or which are otherwise set forth in a writing intended by the parties as a final expression of their agreement with respect to such terms as are included therein may not be contradicted by evidence of any prior agreement or of a contemporaneous oral agreement but may be explained or supplemented
>
> **(a)** By course of performance, course of dealing, or usage of trade (section 1–303); and
>
> **(b)** By evidence of consistent additional terms unless the court finds the writing to have been intended also as a complete and exclusive statement of the terms of the agreement.

The parol evidence rule is intended to give certainty to written agreements entered into with care and formality and to protect against perjury. It provides that terms set forth in a final writing (also known as a partially integrated writing) cannot be contradicted by evidence of any alleged prior agreement or contemporaneous oral agreement but can be supplemented by evidence of consistent additional terms unless the court deems the final writing so meticulously well-crafted as to be "a complete and exclusive statement of the terms of the agreement." Such "final, complete and exclusive" contracts (also referred to as fully integrated) cannot be supplemented by evidence of consistent additional terms. However, all final writings, whether partially or fully integrated, can be explained or supplemented by relevant course of performance, course of dealing or trade usage.

UCC section 2–202 is reducible to three essential tenets:

1. Evidence extrinsic to a final writing will be excluded if it contradicts the terms of a final writing and is contained in a prior or contemporaneous oral agreement.

2. A final writing that is deemed by the court to be only partially integrated may be supplemented by evidence of consistent additional terms, but a final writing that is deemed by the court to be fully integrated ("final, complete and exclusive") cannot be supplemented by such evidence.

3. Unless carefully negated in the contract, course of performance, course of dealing and trade usage are freely admissible to explain or supplement both partially integrated and fully integrated writings.

The parol evidence rule can become confounding because it makes a distinction between a "final writing" (partially integrated) and a writing that is "final" but also so meticulously well-crafted as to be deemed by the court as "intended also as a complete and exclusive statement of the terms of the agreement" (fully integrated). In other words, it contemplates two separate levels of finality. Most routine contracts are apt to be deemed final but only partially integrated, and therefore capable of supplementation by evidence of any consistent additional terms. By contrast, a fully integrated (or final, complete, and exclusive) contract is so comprehensive and carefully rendered as to be effectively resistant to supplementation even by consistent, additional terms.

Courts use a multi-factored approach to determine the extent of a given writing's integration. Relevant factors include whether both parties were represented by counsel, the sophistication of the transaction, the price, the amount of time available to comport the writing to negotiations and the presence or absence of a merger or integration clause. A merger or integration clause is a provision in the contract that recites that it is the parties' "final, complete and exclusive understanding." Because a merger clause is usually boilerplate, its presence (or absence) in and of itself is not dispositive, although many courts consider it to constitute a rebuttable presumption of complete integration.

Partially integrated writings (but not fully integrated writings) can be explained or supplemented by evidence of consistent additional terms. All final writings, whether partially or fully integrated, can be explained or supplemented by evidence relevant to the parties' course of performance, course of dealing, and trade usage (the triplets) as long as that evidence has not been carefully negated or displaced in the contract. The problem here is that sometimes evidence relevant to the triplets actually does contradict the writing. Even in those instances, courts have demonstrated a willingness to allow the evidence in, glossing over the fact that it is contradictory under the guise of its serving to "explain" the writing.

To assess admissibility under the parol evidence rule, the court will first categorize the parties' contract. Is it a final writing? The parol evidence rule protects only final writings. If so, is that final writing partially or fully integrated? Partially integrated contracts can be supplemented by evidence of consistent additional terms. Fully integrated contracts cannot. Next, the court will categorize the given proffer (meaning the term(s) that a party seeks to introduce into evidence) and that term's relationship to the final writing. Does that proffer that pertains to an alleged prior or contemporaneous oral agreement reached by the parties contradict the final writing's terms? If so, it is inadmissible. By contrast, is the proffer supplemental? In that case, it is admissible, unless the writing has been deemed fully integrated. Is the proffer merely explanatory (i.e., interpreting existing terms)? In that case, the evidence will nearly always be admissible for that purpose. Finally, is the proffer relevant to the triplets? If so, the court will err in favor of its admissibility no matter even that the parties' final writing is fully integrated unless that proffered aspect of the parties' course of performance, course of dealing or applicable trade usage had been carefully negated in the contract.

One last point must be made regarding the parol evidence rule—sometimes it does not apply. First, as we will see immediately below, it does not apply to agreements that are struck *after* execution of the written agreement (i.e., modifications). This is because the parol evidence rule, by its terms, only applies to agreements entered *before* or *simultaneously* with execution of the written contract, not *after*. Moreover, the parol evidence presupposes a *valid* agreement in the first place. So, if there are facts showing that the agreement as a whole is invalid, then the parol evidence rule will not bar such evidence from being admitted. Thus, for instance (and under section 1–103), evidence that the agreement was procured by fraud, mistake or duress will be admissible, notwithstanding the parol evidence rule. Another related possibility is that the parties agreed to an oral condition precedent to the agreement's validity—say, for example, that just before Wayne signed an agreement to purchase Paula's Picasso painting for $1 million, Wayne said orally that he wanted his obligation to purchase the painting to be subject to the condition that he have the painting authenticated by an expert as a genuine Picasso. Most courts will allow evidence of such oral conditions to be admitted, since it is a threshold predicate for the contract taking effect and becoming valid in the first place.

APPLYING THE CODE

Problem 3-10: Applying the Parol Evidence Rule

A) Buyer, Paula American Bakeries, Inc., began negotiations with seller, David Commercial Ovens, Inc., for the purchase of a commercial grade oven. Early on, they agreed in writing that the price would be $110,000. Later, they orally agreed that Paula American Bakeries, Inc.'s duty to pay was conditioned on it getting financing from a bank. At the end of negotiations, the parties signed a writing that was complete on its face and did not contain a merger clause. The contract price was stated to be $120,000 and the financing condition did not appear in the writing. Paula American Bakeries, Inc., now seeks to introduce evidence of the lower price and the agreed upon financing condition. What result?

B) Wayne Fertilizer Co. manufactures and markets mixed fertilizer comprised of several compounds including phosphate. Kevin Nitrogen Co. produces and sells phosphate. The parties entered into a five-year contract whereby Kevin Nitrogen Co. was to provide Wayne Fertilizer Co. with a minimum of 40,000 tons of phosphate each year at the price of $90 per ton. When phosphate prices fell, Wayne Fertilizer Co. ordered only part of the scheduled tonnage and demanded a lower price for it. Kevin Nitrogen Co. refused. At the ensuing lawsuit, Wayne Fertilizer Co.'s lawyer sought to introduce expert testimony that in the phosphate industry a contract's stated quantity and price terms "are mere estimates, meant to be adjusted based on the market." Kevin's lawyer immediately objected, declaring, *"Your Honor, such testimony is barred by the parol evidence rule."* What is the basis for that objection? How should the court rule? Why?

G. Post-Contract Modifications: DCC Section 2-209.

READING THE CODE

> **DCC SECTION 2-209: Modification, Rescission and Waiver**
>
> **(1)** An agreement modifying a contract within this Article needs no consideration to be binding.
>
> **(2)** A signed agreement which excludes modification or rescission except by a signed writing cannot be otherwise modified or rescinded, but except as between merchants such a requirement on a form supplied by the merchant must be separately signed by the other party.
>
> **(3)** The requirements of the statute of frauds section of this Article (section 2-201) must be satisfied if the contract as modified is within its provisions.
>
> **(4)** Although an attempt at modification or rescission does not satisfy the requirements of subsection (2) or (3) it can operate as a waiver.
>
> **(5)** A party who has made a waiver affecting an executory portion of the contract may retract the waiver by reasonable notification received by the other party that strict performance will be required of any term waived, unless the retraction would be unjust in view of a material change of position in reliance on the waiver.

Sometimes the parties will change or modify their contract after the deal is finalized. When you are presented with a change in terms alleged to have occurred **after** the contract was struck, turn to section 2-209. By contrast, when the alleged change in terms is said to have occurred in the negotiation phase, **before** or as the final deal was being struck, apply section 2-202.

Consistent with Article 2's attempt to discard undue formalism, consideration is not needed to render a post-contract modification enforceable. Section 2-209(1) represents a departure from the common law of contract's pre-existing duty rule, which required that post-contract changes be supported by independent consideration.

While post-contract modifications need not be supported by consideration, they do have to be in writing in two circumstances: 1) if the original contract requires that all modifications be in writing, or 2) if the contract, as modified, is within the statute of frauds. Section 2–209 incorporates the statute of frauds (section 2–201) into its terms. Hence, if the contract, as modified, is for the sale of goods for $500 or more, the change must be evidenced in a valid writing. If the alleged modification is not contained in a valid writing, check to see if one of the exceptions to the statute of frauds applies. Run through the reply doctrine, specially manufactured goods, admissions, partial payment and partial acceptance exceptions to see if any one of those is available on your facts to take the modification out of the writing requirement.

The Official Comments to section 2–209 emphasize that all post-contract modifications must meet the test of good faith imposed by Article 2. Comment 2 provides that the use of bad faith to evade contract performance is prohibited, "and the extortion of a 'modification' without legitimate commercial reason is ineffective as a violation of the duty of good faith." It goes on to suggest that a market shift could provide such a reason. Section 1–201(b)(20) in turn defines good faith to mean "honesty in fact and the observance of reasonable commercial standards of fair dealing."

APPLYING THE CODE

Problem 3-11: Post-Contract Modifications

Buyer Wayne Improvements, Inc., a general contractor, contracted with Kevin, the owner of Transit-Mixed Concrete Company, for the purchase of 200 cubic yards of concrete at a price of $40 per cubic yard. Shortly thereafter, Kevin discovered that the deal was unprofitable and threatened to terminate the contract unless Wayne agreed to an upward price adjustment of $10 per cubic yard. Wayne was under serious time constraints and reluctantly accepted the modification to the price term. Is the modification valid?

Test Your Knowledge

To assess your understanding of the material in this chapter, click here to take a quiz.

4

The Content of the Article 2 Contract

Gap-Fillers, Output, Requirements, and Exclusive Dealings Contracts

Key Concepts

- The applicability of Article 2's gap-fillers when a contract term is unspecified
- The controlling nature of express terms in a contract
- The way to resolve ambiguities within a contract for the sale of goods
- The relevance of course of performance, course of dealing and usage of trade in supplementing missing terms
- How to fill in a missing price term in an Article 2 contract
- How to fill in a missing term related to time, place and manner in an Article 2 contract
- The role of an open quantity term output contract
- The role of an open quantity term requirements contract
- The relevance of an exclusive dealings contract
- The requirement of using best efforts in an exclusive dealings contract

Once a contract for the sale of goods has been formed, questions can arise as to its precise content. Sometimes, for example, one or more of the deal's terms are ambiguous or missing. Article 2, in the sections contained in the 2–300s, provides an approach for assessing the contract's content, filling any gaps, and resolving any ambiguities.

Set forth below is a methodology for discerning the Article 2 contract's terms:

- **Express terms control.** The contract's express provisions are binding unless found to be unconscionable (*see* section 2–302) or in violation of applicable law (*see* section 1–103).

- **If terms are missing, apply this three-step approach:**

  1. Did the parties intend to contract with finality no matter the absence of certain term(s)? If so, proceed to step 2.

  2. Go to the triplets (relevant course of performance, course of dealing or trade usage) to supply the missing term(s) (*see* section 1–303 and section 2–208).

  3. If the triplets are unavailing, go to the Article 2 gap-fillers, contained in the section 2–300s.

- **Article 2's gap-fillers: Article 2 supplies the following terms when there is a gap in the contract that cannot be filled by the triplets.**

  1. When price is unspecified: DCC section 2–305

  2. When time for delivery is unspecified: DCC section 2–309

  3. When place for delivery is unspecified: DCC section 2–308

  4. When manner of delivery is left open: DCC section 2–307

  5. When other specifications as to delivery are left open: DCC section 2–311

  6. When time and place for payment is left open: DCC section 2–310

  7. When quantity is left to be defined by seller's output or buyer's requirements: DCC section 2–306

  8. When an unforeseen event renders performance impossible or impracticable: DCC sections 2–508, 2–613–616 (*see* chapter five)

9. When the quality of the goods is undefined: Article 2's warranty provisions (DCC sections 2–312–318) (*see* chapter six)

A. Working with Article 2's Gap-Fillers

Sometimes, whether by design or inadvertence, the parties to an Article 2 contract leave terms unspecified or absent. In those instances, before resorting to Article 2's gap-fillers, be sure to ascertain first whether the parties intended to close the deal, no matter the absence of a term or terms. You will be able to glean that intent from the document itself as well as the parties' words and conduct. If it is clear that the parties intended to contract with finality, determine next whether their course of performance, course of dealing or applicable trade usage (the triplets) can supply the missing term or terms. (*See* chapter one for a detailed discussion of the triplets.) If the triplets are unavailing, turn to Article 2's gap-fillers. Each of those is discussed below.

B. When Price Is Unspecified: DCC Section 2–305

READING THE CODE

> **DCC SECTION 2–305: Open Price Term**
>
> (1) The parties if they so intend can conclude a contract for sale even though the price is not settled. In such a case the price is a reasonable price at the time for delivery if
>
>   (a) nothing is said as to price; or
>
>   (b) the price is left to be agreed by the parties and they fail to agree; or
>
>   (c) the price to be fixed in terms of some agreed market or other standard as set or recorded by a third person or agency and it is not so set or recorded.
>
> (2) A price to be fixed by the seller or by the buyer means a price for him or her to fix in good faith.
>
> (3) When a price left to be fixed otherwise than by agreement of the parties fails to be fixed through fault of one party the other may at his or her option treat the contract as cancelled or himself or herself fix a reasonable price.

> **(4)** Where, however, the parties intend not to be bound unless the price be fixed or agreed and it is not fixed or agreed there is no contract. In such a case the buyer must return any goods already received or if unable so to do must pay their reasonable value at the time of delivery and the seller must return any portion of the price paid on account.

Sometimes the price for the goods contracted for is left open. Recall that the statute of frauds (section 2–201) requires only that contracts within its scope contain some reference to quantity. All other terms, including price, can be supplied, assuming of course that the parties intended to close the deal no matter the absence of a precise price term.

There are several reasons why price might not be specified in the contract. For example, in industries where price fluctuates the parties might want to wait until performance comes due to set the price and then, at that point, find that they cannot agree. Other times the parties intend to rely on prevailing market rates or a designated expert to supply price and that market index or expert is now unavailable. Alternatively, albeit less frequently, price is not a concern and buyer wants the goods no matter their ultimate cost. In still other cases, the parties have a range in mind for price and need to close the deal without having set the exact price.

Section 2–305 leaves the parties to a contract that does not contain a price term somewhat vulnerable. In the absence of any contractual safeguards, section 2–305 permits the imposition of a "reasonable price at the time of delivery." Notice that a "reasonable price" is not necessarily the market price. "Reasonableness" is subject to multiple interpretations and can turn on the lens of the given observer. Hence, it is best to build safeguards into the contract to temper or rein in the scope of any price that is eventually set. In a contract where price is left open, the parties are best advised to stipulate the procedure or mechanism to be used to eventually set the price. For example, to determine the price for the goods contracted for, the parties could designate an expert and alternate expert in the event that the specified price arbiter becomes unavailable. Alternatively, the parties could stipulate a relevant market, trade journal or independent reference point to impose a price term. Further, it is always wise to set forth in the contract a floor and ceiling for price. Additionally, it is certainly permissible for the parties to close the deal but in doing so, agree to reconvene at a designated later time and place to arrive at a price term and then, if price fails to be set through no fault of either party, deem the contract terminated.

APPLYING THE CODE

Problem 4-1: Supplying a Missing Price Term

David, in the market for a sport fishing boat, stopped into Tidewater Yachts, Inc. There he spoke with Wayne, a sales representative, who took David for a ride on a new model sport fishing boat known as the 4000 Trophy Convertible. Wayne told David that the boat had been released in limited edition, and that if David was interested he should act quickly. David loved the boat. When he asked about its price, Wayne told him that he would have to contact the manufacturer but it was about $120,000 and would not be higher than $130,000. David hesitated but, not wanting to lose the boat to some other buyer, signed a sales agreement for its purchase. The agreement contained no mention of price.

A) Did David just make a big mistake? What safeguards could have been included in the contract to protect David?

B) Suppose that the following week Wayne telephoned David to indicate that the price for the boat is actually $140,000. Is David bound by that price? Which other provisions of Article 2, already covered, might apply here? How would the parol evidence rule be relevant to your answer? (See section 2–202, discussed in Chapter 3.)

C) Suppose now that David tells Wayne, "*Sorry, but that's more than I bargained for. I don't want the boat.*" Wayne sues. You are the judge's law clerk. What would your bench memo to the court look like?

UCC provisions containing other gap-fillers for time, place, manner and other specifications relating to delivery and payment follow.

C. Time for Delivery: DCC Section 2–309

READING THE CODE

> ### ■ DCC SECTION 2–309: Absence of Specific Time Provisions; Notice of Termination
>
> **(1)** The time for shipment or delivery or any other action under a contract if not provided in this Article or agreed upon shall be a reasonable time.
>
> **(2)** Where the contract provides for successive performances but is indefinite in duration it is valid for a reasonable time but unless otherwise agreed may be terminated at any time by either party.
>
> **(3)** Termination of a contract by one party except on the happening of an agreed event requires that reasonable notification be received by the other party and an agreement dispensing with notification is invalid if its operation would be unconscionable.

D. Place for Delivery: DCC Section 2–308

READING THE CODE

> ### ■ DCC SECTION 2–308: Absence of Specified Place for Delivery
>
> Unless otherwise agreed
>
> **(a)** the place for delivery of goods is the seller's place of business or if he or she has none his or her residence; but
>
> **(b)** in a contract for sale of identified goods which to the knowledge of the parties at the time of contracting are in some other place, that place is the place for their delivery; and
>
> **(c)** documents of title may be delivered through customary banking channels.

E. Manner of Delivery: DCC Section 2–307

READING THE CODE

> **DCC SECTION 2–307: Delivery in Single Lots or Several Lots**
>
> Unless otherwise agreed all goods called for by a contract for sale must be tendered in a single delivery and payment is due only on such tender but where the circumstances give either party the right to make or demand delivery in lots the price if it can be apportioned may be demanded for each lot.

F. Other Specifications Relating to Delivery: DCC Section 2–311

READING THE CODE

> **DCC SECTION 2–311: Options and Cooperation Respecting Performance**
>
> (1) An agreement for sale which is otherwise sufficiently definite (subsection (3) of section 2–204) to be a contract is not made invalid by the fact that it leaves particulars of performance to be specified by one of the parties. Any such specification must be made in good faith and within limits set by commercial reasonableness.
>
> (2) Unless otherwise agreed specifications relating to assortment of the goods are at the buyer's option and except as otherwise provided in subsections (1)(c) and (3) of section 2–319 specifications or arrangements relating to shipment are at the seller's option.
>
> (3) Where such specification would materially affect the other party's performance but is not seasonably made or where one party's co-operation is necessary to the agreed performance of the other but is not seasonably forthcoming, the other party in addition to all other remedies
>
>   (a) is excused for any resulting delay in his or her own performance; and
>
>   (b) may also either proceed to perform in any reasonable manner or after the time for a material part of his or her own performance

> treat the failure to specify or to cooperate as a breach by failure to deliver or accept the goods.

G. Time for Payment: DCC Section 2–310

READING THE CODE

> **DCC SECTION 2–310: Open Time for Payment or Running of Credit; Authority to Ship Under Reservation**
>
> Unless otherwise agreed
>
> **(a)** payment is due at the time and place at which the buyer is to receive the goods even though the place of shipment is the place of delivery; and
>
> **(b)** if the seller is authorized to send the goods he or she may ship them under reservation, and may tender the documents of title, but the buyer may inspect the goods after their arrival before payment is due unless such inspection is inconsistent with the terms of the contract (section 2–513); and
>
> **(c)** if delivery is authorized and made by way of documents of title otherwise than by subsection (b) then payment is due regardless of where the goods are to be received (i) at the time and place at which the buyer is to receive delivery of the tangible documents or (ii) at the time the buyer is to receive delivery of the electronic documents and at the seller's place of business or if none, the seller's residence; and
>
> **(d)** where the seller is required or authorized to ship the goods on credit the credit period runs from the time of shipment but post-dating the invoice or delaying its dispatch will correspondingly delay the starting of the credit period.

APPLYING THE CODE

Problem 4-2: Supplying Terms Relevant to Time, Place, Manner and Other Specifications Relating to Delivery and Payment

Kevin owns and operates a brickyard in rural Massachusetts. Paula is the project manager for a small residential subdivision just outside Boston. In early July she contracts with Kevin for the purchase of six cubes of brick (there are 500 bricks in a cube) at $400 per cube. During negotiations, she indicates that she will need delivery completed by October 1. The parties' contract is silent as to the time, place and manner of delivery and payment.

A) Suppose that Kevin delivers all six cubes to Paula's job site on July 10. He demands payment in full and Paula's assistant remits full payment. When Paula returns to the office she is dismayed and telephones Kevin to say, "*Why are these bricks here? We assumed that we'd be picking them up at your brickyard. For that matter, we can't possibly store all of these bricks at one time. What were you thinking?*" Has Kevin breached the contract? Should payment have been remitted? Which additional facts would you need to learn to answer that question?

B) Suppose that the custom in the brick industry is for shipment in increments of two cubes per delivery, delivery to buyer's place of business. Is that custom binding? What if the parties wanted to displace or negate relevant trade usage? Could they do so?

H. Open Quantity Term: Output and Requirements Contracts: DCC Section 2–306

READING THE CODE

> **DCC SECTION 2–306: Output, Requirements and Exclusive Dealings**
>
> (1) A term which measures the quantity by the output of the seller or the requirements of the buyer means such actual output or requirements as may occur in good faith, except that no quantity unreasonably disproportionate to any stated estimate or in the absence of a stated estimate to any normal or otherwise comparable prior output or requirements may be tendered or demanded.
>
> (2) A lawful agreement by either the seller or the buyer for exclusive dealing in the kind of goods concerned imposes unless otherwise agreed an obligation by the seller to use best efforts to supply the goods and by the buyer to use best efforts to promote their sale.

While contracts for the sale of goods within the scope of the statute of frauds must contain some reference to quantity, it is permissible for the parties to specify that quantity is to be determined on the basis of the seller's output (an output contract) or the buyer's requirements (a requirements contract).

DCC section 2–306 governs output and requirements contracts. It is best analyzed in the context of four essential inquiries:

1. **What is an output contract?** In an output contract, quantity is determined on the basis of the seller's output or production. For example, buyer promises to purchase half of the pizza dough seller makes on a weekly basis, or buyer agrees to buy 25% of seller's wheat crop harvested each year during the months of September and October. The hallmark of an output contract is reducible to the rhyme, *"What will the giver deliver?"* or *"If you make it, I'll take it."*

2. **What is a requirements contract?** In a requirements contract, quantity is determined on the basis of the buyer's needs. To remember that, think: *"What do you require buyer?"* For example, seller promises to supply buyer with 25% of its weekly needs for mozzarella cheese or a designated percentage of the bricks needed to complete construction of buyer's home.

3. **When quantity is determined by seller's output or buyer's requirements, what is the potential for abuse?** Sometimes a seller in an output contract or a buyer in a requirements contract will take advantage of a market shift and manipulate its respective output or requirements. Abuse can arise when a seller's output or buyer's requirements are not actual (for example, to take advantage of a market shift in its favor buyer precipitously increases its requirements to stockpile the goods or, now that the market has shifted in seller's favor, seller suddenly speeds up its production to yield exceedingly high output). Alternatively, a seller might suddenly cease production or buyer might claim to no longer have a need for the goods. Thus, abuse can be found in the presence of a wholesale withdrawal by either buyer or seller.

4. **How does section 2–306 protect against abuse?** To protect against abuse or manipulation, all output and requirements must be actual and must be made in good faith. In addition, even if actual and rendered in good faith, any output or requirement must not be unreasonably disproportionate to any stated estimate or otherwise standard or comparable prior output or requirements.

APPLYING THE CODE

Problem 4-3: Output and Requirements Contracts

David is a builder-developer seeking more efficient energy sources for the buildings that his company, Source Development, owns and builds. Wayne is the owner and operator of Green Efficiency, a company that manufactures a new type of hydrogen generator able to quickly and cheaply utilize solar energy. David contracted with Wayne for the purchase of 75% of the hydrogen generators made by Green Efficiency for a designated two-year period at a price of $25,000 per generator. For the first several months, Green Efficiency produced on average four generators per month. Shortly thereafter the hydrogen market dropped, rendering hydrogen prices at an all-time low. On the open market, the contracted-for generators now sell for only $14,000 per unit. Green Efficiency, seeking to maximize the opportunity presented by its contract with Source Development, sped up its production lines so that it is now on schedule to produce eight generators per month.

A) What kind of contract did the parties enter into? How do you know that?

B) As counsel for Source Development, what sorts of contract provisions would you have sought to include?

C) Is Source Development obliged to accept and pay for Green Efficiency's higher yield? Which additional facts would you need to learn to determine the answer?

I. The Exclusive Dealing Output or Requirements Contract: DCC Section 2–306

Sometimes a section 2–306 output or requirements contract will be an exclusive dealing contract. For example, an exclusive dealing requirements contract would oblige buyer to purchase only from seller all of buyer's needs for a particular good. An exclusive dealing output contract would oblige seller to sell its entire output of a designated good only to buyer. Built into every exclusive dealing output or requirements contract is an element of vulnerability. Hence, section 2–306(2) provides that unless otherwise agreed, every exclusive dealing output and requirements contract obliges the parties to do even more than perform in good faith. Each must use best efforts and be particularly diligent. In an exclusive dealing arrangement, seller impliedly promises to use best efforts to supply the goods, and buyer implicitly promises to use best efforts to promote their sale.

APPLYING THE CODE

Problem 4-4: Exclusive Dealing Contract

Paula is the sole owner of the Ballantine Brewery, located in Newark, New Jersey. Kevin owns and operates Super Fresh Supermarket. Two years ago, Paula and Kevin entered into a contract wherein Super Fresh would become the sole seller of Ballantine beer. Initially, Kevin launched a significant ad campaign to promote the beer label at his stores, sponsored various promotional events and created appealing displays for the product on the supermarkets' shelves. A few months in, noticing that the brand was underperforming, Kevin discontinued the ad campaign, cancelled the remaining promotional events and put the beer on the back shelves of display cases. Sales continued to decline, to the extent that the brewery was eventually forced into bankruptcy. Paula has sued Kevin for breach of contract.

A)   What kind of contract is this?

B)   Has Super Fresh breached the contract? Which additional facts would you need to learn to better answer that question?

C)   How could Paula have better protected Ballantine's interests?

Test Your Knowledge

To assess your understanding of the material in this chapter, click here to take a quiz.

5

More About the Content of the Contract

Excuse Doctrine as a Gap-Filler

Key Concepts

- When goods are identified to an Article 2 contract
- The events that render a party's performance impossible due to casualty to goods
- The events that render a party's performance impracticable due to unforeseeability
- The risk of loss of casualty to goods and when it passes from seller to buyer
- The determination of fault in assessing risk of loss
- The difference between a shipment contract and a destination contract
- The failure of means of payment or method of delivery

Sometimes an unforeseen event renders a party's performance of an Article 2 contract impossible or, while not impossible, nonetheless impracticable. In such instances, when will that party be excused from performing and thereby relieved of its contracted-for obligations? Article 2 answers that question in the context of its provisions on excused non-performance. We consider those as gap-fillers because the parties typically will not have addressed in their contract the matter of how to proceed in the event that an unforeseen contingency or calamity renders performance impossible or impracticable. Do you see why?

Set forth below is the checklist of Article 2 sections relevant to answering the question of when a seller's performance obligation will be excused now that an unforeseeable circumstance has occurred to render that performance either impossible or impracticable.

- **Impossibility of performance:** DCC section 2–613 applies when goods identified to the contract have suffered casualty through no fault of either party and before the risk of loss passed to buyer.

- **Risk of loss:** DCC section 2–509 sets forth rules relevant to the question of when the risk of loss of casualty to identified goods has passed from seller to buyer.

- **Impracticability of performance:** DCC section 2–615 applies when seller's performance has been rendered exceedingly difficult or impracticable because of the occurrence of some event not foreshadowed in the parties' bargaining process, such as a labor strike, embargo and governmental moratorium.

- **Failure of means of payment or method of delivery:** DCC section 2–614 applies when a matter secondary to the heart of the contract, such as the means of payment or method of delivery for the goods, is no longer available.

A. Impossibility of Performance: DCC Section 2–613

READING THE CODE

DCC SECTION 2–613: Casualty to Identified Goods

Where the contract requires for its performance goods identified when the contract is made, and the goods suffer casualty without fault of either party before the risk of loss passes to the buyer, or in a proper case under a "no arrival, no sale" term (section 2–324) then

(a) if the loss is total the contract is avoided; and

(b) if the loss is partial or the goods have so deteriorated as no longer to conform to the contract the buyer may nevertheless demand inspection and at his or her option either treat the contract as avoided or accept the goods with due allowance from the contract price for the deterioration or the deficiency in quantity but without further right against the seller.

DCC section 2–613 applies when the goods identified to the contract suffer damage or devastation through no fault of either party and before the risk of that loss has passed to the buyer. For example, seller contracts with buyer for the sale of the famous ball gown that Princess Diana wore when, in an iconic historical moment, she danced with John Travolta at a State Department dinner. Shortly thereafter, a fire breaks out at the warehouse where the gown has been stored, destroying the gown. If the elements of section 2–613 are satisfied and the loss is total, seller will be excused from his performance obligation and released without liability from the terms of the contract. If the loss is only partial, buyer has the option to either avoid the contract in its entirety or accept the non-damaged goods with an appropriate reduction in price. By contrast, if the elements needed to plead excuse are not satisfied, seller will be liable for breach of contract irrespective of whether the loss is total or partial and no matter that the contracted-for goods are no longer available.

Use this three-step technique to handle questions related to casualty to identified goods.

1. **Are the goods contracted-for "identified" to the contract?** A good is identified when it is distinguishable from the field of similarly situated goods. In the example above, the ball gown is identified to the contract. It is only that iconic ball gown, and no other ball gown, that will satisfy the contract's terms.

2. **If the contracted-for goods are identified to the contract, have they suffered damage or devastation through no fault of either party?** Official Comment 1 to DCC section 2–613 defines fault to include negligence in addition to willful wrong. Fault is liberally defined to encourage the parties to exercise reasonable care with respect to the goods contracted for. If the identified goods have suffered casualty as a proximate cause of seller's carelessness, seller will not be excused and will be liable for breach of contract.

3. **Has the no-fault casualty to identified goods occurred before the risk of that loss passed to the buyer?** If the risk of loss had already passed from seller to buyer at the time that the goods are destroyed or damaged, excuse doctrine does not apply and buyer must remit payment for the goods (no matter that they are compromised or no longer exist). In those instances, the presumption is that the buyer insured the goods and that insurance will cover the loss. By contrast, if the risk of loss had not yet passed from seller to buyer at the time of the casualty to

the identified goods, excuse doctrine does apply to relieve seller of his performance obligation.

DCC section 2–509 applies to answer the question of when the risk of loss passes from seller to buyer.

READING THE CODE

DCC SECTION 2–509: Risk of Loss in the Absence of Breach

(1) Where the contract requires or authorizes the seller to ship the goods by carrier

    (a)   if it does not require him or her to deliver them at a particular destination, the risk of loss passes to the buyer when the goods are duly delivered to the carrier even though the shipment is under reservation (section 2–505); but

    (b)   if it does require him or her to deliver them at a particular destination and the goods are there duly tendered while in the possession of the carrier, the risk of loss passes to the buyer when the goods are there duly so tendered as to enable the buyer to take delivery.

(2) Where the goods are held by a bailee to be delivered without being moved, the risk of loss passes to the buyer

    (a)   on the buyer's receipt of possession or control of a negotiable document of title covering the goods; or

    (b)   on acknowledgment by the bailee of the buyer's right to possession of the goods; or

    (c)   after his or her receipt of possession or control of a non-negotiable document of title or other direction to deliver in a record, as provided in subsection (4)(b) of section 2–503.

(3) In any case not within subsection (1) or (2), the risk of loss passes to the buyer on his or her receipt of the goods if the seller is a merchant; otherwise the risk passes to the buyer on tender of delivery.

(4) The provisions of this section are subject to contrary agreement of the parties and to the provisions of this Article on sale on approval (section 2–327) and on effect of breach on risk of loss (section 2–510).

DCC section 2–509 provides four answers to the question *"when does the risk of loss pass from seller to buyer?"*

1. In a **shipment contract**, the risk of loss passes once seller places conforming goods into the hands of the carrier. Section 2–509(1)(a). A shipment contract arises whenever the contract requires shipment of the goods without the added specification that seller assure the goods' arrival at a particular destination. In commercial exchanges, the term "F.O.B. (free on board) seller's place of business" is a shorthand reference to the fact that this is a shipment contract.

2. In a **destination contract**, the risk of loss does not pass from seller to buyer until the conforming goods arrive at their specified destination, so tendered as to enable buyer to take delivery. Section 2–509(1)(b). A destination contract arises whenever the contract specifies that seller assure the goods' arrival at the particular destination. In commercial exchanges, the term "F.O.B. (free on board) buyer's place of business" is a shorthand reference to the fact that this is a destination contract.

3. If the goods are in a **warehouse or other storage facility** and are to be delivered without being moved, then the risk of loss passes from seller to buyer on buyer's receipt of a document of title covering the goods. DCC section 2–509(2).

4. In **all other instances**, the risk of loss passes from seller to buyer on buyer's receipt of the goods if seller is a merchant or, if seller is a non-merchant, on seller's tender of delivery, no matter that buyer is not yet in receipt of the goods. DCC section 2–509(3). This catch-all provision applies when, for example, the goods are to be picked up at seller's place of business.

APPLYING THE CODE

Problem 5-1: Identifying Identified Goods

A) David, a farmer, contracted with Paula, the owner of a Chipotle franchise, for the sale of "ten bushels of yellow corn." Is corn identified to the contract? Why or why not? If David's crop suffers locust infestation, is David excused from the contract? If not, what is David obliged to do?

B) David contracts with Paula to sell "organic yellow corn grown during the upcoming growing season on the rear twenty acres of Mill Creek Farm." Is the corn identified to the contract? Why or why not? If the specified acreage suffers devastation by locust infestation, what result?

Problem 5-2: Finding Fault

Kevin, a rodeo operator, contracted with Wayne, a rancher, and agreed to pay $50,000 for the prize bull Ferdinand. On the day before Kevin was to pick up the bull, Wayne's farmhand left the barn door open. Ferdinand escaped the premises and is nowhere to be found. Will excuse doctrine relieve Wayne from his performance obligation?

Problem 5-3: Knowing When the Risk of Loss Has Passed

Paula, a New York manufacturer and seller, contracted with David, a North Carolina designer and buyer, for the sale of textiles. The contract stated that it is "F.O.B. New York." The textiles were stolen in transit. Will Paula be excused from her performance obligation? What about David?

Problem 5-4: Knowing When the Risk of Loss Has Passed

Wayne, a California winemaker, contracted with Kevin, owner of a specialty wine shop in Maryland, to sell Kevin Wayne's entire stock of Caberlot, a wine that only Wayne makes using the rarest grapes in the world. The contract stated that it is "F.O.B. Maryland." The carrier's cooling system malfunctioned, significantly damaging the Caberlot. Will Wayne be excused from his performance obligation?

Problem 5-5: Knowing When the Risk of Loss Has Passed

David, the owner of Fargo Oil Company and seller, contracted with Paula, chief operating officer of Triple Flow gas stations and buyer, for the sale of 2,500 barrels of canola-infused diesel fuel, a specialty hybrid brand. The contract specified that Triple Flow was to siphon the goods from Fargo's holding tank at a port in Perth Amboy, New Jersey. When the goods were ready for retrieval, but before Paula had received the relevant documents of title authorizing Triple Flow's retrieval, a fire broke out at the port, destroying the goods. Will Fargo be able to successfully claim excuse?

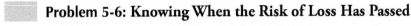

Problem 5-6: Knowing When the Risk of Loss Has Passed

Wayne, a sports memorabilia collector and seller, contracted with Kevin, another collector and buyer, for the sale of Barry Bond's 700th hit baseball. The parties agreed that Kevin would pick up the baseball at Wayne's home once Kevin's check for the baseball cleared. The check cleared and Wayne phoned Kevin to tell him, "*Congratulations, buddy. It's all yours. You can pick it up anytime this week.*" Before Kevin had a chance to pick up the ball, it disappeared. Wayne does not know what happened but suspects that it may have been stolen by a guest at a recent party that Wayne hosted. Will Wayne be able to successfully claim excuse?

B. Impracticability of Performance: DCC Section 2–615

READING THE CODE

DCC SECTION 2–615: Excuse by Failure of Presupposed Conditions

Except so far as a seller may have assumed a greater obligation and subject to the preceding section on substituted performance:

(a) Delay in delivery or non-delivery in whole or in part by a seller who complies with paragraphs (b) and (c) is not a breach of his or her duty under a contract for sale if performance as agreed has been made impracticable by the occurrence of a contingency the non-occurrence of which was a basic assumption on which the contract was made or by compliance in good faith with any applicable foreign or domestic governmental regulation or order whether or not it later proves to be invalid.

(b) Where the causes mentioned in paragraph (a) affect only a part of the seller's capacity to perform, he or she must allocate production and deliveries among his or her customers but may at his or her option include regular customers not then under contract as well as his or her own requirements for further manufacture. He or she may so allocate in any manner which is fair and reasonable.

> **(c)** The seller must notify the buyer seasonably that there will be delay or non-delivery and, when allocation is required under paragraph (b), of the estimated quota thus made available for the buyer.

DCC section 2–615 applies when seller's performance, while not impossible, is rendered exceedingly difficult or commercially impracticable because of the occurrence of some unforeseeable event. That event, to form the basis for excusable non-performance, must not have been foreshadowed in the bargaining process. The greater the inference that the problem complained of was predictable, the lesser the inference that the impracticability doctrine will apply to relieve seller from its performance obligation. The idea here is that when the given event was foreseeable during the contract's formation, seller is presumed to have assumed the risk of its occurring, promising to perform notwithstanding its occurrence. Moreover, Official Comment 4 provides that "increased cost alone does not excuse performance unless the rise in cost is due to some unforeseen contingency which alters the essential nature of the performance." Similarly, a market shift will not excuse performance unless attributable to some unforeseeable event such as a governmental moratorium or embargo.

APPLYING THE CODE

Problem 5-7: Impracticability Doctrine

Paula, a manufacturer, sold David three pieces of factory equipment, with a delivery date of October 1. Shortly thereafter, a union strike was called, slowing down production lines and rendering it exceedingly difficult for her to order components necessary to complete the equipment's manufacture. Does excuse apply to relieve Paula of her performance obligation?

Problem 5-8: Impracticability Doctrine

Kevin, a grower, agreed to sell Wayne his output of cotton for fall delivery at $2.00 per pound. During the summer, the market price of cotton rose to $3.00 per pound. Kevin failed to deliver and claimed excuse. What result?

Problem 5-9: Impracticability Doctrine

David is the purchasing agent for the Lexington, Kentucky, public school system. He entered into a five-year contract with Paula, operator of Maple Farms, to supply milk for the school district at a price of 73 cents per container. One year into the contract the price of raw milk tripled, thereby tripling Paula's production costs. She seeks to avoid the contract, arguing that the opening of U.S. trade with Cuba has skewed the milk market. What result?

C. When the Means of Delivery or Payment Fails: DCC Section 2–614

READING THE CODE

DCC SECTION 2–614: Substituted Performance

(1) Where without fault of either party the agreed berthing, loading, or unloading facilities fail or an agreed type of carrier becomes unavailable or the agreed manner of delivery otherwise becomes commercially impracticable but a commercially reasonable substitute is available, such substitute performance must be tendered and accepted.

(2) If the agreed means or manner of payment fails because of domestic or foreign governmental regulation, the seller may withhold or stop delivery unless the buyer provides a means or manner of payment which is commercially a substantial equivalent. If delivery has already been taken, payment by the means or in the manner provided by the regulation discharges the buyer's obligation unless the regulation is discriminatory, oppressive or predatory.

If the agreed upon means of payment is no longer available because of governmental regulation, seller is within its rights to withhold or stop delivery until buyer provides a commercially equivalent way to pay. If the contractually-specified manner of delivery is no longer available but a commercially reasonable substitute is available, performance will not be excused and that substitute must be tendered and accepted.

APPLYING THE CODE

 Problem 5-10: Failure of Carrier or Means of Payment

Kevin, produce manager for Whole Foods, contracted with Fresco Farmers, a Mexican corporation, for the purchase of 2,000 cases of mangoes and agreed to pay the price in Mexican pesos drawn on Banco Primero. Shortly thereafter, Banco Primero failed and was closed by order of the Mexican government. At the same time, the Mexican peso was devalued by 25%. What are Kevin's options?

Test Your Knowledge

To assess your understanding of the material in this chapter, click here to take a quiz.

6

More About the Content of the Contract
Determining the Quality of the Goods

Key Concepts

- The requirement that the seller of goods warrant that he or she has good and rightful title
- The affirmations of fact that constitute an express warranty in an Article 2 contract
- The intersection between express warranties and the parol evidence rule
- The difference between fact and opinion in a seller's representations about goods
- The circumstances when the implied warranty of merchantability applies to a given transaction
- The circumstances when the implied warranty of fitness for a particular purpose applies to a given transaction
- The heightened warranty standards that merchants are held to
- The need to construe warranties cumulatively within an Article 2 contract
- The events that give rise to disclaiming or modifying warranties
- The limitations of warranties when the goods are used by someone other than the buyer

---

In this chapter, we consider how to determine the quality of the goods contracted for. Article 2's provisions on warranties (sections 2–312 through 2–318) set forth the quality standards that the seller of goods is sometimes obliged to meet. We assess those sections on warranties as gap-fillers relevant to the contract's content because they will sometimes be imputed to the seller of goods in the absence of any specific provision on point in the contract.

Set forth below is a checklist of issues relevant to determining the quality of the goods contracted for:

- **The warranty of title:** DCC section 2–312 provides that a seller warrants that she has good and rightful title to the goods.

- **Express warranties:** DCC section 2–313 provides that a seller is bound by her affirmations of fact about those goods that help to form the basis of the bargain.

- **The implied warranty of merchantability:** DCC section 2–314 provides that a merchant seller implicitly promises that the goods contracted for are merchantable, meaning that they would pass without objection in the industry or trade in which those goods are routinely dealt.

- **The implied warranty of fitness for a particular purpose:** DCC section 2–315 provides that a seller who knows or should know of a buyer's particular purpose for the goods and that the buyer is relying on seller's expertise to select suitable goods implicitly promises that the goods are suitable for that purpose.

- **Construe warranties cumulatively:** DCC section 2–317 indicates that more than one warranty can apply to the given circumstances and that warranties are to be construed as cumulative.

- **Disclaimers of warranties:** DCC section 2–316 indicates how express or implied warranties regarding the quality of the goods contracted for might be disclaimed or modified.

- **The limitation of privity:** DCC section 2–318 applies to assess whether the given warranty applies when the user of the goods contracted for is not the buyer but the buyer's family member, guest, employee or invitee.

A. The Warranty of Title: DCC Section 2–312

READING THE CODE

> ### ■ DCC SECTION 2–312: Warranty of Title and Against Infringement
>
> **(1)** Subject to subsection (2) there is in a contract for sale a warranty by the seller that
>
>   **(a)** the title conveyed shall be good, and its transfer rightful; and
>
>   **(b)** the goods shall be delivered free from any security interest or other lien or encumbrance of which the buyer at the time of contracting has no knowledge.
>
> **(2)** A warranty under subsection (1) will be excluded or modified only by specific language or by circumstances which give the buyer reason to know that the person selling does not claim title in himself or herself or that he or she is purporting to sell only such right or title as he or she or a third person may have.
>
> **(3)** Unless otherwise agreed a seller who is a merchant regularly dealing in goods of the kind warrants that the goods shall be delivered free of the rightful claim of any third person by way of infringement or the like but a buyer who furnishes specifications to the seller must hold the seller harmless against any such claim which arises out of compliance with the specifications.

Every seller of goods warrants or promises that he owns the goods contracted for and has the power to sell those goods. In other words, the seller of goods promises that the title conveyed to the buyer is good and free of any outstanding liens or claims that could be asserted by others. Section 2–312 works in tandem with Article 9 of the UCC, which applies whenever a creditor has a security interest or lien in debtor's goods to collateralize or back up the creditor's extension of value to that debtor.

APPLYING THE CODE

Problem 6-1: The Warranty of Title

David, a farmer, borrowed $12,000 from Bank, granting Bank a security interest in David's tractor to collateralize the loan. The parties' security agreement (their contract) provides that David is prohibited from selling or otherwise disposing of the tractor without Bank's prior written approval. Later, and unbeknownst to Bank, David contracts with Kevin for the sale of the tractor. Kevin is unaware of Bank's lien. Has David breached the warranty of title?

B. Express Warranties: DCC Section 2–313

READING THE CODE

DCC SECTION 2–313: Express Warranties by Affirmation, Promise, Description, Sample

(1) Express warranties by the seller are created as follows:

   (a) Any affirmation of fact or promise made by the seller to the buyer which relates to the goods and becomes part of the basis of the bargain creates an express warranty that the goods shall conform to the affirmation or promise.

   (b) Any description of the goods which is made part of the basis of the bargain creates an express warranty that the goods shall conform to the description.

   (c) Any sample or model which is made part of the basis of the bargain creates an express warranty that the whole of the goods shall conform to the sample or model.

(2) It is not necessary to the creation of an express warranty that the seller use formal words such as "warrant" or "guarantee" or that he or she have a specific intention to make a warranty, but an affirmation merely of the value of the goods or a statement purporting to be

merely the seller's opinion or commendation of the goods does not create a warranty.

A seller of goods could create an express warranty in any one of three ways: 1) by what she says about the goods, whether orally or in writing; 2) by providing a description of the goods through, for example, a brochure, pictures or charts of technical specifications or 3) by providing a sample or model of the goods. A sample is actually drawn from the bulk of the goods themselves while a model is presented as a replica of the goods.

There are four important connections to make about DCC section 2–313 and express warranties.

1. To qualify as an express warranty, seller's representation about the goods must be more than mere opinion or puffery. It must be a statement of fact that becomes part of the basis of the bargain. As Official Comment 3 points out, it is presumed that seller's affirmations of fact about the goods are part of the bargain that is struck. It is not necessary that seller had the intent to create an express warranty.

2. Consistent with Article 2's aim to honor substance over form, creation of an express warranty does not depend on seller's use of magic words such as "*I promise*" or "*We warrant*" or "*I guarantee.*"

3. Any statements of fact that seller makes to buyer *after* the deal is struck do not qualify as express warranties. (Remember that an express warranty, to be such, must be part of the basis of the bargain that is struck.) Instead, post-contract promises about the goods' quality are analyzed as post-contract modifications within the scope of section 2–209, discussed in chapter three.

4. DCC section 2–313 will often coincide with DCC section 2–202, the parol evidence rule (discussed in Chapter Three). For example, seller might make various statements relevant to the goods' quality during the negotiation phase of the deal and then seek to disavow those statements once the deal is struck and a written agreement is signed. In those instances, the parol evidence can become relevant to determine when and whether those statements would be admissible to establish the quality of the goods contracted for.

APPLYING THE CODE

Problem 6-2: Express Warranties

Paula, needing new windows for her home, contacted Bella Windows Co. Wayne, the sales representative, came to her home and suggested the "*Bella model 250, easy-slide window.*" He indicated the model 250 has a "*fiberglass finish that is the most durable in the industry and will look beautiful for years to come.*" He showed Paula a model of what he described as the window's "*revolutionary hardware design, with its comfort grip for easy use and smooth operation.*" Paula found the model easy to use. Paula ordered the windows. The windows were installed. Paula found them difficult to open and shut. Then, during a rainstorm, one of the windows shattered. A local repairperson who fixed the window told her that while fiberglass is strong, it is less shatter-resistant than vinyl. Paula is not happy with the windows. Advise her on how best to proceed.

C. The Implied Warranty of Merchantability: DCC Section 2–314

READING THE CODE

DCC SECTION 2–314: Implied Warranty: Merchantability; Usage of Trade

(1) Unless excluded or modified (section 2–316), a warranty that the goods shall be merchantable is implied in a contract for their sale if the seller is a merchant with respect to goods of that kind. Under this section the serving for value of food or drink to be consumed either on the premises or elsewhere is a sale.

(2) Goods to be merchantable must be at least such as

(a) pass without objection in the trade under the contract description; and

(b) in the case of fungible goods, are of fair average quality within the description; and

> **(c)** are fit for the ordinary purposes for which such goods are used; and
>
> **(d)** run, within the variations permitted by the agreement, of even kind, quality and quantity within each unit and among all units involved; and
>
> **(e)** are adequately contained, packaged, and labeled as the agreement may require; and
>
> **(f)** conform to the promises or affirmations of fact made on the container or label if any.
>
> **(3)** Unless excluded or modified (DCC section 2–316) other implied warranties may arise from course of dealing or usage of trade.

Four elements are essential to the application and understanding of the implied warranty of merchantability:

1. The warranty applies only to contracts for the sale of goods, and not for services.

2. Seller must be a merchant as that term is defined in section 2–104.

3. That merchant seller implicitly promises that the goods contracted for are suitable for their customary or usual purposes.

4. The warranty must not have been modified or otherwise disclaimed pursuant to section 2–316, discussed *infra*.

The Official Comments to section 2–314 indicate that goods sold by a merchant "in a given line of trade must be of a quality comparable to that generally acceptable in that line of trade." Official Comment 2. Hence, the meaning of merchantability depends on custom, industry practice and trade usage. The parties' relevant course of performance and course of dealing can also set standards of merchantability. Moreover, price is a relevant gauge of the quality of the goods contracted for, insofar as most buyers expect to get what they pay for. Official Comment 7.

DCC section 2–314 also applies to the sale of food or drink. Previously, liability would attach only when the problem complained of was caused by a foreign substance like, for example, the presence of a nail in a bowl of chili. Liability would not attach when a natural by-product caused the harm complained of, for example, a bone fragment in a hamburger. Today, most courts will impose liability irrespective of whether the offending particle was foreign or natural if, because of the way the food was processed or the size and nature of the substance, or both, a reasonable user would not reasonably have anticipated the substance's presence.

APPLYING THE CODE

Problem 6-3: The Implied Warranty of Merchantability

Kevin is a pre-school teacher. He goes to David's Hobby store and purchases bags of small pom poms, wooden ice cream sticks, Forever-Stick glue, small cardboard containers and buttons. Kevin uses them in class to have his students make decorative jewelry boxes for Mother's Day. To Kevin's disappointment, the glue does not work. The small pom poms, sticks and buttons would not adhere to the cardboard boxes. What is more, the boxes collapsed in the process of the children's decorating them. To try to make some use of the purchases, Kevin brings the remaining buttons home but finds that they break when used to fasten garments. Has the implied warranty of merchantability been breached? Explain.

D. The Implied Warranty of Fitness for a Particular Purpose: DCC Section 2–315

READING THE CODE

DCC SECTION 2–315: Implied Warranty: Fitness for Particular Purpose

Where the seller at the time of contracting has reason to know any particular purpose for which the goods are required and that the buyer is relying on the seller's skill or judgment to select or furnish suitable goods, there is unless excluded or modified under the next section an implied warranty that the goods shall be fit for such purpose.

The implied warranty of fitness for a particular purpose will apply when: 1) seller knows or has reason to know of the particular purpose that buyer has in mind for the goods and 2) buyer actually relies on seller's expertise to select suitable goods. This is the only warranty that depends for its successful assertion on buyer's demonstration of reliance in fact on seller's judgment. Hence, the greater the buyer's reliance on its own independent research and judgment, the lesser the inference that buyer actually relied on seller's expertise to make this purchase.

Official Comment 1 states that the question of whether or not this warranty arises in a given case is one of fact to be determined by an assessment of the circumstances of the contracting. The relevant consideration becomes whether "the circumstances are such that the seller has reason to realize the purpose intended or that the reliance exists." Official Comment 1. The buyer, in turn, must actually be relying on the seller.

There is a significant difference between "particular purpose" and "ordinary purpose." As Official Comment 2 points out, particular purpose "envisages a specific use by the buyer which is peculiar to the nature of his business whereas the ordinary purposes for which goods are used are those envisaged in the concept of merchantability and go to uses which are customarily made of the goods in question." For instance, shoes are typically used for walking in ordinary, customary circumstances, but a seller may know or have reason to know that a particular pair was selected for mountain climbing on especially slippery terrain.

Notice that section 2–315 is not limited to merchant sellers. As Official Comment 4 points out, "Although normally the warranty will arise only where the seller is a merchant with the appropriate 'skill or judgment,' it can arise as to non-merchants where this is justified by the particular circumstances."

APPLYING THE CODE

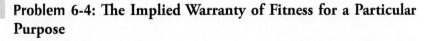

Problem 6-4: The Implied Warranty of Fitness for a Particular Purpose

Assume the same set of facts as those contained in problem 6-3, only now suppose that Kevin enters David's Hobby store having done some research. He asks about Forever-Stick, a glue that he read works on all surfaces. He tells David about the project he has in mind for his class and what he has read about Forever-Stick. David says, "Forever Stick is very strong," and shows Kevin where to find it in the store. Kevin purchases it. Has an implied warranty of fitness for a particular purpose been made? Explain.

E. Warranties Are to Be Construed Cumulatively: DCC Section 2–317

READING THE CODE

> ### ■ DCC SECTION 2–317: Cumulation and Conflict of Warranties Express or Implied
>
> Warranties whether express or implied shall be construed as consistent with each other and as cumulative, but if such construction is unreasonable the intention of the parties shall determine which warranty is dominant. In ascertaining that intention the following rules apply:
>
> (a) Exact or technical specifications displace an inconsistent sample or model or general language of description.
>
> (b) A sample from an existing bulk displaces inconsistent general language of description.
>
> (c) Express warranties displace inconsistent implied warranties other than an implied warranty of fitness for a particular purpose.

Often, more than one warranty will apply to a given set of facts. Section 2–317 provides that whenever possible, warranties should be interpreted as cumulative and as consistent with each other. Sometimes, however, consistent construction is just not possible. For example, suppose that fabric is described as "patterned" and that, when buyer requests a sample she is given a swatch that is plaid. Later, when the fabric arrives, it is polka-dotted. In that case, the sample would displace the general language of description and an express warranty would have been breached unless additional facts can support a contrary conclusion.

F. Disclaiming Warranties: DCC Section 2–316

READING THE CODE

> ■ **DCC SECTION 2–316: Exclusion or Modification of Warranties**
>
> **(1)** Words or conduct relevant to the creation of an express warranty and words or conduct tending to negate or limit warranty shall be construed wherever reasonable as consistent with each other; but subject to the provisions of this Article on parol or extrinsic evidence (section 2–202) negation or limitation is inoperative to the extent that such construction is unreasonable.
>
> **(2)** Subject to subsection (3), to exclude or modify the implied warranty of merchantability or any part of it the language must mention merchantability and in case of a writing must be conspicuous, and to exclude or modify any implied warranty of fitness the exclusion must be by a writing and conspicuous. Language to exclude all implied warranties of fitness is sufficient if it states, for example, that "There are no warranties which extend beyond the description on the face hereof."
>
> **(3)** Notwithstanding subsection (2)
>
> **(a)** unless the circumstances indicate otherwise, all implied warranties are excluded by expressions like "as is", "with all faults" or other language which in common understanding calls the buyer's attention to the exclusion of warranties and makes plain that there is no implied warranty; and
>
> **(b)** when the buyer before entering into the contract has examined the goods or the sample or model as fully as he or she desired or has refused to examine the goods there is no implied warranty with regard to defects which an examination ought in the circumstances to have revealed to him or her; and
>
> **(c)** an implied warranty can also be excluded or modified by course of dealing or course of performance or usage of trade.
>
> **(4)** Remedies for breach of warranty can be limited in accordance with the provisions of this Article on liquidation or limitation of damages and on contractual modification of remedy (sections 2–718 and 2–719).

(5) The implied warranties of merchantability and fitness shall not be applicable to a contract for the sale of human blood, blood plasma or other human tissue or organs from a blood bank or reservoir of such other tissues or organs. Such blood, blood plasma or tissue or organs shall not for the purposes of this Article be considered commodities or goods subject to sale or barter, but shall be considered as medical services.

Often, the seller of goods will attempt to negate or displace any warranties that might otherwise apply. Section 2–316 makes plain that when the language of a disclaimer and the language of an express warranty conflict, the express warranty controls. For example, suppose that the contract states that buyer has agreed to purchase a dryer. The contract also recites that "seller hereby disclaims all warranties." When a washer arrives instead, seller has breached the contract and cannot rely on the warranty disclaimer to justify its non-conforming tender.

The implied warranty of merchantability can be disclaimed orally or in writing, but the language of disclaimer must mention the word "merchantability" and the disclaimer, if in writing, must be conspicuous. A disclaimer of the implied warranty of fitness for a particular purpose need not use specific language but it must be in a conspicuous writing.

Implied warranties are excluded when the goods in question are described as "irregular", "as is", "with all faults" or by other language or circumstances that commonly would be understood as signaling to the buyer that no implied warranties exist. For example, buyer goes to a used car lot and buys a car that had a sign on its windshield indicating, "AS IS." That sort of language, taken in context, should alert buyer to the fact that there might well be risks associated with the purchase and that buyer should take care to carefully inspect the car.

G. The Limitation of Privity: DCC Section 2–318

READING THE CODE

> **DCC SECTION 2–318: Third Party Beneficiaries of Warranties Express or Implied**
>
> *(States to select one alternative.)*
>
> **Alternative A**
>
> A seller's warranty whether express or implied extends to any natural person who is in the family or household of his buyer or who is a guest in his home if it is reasonable to expect that such person may use, consume or be affected by the goods and who is injured in person by breach of the warranty. A seller may not exclude or limit the operation of this section.
>
> **Alternative B**
>
> A seller's warranty whether express or implied extends to any natural person who may reasonably be expected to use, consume or be affected by the goods and who is injured in person by breach of the warranty. A seller may not exclude or limit the operation of this section.
>
> **Alternative C**
>
> A seller's warranty whether express or implied extends to any person who may reasonably be expected to use, consume or be affected by the goods and who is injured by breach of the warranty. A seller may not exclude or limit the operation of this section with respect to injury to the person of an individual to whom the warranty extends.

Sometimes someone other than the buyer of the goods will suffer harm when the goods are not as warranted. For example, it may be that the buyer's child, employee or house guest is injured when the goods fail to comport with the specifications warranted. Questions of privity arise in those instances and are governed by section 2–318.

Section 2–318 gives states three options to choose from. Alternative A takes the narrowest approach to questions of horizontal privity and extends warranty protection to personal injuries sustained by members of buyer's family, household and household guests. Alternative B extends warranty protection for personal injuries to a broader group, including persons who might reasonably be expected to come into contact with the goods. For example, buyer's landscaper, injured by a defective garden hose, would be protected under Alternative B but not Alternative A. Alternative C, the most generous of the alternatives presented, extends warranty protection to an expanded group. "Any" person is protected, not just "natural" persons. Therefore, business entities are protected, as well as individuals. Moreover, Alternative C includes protection for economic as well as personal injury.

Section 2–318 does not address questions of vertical privity, such as whether an aggrieved buyer can proceed against the manufacturer of the product when the manufacturer is not that buyer's seller. Those questions are addressed by consumer protection statutes, judge-made doctrine, tort law, products liability and design defect law.

APPLYING THE CODE

Problem 6-5: A Review of Warranties

Assume the same set of facts as those contained in problems 6-3 and 6-4. Add that the parties' retail agreement indicates that "*this writing displaces any and all warranties, whether express or implied.*" The Forever-Stick glue proves ineffective for Kevin's project (the decorative Mother's Day containers) and the buttons Kevin purchased break when used for fastening. Additionally, Kevin's classroom assistant Wayne gets some of the glue on his fingers and they stick together so tightly that Wayne requires surgery. Which warranties were made, and which were disclaimed? Would Wayne be able to proceed against David's Hobby store for the injuries he sustained?

Test Your Knowledge

To assess your understanding of the material in this chapter, click here to take a quiz.

7

Performance of the Article 2 Contract

Key Concepts

- Seller's performance obligations under an Article 2 contract
- Buyer's performance obligations under an Article 2 contract
- When a party to an Article 2 contract requires assurances that performance will be completed
- The seller's duty to tender conforming goods in a timely manner
- The buyer's right to inspect goods prior to acceptance
- The buyer's obligation to accept and pay for conforming goods
- The actions that constitute acceptance of goods and whether buyer has indeed accepted
- The imposition on buyer to notify seller of non-conforming goods
- The burden on buyer to prove non-conformity at the time of tender
- The circumstances that allow a buyer to revoke acceptance of goods
- The events that may justify buyer's acceptance of non-conforming goods
- The circumstances that allow a buyer to reject goods and the role of the perfect tender rule
- The standard for cure when seller is permitted the right to remedy an improper tender

In this chapter, we explore the component parts of buyer and seller performance of an Article 2 sales contract. The parties' performance obligations are contained in the 2–500s and 2–600s of the statute. Stated most succinctly, seller performs by getting the right goods to the right place at the right time. Buyer performs by accepting the conforming goods and paying for them. Often, however, something goes wrong on the road to performance of the contract. In that case, several Article 2 sections intersect to provide a framework for analysis.

Sometimes a party to an Article 2 contract will have concerns about the other party's capacity or willingness to properly perform. In such cases, section 2–609 can be helpful. It allows a party with "reasonable grounds for insecurity" with respect to the other party's performance to make a written demand for adequate assurances that performance will be completed. The party making the demand is permitted to suspend its own performance until reassurances are forthcoming, as long as that suspension is "commercially reasonable." The recipient of the demand has thirty days from its receipt to provide adequate assurances. Failure to do so constitutes a breach.

Set forth below is a checklist to use when assessing the parties' performance obligations:

- Begin with section 2–503, which imposes upon seller the duty to tender conforming goods in a timely manner.

- Once seller has tendered delivery, turn to sections 2–513 and 2–512, which apply to buyer's right to inspect the goods tendered. Buyer will know whether seller's tender is conforming by inspecting the goods in accordance with sections 2–512 and 2–513.

- If seller tendered conforming goods on time, buyer is obliged to accept those goods (acceptance in this context is defined in section 2–606) and pay for them, in accordance with section 2–607.

- If seller failed to tender conforming goods on time, buyer's options depend on whether or not buyer accepted those goods. Apply section 2–606 to determine whether, by his words or conduct, buyer can be deemed to have accepted the goods.

- If seller tendered non-conforming goods and buyer has accepted those goods under section 2–606, apply section 2–607 to assess the consequences of acceptance. A buyer who has accepted: i) must remit payment for the goods (no matter their non-conformity), ii) loses the right to reject the goods under section 2–601 and instead can try to revoke the acceptance under section 2–608, iii) must notify seller of the goods' non-conformity or be barred from any remedy and iv) bears the burden of proving that the goods were non-conforming at the time of tender.

- If seller tendered non-conforming goods and buyer has accepted those goods under section 2–606, buyer cannot reject the goods under section 2–601 but can try to revoke his acceptance under section 2–608.

- If seller tendered non-conforming goods and buyer has not accepted those goods under section 2–606, buyer can reject the goods by complying with sections 2–601 to 2–605.

- Finally, a seller who tenders non-conforming goods and now faces buyer's rejection or revocation of those goods will sometimes have the opportunity to cure or correct the defect(s) complained of. Apply the standard for cure set forth in section 2–508 to determine if seller in this case can be given that second chance to get the right goods to buyer.

A. Seller's Performance Obligation: To Get the Right Goods to the Right Place at the Right Time: DCC Section 2–503

READING THE CODE

DCC SECTION 2–503: Manner of Seller's Tender of Delivery

(1) Tender of delivery requires that the seller put and hold conforming goods at the buyer's disposition and give the buyer any notification reasonably necessary to enable him or her to take delivery. The manner, time and place for tender are determined by the agreement and this Article, and in particular

　(a) tender must be at a reasonable hour, and if it is of goods they must be kept available for the period reasonably necessary to enable the buyer to take possession; but

　(b) unless otherwise agreed the buyer must furnish facilities reasonably suited to the receipt of the goods.

(2) Where the case is within the next section respecting shipment tender requires that the seller comply with its provisions.

(3) Where the seller is required to deliver at a particular destination tender requires that he or she comply with subsection (1) and also in any appropriate case tender documents as described in subsections (4) and (5) of this section.

(4) Where goods are in the possession of a bailee and are to be delivered without being moved

    (a) tender requires that the seller either tender a negotiable document of title covering such goods or procure acknowledgment by the bailee of the buyer's right to possession of the goods; but

    (b) tender to the buyer of a non-negotiable document of title or of a record directing the bailee to deliver is sufficient tender unless the buyer seasonably objects, and except as otherwise provided in Article 9 receipt by the bailee of notification of the buyer's rights fixes those rights as against the bailee and all third persons; but risk of loss of the goods and of any failure by the bailee to honor the non-negotiable document of title or to obey the direction remains on the seller until the buyer has had a reasonable time to present the document or direction, and a refusal by the bailee to honor the document or to obey the direction defeats the tender.

(5) Where the contract requires the seller to deliver documents

    (a) he or she must tender all such documents in correct form, except as provided in this Article with respect to bills of lading in a set (subsection (2) of section 2–323); and

    (b) tender through customary banking channels is sufficient and dishonor of a draft accompanying or associated with the documents constitutes non-acceptance or rejection.

The most important takeaway from section 2–503 is that seller performs by making conforming goods reasonably available to buyer. The goods tendered must conform with respect to both quality and quantity. Seller makes goods reasonably available when seller notifies buyer of their availability and holds them for a reasonable period of time to allow buyer to retrieve them or ships them pursuant to buyer's instructions.

B. Determining Whether Seller Tendered Conforming Goods: Buyer's Right to Inspect: DCC Sections 2–512 and 2–513

READING THE CODE

> ### ■ DCC SECTION 2–512: Payment by Buyer Before Inspection
>
> **(1)** Where the contract requires payment before inspection non-conformity of the goods does not excuse the buyer from so making payment unless
>
> **(a)** the non-conformity appears without inspection; or
>
> **(b)** despite tender of the required documents the circumstances would justify injunction against honor under this subtitle (section 5–109(b)).
>
> **(2)** Payment pursuant to subsection (1) does not constitute an acceptance of goods or impair the buyer's right to inspect or any of his or her remedies.

> ### ■ DCC SECTION 2–513: Buyer's Right to Inspection of Goods
>
> **(1)** Unless otherwise agreed and subject to subsection (3), where goods are tendered or delivered or identified to the contract for sale, the buyer has a right before payment or acceptance to inspect them at any reasonable place and time and in any reasonable manner. When the seller is required or authorized to send the goods to the buyer, the inspection may be after their arrival.
>
> **(2)** Expenses of inspection must be borne by the buyer but may be recovered from the seller if the goods do not conform and are rejected.
>
> **(3)** Unless otherwise agreed and subject to the provisions of this Article on C.I.F. contracts (subsection (3) of section 2–321), the buyer is not entitled to inspect the goods before payment of the price when the contract provides
>
> **(a)** for delivery "C.O.D." or on other like terms; or

> **(b)** for payment against documents of title, except where such pay-
> ment is due only after the goods are to become available for
> inspection.
>
> **(4)** A place or method of inspection fixed by the parties is presumed to
> be exclusive but unless otherwise expressly agreed it does not post-
> pone identification or shift the place for delivery or for passing the
> risk of loss. If compliance becomes impossible, inspection shall be as
> provided in this section unless the place or method fixed was clearly
> intended as an indispensable condition failure of which avoids the
> contract.

Section 2–513 provides that unless otherwise agreed in the contract or prescribed by the circumstances, buyer has the right to inspect seller's tender before having to remit payment for the goods. A "C.O.D." or "cash on delivery" transaction is one of those circumstances where buyer must pay for the goods on delivery, even before inspecting them, unless the goods' defect is in plain view and detectable on sight. Section 2–512 provides that in "C.O.D." transactions, buyer's payment for the goods does not qualify as acceptance of those goods.

By analogy, a buyer who purchases goods online typically remits payment at the time of purchase, before the goods arrive for inspection. Whether buyer is obliged to pay on delivery or pay in advance, buyer's payment alone does not mean that buyer has accepted the goods. Whether he chooses to exercise the opportunity or not, buyer must be afforded a reasonable opportunity to inspect the goods tendered before buyer can be found to have accepted those goods. Acceptance and the consequences of acceptance are contained in sections 2–606 and 2–607 and discussed later in this chapter. Buyer cannot be deemed to have accepted and suffer the rather significant consequences of acceptance until buyer has had a meaningful chance to examine the goods.

DCC section 2–513 sets forth four important guideposts relevant to buyer's right to inspect:

1. Unless the contract states otherwise, buyer bears the cost of inspection. If the goods turn out to be non-conforming, buyer can recover those costs as incidental damages under section 2–715.

2. The parties are free to stipulate in their contract the designated time, place and manner of inspection.

3. In the absence of a contract provision on point, buyer is within its rights to inspect at any reasonable place and time and in any reasonable manner. What is or is not reasonable depends on the circumstances and on the parties' course of performance, course of dealing and industry custom (the triplets).

4. Inspection is not mandatory, but a buyer who declines the opportunity to inspect the goods tendered or who fails to inspect in a timely manner will suffer the consequences of having accepted the goods, no matter their non-conformity, and may be precluded from a remedy. The consequences of acceptance are set forth in section 2–607, discussed later in this chapter.

APPLYING THE CODE

Problem 7-1: Inspection

A) Kevin purchases a copy machine for his office, "C.O.D." The machine arrives in a large cardboard box that is partially dented. Kevin refuses to pay for the machine, no matter the courier's assurances that, "*these boxes always get dented. There's nothing wrong with the machine. It's surrounded by yards of bubble wrap.*" Is Kevin within his rights to refuse to remit payment?

B) Assuming the same set of facts as those contained in Part (A), would Kevin have made a mistake by remitting payment to the courier?

C) Paula is the chief purchasing agent for Luxury by Design, a custom furniture-making company. She contracts with David, owner of Rossi Fabrics, for the purchase of 2,000 yards of Japanese silk fabric. The contract stipulates that a sample of the goods tendered is to be examined for quality by industry expert May Tago. When the time for delivery arrives, the parties learn that May Tago is out of the country for the rest of the year. What result? Which additional facts would you need to learn?

D) Now assume that in Part (C) the contract was silent as to inspection. When the time for delivery arrives, Paula insists that they first be inspected by May Tago, the silk fabric industry's leading expert who is particularly adept at gauging the quality of Japanese silks. When she learns that May Tago is out of the country for the rest of the year, she tells David that "the deal is off." Is Paula within her rights?

C. When Seller Has Tendered Conforming Goods, Buyer Must Accept and Pay for Them: DCC Section 2–606

READING THE CODE

> **DCC SECTION 2–606: What Constitutes Acceptance of Goods**
>
> **(1)** Acceptance of goods occurs when the buyer
>
>   **(a)** after a reasonable opportunity to inspect the goods signifies to the seller that the goods are conforming or that he or she will take or retain them in spite of their non-conformity; or
>
>   **(b)** fails to make an effective rejection (subsection (1) of section 2–602), but such acceptance does not occur until the buyer has had a reasonable opportunity to inspect them; or
>
>   **(c)** does any act inconsistent with the seller's ownership; but if such act is wrongful as against the seller it is an acceptance only if ratified by him or her.
>
> **(2)** Acceptance of a part of any commercial unit is acceptance of that entire unit.

Note first that acceptance here, in the context of assessing the parties' performance obligations under section 2–606, is very different from acceptance as that term is defined in the formation phase of the contract under section 2–206. Section 2–206, discussed earlier, applies to determine how assent of an offer can be manifested in order to close the deal. By contrast, section 2–606 is relevant to the determination of whether a buyer to a sales contract has actually accepted seller's tender of the goods that are the subject of the transaction. In short, section 2–206 "acceptance" is about *formation* of the contract, whereas section 2–606 "acceptance" is about *performance* of the contract. Acceptance here means that buyer exercises dominion and control over the goods (by, for example, storing, using or cleaning them) or does any other act inconsistent with seller's ownership (such as displaying the goods in a shop window, listing them on e-Bay or lending them to another).

When buyer's inspection reveals that the goods are conforming, section 2–606 obliges buyer to accept and pay for those goods. Moreover, buyer can be deemed to have accepted even when the goods tendered are non-conforming. In those instances, buyer may have accepted by words, conduct or by default, simply by failing to properly reject non-conforming goods as prescribed by sections 2–601 to 2–605, covered later in this chapter.

DCC section 2–606, when synthesized with DCC sections 2–607, 2–512 and 2–513, is reducible to several essential precepts:

1. Buyer will know whether seller has tendered conforming goods by inspecting the tender. *See* section 2–512 and 2–513, previously discussed in this chapter, on inspection.

2. Buyer always has the right to inspect the goods before buyer can be deemed to have accepted those goods, but is not required to accept. When the contract provides that price is due on delivery (a "C.O.D." or "cash on delivery transaction"), buyer's payment for the goods is not acceptance of the goods. Buyer is still afforded the opportunity to inspect, whether in accord with the contract's specifications or, if the contract is silent, within a reasonable time and in a reasonable place and manner, before buyer can be deemed to have accepted the goods. Sections 2–512 and 2–513.

3. When, having inspected, buyer determines that the goods are conforming, buyer must accept and pay for those goods. Section 2–607.

4. Sometimes, once seller has tendered, buyer will decline to inspect, or fail to inspect in a timely manner. In those instances, once the time for inspection has passed, buyer will be deemed to have accepted the goods even when they are non-conforming. Section 2–606.

5. Buyer's acceptance can be manifested overtly, by words.

6. Buyer's acceptance can also be manifested implicitly, by conduct. Notice that section 2–606 provides that acceptance occurs whenever buyer signifies to seller that the goods are conforming or that the goods are acceptable no matter their non-conformity. Sometimes, buyer's mere silence after the time

for inspection has passed will be deemed acceptance. Other times, buyer may not have overtly signaled to seller that the goods are acceptable but by his conduct, shows that they are. For example, buyer uses the goods.

7. A buyer who fails to accomplish a proper rejection of non-conforming goods will be deemed to have accepted those goods. *See* sections 2–601 to 2–605, which are discussed later in this chapter.

8. A buyer who has accepted the goods bears several consequences, set forth in the next section to be discussed, section 2–607.

APPLYING THE CODE

Problem 7-2: Acceptance

A) Wayne, who owns Hillcrest Stables in Pennsylvania, buys a racehorse at auction from Yonkers Raceway in New York. Rather than bring his veterinarian to the auction, Wayne transports the horse to Hillcrest Stable where Wayne's veterinarian will examine it. That is unusual, since racehorse buyers typically bring a veterinarian to the auction site to inspect the horses. Has Wayne accepted the horse?

B) David buys two flat-screen televisions from Best Buy Online. The goods are delivered. David is on an extended vacation and the televisions remain unopened in their boxes for several weeks. Has David accepted?

C) Kevin purchases living room furniture from IKEA. Once he assembles the furniture, he notices that the sofa's fabric is torn and that the legs on the coffee table wobble. Has Kevin accepted?

D. The Consequences of Acceptance: DCC Section 2–607

READING THE CODE

> ### DCC SECTION 2–607: Effect of Acceptance; Notice of Breach; Burden of Establishing Breach After Acceptance; Notice of Claim or Litigation to Person Answerable over
>
> **(1)** The buyer must pay at the contract rate for any goods accepted.
>
> **(2)** Acceptance of goods by the buyer precludes rejection of the goods accepted and if made with knowledge of a non-conformity cannot be revoked because of it unless the acceptance was on the reasonable assumption that the non-conformity would be seasonably cured but acceptance does not of itself impair any other remedy provided by this Article for non-conformity.
>
> **(3)** Where a tender has been accepted
>
>   **(a)** the buyer must within a reasonable time after he or she discovers or should have discovered any breach notify the seller of breach or be barred from any remedy; and
>
>   **(b)** if the claim is one for infringement or the like (subsection (3) of section 2–312) and the buyer is sued as a result of such a breach he or she must so notify the seller within a reasonable time after he or she receives notice of the litigation or be barred from any remedy over for liability established by the litigation.
>
> **(4)** The burden is on the buyer to establish any breach with respect to the goods accepted.
>
> **(5)** Where the buyer is sued for breach of a warranty or other obligation for which his or her seller is answerable over
>
>   **(a)** he or she may give his or her seller written notice of the litigation. If the notice states that the seller may come in and defend and that if the seller does not do so he or she will be bound in any action against him or her by his or her buyer by any determination of fact common to the two litigations, then unless the seller after seasonable receipt of the notice does come in and defend he or she is so bound.
>
>   **(b)** if the claim is one for infringement or the like (subsection (3) of section 2–312) the original seller may demand in writing that his or her buyer turn over to him or her control of the litigation including settlement or else be barred from any remedy over and

> if he or she also agrees to bear all expense and to satisfy any ad-
> verse judgment, then unless the buyer after seasonable receipt
> of the demand does turn over control the buyer is so barred.
>
> **(6)** The provisions of subsections (3), (4) and (5) apply to any obligation
> of a buyer to hold the seller harmless against infringement or the like
> (subsection (3) of section 2–312).

Buyer must pay at the contract rate for any goods accepted, even when the goods are non-conforming. Moreover, a buyer who has accepted the goods loses the right to reject those goods. Acceptance and rejection are mutually exclusive. In other words, buyer cannot have it both ways. Buyer cannot signal (whether by words or sheer failure to object) that the goods are suitable and then later successfully reject those goods. A buyer who has accepted non-conforming goods can try instead to revoke that acceptance under section 2–608, discussed in the next section, but cannot reject.

A buyer who has accepted the goods bears the burden of proving that the goods were non-conforming when tendered. (By contrast, when buyer rightfully rejects seller's tender because of the goods' non-conformity, it is the seller who bears the burden of proving that the goods were conforming when tendered.) A buyer who has accepted goods and now alleges that those goods were non-conforming when tendered can sometimes face an insurmountable hurdle. The presumption is that the tender was conforming, hence prompting buyer's acceptance of the goods. Why else would buyer have accepted? Additionally, a buyer who has accepted the goods only to later assert that they are non-conforming, must be prepared to rebut the inference that it was buyer who actually caused or contributed to the problem now complained of. It is very difficult for buyer to rebut those presumptions.

Perhaps most significantly, a buyer who is deemed to have accepted seller's tender must seasonably notify seller of the non-conformity **or be barred from any remedy**. Stated differently, a buyer who has accepted the goods must object (whether to their quality, quantity or for any other reason) in a timely manner or forever hold his peace. That is a very harsh and sometimes drastic consequence but a consequence of acceptance nonetheless. Hence, an attorney representing an aggrieved buyer is best advised to be alert to this potential consequence of her client's acceptance or run the risk of a later malpractice lawsuit.

APPLYING THE CODE

Problem 7-3: Consequences of Acceptance

Paula purchased the Espresso Deluxe, an espresso and cappuccino machine for her café. Once installed, she saw that the espresso filter for the machine did not work. She called the seller, who indicated that he would retrieve the machine in a few days. In the meantime, she uses it during the café's busy time to foam milk. What are the risks of her doing so?

E. Buyer Who Accepts Cannot Reject but Can Try to Revoke That Acceptance: Revocation Under DCC Section 2–608

READING THE CODE

DCC SECTION 2–608: Revocation of Acceptance in Whole or in Part

(1) The buyer may revoke his or her acceptance of a lot or commercial unit whose non-conformity substantially impairs its value to him or her if he or she has accepted it

   (a) on the reasonable assumption that its non-conformity would be cured and it has not been seasonably cured; or

   (b) without discovery of such non-conformity if his or her acceptance was reasonably induced either by the difficulty of discovery before acceptance or by the seller's assurances.

(2) Revocation of acceptance must occur within a reasonable time after the buyer discovers or should have discovered the ground for it and before any substantial change in condition of the goods which is not caused by their own defects. It is not effective until the buyer notifies the seller of it.

(3) A buyer who so revokes has the same rights and duties with regard to the goods involved as if he or she had rejected them.

It is difficult for a buyer who has accepted goods to undo or revoke that acceptance. The presumption, difficult to rebut, is that the goods *were* conforming when tendered, hence prompting buyer to accept them in the first place. Otherwise, why would buyer have accepted non-conforming goods? A buyer who seeks to revoke acceptance must have an answer to that very good question.

Section 2–608 sets forth three circumstances that might justify buyer's acceptance of non-conforming goods. First, buyer might have been duped into accepting based on seller's assurances that the defects would be cured, only to have seller renege on those assurances or otherwise fail to correct the defects. For example, buyer complains to seller of a problem with the goods and seller responds by promising to send a repair person or a replacement only to then, after a significant time has elapsed, fail to do either.

Second, it might be that the defects were latent and did not manifest until acceptance had already occurred. For example, buyer purchased tulip bulbs that seemed fine, only to see months later that they failed to grow. Or perhaps buyer picks up his new car from the dealership, drives it for some distance and only then learns that the car's engine fails at speeds of 50 M.P.H. or more.

Third, it could be that buyer's acceptance was based on seller's vociferous assurances that there were no defects, so that those assurances essentially precluded buyer from inspecting as thoroughly as buyer had hoped. For example, when buyer arrives at the car dealership to pick up his brand new vehicle the dealer tells him, "Go take this beauty out and enjoy the day. This car is perfect. I already checked out every nook and cranny. Stop obsessing and hit the open road! Now get out of here!" That buyer may well have been precluded from inspecting as carefully as he would have but for the seller's assurances.

In addition to demonstrating that the circumstances at hand fall into one of the three settings described above, a buyer who has accepted goods now alleged by that buyer to be non-conforming must rebut the inference that buyer's use contributed to or compounded the harm now complained of. Revocation will not reside for any slight defect in the goods' quality or quantity. Revocation depends on buyer's demonstrating that the goods' defect(s) represents a substantial impairment in value to that buyer. The good news for an aggrieved buyer is that "substantial impairment in value" is defined subjectively. The Official Comments to section 2–608 provide that the relevant question is whether, because of the goods' non-conformity, *this buyer, in fact,* suffered a substantial impairment in value in view of the particular uses and purposes that this buyer intended for the goods. It does not matter that seller might not actually know or have reason to know of buyer's particular needs or intended purposes for the goods.

A buyer who intends to revoke his or her acceptance must give seller notice of that intent within a reasonable time after buyer discovers or should have discovered the problem complained of. The Official Comments make plain that it is safest for buyer to act promptly and to particularize the basis for the alleged non-conformity to give seller a chance to cure (pursuant to section 2–508, discussed later in this chapter). Certainly, buyer must act before the goods have undergone a substantial change in value not attributable to their defects.

APPLYING THE CODE

Problem 7-4: Revocation of Acceptance

A) Wayne bought wood panels for the walls of his art gallery. Once up, he and his staff hung the gallery's paintings on the panels. Within a few weeks, Wayne noticed that several of the panels had chipped. He sent a photo of the damage to seller, who replied, *"But that's hardly even noticeable."* Wayne replied, *"Our gallery's patrons are discerning and see everything. The chips will be noticeable to them and to us."* The parties are at an impasse. How should Wayne proceed? Which additional facts would you need to learn to support your answer?

B) Kevin bought a Renato Series 550 automobile. Shortly after driving it off the dealer's lot, a small piece of chrome fell off the car's door. Kevin immediately drove the car back to the dealership. The dealer took a look and said, *"Not a big deal. That happens sometimes because of this model's slight bend. We keep extra chrome strips on hand for that very reason."* The dealer snapped on the missing piece and Kevin drove the car home. Later that month, on a drive from Maryland to New York, the rest of the car's chrome trim fell off. When Kevin brought the car back to the dealership, the dealer said, *"You must have been going crazy speeds for this to happen."* Kevin assured the dealer that he had abided the speed limit throughout. The dealer replied, *"Well, whatever you did, we can't fix this."* What should Kevin do at this point? Which additional facts would be helpful to learn?

F. When Goods Are Non-Conforming and Buyer Has Not Accepted, Buyer Is Within Its Rights to Reject the Tender: Rejection Under DCC Section 2–601

READING THE CODE

> **DCC SECTION 2–601: Buyer's Rights on Improper Delivery**
>
> Subject to the provisions of this Article on breach in installment contracts (section 2–612) and unless otherwise agreed under the sections on contractual limitations of remedy (sections 2–718 and 2–719), if the goods or the tender of delivery fail in any respect to conform to the contract, the buyer may
>
> **(a)** reject the whole; or
>
> **(b)** accept the whole; or
>
> **(c)** accept any commercial unit or units and reject the rest.

Suppose that seller tenders non-conforming goods. Buyer learns of the non-conformity as a result of buyer's inspection of those goods pursuant to sections 2–513 and 2–512, discussed earlier in this chapter. Buyer takes care to avoid accepting those defective goods, mindful of the expansive definition of acceptance set forth in section 2–606 and the adverse consequences of acceptance contained in section 2–607.

A buyer who has not yet accepted non-conforming goods is within its rights to reject the tender. Rejection, when accomplished properly, places buyer in the same remedial position as if seller never performed at all. (The range of remedies available to a buyer who properly rejects non-conforming goods will be discussed in Chapter 8.)

Section 2–601 embraces the so-called "perfect tender rule" and makes rejection available for any non-conformity in quality or quantity, however slight. In other words, buyer has the right to perfect tender. Notice that the standard for rejection is far more generous to buyer than the standard that must be met for buyer to successfully revoke its acceptance under section 2–608. It is much more difficult for a buyer who has accepted goods to undo or revoke that acceptance on the basis of some non-conformity than it is for a buyer who never accepted the goods to reject a non-conforming tender. Do you see why? A buyer who did after all accept the goods now alleged to be non-conforming must overcome the inference that the goods were conforming when tendered (hence prompting buyer to accept) and suffered as a consequence of something that buyer did or failed to do. A buyer is not within his rights to revoke for any defect, however slight. Instead, the buyer who seeks to revoke his acceptance must show that the non-conformity complained of represents a substantial impairment in value to him or her and that buyer's acceptance was basically duped because the goods' latent defects took time to manifest, seller promised to correct the problem but never does or seller's aggressive assurances or other diversionary tactics at the time and place for tender deprive buyer of the opportunity to inspect or to inspect as fully as he desired. *See* section 2–608.

APPLYING THE CODE

Problem 7-5: Rejection

A)   David, a builder-developer, purchased 1,400 board feet of Rosewood lumber, Grade AAAA (the highest grade). The shipment arrives, and David's construction crew inspects and discovers that the order is short 10 board feet. Otherwise, its quality is as promised. Is David within his rights to reject the goods?

B)   What if the shortfall would ordinarily be meaningless to David, but he decides to use it as a way to renege on the deal because, thanks to a market shift, he is now able to buy comparable lumber on the open market at a cheaper rate? Is he within his rights to reject the tender?

C)   Suppose instead that David's crew does not realize the shortfall until several weeks have passed and they have had a chance to more carefully sort and weigh the lumber. A different result? What does your answer turn on?

G. Procedures for Rightful Rejection: DCC Sections 2–602 to 2–605

READING THE CODE

> **DCC SECTION 2–602: Manner and Effect of Rightful Rejection**
>
> **(1)** Rejection of goods must be within a reasonable time after their delivery or tender. It is ineffective unless the buyer seasonably notifies the seller.
>
> **(2)** Subject to the provisions of the two following sections on rejected goods (sections 2–603 and 2–604),
>
> **(a)** after rejection any exercise of ownership by the buyer with respect to any commercial unit is wrongful as against the seller; and
>
> **(b)** if the buyer has before rejection taken physical possession of goods in which he or she does not have a security interest under the provisions of this Article (subsection (3) of Section 2–711), he or she is under a duty after rejection to hold them with reasonable care at the seller's disposition for a time sufficient to permit the seller to remove them; but
>
> **(c)** the buyer has no further obligations with regard to goods rightfully rejected.
>
> **(3)** The seller's rights with respect to goods wrongfully rejected are governed by the provisions of this Article on Seller's remedies in general (section 2–703).

> **DCC SECTION 2–603: Merchant Buyer's Duties as to Rightfully Rejected Goods**
>
> **(1)** Subject to any security interest in the buyer (subsection (3) of Section 2–711), when the seller has no agent or place of business at the market of rejection a merchant buyer is under a duty after rejection of goods in his or her possession or control to follow any reasonable instructions received from the seller with respect to the goods and in the absence of such instructions to make reasonable efforts to sell them for the seller's account if they are perishable or threaten to decline in

value speedily. Instructions are not reasonable if on demand indemnity for expenses is not forthcoming.

(2) When the buyer sells goods under subsection (1), he or she is entitled to reimbursement from the seller or out of the proceeds for reasonable expenses of caring for and selling them, and if the expenses include no selling commission then to such commission as is usual in the trade or if there is none to a reasonable sum not exceeding ten per cent on the gross proceeds.

(3) In complying with this section the buyer is held only to good faith and good faith conduct hereunder is neither acceptance nor conversion nor the basis of an action for damages.

DCC SECTION 2–604: Buyer's Options as to Salvage of Rightfully Rejected Goods

Subject to the provisions of the immediately preceding section on perishables, if the seller gives no instructions within a reasonable time after notification of rejection the buyer may store the rejected goods for the seller's account or reship them to him or her or resell them for the seller's account with reimbursement as provided in the preceding section. Such action is not acceptance or conversion.

DCC SECTION 2–605: Waiver of Buyer's Objections by Failure to Particularize

(1) The buyer's failure to state in connection with rejection a particular defect which is ascertainable by reasonable inspection precludes him or her from relying on the unstated defect to justify rejection or to establish breach

  (a) where the seller could have cured it if stated seasonably; or

  (b) between merchants when the seller has after rejection made a request in writing for a full and final written statement of all defects on which the buyer proposes to rely.

(2) Payment against documents made without reservation of rights precludes recovery of the payment for defects apparent in the documents.

Taken together, the procedures required for buyer to accomplish a rightful rejection yield four bright line rules:

1. When seller's tender is non-conforming, buyer must give seller seasonable notice of his desire to reject the goods. Section 2–602. What is or is not timely notice depends on what the contract says and, in the absence of a contract provision on point, the parties' course of performance, course of dealing and industry custom (the triplets).

2. Buyer must specify the reasons for rejection whenever the defect is curable or seller requests that buyer particularize the basis for its rejection. A buyer who fails to specify the basis for a curable non-conformity or who fails to provide specifics in response to seller's request for those loses the right to reject as well as the right to establish a breach of contract. Section 2–605. The takeaway is that buyer should always specify the basis for rejection, whether buyer deems the defects curable or not and whether seller requests particularization or not. Doing so closes the door to seller's assertion that if it had only known of the grounds for rejection it could have done something to make things right for buyer and thereby preserve the essence of the deal.

3. Once buyer gives timely notice of its desire to reject non-perishable goods on the basis of their non-conformity, buyer typically is obliged to await seller's instructions on what to do with the goods. If no instructions are forthcoming, section 2–604 allows buyer to store, ship or resell the goods on seller's behalf. The expenses of storage, shipment or resale are recoverable as part of buyer's incidental or out-of-pocket expenses occasioned by seller's breach. *See* section 2–715, discussed in chapter 9.

4. When the non-conforming goods are perishable and buyer is a merchant, buyer must make reasonable efforts to resell the goods on seller's account if seller has no agent or place of business at the site of rejection. Section 2–603 imposes this affirmative duty to mitigate only when: i) the goods threaten to decline quickly in value (they are perishable); ii) buyer is a merchant (and presumably familiar with the local market) and iii) seller would presumably have significant difficulty reselling in view of the exigencies of time and the disadvantages of being without an agent in the locale. Note that in those circumstances the merchant buyer must at least make a good faith attempt to resell on seller's behalf. Buyer is not obliged

to succeed at that effort, but must at least try, unless the circumstances are such as to justify the conclusion that any such effort would be fruitless.

APPLYING THE CODE

Problem 7-6: Procedures for Rightful Rejection

A) Paula, an accomplished pianist, contracted with Yamaha to buy a baby grand piano, "C.O.D." The piano arrived on time, was assembled by seller and seemed fine. It had yet to be tuned however (a process that could only occur a week or two after delivery, to allow the instrument to settle). Ten days after delivery, Paula's tuner Fred tuned the piano and reported to Paula that the G sharp key was slightly off pitch, no matter several attempts to get it pitch perfect. Paula is quite upset because even the slightest variation in pitch is detectable in modern concert halls. She decides that she no longer wants the piano. What are her rights? How should she proceed?

B) Kevin, a local crabber whose sole business is near Baltimore, Maryland, contracts with David, a seafood distributor in Richmond, Virginia, for the sale of 100 dozen blue crabs, a delicacy of the Chesapeake Bay. The crabs arrive in Richmond and David sees that they are soft-shell crabs. He does not want them. How should David proceed?

H. Seller's Right to Cure: DCC Section 2–508

READING THE CODE

> **DCC SECTION 2–508: Cure by Seller of Improper Tender or Delivery; Replacement**
>
> **(1)** Where any tender or delivery by the seller is rejected because non-conforming and the time for performance has not yet expired, the seller may seasonably notify the buyer of his or her intention to cure and may then within the contract time make a conforming delivery.

> **(2)** Where the buyer rejects a non-conforming tender which the seller had reasonable grounds to believe would be acceptable with or without money allowance the seller may if he or she seasonably notifies the buyer have a further reasonable time to substitute a conforming tender.

Suppose that seller tenders non-conforming goods. Recall that if buyer has not yet accepted the goods he is within his rights to reject them. (*See* sections 2–601 to 2–605). If buyer has accepted, buyer cannot reject but, in certain circumstances, can revoke the acceptance. (*See* section 2–608). When buyer rightfully rejects the goods under sections 2–601 to 2–605, the seller may have the opportunity to cure or correct the problem(s) that buyer complains of pursuant to 2–508. Section 2–508 tells us that if the contractually-provided time for performance has not yet come due, seller has an unrestricted right to cure. In other words, when seller tenders delivery earlier than contractually specified and buyer rightfully rejects in response to the goods' defects, seller is entitled to a second chance to get it right by tendering conforming goods by the time specified in the contract. Article 2 liberally assures that right in order to preserve the essence of the deal and afford seller the chance to mitigate any harm done.

When seller tenders non-conforming goods on the contract's due date, so that the time for performance has arrived, seller is not given an unfettered right to cure. Instead, seller may cure only if she had a reasonable basis for believing that the tender, albeit non-conforming, would nonetheless be acceptable to buyer. When would seller have those reasonable grounds? Official Comment 2 provides that reasonable grounds can be based on the parties' previous course of dealing, course of performance, or usage of trade as well as the given circumstances surrounding the making of the contract. Comment 2 adds that, "The seller is charged with commercial knowledge of any factors in a particular sales situation which require him to comply strictly with his obligations under the contract."

Section 2–508 does not prescribe how cure is to be accomplished. The case law provides that seller can cure by tendering a conforming replacement or, if appropriate, by repairing the defect.

APPLYING THE CODE

Problem 7-7: Seller's Right to Cure

A) Wayne purchased a 90" flat screen Smart TV from David's Appliances. David promised delivery by January 25, in time for the Super Bowl. The TV was delivered to Wayne on January 20. Wayne installed it and found that some of the Smart TV features did not function. He contacted David and said, "*I want my money back. This TV doesn't work the way it's supposed to.*" What are the parties' rights and duties?

B) Suppose instead that David tenders delivery on January 25. Would your answer change?

Test Your Knowledge

To assess your understanding of the material in this chapter, click here to take a quiz.

8

Buyer's Remedies for Seller's Breach of Contract

Key Concepts

- Buyer's available remedies when seller breaches its performance obligations
- The continued applicability of law and equity for buyer's remedies
- The right to cancel a contract and signal intent to pursue future remedies
- The right for buyer to receive any deposit that was remitted to seller
- When cover is available as a remedial option
- When specific performance would be permitted for a buyer in need of goods
- When money damages may be awarded to a buyer for the difference between market price and contract price
- When money damages may be awarded to a buyer for the difference in value of defective goods
- When buyer is entitled to incidental or consequential damages
- The ability to modify remedial entitlements subject to the unconscionability doctrine

If seller has breached its performance obligations, buyer is within its rights to pursue a remedy. We begin our treatment of buyer's remedies by noting first that the purpose of UCC-available remedies is to make the aggrieved party whole and not to punish. *See* section 1–305. While punitive damages are sometimes available by application of supplemental principles of law and equity under section 1–103, as a general matter Article 2's remedial provisions aim to give the party who was wronged the benefit of the bargain struck rather than mete out penalties for wrongful conduct or non-performance.

A host of circumstances can trigger buyer's remedial entitlements. For example, seller might fail to tender the goods contracted for, or fail to tender conforming goods on time. Alternatively, seller might repudiate before the time for performance comes due.

Buyer's remedial options are indexed in section 2–711 and then elaborated upon in various sections found in the section 2–700s. Buyer's remedial options include:

- The right to cancel the contract, pursuant to section 2–711. Cancellation is a remedy. It calls the contract off. Moreover, a buyer who cancels signals to seller that buyer views seller's failure to perform properly as a breach of contract and that buyer is likely to pursue additional remedies against seller. Cancellation differs from termination. A deal is terminated for amicable reasons. For example, seller rightly pleads excuse or, in an output or requirements contract, the deal comes to its stated end or, if open-ended, the parties agree to terminate. When a deal is terminated, litigation is not on the horizon. By contrast, cancellation is a remedy, portending a litigious outcome for seller's alleged breach of contract.

- The return of any deposit that buyer had remitted to seller, recoverable under section 2–711.

- Cover, available under section 2–712, which allows an aggrieved buyer without the goods contracted for to procure a substitute on the open market.

- Specific performance, pursuant to section 2–716, available when the goods are unique or in "other proper circumstances," allows the court to compel the breaching seller to tender the contracted-for goods to buyer.

- Money damages under section 2–713, which award the buyer who is without the goods contracted for the difference between market price and contract price at the time and place that buyer learns of the breach.

- Money damages under section 2–714, which award the buyer who has accepted non-conforming goods either the difference between the value of the goods as warranted and their actual value in view of their defects or recovery for any loss resulting in the ordinary course from seller's breach.

- Incidental and consequential damages, available under section 2–715, to allow buyer to recover, in addition to its direct measure of recovery, any out-of-pocket losses or reasonably foreseeable consequential damages.

- Add to this analysis consideration of whether the parties, in their contract, modified, displaced or limited any of the remedial entitlements otherwise assured by Article 2. Section 2–719 allows for that possibility, subject to certain limitations including the unconscionability doctrine.

Set forth below is a checklist of issues relevant to consideration of buyer's remedial options when seller has breached its performance obligations in a contract for the sale of goods:

- Is buyer without conforming goods, either because seller failed to deliver or tendered non-conforming goods which buyer rightfully rejected pursuant to sections 2–601 to 2–605? Alternatively, if buyer accepted non-conforming goods, has buyer succeeded in rightfully revoking that acceptance under section 2–608?

- If buyer is without conforming goods, still has a need for those goods and a reasonable substitute for the goods contracted for is available on the market, buyer is within its rights to cover under section 2–712. A buyer who rightfully covers is entitled to the difference between the contract price and the cover price plus any incidental and consequential damages under section 2–715.

- If buyer is without conforming goods, still has a need for those goods and a reasonable substitute is not available on the market, either because the goods are unique or cover is impracticable, buyer might succeed in an action for specific performance under section 2–716. In that case, the court will order that seller remit to buyer the goods that are the subject matter of the transaction. Buyer is also entitled here to recovery for any incidental or consequential losses under section 2–715.

- When seller fails to tender conforming goods and buyer no longer has a need for the goods, neither cover nor specific performance make sense as appropriate remedial options. Instead, a buyer without the goods is entitled to money damages under section 2–713. Section 2–713 awards the aggrieved buyer the difference between the contract price and the market price at the time and place that buyer learns of the breach, together with any incidental or consequential losses under section 2–715.

- When seller has tendered non-conforming goods, buyer has accepted those goods (acceptance is defined in section 2–606), and the circumstances are such that buyer cannot revoke that acceptance (revocation is defined in section 2–608), buyer is entitled to money damages under section 2–714. Section 2–714 awards the buyer who has accepted non-conforming goods the difference between the value of the goods as warranted and their actual value in view of their defects at the time and place of acceptance, together with any incidental or consequential losses under section 2–715.

Keep in mind that freedom of contract allows the parties to waive, modify or displace any of the remedial entitlements contained in Article 2. Section 2–719 specifically allows for that possibility, subject to certain constraints including the unconscionability doctrine in section 2–302.

A. When Buyer Is Without Conforming Goods and Still Needs Them: The Availability of Cover as a Remedial Option: DCC Section 2–712

READING THE CODE

▪ DCC SECTION 2–712: "Cover"; Buyer's Procurement of Substitute Goods

(1) After a breach within the preceding section the buyer may "cover" by making in good faith and without unreasonable delay any reasonable purchase of or contract to purchase goods in substitution for those due from the seller.

(2) The buyer may recover from the seller as damages the difference between the cost of cover and the contract price together with any incidental or consequential damages as hereinafter defined (section 2–715), but less expenses saved in consequence of the seller's breach.

(3) Failure of the buyer to effect cover within this section does not bar him or her from any other remedy.

Cover as a remedy is available when seller has repudiated the contract, failed to deliver or tendered non-conforming goods, prompting buyer to rightfully reject or, when buyer has accepted, to properly revoke that acceptance. Cover allows the aggrieved buyer to go into the market to procure goods in substitution for those contracted for. Cover is a viable option for the aggrieved buyer when he continues to have a need for the goods no matter seller's failure to perform properly and there is a reasonable commercial equivalent for the goods that is available on the open market.

The buyer who successfully covers is entitled to the difference between the contract price and cover price, together with any incidental and consequential damages. Typically, there will be a difference between the contract price and cover price. Seller may have failed to perform because, when the time for performance arrived, the market had shifted to seller's advantage, allowing seller to reap more for the goods on the open market than she would under the contract. The same market shift that favors seller works to the detriment of buyer. By awarding the buyer who covers the difference between the contract price and the market price, buyer is given the benefit of the bargain originally struck with the breaching seller.

Section 2–712 provides that the buyer who covers need not procure goods identical to those contracted-for. Still, the substituted goods must be a reasonable commercial equivalent for those that were the subject matter of the contract. Buyer cannot use cover to unreasonably upgrade or otherwise exploit the opportunity to reap a windfall. Cover must be exercised in good faith.

Further, exercising the cover remedy is not mandatory but if a reasonable commercial equivalent for the goods contracted-for does exist, a buyer who declines the opportunity to cover will have his damages award reduced based on the losses that could have been avoided had he covered. Cover, at bottom, is intended to be a mitigation principle, available as a way for buyer to reduce rather than compound his losses.

Finally, cover as a remedial option is not limited to merchants. Official Comment 4 to section 2–712 provides that non-merchants can exercise the right to cover. Note, however, that a non-merchant is often at a considerable disadvantage when it comes to procuring a good that is more sophisticated or outside the norm. Do you see why? The difficulties that buyer might experience when attempting to cover can be a basis for an award of specific performance to the aggrieved buyer. *See* section 2–716, discussed later in this chapter.

APPLYING THE CODE

Problem 8-1: Cover Under Section 2–712

A) Wayne, a baker, had two delivery trucks. When one was stolen, he contracted with Acme for a new truck. Wayne paid $5,000 of the $40,000 contract price, with the balance due on delivery. Acme promised to deliver within two weeks. Acme failed to deliver on time and indicated that the truck would not be available for another month. Wayne cancelled the contract and promptly purchased a somewhat similar truck from another dealer for $55,000. What may Wayne recover from Acme? Which additional facts would you need to learn to support your answer?

B) Kevin owns a local Blinkos copy and printing center. He contracts with Memorex for the sale of toner and developer for the shop's high-speed copier. When Memorex failed to deliver, Kevin experienced difficulty finding a substitute source for the goods contracted-for. Counsel Kevin, indicating which additional facts you would need to learn.

B. When Buyer Is Without Conforming Goods, Still Needs Them and Cannot Cover: Specific Performance Under DCC Section 2–716

READING THE CODE

> **DCC SECTION 2–716: Buyer's Right to Specific Performance or Replevin**
>
> **(1)** Specific performance may be decreed where the goods are unique or in other proper circumstances.

Sometimes, in equity, the court will be persuaded to decree that the breaching seller must tender the contracted-for goods to buyer. As you might imagine, courts tend to be reluctant to award specific performance because of the burdens that such a decree puts upon the judicial system. If seller fails to comply with the court's order, the matter will be back on the court's docket. To enforce its decree, the court may have to issue a contempt order against seller and compel the sheriff to recover the goods on buyer's behalf. Judges hope to avoid those impositions on often already-crowded dockets and overtaxed law enforcement agents. Hence, at common law, specific performance is considered an extraordinary remedy, available only when the goods are unique so that no substitute will do.

Article 2 liberalizes the common law standard for specific performance. Section 2–716 provides that specific performance is available when the goods are unique or "in other proper circumstances." Goods are unique when they have been identified to the contract, distinguishable from the world of similarly situated goods and not capable of ready substitute. For example, works of art, rare coins and limited edition stamps are unique.

Section 2–716 also allows for the possibility of an award to buyer of specific performance in "other proper circumstances." The case law has found those proper circumstances when, no matter that the goods are not unique, buyer has a significant degree of difficulty in covering based on the totality of the circumstances. Specific performance has also been awarded when buyer, having contracted with the seller for goods, enters into a contract to sell those goods to a third party. Seller's nonperformance renders buyer liable to that third party for breach of contract.

The buyer who succeeds in its suit for specific performance is also entitled to incidental or consequential damages under section 2–715.

APPLYING THE CODE

Problem 8-2: Specific Performance Under Section 2–716

A)   David, a horse breeder, enters into a contract with Wayne, the owner of Elite Stables, promising to sell Wayne the prize horse Seamuffin. Prior to the specified delivery date, David receives a better offer for the horse from Paula, an investor. He reneges on the contract with Wayne. Advise Wayne on how best to proceed.

B)   Paula purchased a used GE Electric Transformer at a relatively low price from Ace Equipment. Once the contract was signed, she entered into a contract to sell the transformer to Aqua Chemicals for a considerably higher price. Thereafter, Ace Equipment failed to deliver. Advise Paula. Which additional facts are important to your answer?

C) Kevin, chief operating officer for Public Service and Gas, a public utility, contracted to buy 50% of Apex's production of natural gas at a fixed price with escalation over a fifteen-year period. The price of natural gas rose beyond the scope of the escalation provision and, after five years, Apex repudiated. Kevin sues. How might the court rule?

C. When Buyer Is Without Conforming Goods and No Longer Has a Need for Them: Money Damages Under DCC Section 2–713

READING THE CODE

> **DCC SECTION 2–713: Buyer's Damages for Non-Delivery or Repudiation**
>
> **(1)** Subject to the provisions of this Article with respect to proof of market price (section 2–723), the measure of damages for non-delivery or repudiation by the seller is the difference between the market price at the time when the buyer learned of the breach and the contract price together with any incidental and consequential damages provided in this Article (section 2–715), but less expenses saved in consequence of the seller's breach.
>
> **(2)** Market price is to be determined as of the place for tender or, in cases of rejection after arrival or revocation of acceptance, as of the place of arrival.

Suppose that seller has breached the contract by failing to tender conforming goods on time. It may be that circumstances are such that buyer now no longer has a need or use for the goods. In that case, neither cover nor specific performance is helpful. Instead, the aggrieved buyer may elect to pursue money damages from the breaching seller. Section 2–713 applies to give buyer the benefit of the bargain that was struck by awarding the buyer, who is without the goods contracted for, the difference between the contract price and the market price at the time and place that buyer learns of the breach. In addition to that direct measure of recovery, buyer is entitled to incidental and consequential damages under section 2–715.

There is apt to be a difference here between purchase price and market price at the time of breach. Do you see why? Often, seller reneges on its contract with buyer because, as a result of a market shift, seller can now reap a premium for the goods on the open market. The same market shift that works to seller's advantage will work to buyer's disadvantage. Contracts are locked in to allocate risks, principal among those the risk that after the contract is signed the market will shift. Parties lock in price terms to protect against that risk. Hence, buyer is entitled to the benefit of its bargain with seller no matter the post-contract market change.

APPLYING THE CODE

Problem 8-3: Money Damages Under Section 2–713

David runs American Bakeries Company. Rising gasoline prices have prompted him to want to convert his fleet of more than 3,000 motor vehicles so that they operate on propane. He enters into a contract with Empire Gas for the purchase of 3,000 conversion units at a price of $1,200 per unit. Thereafter, as gasoline prices continue to rise, the market for conversion units has risen, driving the price for the goods to $1,800 per unit. Empire Gas repudiates the contract. Advise David on his remedial options and how best to proceed.

D. When Buyer Has Accepted Non-Conforming Goods and Cannot Revoke That Acceptance: Money Damages Under DCC Section 2–714

READING THE CODE

> **DCC SECTION 2–714: Buyer's Damages for Breach in Regard to Accepted Goods**
>
> **(1)** Where the buyer has accepted goods and given notification (subsection (3) of Section 2–607) he or she may recover as damages for any non-conformity of tender the loss resulting in the ordinary course of events from the seller's breach as determined in any manner which is reasonable.
>
> **(2)** The measure of damages for breach of warranty is the difference at the time and place of acceptance between the value of the goods accepted and the value they would have had if they had been as warranted, unless special circumstances show proximate damages of a different amount.
>
> **(3)** In a proper case any incidental and consequential damages under the next section may also be recovered.

Sometimes, either intentionally or inadvertently, buyer accepts the goods delivered no matter their non-conformity. Recall that acceptance is defined in section 2–606. A buyer who has accepted the goods suffers consequences outlined in section 2–607 and discussed earlier. Significantly, section 2–607 provides that the buyer who has accepted must prove that the goods were non-conforming at the time and place of tender. It can be difficult to sustain that burden, particularly in the face of seller's likely assertion that buyer's use caused or contributed to the defects now complained of.

A buyer who accepts the goods loses the right to reject them under section 2–601 but might be able to revoke the acceptance under section 2–608. When revocation is unavailable or inapplicable, a buyer who has accepted non-conforming goods can pursue remedies under section 2–714. Section 2–714(1) provides that buyer may recover for any losses resulting from seller's breach in the ordinary course. The statute is deliberately vague here, allowing for it to be applied malleably depending on the given facts and circumstances.

More often, the buyer who accepted non-conforming goods will pursue the remedy contained in section 2–714(2). That section applies when buyer has a claim for breach of warranty against seller. For example, perhaps the goods are not as expressly warranted (pursuant to section 2–313). Maybe they are not fit for their ordinary purposes and therefore betray the guarantees of the implied warranty of merchantability set forth in section 2–314. Perhaps seller knew or had reason to know of buyer's particular purposes for the goods, buyer relied on seller's judgment in selecting suitable goods and the goods are actually unfit for those purposes. In those cases, buyer will have a claim for breach of the implied warranty of fitness for a particular purpose under section 2–315.

Section 2–714(2) provides that in a successful claim for breach of warranty, buyer's damages are to be measured by the difference between the value of the goods as warranted and their value in view of their defects at the time and place of acceptance, plus any incidental or consequential damages under section 2–715. The goods' value as warranted is typically the contract price. The goods' value in their defective condition is usually considerably less than the contract price, and sometimes will be of no value.

APPLYING THE CODE

Problem 8-4: Money Damages Under DCC Section 2–714

Wayne contracted with Boz Dash Guitar Company for the purchase of a Damien Rice Red Guitar (a high quality electric guitar) at a purchase price of $2,400. The guitar arrived and Wayne remitted the balance due. Shortly thereafter, during a practice session, two of the guitar's strings snapped. Wayne replaced them. Then, while performing at a benefit concert, two of the guitar's tuners (those silver knobs at the top of the instrument used to adjust the strings) broke off. Wayne comes to you seeking counsel on how best to proceed. Provide counsel to Wayne, indicating which additional facts you would need to learn.

E. Buyer's Incidental and Consequential Damages: DCC Section 2–715

READING THE CODE

> **DCC SECTION 2–715: Buyer's Incidental and Consequential Damages**
>
> **(1)** Incidental damages resulting from the seller's breach include expenses reasonably incurred in inspection, receipt, transportation and care and custody of goods rightfully rejected, any commercially reasonable charges, expenses or commissions in connection with effecting cover and any other reasonable expense incident to the delay or other breach.
>
> **(2)** Consequential damages resulting from the seller's breach include
>
> > **(a)** any loss resulting from general or particular requirements and needs of which the seller at the time of contracting had reason to know and which could not reasonably be prevented by cover or otherwise; and
> >
> > **(b)** injury to person or property proximately resulting from any breach of warranty.

In addition to its direct measure of recovery, an aggrieved buyer is within its rights under section 2–715 to pursue recovery for any incidental and consequential losses occasioned by seller's breach.

Incidental damages are those out-of-pocket expenses that buyer incurred as a result of seller's failure to perform properly. Those out-of-pocket or administrative costs might include:

- Reasonable expenses incurred by buyer in rejecting the goods (under section 2–601 to section 2–605) or revoking any acceptance of non-conforming goods (under section 2–608), such as storage costs or shipping costs.

- Reasonable expenses incurred by covering or procuring goods in substitution for the goods contracted for under section 2–712, such as search fees and travel costs.

- Costs of inspection under section 2–513.

Consequential damages are compensable for any loss sustained by buyer as a reasonably foreseeable consequence of seller's breach. Those might include buyer's lost profits or any other predictable losses suffered as a result of buyer's lost opportunity to put seller's performance to its intended purpose.

APPLYING THE CODE

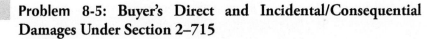

Problem 8-5: Buyer's Direct and Incidental/Consequential Damages Under Section 2–715

Paula, a baker, decides to expand her business. She explains that to Rolf Ovens, a manufacturer of commercial-grade ovens. Rolf agrees on May 1 to deliver an oven of specified capacity by Nov. 1 for $60,000. After the contract was signed, Paula spent $80,000 expanding the bakery and preparing for the new oven. She also entered into six new contracts with retailers for the delivery of bread for the expanded bakery. Rolf failed to deliver the oven on Nov. 1 and, in fact, had sold it to another buyer for $70,000. Paula promptly purchased a substitute oven for $72,000 and the oven was installed on Feb. 1. Paula wishes to sue Rolf for breach of contract. Outline the analysis that would afford her maximum.

Test Your Knowledge

To assess your understanding of the material in this chapter, click here to take a quiz.

9

Seller's Remedies for Buyer's Breach of Contract

Key Concepts

- Seller's available remedies when buyer fails to perform properly
- The continued applicability of law and equity for seller's remedies
- The right to cancel the contract and signal intent to pursue future remedies
- When seller is permitted to resell goods on a breaching buyer's behalf
- When a seller may recover the contract price in an action for the price
- When money damages may be awarded to a seller
- When seller is entitled to incidental or consequential damages
- The ability to modify remedial entitlements subject to the unconscionability doctrine

In this chapter, we consider Article 2's remedial consequences for the buyer who fails to perform properly. Buyer could betray her performance obligations by, for example, failing to pay for conforming goods, wrongfully repudiating, wrongfully rejecting the goods or wrongfully revoking her acceptance of the goods. Just as section 2–711 catalogues buyer's remedial options, section 2–703 provides the menu of seller's remedial rights.

A seller confronted with buyer's nonperformance can:

- Cancel the contract under section 2–703(f).

- Resell the goods on the breaching buyer's account under section 2–706.

- Sometimes recover the contract price in an action for the price under section 2–709.

- Recover money damages under section 2–708.

- Recover for incidental and consequential damages under section 2–710.

- Add to this analysis consideration of whether the parties, in their contract, modified, displaced or limited any of the remedial entitlements otherwise assured by Article 2. Section 2–719 allows for that possibility, subject to certain limitations including the unconscionability doctrine.

A. Resale: DCC Section 2–706

READING THE CODE

> **DCC SECTION 2–706: Seller's Resale Including Contract for Resale**
>
> **(1)** Under the conditions stated in section 2–703 on seller's remedies, the seller may resell the goods concerned or the undelivered balance thereof. Where the resale is made in good faith and in a commercially reasonable manner the seller may recover the difference between the resale price and the contract price together with any incidental damages allowed under the provisions of this Article (section 2–710), but less expenses saved in consequence of the buyer's breach.
>
> **(2)** Except as otherwise provided in subsection (3) or unless otherwise agreed resale may be at public or private sale including sale by way of one or more contracts to sell or of identification to an existing contract of the seller. Sale may be as a unit or in parcels and at any time and place and on any terms but every aspect of the sale including the method, manner, time, place and terms must be commercially reasonable. The resale must be reasonably identified as referring to the broken contract, but it is not necessary that the goods be in existence or that any or all of them have been identified to the contract before the breach.
>
> **(3)** Where the resale is at private sale the seller must give the buyer reasonable notification of his or her intention to resell.

(4) Where the resale is at public sale

    (a) only identified goods can be sold except where there is a recognized market for a public sale of futures in goods of the kind; and

    (b) it must be made at a usual place or market for public sale if one is reasonably available and except in the case of goods which are perishable or threaten to decline in value speedily the seller must give the buyer reasonable notice of the time and place of the resale; and

    (c) if the goods are not to be within the view of those attending the sale the notification of sale must state the place where the goods are located and provide for their reasonable inspection by prospective bidders; and

    (d) the seller may buy.

(5) A purchaser who buys in good faith at a resale takes the goods free of any rights of the original buyer even though the seller fails to comply with one or more of the requirements of this section.

(6) The seller is not accountable to the buyer for any profit made on any resale. A person in the position of a seller (section 2–707) or a buyer who has rightfully rejected or justifiably revoked acceptance must account for any excess over the amount of his or her security interest, as hereinafter defined (subsection (3) of section 2–711).

A seller who still has the goods contracted for, whether because buyer wrongfully cancelled or repudiated the contract, wrongfully rejected or revoked acceptance of the goods, is within its rights to resell those goods on the breaching buyer's behalf. It is important to note that resale is an option and not a mandate for the aggrieved seller.

Resale on seller's side is analogous to cover on buyer's side. Recall that cover, prescribed by section 2–712, allows buyer to procure goods in substitution for those that seller fails to deliver properly, entitling buyer to recover the difference between the contract price and the cover price. Resale allows the aggrieved seller, now stuck with the goods that buyer wrongfully refuses to accept, to resell them and recover the difference between the contract price and the resale price. Like cover on buyer's side, seller's right to resell is meant to afford seller the opportunity to mitigate or cut its losses. While seller is not required to resell on the defaulting buyer's behalf, a seller who declines to do so when resale could have spared seller some of its losses may suffer a set-off or reduction in its damages award.

A seller who chooses to resell the goods contracted for must accomplish the resale in good faith and in a commercially reasonable manner. What is or is not reasonable will depend on the totality of the surrounding circumstances and will be informed by the parties' course of performance, course of dealing and trade usage (the triplets).

A seller who successfully resells is entitled to the difference between the contract price and the resale price, plus any incidental or consequential damages under section 2–710. Often, there will be a difference between those two metrics. Buyer may have walked away from the contract because of a post-contract market shift that renders the market price for the goods contracted for considerably less than the contract price. The same market shift that redounds to buyer's advantage will render it likely that seller will experience a shortfall when it resells those goods to a third party.

APPLYING THE CODE

Problem 9-1: Seller's Right to Resell

David, owner of Aero Aircraft, contracted with Kevin for the sale of a Gulfglow IV private jet, purchase price $32 million. Kevin repudiated the contract, likely because after the contract was signed the new Airbus 360 was released, a cheaper and more fuel-efficient alternative to the Gulfglow.

A) Counsel David on how best to proceed. How viable is resale as a remedial option? Which additional facts would you need to learn?

B) Assume that David does resell to his friend Wayne at private sale. Wayne purchases the Gulfglow IV for $20 million. What factors are relevant to consideration of David's damages award?

B. Seller's Action for the Price: DCC Section 2–709

READING THE CODE

> ### ■ DCC SECTION 2–709: Action for the Price
>
> **(1)** When the buyer fails to pay the price as it becomes due the seller may recover, together with any incidental damages under the next section, the price
>
> **(a)** of goods accepted or of conforming goods lost or damaged within a commercially reasonable time after risk of their loss has passed to the buyer; and
>
> **(b)** of goods identified to the contract if the seller is unable after reasonable effort to resell them at a reasonable price or the circumstances reasonably indicate that such effort will be unavailing.
>
> **(2)** Where the seller sues for the price he or she must hold for the buyer any goods which have been identified to the contract and are still in his or her control except that if resale becomes possible he or she may resell them at any time prior to the collection of the judgment. The net proceeds of any such resale must be credited to the buyer and payment of the judgment entitles him or her to any goods not resold.
>
> **(3)** After the buyer has wrongfully rejected or revoked acceptance of the goods or has failed to make a payment due or has repudiated (section 2–610), a seller who is held not entitled to the price under this section shall nevertheless be awarded damages for non-acceptance under the preceding section.

When buyer wrongfully rejects, revokes or repudiates, so that seller has the conforming goods contracted for, sometimes that aggrieved seller will be entitled to recover the contract price from the breaching buyer. Seller, in turn, tenders the goods to buyer. Seller's action for the price is analogous to buyer's action for specific performance under section 2–716. Whereas specific performance has the court ordering that seller come forth with the goods that are the subject matter of the contract, an action for the price has the court decreeing that buyer must remit the purchase price for the goods and in turn presumably accept those goods that it paid for.

Like specific performance on buyer's side, seller's action for the price is out of the norm and dependent for its success on several predicates. First, seller's action for the price is deemed premature until the time for payment has come due and buyer has failed to pay. Seller does not have an anticipatory right to the price.

Second, once the time for payment has come due and buyer has not paid, seller's action for the contract price will reside only if one of three circumstances is present. Either:

- Buyer accepted the goods under section 2–606 and failed to pay for them.

- The risk of loss of conforming goods had passed to buyer and the goods are damaged or destroyed thereafter. Recall that section 2–509 indicates how and when the risk of loss passes from seller to buyer. Once that risk has passed, any damage or devastation to the goods is buyer's problem (hopefully buyer has insurance) and buyer is obliged to pay for the goods at the contract rate.

- Buyer wrongfully refused conforming goods and seller is unable to resell those goods under section 2–706 after a reasonable attempt to do so or seller can show that under the circumstances any attempt to resell would be futile. When goods are customized, quickly perishable or specially manufactured for buyer, often seller will not be able to resell those goods on buyer's behalf. Similarly, goods that suffer obsolescence shortly after buyer's breach will be difficult for seller to resell.

A seller who succeeds with an action for the price is also entitled to recovery for its incidental and consequential losses under section 2–710.

APPLYING THE CODE

Problem 9-2: Seller's Action for the Price

A) Paula, a New York seller, agreed to sell Wayne, a Texas buyer, 3,000 units of Flake's cakes for $30,000, with delivery to be in three equal monthly installments. The contract specified that it was "F.O.B. New York" and that Wayne was to pay the price of each installment fifteen days after delivery. Paula shipped and Wayne received but failed to pay for the first installment. Paula shipped the second installment, but it was damaged in transit by excessive heat while in the carrier's possession. Wayne refused to accept the available portion of the second installment and repudiated the balance of the contract. What are Paula's remedial rights?

B) Kevin contracted with David for the purchase of a high-end briefcase embossed with David's initials. Before Kevin began performance, David telephoned Kevin to tell him that he had decided against such an extravagant purchase. Kevin nonetheless embossed and packaged the briefcase, shipping it to David. Kevin intends to sue David for the contract price. What result?

C. Seller's Right to Money Damages: DCC Section 2–708

READING THE CODE

DCC SECTION 2–708: Seller's Damages for Non-Acceptance or Repudiation

(1) Subject to subsection (2) and to the provisions of this Article with respect to proof of market price (section 2–723), the measure of damages for non-acceptance or repudiation by the buyer is the difference between the market price at the time and place for tender and the unpaid contract price together with any incidental damages provided in this Article (section 2–710), but less expenses saved in consequence of the buyer's breach.

(2) If the measure of damages provided in subsection (1) is inadequate to put the seller in as good a position as performance would have done then the measure of damages is the profit (including reasonable overhead) which the seller would have made from full performance by the buyer, together with any incidental damages provided in this Article (section 2–710), due allowance for costs reasonably incurred and due credit for payments or proceeds of resale.

Section 2–708 sets forth the customary measure of money damages available to a seller who seeks redress for buyer's failure to perform and does not or cannot resell the goods contracted for under section 2–706 and does not have an action for the price under section 2–709. The aggrieved seller is entitled to the difference between the contract price and the market price at the time and place of tender, plus any incidental or consequential losses under section 2–710. Note that there is apt to be a difference between those two metrics, mindful that a market shift in buyer's favor might have precipitated buyer's breach. The same market shift that favors buyer will work to seller's detriment. Seller nonetheless is entitled to the benefit of its market.

Section 2–708(2) applies when the direct measure of recovery prescribed by section 2–708(1) is inadequate, typically because the aggrieved seller is a "lost volume seller." When seller has a seemingly inexhaustible supply of goods that are the subject matter of this contract, so that buyer's breach is not the necessary predicate to seller's resale, the measure of damages permitted under section 2–706 will not make seller whole. Instead, because of buyer's breach, seller has suffered lost profits. Those are recoverable under section 2–708(2).

EXAMPLES AND EXPLANATIONS

For example, suppose that Paula has a vast fleet of sailboats. David contracted with Paula for the purchase of one of those boats for $30,000 and then failed to accept the boat. Paula sells the boat to Kevin for $30,000 or close to it. The resale measure of damages under section 2–706 would give Paula the difference between the contract price and resale price. That differential will be inadequate when, given her volume of boats, Paula could have closed the deal with Kevin irrespective of David's breach. In other words, had David performed, Paula would have closed two deals instead of just one. In those instances, section 2–708(2) awards Paula her lost profits. Official Comment 2 to section 2–708 states that "profit" is the "list price minus the cost to manufacturer" or the "list price minus cost to the dealer."

APPLYING THE CODE

Problem 9-3: Seller's Right to Money Damages

A) Wayne, a Hawaii-based grower and seller of pineapples, contracts with Kevin, a Texas buyer, for the sale of 50 cases of Maui Gold Pineapples, purchase price $50 per case. Thereafter, Kevin repudiates. The price in Texas for a case of Maui Gold Pineapples approximates $30 per case. What is Wayne's measure of damages?

B) When would Wayne be able to avail himself of the measure of recovery set forth in section 2–708(2)?

D. Seller's Incidental and Consequential Losses: DCC Section 2–710

READING THE CODE

> **DCC SECTION 2–710: Seller's Incidental Damages**
>
> Incidental damages to an aggrieved seller include any commercially reasonable charges, expenses or commissions incurred in stopping delivery, in the transportation, care and custody of goods after the buyer's breach, in connection with return or resale of the goods or otherwise resulting from the breach.

Section 2–710 specifically provides that in addition to its direct measure of recovery (whether under the section 2–706 resale formula, an award of the contract price under section 2–709 or money damages under section 2–708), an aggrieved seller is entitled to recover from the breaching buyer any out-of-pocket costs incurred as a reasonable incident of buyer's breach. Those could include search costs to find a substitute buyer and shipping costs.

Section 2–710 does not specifically provide for the aggrieved seller to recover consequential damages, or those reasonably foreseeable losses suffered by seller as a consequence of buyer's breach. Nonetheless, the case law has demonstrated a willingness to award those when seller can demonstrate, for example, that it suffered quantifiable loss of goodwill or lost or foregone opportunities as a reasonable consequence of buyer's breach.

EXAMPLES AND EXPLANATIONS

For example, suppose that Paula's bread shop is the exclusive supplier of semolina bread for Frank Sinatra. Later, Mr. Sinatra wrongfully cancels the contract. In addition to recovering a direct measure of damages, Paula is entitled to recovery for incidental losses and could be entitled to recovery for any demonstrable losses occasioned as a reasonably foreseeable consequence of Mr. Sinatra's breach. For example, perhaps Paula suffers a quantifiable loss of business that she can prove is attributable to the loss in status and prestige that her shop has suffered as a reasonably foreseeable consequence of Mr. Sinatra's breach. Perhaps Paula can quantify the opportunities lost now that she can no longer use Mr. Sinatra's endorsement.

10

Putting It All Together

Article 2 Review and Problems

Key Concepts

- Analysis of Article 2 contracts for the sale of goods
- The scope of Article 2's application to a given transaction
- How to determine the formation of an Article 2 contract
- How to analyze the content of an Article 2 contract
- How to understand the performance obligations of parties to an Article 2 contract
- What remedies apply to an aggrieved buyer of an Article 2 contract
- What remedies apply to an aggrieved seller of an Article 2 contract

Set forth below is a methodology for successfully synthesizing and analyzing Article 2 contracts for the sale of goods:

- First, whether on a law school exam, the bar exam or in practice, begin by determining whether Article 2 applies to the given transaction. Article 2 applies to contracts for the sale of goods. "Goods," as defined by section 2–105, are all things movable. A "sale" of goods under section 2–106 involves the passing of title to those goods from seller to buyer in exchange for a price.

- If the transaction is within Article 2's scope, examine its given facts in accordance with the following four tiers of analysis. First, was a valid contract formed, in accordance with the requirements set forth in the 2–200s of Article 2? Second, if a valid contract was formed, what is the content of that contract? Go primarily to the 2–300s to determine the deal's content. Third, have the parties satisfied their respective performance obligations? Those are contained in the 2–500s and 2–600s. Fourth, if buyer or seller has failed to perform properly and is in breach of contract, which remedial entitlements apply? Buyer and seller remedies are contained in the 2–700s.

- **A checklist for the first tier of analysis: formation of the contract (the 2–200s):**

  - Was an offer for the purchase or sale of goods made?

  - Does that offer qualify as a "firm offer" so that section 2–205 applies?

  - Has there been an appropriate acceptance of the offer under section 2–206?

  - Do the terms of the offer and terms of the assent fail to match up so that there is a "battle of the forms?" If so, go to section 2–207 to assess whether a contract has nonetheless been formed and, if it has, what to do with the variant terms.

  - Does the deal have to be authenticated by an appropriate writing under section 2–201's statute of frauds? If so, is there an appropriate writing that binds the party against whom enforcement is now sought? If not, do any of the exceptions to the statute of frauds apply?

  - Is the deal contained in a final writing that one of the parties now seeks to supplement or contradict as a consequence of some alleged sidebar understanding reached by the parties before or at the time that this deal is formed? If so, turn to section 2–202 and the parol evidence rule.

  - Does a party to the contract allege a post-formation change in the deal? If so, apply section 2–209 on contract modification.

- **A checklist for the second tier of analysis: content of the contract (the 2–300s):**

  - Have the parties expressly agreed on all terms? If so, their express terms control.

■ If there are gaps or missing terms in the agreement, did the parties nonetheless intend to close the deal with finality? Only if the answer is yes, proceed to the parties' course of performance, course of dealing and trade usage (the triplets), in that order to supply the missing term or terms. If the triplets are unavailing, turn to Article 2's gap-filler provisions, contained in sections 2–305 to 2–311.

■ Be sure to be able to identify requirements, output and exclusive dealing contracts for the sale of goods, and the standards that apply to each under section 2–306.

■ To determine the quality of the goods contracted for, consult the contract's express terms in conjunction with Article 2's sections on warranties. The agreement's express description of the goods, for example, creates an express warranty under section 2–313. Express warranties can also be found in the affirmations of fact that seller makes when those statements form part of the basis of the bargain struck. Express warranties also include any blueprint or technical specifications that seller provides about the goods. When seller is a merchant, she impliedly promises that the goods are merchantable, or suitable for their ordinary purposes, under section 2–314. When seller knows of buyer's particular needs for a good and that buyer is relying on seller's judgment to select the good suitable for those needs, the implied warranty of fitness for a particular purpose under section 2–315 provides that the goods must be suitable for those specialized needs. When evaluating what the seller promised, whether express or implied, about the goods' quality, take a cumulative approach under section 2–317. More than one warranty is likely to apply. Remember to assess whether any warranties have been effectively disclaimed or modified under section 2–316. When a remote buyer suffers harm as a proximate cause of the goods' betrayal of promised quality standards, apply section 2–318 on privity together with supplemental principles of common law, such as products liability law.

■ When an unforeseen contingency or calamity renders seller's performance impossible or impracticable, the parties' contract is apt to be silent on how the parties are to proceed. In those cases, turn to Article 2's sections on excuse doctrine to determine whether seller will be released or discharged from its contractual obligations. Impossibility of performance is covered in section 2–613 and impracticability in section 2–615. Integrate section 2–509 here to ascertain when the risk of loss passed from seller to buyer, and section 2–614 to determine the protocol for a claim of excuse.

- **A checklist for the third tier of analysis: performance of the contract (the 2–500s and 2–600s):**

  - Under section 2–503, seller performs by tendering the right goods to the right place at the right time and buyer performs by accepting the goods and remitting the contracted-for price for the goods.

  - To ascertain whether seller has satisfied its performance obligation, buyer is afforded the opportunity to inspect the goods under sections 2–512 and 2–513 prior to its being deemed to have accepted them under section 2–606.

  - To know buyer's entitlements when the goods are non-conforming, first determine whether or not buyer has already accepted the goods under section 2–606.

  - If buyer has not accepted the goods under section 2–606, buyer is within its rights to reject them for any defect, however slight, as long as it comports with the protocol for rightful rejection contained in sections 2–601 to 2–605.

  - If buyer has accepted the goods under section 2–606, buyer can try to revoke that acceptance under section 2–608 only if the problem complained of represents a substantial impairment in value to the buyer and the circumstances are such that buyer's acceptance of the albeit non-conforming goods is justifiable.

  - Whether buyer rightfully rejects or revokes, consider whether seller is entitled to exercise its right to cure the defects that seller complains of under section 2–508.

- **A checklist for the fourth tier of analysis: remedies (the 2–700s):**

  - Buyer's remedies for seller's breach are indexed in section 2–703 and include cancellation, refund of any down payment or deposit, cover under section 2–712, money damages under section 2–713 and specific performance under section 2–716. Add to buyer's direct measure of recovery any incidental or consequential losses suffered under section 2–715.

- Seller's remedies for buyer's breach are indexed in section 2–711 and include cancellation, resale under section 2–706, an action for the price under section 2–709 and money damages under section 2–708. Add to seller's direct measure of recovery any incidental or consequential losses suffered under section 2–710.

- Keep in mind that the parties' remedial entitlements may be modified in the contract, an allowable exercise of freedom of contract under section 2–719, subject to the unconscionability doctrine under section 2–302.

APPLYING THE CODE

Review Problem 10-1:

Kevin, a Maryland wine producer, took a telephone order from Trader Jay's, a California-based food emporium, for 400 cases of wine. Kevin mailed Trader Jay's a confirmation of the order, which indicated that the wine would be shipped in a single delivery by Sept. 1, purchase price C.O.D., F.O.B. California. Trader Jay's did not object to the contents of the confirmation, but phoned Kevin to indicate that it wanted 200 cases delivered in November and 200 cases delivered in December, in time for the holiday rush. Kevin tendered delivery of all 400 cases on Sept. 1. Trader Jays's assistant remitted payment when the shipment arrived. Trader Jay was dismayed by the early shipment but instructed his staff to store the cases in a local warehouse until November.

In November, Trader Jay began stocking his store's shelves with the wine. Soon, disgruntled customers began returning the wine, complaining that it had soured, a consequence most typical of exposure to high temperatures. Trader Jay is exceedingly upset, particularly because Trader Jay's brand depends on quality.

Advise Trader Jay on his rights and liabilities. State which additional facts you would need.

Review Problem 10-2:

Paula, sales agent for Centrex Lighting, negotiated a contract whereby her company would design and manufacture a lighting system for One Oak, a trendy nightspot in Los Angeles. The contract price was set at $200,000. One Oak's manager remitted a $5,000 down payment and indicated that the club was looking to "liven up" the space but also give its guests "the vibe they expect when they walk in the door." Paula completed the design and sent the blueprints to One Oak, who never responded. Months later, she and her team arrived to install the lighting. The next day, One Oak's manager phoned to say, *"It's too bright. This is not Wal-Mart. This is One Oak."* Paula's team returned, used lesser wattage and still the manager complained. Paula is uncertain how best to proceed. She seeks your counsel. Advise Paula, indicating which additional facts you would need.

Review Problem 10-3:

Wayne is an interior decorator. On Sept. 1, he went to see David, a carpenter known for his artistically inspired, unusual hand-carved designs, and indicated that he wished to purchase six dining room chairs for his home. He noted that he needed them by early December and added that they should be "sturdy and cheery," to accommodate his young and very active children. David responded, *"My work is bold and it endures. You will love what I create."* David added that he seldom creates sets of items but that he would accommodate Wayne's request as a "professional courtesy." Wayne left the design to David's discretion, with the price to be determined once manufacture was close to completion.

One week later, David sent Wayne a written confirmation, which stated that *"six chairs will be completed by Dec. 1 for buyer to pick up at David's studio."* In November, David telephoned Wayne to tell him that the work was near completion and that he wished to finalize the price. The parties orally agreed on a price of $500 per chair.

On Dec. 1, the work was complete. Wayne arrived at the showroom and was dismayed to find that various explicit battle scenes had been carved into each piece and that each of the six chairs was different.

Wayne indicated that the chairs were unsuitable. When David responded that he had been given artistic license, Wayne replied, *"Well, I don't remember that."* Wayne left the showroom without paying for or taking the chairs.

David comes to you for legal advice. Discuss the relevant issues raised and their likely outcomes.

Review Problem 10-4:

Paula, a professional golfer, went to Foot Solutions, Inc., a specialty footwear shop, to inquire about the "Winning Support" brand of customized golf shoes. She explained that her feet have a tendency to pronate (turn inward) and that she needs substantial ankle support. The salesperson said, *"That brand has the most support."* The salesperson took an imprint of Paula's feet for purposes of molding the insoles. The price would be approximately $600.

The next day, Foot Solutions, Inc., sent Paula a written confirmation indicating that the shoes would be delivered within one month.

The shoes arrived on time, with a bill for $925 attributable to mounting labor costs in the plastics industry. Paula used the shoes without incident until, two weeks later, her right foot pronated so badly that her ankle twisted, prompting her to sit out the rest of the golf tour.

Advise Paula, stating which additional facts you would need.

11

CISG

United Nations Convention on Contracts for the International Sale of Goods

Key Concepts

- The similarities and differences between Article 2 and the CISG
- The scope of the CISG
- Formation under the CISG
- Content under the CISG
- Performance under the CISG
- Remedies available under the CISG

In this chapter, we consider the primary law applicable to the international sale of goods. That law, the United Nations Convention on Contracts for the International Sale of Goods, or "CISG," was promulgated in 1980 by the United Nations Commission on International Trade Law (UNCITRAL). The United States ratified the CISG in 1980. The CISG has been ratified by 85 nations and, unless expressly negated, it governs contracts for the sale of goods between parties from member nations. The most significant trading sovereigns to not yet ratify the CISG are India, the United Kingdom, Hong Kong, Taiwan and South Africa.

The CISG applies to international contracts for the sale of goods. It has taken on added resonance with the proliferation of multinational businesses and the growing internationalization of trade. While some of the CISG replicates Article 2, it also reflects international norms.

The CISG is comprised of 101 Articles. Its most noteworthy provisions and points of departure from Article 2 of the UCC are set forth below. Our discussion of the

CISG will follow the organizational guideposts that we employed to study Article 2: Formation, Content, Performance, Breach and Remedies.

A. The Scope of the CISG

The CISG applies to contracts for the sale of commercial goods. Article 1. While the document fails to define either "sale" or "goods," it is well-settled that the CISG does not apply to contracts for the sale of realty and intangibles. Significantly, the CISG does not apply to contracts for the sale of consumer goods, unless the seller neither knew nor had reason to know that the goods were bought for "personal, family or household use." Article 2. The justification for the exclusion of intended consumer transactions from the CISG's scope is that consumer-based regulatory regimes and legal cultures vary from nation to nation. When the given contract involves the sale of commercial goods and the provision of services, the CISG will apply when the provision of goods represents a preponderant part of the deal. Article 3(2).

It is important to note that the CISG embraces the norm of "freedom of contract." Thus, it allows the parties in their written contract to displace any of the CISG's provisions or exclude application of the CISG in its entirety. Article 6.

Many CISG provisions comport in content to their counterparts in Article 2 of the UCC. The CISG provisions that depart in significant measure from Article 2 of the UCC are taken up in this chapter.

B. Formation Under the CISG

1. The Statute of Frauds

CISG Article 11 provides that a "contract of sale need not be concluded in or evidenced by writing." Hence, there is no statute of frauds applicable to contracts within the CISG's scope. Article 12, however, allows member states whose own law requires that contracts for the sale of goods be in writing to impose a writing requirement where a party has its place of business in that state.

2. The Battle of the Forms

Recall that under the UCC's section 2–207(1), a contract for the sale of goods will be locked in on the offeror's terms no matter that some of the terms contained in the offeree's definite expression of assent are additional to or different from the terms contained in the offer, as long as that assent is not expressly made conditional on the offeror's agreement to its variant terms. Section 2–207(2) adds that even between merchants, variant terms in an assent will drop out if they materially alter the contract. Article 19 of the CISG alters those provisions but only slightly. It provides that an assent that contains additional or different terms qualifies as an acceptance as long as those variant terms do not materially alter the terms of the offer. If they do, the assent is a rejection of the offer and instead a counteroffer.

3. Post-Contract Modifications

Article 29 of the CISG differs considerably from section 2–209 of the UCC. Unlike section 2–209, Article 29 does not impose a good faith obligation on contract modifications. Moreover, since the CISG does not impose a writing requirement on contracts within its scope, Article 29 does not oblige modifications to be in writing.

C. Content Under the CISG

Like Article 2, the CISG includes a number of gap-fillers to supply terms missing from the contract. Those largely mirror their Article 2 counterparts with one important distinction. The CISG is unclear about how best to proceed in the absence of a price term. While Article 55 suggests that a contract can be concluded with finality even in the absence of a price term, Article 14 states that an offer must be sufficiently definite and is sufficiently definite when it contains a price term. Courts have reconciled this seeming contradiction by placing a gloss on Article 14, interpreting it to read that while an offer is sufficiently definite if it includes a price term, it does not have to contain a price term to be definite. Hence, a missing price term in a contract otherwise definitely concluded is to be supplied by imposing the price customarily affixed in the trade at the time of contract's closing.

D. Performance Under the CISG

Article 30 obliges seller to tender conforming goods in accordance with the contract's terms. Article 35 requires that the tender comport with the description of the goods set forth in the contract. Article 53 requires buyer to pay for conforming goods.

Unlike section 2–601 of the UCC, the CISG does not contain a perfect tender rule. Hence, buyer must accept goods no matter their slight non-conformities. Pursuant to Article 49, only defects that are tantamount to a "fundamental breach" may be rightfully rejected.

The CISG does not allocate the burden of proof with respect to conformity or non-conformity of goods. Applicable case law has applied the UCC to transactions within the CISG's scope to rule that a buyer who has accepted non-conforming goods bears the burden of proving that the goods were non-conforming when tendered.

E. Remedies Under the CISG

The range and nature of remedies available under the CISG mirrors much of the UCC's remedies scheme. Unlike the UCC, however, the CISG does not distinguish between remedies available to the buyer who has accepted and the buyer who has rightfully rejected, revoked or never accepted at all. Instead, Articles 74, 75 and 76 of the CISG use the concept of "avoidance" of the contract. Rather than hinge on whether the non-breaching party has accepted or not, the range of remedies available to that party are determined by whether it successfully avoided the contract or not.

"Avoidance" is analogous to "cancellation" under the UCC. Under Articles 49, 25 and 26, a contract can be avoided for "fundamental breach." Once avoided, the non-breaching party can demand conforming performance or proceed for damages. If avoidance is not available or the non-breaching party chooses not to avoid the contract, it is permitted under Article 74 to accept the tender and sue for damages.

Article 76 sets forth the non-breaching party's measure of money damages as the difference between the contract price and "current price." It deems "current price" the market price at the time when the buyer received possession of the goods.

Article 50 allows the buyer the opportunity to reduce the price due to the seller when the goods are non-conforming. Reduction of the price is determined by the difference between the value of the goods had they conformed to contract specifications and their value on the date of delivery.

Article 46 awards specific performance to the aggrieved buyer in circumstances broader than those available under the UCC. It provides that "the buyer may require performance by the seller . . . unless the buyer has resorted to a remedy which is inconsistent with this requirement." Article 62 makes the same remedy available to the aggrieved seller.

Test Your Knowledge

To assess your understanding of the material in this chapter, click here to take a quiz.

PART II

Secured Transactions:
Article 9

12

Introduction to Article 9

Key Concepts

- The scope of Article 9
- The definition of a security interest
- The need for secured transactions law
- The exclusions from Article 9's coverage

Article 9 of the UCC greatly simplified and unified the prior law regarding consensual liens in personal property. Previously, consensual liens in personal property consisted of lots of different common law devices such as pledges, chattel mortgages, conditional sales, trust receipts, factor's liens, and warehousing governed by separate laws. Now consensual liens in personal property are "security interests" governed by Article 9.

We will cover the basic Article 9 concepts in roughly the order that they are presented in the provisions of Article 9: **Introduction/Definitions, Attachment (Creation of the Security Interest), Perfection, Priority, and Default.**

A. Secured Transactions—Introduction and Definition

Article 9 is entitled "Secured Transactions." Two words—"secured" and "transactions." First, "transactions." A secured transaction is, of course, a kind of "transaction" or contract between two parties. You still know what "contracts" (or transactions) are from your first-year Contracts course.

Second, "secured." Section 9–109 explains why the transaction is called a "secured" one:

READING THE CODE

> ### TEX. BUS. & COM. CODE ("TEX. BCC") SECTION 9.109(a): Scope
>
> . . . [T]his chapter [i.e., Article 9] applies to . . . a transaction . . . that creates a security interest in personal property . . . by contract.[1]

So, it's called a "secured transaction" because it's a transaction that creates a thing called a "security interest" in personal property. By the way, you still know what "property" is from your first-year Property course. You probably focused more on "real" property (land or real estate) than "personal" property (everything else—like goods, IP rights, contract rights, stocks, etc.). We'll talk more about that a little later.

Next, let's define "security interest." "Security interest" is a term that is defined in the Article 1 definitions (some of which apply to Article 9, just as well as to Article 2 and Articles 3 and 4). Specifically, "security interest" is defined in section 1–201(b)(35):

READING THE CODE

> ### TEX. BCC SECTION 1.201(b)(35): General Definitions
>
> **(35)** "Security interest" means an interest in personal property . . . which secures payment or performance of an obligation.

So, the "security interest" is a type of property interest (albeit in personal property). It's not the whole bundle of sticks—i.e., it's not full 100% title to the personal property. Instead, the security interest is a limited type of property interest, only granted to someone in order to "secure" payment of an "obligation." The Code does not define the term "obligation." Most of the time, the obligation we are talking

---

1   Tex. Bus. & Com. Code Ann. section 9.109(a). All of the quoted UCC sections in the materials on Secured Transactions are from the Texas version of the UCC (because Wayne fancies himself a "Long Tall Texan"; *see* https://www.youtube.com/watch?v=n0woy8L3F5s. Oh, also because we can quote it for free. The Texas version of the UCC is codified in the Texas Business and Commerce Code. Texas Business and Commerce Code will be abbreviated to "Tex. BCC" in the text throughout. Note that Texas does a couple of quirky things with its version of the UCC. One is that it calls an "Article" a "chapter," as you can see from the language of section 9–109(a) above. Another thing is that it decimalizes the sections, instead of hyphenating them like the model UCC does. So, UCC section 9–109 is "9.109" in Texas. ¯_(ツ)_/¯

about is a debt, i.e., money owed to a creditor on a prior loan or credit obligation. But in theory, it could be any type of obligation—such as obligations of a tenant under an apartment lease, obligations of a contractor to pay a subcontractor, or any other type of contractual obligation of payment or performance.

So, how does the security interest "secure" payment of the obligation, or, what does that mean? This is bound up in the nature of the limited property interest that is the "security interest." The interest is contingent. It is an "only if" type of interest. The creditor, who receives the interest, hopes he will never have to use it, hopes that the borrower will just pay the debt back according to its terms. But, if there is a default on the debt, then the contingent security interest takes effect. Once there is a default, the creditor with a security interest then (and usually only then) has the right to take control of the property and either sell it for cash, or collect payments on it (depending on the type of property the security interest is in, a subject we will talk about more in the next section).

Hopefully, you can see now why a security interest makes the creditor more "secure" (and thus why it's called a "security" interest). Because it makes it more likely that the creditor will get paid. The creditor is more "secure" in knowing he will get paid something if the debtor stops making payments on the loan, because the creditor, upon default, can then take the personal property and use it (sell it) to get money to help pay off the debt. This "taking" of the property pursuant to the security interest is often called a "repossession" (if it's the right kind of property).

EXAMPLES AND EXPLANATIONS

> So, to take an example:
>> David buys a brand new Chevy El Camino SS on credit from Kevin Chevrolet Co. (KCC), for $35,000. As part of the deal, David signed a contract (1) promising to pay KCC the $35,000 with interest in 60 monthly payments and (2) giving KCC a lien (a/k/a "a security interest") on the El Camino.
>
> In Article 9 terms, what has happened is that David has entered into a "secured transaction" with KCC. This is because David granted a "security interest" in the personal property (in this case, the El Camino) to KCC by contract, and the security interest granted secures David's payment of his obligation to KCC (the $35,000 car loan). Of course, KCC hopes David will just make the 60 payments under the loan schedule. But, KCC is more "secure" knowing that if David misses a payment, KCC can exercise its

right under the security agreement to repossess the El Camino and have a foreclosure sale. KCC can then use the money it gets from the sale to help pay David's debt. That's the essence of the secured transaction.

APPLYING THE CODE

Problem 12-1: Definition/Existence of a Security Interest

A) Paula Printing Press purchased a new Model XJ-47 printing machine from Wayne Manufacturing. The price of the machine was $15,000. Wayne Manufacturing offered in-house financing, allowing Paula the option to make payments on the $15,000 purchase price, in monthly installments over a 3-year period. The contract consisted solely of the terms regarding the identification of the Model XJ-47 machine as the sale item, and the schedule of payment installments. Does Wayne Manufacturing have a security interest in the machine? That is, if Paula makes the first six monthly payments but then defaults, can Wayne repossess the machine?

B) Does it change your answer if the contract between Paula Printing Press and Wayne Manufacturing included not only the identification of the Model XJ-47 machine as the sale item, and the schedule of payment installments, but also a clause providing that *"Paula Printing Press hereby grants to Wayne Manufacturing a security interest in the Model XJ-47 to secure the payment and performance of the obligation to pay the Model XJ-47 purchase price?"* Why or why not?

C) Say that Paula Printing Press purchased the Model XJ-47 for cash instead of making payments. Subsequently, Paula's apprentice in the printing business begins his own business, Kevin Precision Press. As a favor to Kevin, Paula loans the Model XJ-47 to Kevin for him to use initially while he gets his new business up and running. Does Paula have a security interest in the Model XJ-47? Why or why not?

B. Why Secured Transactions? A Brief Discussion of State Debtor-Creditor Law

It may already seem obvious why a creditor would want to obtain a security interest from a debtor, so that they can be "more secure" in getting more of the debt paid off. After all, debtors sometimes default on payment of the debt, so why not get an extra remedy in the form of a security interest in some property in case that ever happens?

It may surprise you to know that, under the general debtor-creditor law of most states, most creditors have a right to seize some of the debtor's property in order to help pay the debt, whether they had obtained a security interest in the contract or not. Whereas creditors that get a security interest are often called "secured creditors," most creditors that make loans or extend credit do not get a security interest—they are therefore called "unsecured creditors." If an unsecured creditor can eventually seize some property in order to pay the debt, what then are the extra benefits of being a secured creditor by contract in the first place? Some background on the process available to unsecured creditors and the potential problems associated with it will help explain further why a security interest is such a good idea.

Unsecured creditors start out with merely personal claims for the debt against their borrowers (sometimes called *in personam* claims, or personal claims). And, if the debtor does not pay the debt according to its terms, the creditor is entitled to file a lawsuit in a court with jurisdiction and obtain a money judgment. At that point, the unsecured creditor becomes a judgment creditor, but is still usually an unsecured one. The debt has simply now been adjudicated valid by the state court (or federal court, as applicable).

However, once a creditor has become a judgment creditor, then state law usually gives a variety of judgment collection methods to the judgment creditor, most of which are designed to compel the debtor to surrender some of his property or money in satisfaction of the judgment. These take many forms, and go by different names like abstract, execution, attachment, replevin, and garnishment, to name a few. What most of them require is for the judgment creditor to request a writ or other document from the court clerk, and then file it somewhere (such as the county real estate records office) or deliver it to a sheriff with a request to attempt to seize any of the debtor's available property (the sheriff's action in using the writ to then seize property is usually called "*levying*"). When the judgment creditor is successful in having the sheriff seize some of the judgment debtor's property, or in otherwise laying claim to such property by a public filing of some type, then the judgment creditor at that point obtains a judicial lien on such property in order to secure payment of the judgment debt (this lien or claim on such seized assets is sometimes called an *in rem* claim, or claim against property).

At the point that the judgment creditor obtains a judicial lien on some of debtor's assets through one of the processes described above, then they are a "secured" creditor, in some ways similar to an Article 9 secured creditor. The property subject to the judicial lien can be sold at a judicial foreclosure sale, and the money can then be used to help pay off the judgment.

APPLYING THE CODE

Problem 12-2: Unsecured Creditors and Judgment Creditors

A)   David Enterprises is a CPA and financial planning firm, offering advice to clients on their investments, bookkeeping, and taxes. In order to help finance his business expenses, David Enterprises uses a Visa account issued by Paula National Bank. The account has a credit limit of $50,000, and was a "signature" account. David's business is successful at first, but his clients begin leaving in droves when the local paper breaks a story about a Ponzi scheme David has been perpetrating on many of his clients, defrauding them out of thousands of dollars. As a result, David has defaulted on the Visa account. Is Paula National Bank a creditor? Is it a judgment creditor? Does it have any liens or security interests?

B)   What if, after two months of nonpayment, Paula National Bank sues David Enterprises and obtains a default judgment against David for $50,000, plus all applicable interest. Is Paula National Bank a creditor? Does it have any liens or security interests?

C)   What if, after obtaining the $50,000 judgment against David Enterprises, Paula requests a writ of execution to be issued by the court clerk. Paula then delivers the writ to the local sheriff, who seizes all of the office furniture and equipment in David Enterprises' offices. Is Paula National Bank a creditor? Is it a judgment creditor? Does it have any liens or security interests?

Although the availability of judgment collection methods is nice to have, there are big practical problems with it. Unsecured creditors hoping to rely on the judicial lien process face at least two major issues. First, the judgment creditor does not have access to all of debtor's property. Under most state laws, the individual debtor (for reasons of basic humanity and dignity) is allowed to "exempt" certain categories of property from the claims of judgment creditors, the idea being that debtors should not be rendered essentially homeless and penniless for not paying their debts (note that only humans get exemptions, not corporations). These categories of protected property—called "exemptions"—usually include some amount of the value of the debtor's principal residence or home, at least one or more of his cars, a substantial amount of his household furnishings and belongings, and his 401k or other retirement accounts (to name some of the major applicable categories of exemptions). As a practical matter, unless the debtor has "extra" property beyond these typical exemptions (e.g., a second home, or extra real estate, or stock not in retirement accounts, or large amounts of cash in bank accounts), there is nothing for the sheriff to "seize" for the judicial lien—nothing to get. In a lot of judgment debt scenarios, especially consumer debt scenarios, this is the end result of an attempt to obtain a judicial lien. This is why a lot of debtors are considered "judgment-proof." They don't own anything besides exempt property, or property already subject to contractual liens (see next paragraph).

The second big problem with relying on the judicial lien process is that the debtors tend to borrow money from several creditors over any particular period of time. This means there can be lots of other creditors seeking judgments and attempting to obtain judicial liens on what little non-exempt property the debtor has. Not only that, but the debtor may also have granted contractual Article 9 security interests to other creditors. And when more than one creditor has a claim on a particular item of the debtor's property, there are rules for which creditor gets first dibs on the property (it is not generally a "share-and-share-alike" system). These are called rules of priority. And the very first rule of priority in determining secured claims disputes is that the claim that is first in time is first in right. So, if a judgment creditor attempts to obtain a judicial lien on one of debtor's assets, and an Article 9 secured creditor already has a security interest in that same asset, the Article 9 secured creditor is likely going to win—going to take that asset and sell it to pay off its own debt first, leaving the later-acquired judicial lien out of luck.

Therefore, it's good to be an Article 9 secured creditor. Such a creditor gets a contractual security interest in specific property. That property is now earmarked for the secured creditor's debt, and the secured creditor doesn't have to worry about other creditors obtaining judicial liens and seizing the property later. The Article 9 secured creditor has first dibs. Further, if the debtor defaults, the secured creditor doesn't have to first sue on the personal debt obligation before it seeks to recover the assets (although it could.) And, neither does the Article 9 secured creditor have to engage in a search for assets to help pay the debt upon default. It already has such assets earmarked by the grant of the security interest itself. This is why it's good to be an Article 9 secured creditor, all things considered.[2]

APPLYING THE CODE

Problem 12-3: Problems Faced by Unsecured Creditors

Wayne owed $10,000 to Epstein CardBank on his personal Visa credit card. The Epstein CardBank Visa debt was an unsecured debt. Wayne lived in an apartment that he rented. He owned one very used Honda Civic car worth $2,200. He also had modest furnishings, household items, clothing, and one misbehaving dog, Fido. The laws of the state where Wayne lived provide that all of these possessions that Wayne owned were exempt.

A) When Wayne defaults on his Visa payments, what are Epstein's options for getting Wayne to pay the debt?

B) May Epstein repossess any of Wayne's stuff to help pay off the debt?

C) Can Epstein likely improve its position by obtaining a judgment against Wayne and pursuing judgment collection methods? Why or why not?

Problem 12-4: Problems Faced by Judicial Lien Creditors

Paula Health Foods, Inc. owes Kevin State Bank (KSB) $100,000 on a business loan to help with the operating costs of Paula's business. KSB has a security interest in all of Paula's inventory of food items for sale, as well as the equipment she uses to run her store. Paula's business took a

---

2   Although we don't deal with bankruptcy too much in this book on core commercial concepts, it is important to note that an Article 9 secured creditor is also generally much better off in the event the debtor files a bankruptcy case. If the secured creditor has taken all the necessary steps to properly create and protect its security interest, the creditor will generally be entitled to the collateral (or its deemed equivalent), to the same extent as it would be outside of bankruptcy.

serious downturn when some of her vegan items began making people sick, which precipitated several personal injury lawsuits against her. Paula currently owes KSB $100,000. The value of all of the property subject to KSB's security interest is approximately $110,000. All of Paula's other assets besides this are worth approximately $20,000. She owes various suppliers $20,000 and also owes her employees $10,000. The tort victims are claiming a combined amount of approximately $1,000,000. What are the options and sources of payment available to Paula's tort victims, suppliers and employees for payment? What are KSB's options and sources of payment?

C. Scope of Article 9

We saw previously that an Article 9 security interest is defined in section 1–201(b)(35) as an "interest in personal property . . . which secures payment or performance of an obligation." We also defined a "secured transaction" as a transaction that creates a security interest. We did this by looking to another UCC section, section 9–109(a). That section is called the "scope" section. Take another look at that section now, with some additional subsections added:

READING THE CODE

TEX. BCC SECTION 9.109: Scope

(a) . . . [T]his chapter [i.e., Article 9] applies to . . . a transaction . . . that creates a security interest in personal property . . . by contract.

. . . .

(d) This chapter does not apply to:

(1) a landlord's lien . . . .

(2) a lien . . . given by statute or other rule of law for services or materials, [or] . . . . .

(11) the creation or transfer of an interest in or lien on real property . . . .

Section 9–109 provides what kinds of interests Article 9 applies to, and it also provides some specific kinds of interests that Article 9 does not apply to. As we said before, Article 9 applies when a security interest in personal property is created by contract. Note the various elements of that concept:

- A security interest has been granted (not some other kind of interest)

- The interest is in personal property (not some other kind of property, like real property)

- The interest has been granted by contract (i.e., consensually)

Notice also that subsection (d) of section 9–109 provides specifically a few examples of things that Article 9 definitely does *not* apply to. These correspond to the affirmative scope provision in subsection (a), but are included in section 9–109 for clarity. So, notice that Article 9 does not apply to:

- Landlord's liens or other statutory liens (which, of course, are not interests granted by contract)

- Interests or liens in real property (which, of course, is not an interest in personal property)

Incidentally, the law allows for interests in these ways. But they are not, by and large, governed by the provisions of Article 9—they are governed by some other law. For instance, the law allows the creation of liens in real property. This is called a mortgage (or, a "deed of trust" in some states) and is governed by state real property law, but not Article 9 of the UCC.

One last note about scope. What does it mean that Article 9 applies, or doesn't apply, to a particular contract or scenario? It just means the rules of Article 9 (which we will spend the next few chapters learning) don't apply to it. Other law does, just not Article 9 law. So, several Article 9 rules we will learn throughout the next few chapters, including rules on creation and "perfection" of the security interest, do not apply. Other rules may (and probably do) apply, but not the Article 9 ones. We will just focus on the transaction covered by Article 9—the security interest.

APPLYING THE CODE

Problem 12-5: Scope of Article 9

Kevin Lumber Co. (KLC) entered into several transactions this month. For each transaction, identify whether Article 9 applies:

A)   KLC borrowed $85,000 from Epstein National Bank (ENB), and granted a mortgage to ENB on real estate that KLC owned in order to secure payment of the ENB loan.

B)   KLC borrowed $30,000 from Paula State Bank (PSB), and granted a security interest in KLC's inventory of lumber for sale in order to secure the PSB loan.

C)   KLC sold 200 sheets of ¾-inch plywood to Wayne Construction Co. for $1,000 cash.

D)   KLC refused to pay Epstein Lumber Distributors (ELD) $40,000 for a prior shipment of lumber. ELD sued KLC, obtained a default judgment, and levied execution on all of KLC's existing inventory of lumber to secure payment of the judgment.

KLC refused to pay Paula Mechanical Repair, Inc., (PMR) for repairs to KLC's Toyota Large IC Pneumatic Forklift, which repairs were invoiced at $3,500. As a result, PMR retained possession of the forklift pursuant to a state statute that gives a lien to unpaid mechanics who perform repairs on equipment. PMR refuses to release the forklift to KLC and has threatened to sell it if KLC does not pay.

Test Your Knowledge

To assess your understanding of the material in this chapter, click here to take a quiz.

13

Definitions/Concepts

Key Concepts

- The definitions of "security agreement", "collateral," "secured party," "debtor" and "obligor" under Article 9
- The definitions of types of collateral such as, "goods," "consumer goods," "inventory," "farm products," "equipment" and "accounts" under Article 9
- The concept of a purchase-money security interest

In the last chapter, we introduced the subject of secured transactions, and defined conceptually what a secured transaction is—a contract that grants a property interest known as a security interest. We also discussed the general scope of Article 9 of the UCC, and defined the term "security interest." In this chapter, we will spend some time going over some basic definitions and concepts of Article 9. We will use these concepts as building blocks to use as we later learn the primary rules and concepts of Article 9.

A. General Definitions

Recall that a "security interest" is defined as "an interest in personal property . . . which secures payment or performance of an obligation." Section 1–201(b)(35). Recall also that obligation can mean any obligation, whether on a loan, credit, or some other contractual obligation such as a lease. Also, recall that Article 9 applies to "a transaction . . . that creates a security interest in personal property . . . by contract." Tex. BCC section 9.109(a)(1).

Let's add a few more definitions to our vocabulary so that we get a fuller picture of the components of the secured transaction. Article 9 defines the following terms:[1]

READING THE CODE

■ TEX. BCC SECTION 9.102(a): Definitions and Index of Definitions

(74) "Security agreement" means an agreement that creates or provides for a security interest.

(12) "Collateral" means the property subject to a security interest . . . .

(73) (A) "Secured party" means . . . a person in whose favor a security interest is created or provided for under a security agreement, whether or not any obligation to be secured is outstanding . . . .

(28) (A) "Debtor" means . . . a person having an interest, other than a security interest or other lien, in the collateral, whether or not the person is an obligor . . . .

(60) "Obligor" means a person that, with respect to an obligation secured by a security interest in . . . the collateral, . . . owes payment or other performance of the obligation . . . .

EXAMPLES AND EXPLANATIONS

■ Recall Our Prior Example:

David buys a brand new Chevy El Camino SS on credit from Kevin Chevrolet Co. (KCC), for $35,000. As part of the deal, David signed a contract (1) promising to pay KCC the $35,000 with interest in 60 monthly payments and (2) giving KCC a lien (a/k/a "a security interest") on the El Camino.

---

1   Last time we referred to section 1–201, which is the definition section containing definitions that generally apply across the entire nine articles of the UCC. Here, we are referring to section 9–102, which is the Article 9–specific definition section. In general, if you come across a term and want to check to see if it is defined in the Code, you should consult these two sections.

We already know that the type of transaction entered into between David and KCC is a "secured transaction" and that the interest in the El Camino that David is granting to KCC is a "security interest," given to help secure payment of David's loan obligation owed to KCC.

With the new definitions above, now we can add a few more labels into the mix from this example:

1. **Security Agreement.** The contract itself between David and KCC is called a "Security Agreement" under section 9–102(a)(74). It is a contract or agreement that grants a security interest. "Security Agreement" is Article 9's name for this type of contract.

2. **Collateral.** The El Camino is also called "Collateral" under section 9–102(a)(12). It is the "property subject to the security interest." That is, it's what David granted a security interest in, conveyed to KCC to secure payment of David's car loan. Collateral is the stuff that KCC gets to seize or repossess if David defaults on his loan. Being able to get the collateral and sell it to pay off the loan is what makes KCC more "secure."

3. **Secured Party.** KCC is the "Secured Party" under section 9–102(a)(73)(A). David created and granted the security interest in the Collateral (El Camino) in KCC's favor. That is, KCC is the one that has the right to seize and repossess the Collateral when there is a default on David's loan. This makes KCC the Secured Party.

4. **Debtor.** The "Debtor" here is David. Not, strangely enough, because David owes a "debt" to KCC. But rather, under section 9–102(a)(28)(A), the reason David is the Debtor is because he is the one that has an interest in the Collateral (El Camino). At least, he is the one with an interest in it, *besides*, of course, KCC, the Secured Party. Under the Code, the "Debtor" is basically the person that has an interest in the Collateral (usually owns it), and that grants the security interest in it to the Secured Party to secure a debt. Notice that the "Debtor" does *not* have to be the one that owes the debt. Strange but true.

5. **Obligor.** The "Obligor" is David, also. Under section 9–102(a)(59), the "Obligor" is a party that actually owes the money on the secured loan. In other words, the one you would have thought was the "debtor" before you studied the actual Article 9 definitions. Under Article 9, the one that owes

on the debt is the "obligor"—the one "obligated" to pay the debt or loan. Usually, as here, the same person (David) is both "Obligor" (the one who owes the money) and "Debtor" (the one with an interest in the Collateral that conveys a Security Interest in it to Secured Party). But not always, so the Code has the two separate definitions for the two separate concepts.

We will come back to these definitions at several points throughout our discussion of Article 9 and Secured Transactions, as they are referenced in several important concepts.

APPLYING THE CODE

Problem 13-1: Identifying the Security Agreement and the Collateral

Wayne Enterprises ("Wayne") was a multinational firm with an occasionally "batty" CEO (but not so much so that he lacked capacity to contract). Wayne owned a $10 million office building in downtown Chicago, and also millions of dollars of expensive machinery that it used in carrying out its operations. In order to raise money for operations, Wayne borrowed $2 million from First Bank, and granted it interests in several items of property to secure the loan. At closing, Wayne signed the following documents:

A) A "General Loan Agreement" specifying the overall terms of the $2 million loan, and numerous covenants requiring Wayne Enterprises to maintain certain levels of profitability and assets, in order to remain in good standing under the agreement.

B) A "Promissory Note" in the amount of $2 million, by which Wayne promised to pay to the order of First Bank $2 million in installment payments over 10 years, at an interest rate of Prime + 1.5%.

C) A "Deed of Trust" by which Wayne granted First Bank an interest in the office building, for purposes of securing the $2 million loan.

D) A "Machinery Lien Agreement" by which Wayne granted First Bank an interest in the machinery, for purposes of securing the $2 million loan.

However, simply defining the collateral as goods is not enough. There are actually four different sub-categories of goods for purposes of Article 9, and we need to know what these categories are for the reasons discussed above. The four sub-categories of goods are ***Consumer Goods, Inventory, Farm Products, and Equipment.*** They are defined as follows:

READING THE CODE

> ### TEX. BCC SECTION 9.102(a): Definitions and Index of Definitions
>
> **(23)** "Consumer goods" means goods that are used or bought for use primarily for personal, family, or household purposes.
>
> **(48)** "Inventory" means goods, other than farm products, that:
>
> **(A)** are leased by a person as lessor;
>
> **(B)** are held by a person for sale or lease or to be furnished under a contract of service;
>
> **(C)** are furnished by a person under a contract of service; or
>
> **(D)** consist of raw materials, work in process, or materials used or consumed in a business.
>
> **(34)** "Farm products" means goods, other than standing timber, with respect to which the debtor is engaged in a farming operation and which are:
>
> **(A)** crops grown, growing, or to be grown, including . . . crops produced on trees, vines, and bushes . . . .;
>
> **(B)** livestock, born or unborn . . .;
>
> **(C)** supplies used or produced in a farming operation; or
>
> **(D)** products of crops or livestock in their unmanufactured states.
>
> **(33)** "Equipment" means goods other than inventory, farm products, or consumer goods.

There are two things to keep in mind with these definitions. One, it is the Debtor's use of the collateral that matters for purposes of determining what type of collateral the property is. Two, the determination of the type of collateral involved is made at the time the Debtor grants the security interest—not before, and not after. That is, the Secured Party doesn't generally have to monitor how the Debtor uses the property after the security interest is granted.

EXAMPLES AND EXPLANATIONS

Example: Take a Kenmore Elite 41072 front-loading washing machine. It could be classified differently depending on who the debtor is, and when the security interest was granted. Take the following scenarios:

- Wayne buys the washing machine on credit from Sears, granting a security interest in the machine to Sears to secure repayment of the debt. Wayne bought the machine in order to use it in his home for his family to use. The washing machine is consumer goods.

- Kevin buys the same machine from Sears, on the same terms as Wayne. However, Kevin buys the machine in order to use it in the new Laundromat and cleaning service that Kevin is opening for business. The machine is equipment.

- Paula buys the same machine from Sears, on the same terms as Wayne. However, Paula buys the machine (along with many other appliances) in order to put it in the stock of her new electronics and appliances store, Paula's World-Of-Appliances. The machine is inventory.

- Finally, assume Paula likes this model of machine so much that she decides to buy one personally and bring it to her house for her family to use. If she grants a security interest in it as part of this personal household transaction, the machine is consumer goods. Remember that it is *debtor's* use of the collateral *at the time the security interest is granted* that determines its classification.

APPLYING THE CODE

Problem 13-3: Identifying Collateral Categories of Goods

Identify the proper collateral category of goods for each of the following scenarios:

A)   An American Fender Stratocaster electric guitar that Wayne bought for his 15-year old son, who is just learning to play. Wayne uses the Stratocaster as collateral for a loan from First Bank.

B)   Wayne's son, a few years later, has (improbably) made good on his long-standing insistence that he would "make it big" and become a major recording artist. His current band, The Societal Dregs, is currently on a 50-city North American tour, and their album is #1 on the Death Metal charts. Wayne's son uses the same Stratocaster guitar Wayne gave him as collateral for a new loan from Second Bank to Wayne's son.

C)   Kevin's Music Gear Paradise (KMGP) is a music shop and retailer of instruments and musical gear. They currently have 200 American Fender Stratocaster electric guitars available for sale to the public. KMGP uses the Stratocasters as collateral for a loan from First Bank.

D)   KMGP (from previous problem) has recently purchased and installed five iCT250 Ingenico POS (Point-of-Sale) Terminals, for use to process debit and credit card payments from its customers. KMGP uses the Ingenico Terminals as collateral for a loan from First Bank.

E)   KMGP (from previous problem) plans to begin selling a line of guitars it will manufacture itself, the Kevinator Extreme. Currently, KMGP has assembled the individual parts for the Extreme, including 2,000 electrical pickups, 500 maplewood fretboards, 3,000 tuning pegs, 500 solid wood guitar bodies, and 500 sets of D'Addario EXL120 Nickel Super Light Electric Guitar Strings (collectively, "the parts"). None of the guitars are assembled yet. KMGP uses the parts as collateral for a loan from First Bank.

F)   The accounting office for KMGP (from previous problem) employs three people, the CFO and two accounting assistants (KMGP does a thriving business). The office buys pens, notepads, copy paper and toner cartridges for its daily operations (the "supplies"). The office tends to replenish the supplies on a weekly or biweekly basis. KMGP uses the supplies as collateral for a loan from First Bank.

G) David is a farmer who raises hogs and chickens for profit on his farm, E-I-E-I-O-Acre. David uses the hogs and chickens as collateral for a loan from First Bank.

H) David the farmer (from (G) above) regularly gathers the eggs laid by some of the chickens for sale to local farmers' markets. David then uses the eggs as collateral for a loan from First Bank.

I) David the farmer (from (G) above) owns an H&S 170 Grinder-Mixer, which he uses weekly to grind and mix feed for his hogs and chickens. David uses the Grinder-Mixer as collateral for a loan from First Bank.

J) Paula's Payless Car Rental (PPCR) is a car rental company, which offers a fleet of domestic and foreign makes and models of cars and vans for short-term rentals of one month or less. PPCR owns the cars and vans and does not sell them to the public, but only offers them for lease or rental. PPCR uses the cars and vans as collateral for a loan from First Bank.

D. Other Collateral: Accounts

Although goods is a very important category of collateral under Article 9, other types of personal property can also be collateral. Most of them are highly specialized and are beyond the scope of this basic commercial concepts course.[2] We will, however, focus on one more important type of collateral—accounts. Accounts are defined as follows:

---

2   Some of the other collateral categories we are not discussing in detail in this course, but which would be a good idea for us to at least mention to you here, are as follows: (1) instruments (i.e., promissory notes and drafts), section 9–102(a)(47); (2) deposit accounts (i.e., bank accounts), section 9–102(a)(29); (3) chattel paper (a combined payment obligation plus a security interest in goods), section 9–102(a)(11); (4) Investment property (i.e., stocks and bonds in various forms), section 9–102(a)(49); (5) documents (i.e., documents reflecting title to goods, like a warehouse receipt), section 9–102(a)(30); and (6) general intangibles (property that doesn't fit any other category, like an intellectual property right or the right to use a particular website URL address), section 9–102(a)(42).

READING THE CODE

> ### ■ TEX. BCC SECTION 9.102(a): Definitions
>
> **(2)** "Account" . . . means a right to payment of a monetary obligation, whether or not earned by performance, (i) for property that has been or is to be sold, leased, licensed, assigned, or otherwise disposed of, [or] (ii) for services rendered or to be rendered . . . .

An account is a form of monetary obligation. There is no form that an account must take—in fact, there may or may not be any piece of paper involved at all. As the section 9–102(a)(2) definition states, an account is money owed for property that has been sold (or to be sold) or services rendered (or to be rendered). An account is sometimes called an "account receivable" in the commercial world, because it's money that is receivable by the business after it has arranged to sell its property, goods or services. It's like an "IOU," but specifically for the sale of something.

EXAMPLES AND EXPLANATIONS

> **Examples:** Paula's World-of-Appliances is in the business of selling home appliances and various electronic items. When she sells appliances to customers, she takes payment in a variety of ways. She has a loan with First Bank, to which she has granted a security interest in all accounts, that either existed at the time of the original loan or which arise later.
>
> **A)** Paula sells a washing machine to Wayne. In payment, Wayne gives Paula $500 cash. No account involved.
>
> **B)** Paula sells a stereo system to David. David refuses to sign any document, but Paula reluctantly agrees to sell David the stereo anyway. David tells Paula he'll pay her sometime in the next couple of months. David's obligation to Paula is an account. So, it would be part of Paula's "accounts" collateral granted to First Bank.
>
> **C)** Paula enters into a contract to sell 10 washing machines to Kevin's Laundromat Emporium. The contract calls for Kevin to pay $5,000 upon delivery of the machines. Even though Kevin hasn't received the machines yet, upon execution of this contract Paula's contract right to receive Kevin's money would be an "account," since the definition includes money owed for property sold or to be sold.

APPLYING THE CODE

Problem 13-4: Identifying Accounts

Paula Printing (PP) is a commercial printing service company. PP does many types of jobs, both commercial and consumer, big and small. PP takes payment in a wide variety of forms. PP has a current loan with Second Bank, by which she has granted a valid security interest in all of PP's "Accounts" (both currently owned and later acquired). For each of the following transactions or scenarios, indicate whether the customer payment obligation is included in Second Bank's collateral, and why (i.e., is the payment obligation an "Account"?):

A) PP entered into a contract with David Designs (DD), by which PP agreed to print 1,000 brochures for DD and deliver them within 30 days. DD orally agreed to pay the contract price, $5,000, within 60 days from the date of delivery. Before PP began printing the brochures, PP mailed an invoice to DD indicating these terms, with payment due in 60 days.

B) PP made a no-interest $1,000 loan to one of its employees, Wayne, to help him get through a personal family emergency. Wayne orally agreed to pay the $1,000 back within 60 days.

C) PP leased a part of its primary office location to Wayne's Paper Company (WPC). WPC agreed to pay $1,000 monthly in rents for 12 months. (Hint: Compare section 9–102(a)(2) to 9–109(d)(11)).

D) One of PP's newer printing machines, sold to PP by Wayne's Wonderful Machine & Co. (WWMC), has recently stopped functioning properly. It is still under warranty. PP has requested that WWMC repair or replace the machine, but WWMC has refused. PP has spoken to a lawyer, who believes that PP has a valid breach of warranty claim against WWMC worth $2,500.

E) PP recently filed its tax return with the IRS and is entitled to a $3,000 refund. The IRS has not yet paid the refund obligation.

F) PP sold one of its older printing machines to David Designs & Printing (DDP) for $400. DDP orally agreed to pay for the machine within 3 months.

E. Purchase-Money Security Interest

A purchase-money security interest (or PMSI) is a special type of security interest that is favored in certain ways in Article 9 (as we will see later). For now, we just want to briefly define and identify the typical PMSI, so that when we run across it in UCC provisions discussed later, we will know what a PMSI is.

READING THE CODE

> ### TEX. BCC SECTION 9.103: Purchase-Money Security Interest
>
> **(a)** In this section:
>
>   **(1)** "Purchase-money collateral" means goods . . . that secure . . . a purchase-money obligation incurred with respect to that collateral.
>
>   **(2)** "Purchase-money obligation" means an obligation of an obligor incurred as all or part of the price of the collateral or for value given to enable the debtor to acquire rights in or the use of the collateral if the value is in fact so used.
>
> **(b)** A security interest in goods is a purchase-money security interest . . . to the extent that the goods are purchase-money collateral with respect to that security interest . . . .

There are several concepts rolled into section 9–103. The first one is "purchase-money obligation." Basically, purchase-money obligation means a loan or credit or other obligation incurred in order to purchase something (hence the name "purchase-money"). Notice that a purchase-money obligation can be incurred in two ways:

1. **Obligation incurred for price of collateral (direct-financing sellers).** This is referring to a direct-financing seller. So, for example, say that Wayne buys (purchases) a washing machine from Paula's World-of-Appliances. The seller Paula extends credit to Wayne in order to enable him to purchase the machine. Wayne's obligation to Paula is a purchase-money obligation.

2. **Obligation incurred for value given to enable acquisition of collateral (third-party lenders).** Now say that Wayne does not get credit from Paula, but instead goes to First Bank to get a loan to buy the washing machine. The loan is from a third-party lender, who gave value to Wayne

to enable him to acquire (purchase) the washing machine. Assuming that Wayne in fact uses the loan money directly to buy the washing machine, Wayne's obligation to First Bank is a purchase-money obligation.

Section 9–103 next defines the term "purchase-money collateral." This one is simpler. It means that the debtor/obligor gives its purchase-money obligation creditor a security interest in the very goods that it incurred the purchase-money obligation in order to buy. In a word, Wayne grants a security interest in the washing machine to Paula to secure the in-house credit Paula extended to enable Wayne's purchase of that same washing machine. Or, in the second example, Wayne grants a security interest in the washing machine to First Bank to secure the loan that First Bank made to enable Wayne's purchase of that same washing machine. In both instances, the washing machine would be the purchase-money collateral. Basically, the debtor gives its purchase-money lender a security interest in the very thing the lender enabled him to purchase.

Finally, tying this all together, a security in goods is a special PMSI only to the extent that the goods are purchase-money collateral with respect to that interest. So, in both instances above, the security interest in the washing machine would be a PMSI. But, it is generally PMSI only to the extent that "the goods are purchase-money collateral with respect to that security interest."

So, assume, for example, that in order to secure the First Bank loan, Wayne granted a security in the purchased washing machine, but also in a 2008 Honda Accord that he already owned free and clear. First Bank's security interest in the washing machine would be a PMSI, but the security interest in the Honda Accord would not be. The security interest in the Honda Accord would still be a security interest (an interest in the Honda to secure payment of the washing machine loan)—it just wouldn't be the special "PMSI" type of security interest. The reason is that First Bank's loan didn't enable Wayne to purchase the Honda since Wayne already owned it. The loan only enabled Wayne to purchase the washing machine, so only the washing machine security interest is a PMSI.

We will see in a few instances later that PMSIs are given special treatment. The basic reason is that the debtor wouldn't have owned the goods at all if the PMSI creditor hadn't enabled it to buy the goods. Therefore, it makes sense to give favored treatment to such PMSI creditors.

APPLYING THE CODE

Problem 13-5: Identifying Purchase-Money Security Interests

In each of the following scenarios, determine whether the security interest granted is a valid purchase-money security interest (PMSI):

A) Wayne's Western Wear (WWW) bought a life-sized sculpture of John Wayne for display in the front lobby of his clothing and retail store. WWW bought the sculpture from Kevin's Gallery & Studio (KGS) for a purchase price of $30,000. KGS offered company financing to WWW, who thereby purchased the sculpture on credit from KGS. As part of the transaction, Wayne granted a security interest in the sculpture to KGS in order to secure the credit obligation. Is KGS's security interest a PMSI? Why or why not?

B) Assume again that WWW buys the sculpture, except that KGS offers no company credit. Instead, WWW borrows the $30,000 from First Bank, who agrees to loan WWW the money in order to buy the sculpture from KGS. WWW also agrees to grant a security interest in the sculpture to First Bank to secure the loan. First Bank issues a check jointly payable to WWW and KGS, and WWW delivers the check directly to KGS in exchange for the sculpture. Is First Bank's security a PMSI? Why or why not?

C) Same facts as above, except that First Bank's check is issued to WWW alone. WWW deposits the check in his account, but Wayne actually uses the loan money for a personal trip to Vegas. Then, he buys the sculpture a week later from KGS, using a WWW corporate Visa card. Does First Bank have a security interest in the sculpture? Is it a PMSI? Why or why not?

D) Same facts as in (B), except that, in addition to requiring a security interest in the sculpture, First Bank also requires WWW to grant a security interest in its existing inventory of clothing to secure the loan. Does First Bank have a security interest in the sculpture and clothing inventory? Are they both PMSIs? Why or why not as to each?

Finally, say that the facts are changed in that WWW's loan from First Bank was not specifically for the purpose of buying the sculpture, but rather was just a loan for general operating expenses. In order to secure the loan, WWW granted a security interest to First Bank in all of WWW's inventory and equipment. Does First Bank have a security interest in the sculpture? Is it a PMSI? Why or why not?

Test Your Knowledge

To assess your understanding of the material in this chapter, click here to take a quiz.

14

Attachment/Creation of a Security Interest

Key Concepts

- The process of attachment of a security interest
- The necessity of giving value
- The authentication of a security agreement
- The requirement of describing the collateral with particularity
- The role of security interests in after-acquired collateral
- The importance of including future advances of loans as part of the secured transaction
- The definition of "proceeds" and security interests in proceeds under Article 9

So far, we have defined what a security interest is, and who the major players in a secured transaction are (the Debtor and the Secured Party). We have also defined several important concepts, including several types of collateral and the purchase-money security interest concept. Next, we are going to consider the Article 9 concept of "Attachment," which concerns the creation of an enforceable security interest. For the rest of the book we will use the term "attachment" and you will think "creation."

A. What Is Attachment?

Again, attachment is creation. Section 9–203(a) says the same thing another way:

READING THE CODE

> ### ☐ TEX. BCC SECTION 9.203: Attachment and Enforceability of Security Interest. . . .
>
> **(a)** A security interest attaches to collateral when it becomes enforceable against the debtor with respect to the collateral, unless an agreement expressly postpones the time of attachment.

Attachment is important because that is when the security interest becomes *enforceable against the debtor.* We will learn in Chapters 20 and 21 the advantages a creditor gains by having a security interest enforceable against the debtor.

And, in Chapter 19 we will learn that a security interest is not only "enforceable" against the debtor but also "effective" against third parties such as other creditors or buyers of the collateral.

B. What Are the Three Requirements for Attachment?

The three elements of attachment are set out in section 9–203(b):

READING THE CODE

> ### ☐ TEX. BCC SECTION 9.203: Attachment and Enforceability of Security Interest . . . .
>
> **(b)** . . . a security interest is enforceable against the debtor and third parties with respect to the collateral only if:
>
> **(1)** value has been given;
>
> **(2)** the debtor has rights in the collateral. . . ; and
>
> **(3)** one of the following conditions is met:
>
> > **(A)** the debtor has authenticated a security agreement that provides a description of the collateral . . . ; [or]
> >
> > **(B)** the collateral is . . . in the possession of the secured party . . . pursuant to the debtor's security agreement;

We will focus on each of these elements in turn.

C. Value

The first element of attachment is value. Value must be given by the Secured Party in exchange for obtaining the security interest. "Value" is not defined in section 9–203, nor in Article 9 at all. To find a definition of value, you must consult the provisions of Article 1 (which, recall, apply to all Articles of the UCC, including Article 9).

READING THE CODE

TEX. BCC SECTION 1.204: Value

. . . a person gives value for rights if the person acquires them:

(1) in return for a binding commitment to extend credit or for the extension of immediately available credit. . .

(2) as security for, or in total or partial satisfaction of, a preexisting claim. . . . [or]

(4) in return for any consideration sufficient to support a simple contract.

APPLYING THE CODE

Problem 14-1: Attachment: Giving Value

A) Kevin's Custom Cars (KCC) sells a $10,000 car on credit to Epstein who grants KCC a purchase-money security interest in that car. Did KCC give "value" as required by section 9–203(b)(1)?

B) Same facts as (A) except that Epstein borrowed $10,000 from First Bank, granted First Bank a purchase-money security interest in the car, and paid the First Bank loan proceeds to KCC for the car. Who, if anyone, gave value under section 1–204?

C) Same facts as (B), but in addition, Epstein persuaded his brother, Cecil, to grant a security interest in Cecil's yacht to First Bank as additional collateral securing Epstein's car loan. Has First Bank given value for the security interest in the yacht? To whom, and under what subsection if so?

D) Wayne Enterprises (Wayne) owed First Bank $500,000 on an unsecured loan (there was no collateral) payable in monthly installments. Wayne was very late on a couple of loan payments. Wayne and First Bank agreed that, in exchange for First Bank's not insisting on immediate payment, Wayne would grant First Bank a security interest in all of its accounts to secure the $500,000 line of credit. What language in section 1–204 tells you that First Bank gave "value" for the security interest in the accounts?

D. Debtor's Rights in the Collateral

The second element of attachment is that debtor has rights in the collateral. This is a basic property concept. Debtors can only grant a lien such as a security interest in stuff that they have rights in. Usually, this means the debtor owns the stuff. To make a completely obvious point, Wayne cannot grant a security to First Bank in *Paula's* brand new Lamborghini. Wayne doesn't have any rights in Paula's car—only Paula does. Paula owns the car, and so of course, she has sufficient rights in it for a security interest granted by Paula to First Bank to attach. But not Wayne. No rights, no attachment.

In the real world, "rights in the collateral" issues arise in connection with debtors that are business entities. For example, since corporate law treats a corporation as a separate legal entity, Acme Corp cannot grant a security interest in assets belonging to Baker Corp, even if Baker Corp is a wholly owned subsidiary of Acme Corp.

E. Authentication of Security Agreement with Description of Collateral

The third element of attachment, usually, is that the "debtor has authenticated a security agreement that provides a description of the collateral." This is in the nature of a statute-of-frauds type of requirement for security agreements. There are three components here: (i) "authentication," (ii) "security agreement" and (iii) "description of collateral." Since we covered "security agreement" in Chapter 13, let's focus on authentication and description of the collateral.

1. **Authentication (i.e., signed and in writing).** "Authentication" is defined in section 9–102(a)(7). For our purposes, it simply means "to sign." As in, to put a signature on the security agreement in written form (it can also mean other stuff that is the equivalent of signing when the security agreement is done electronically, but we will just focus on signing security agreements in writing and on paper). Therefore, attachment generally requires a *writing* and that the writing be *signed by the debtor.* Like a statute of frauds under contract law.

2. **Security agreement.** And, that writing signed by the debtor must be a "security agreement." Somewhere in the document, it must have "words of grant," that is, it must be a contract that grants a security interest.

3. **Description of the Collateral.** The third element of attachment is that the security agreement must describe the collateral. Just like a real estate mortgage contract must describe the real estate involved (i.e., Redacre), the Article 9 security agreement must describe the collateral involved. It's just that what is a sufficient description of personal property is different from what is a sufficient description of land.

The amount of specificity required for the collateral description in a security agreement is governed by section 9–108:

READING THE CODE

▪ TEX. BCC SECTION 9.108: Sufficiency of Description

(a) Except as otherwise provided in subsections (c) . . . and (e), a description of personal . . . property is sufficient, whether or not it is specific, if it reasonably identifies what is described.

(b) . . . a description of collateral reasonably identifies the collateral if it identifies the collateral by:

  (1) specific listing;

  (2) category; [or]

  (3) except as otherwise provided in subsection (e), a type of collateral defined in [the Uniform Commercial Code] . . . .

> **(c)** A description of collateral as "all the debtor's assets" or "all the debtor's personal property" or using words of similar import does not reasonably identify the collateral. . . . .
>
> . . . .
>
> **(e)** A description only by type of collateral defined in [the Uniform Commercial Code] is an insufficient description of . . . .:
>
> > **(2)** in a consumer transaction, consumer goods . . . .

Notice the ways that section 9–108 regulates the collateral description requirement:

A) **"Reasonable identification" standard.** Subsection (a) provides that that the collateral description is sufficient if it "reasonably identifies what is described." This is a general, overarching standard that applies to the collateral description. It is a flexible standard that gives a court discretion in individual cases, but it is not very helpful in determining **exactly what kind of collateral descriptions will be sufficient.**

B) **Examples of reasonable identification.** Thankfully, subsection (b) of section 9–108 is much more helpful, as it gives specific examples of collateral descriptions that will suffice under the section 9–108(a) standard.

   a. The first example is "specific listing." So, if Paula's World-of-Appliances grants a security interest in her store's inventory to First Bank, the security agreement could list each item of inventory specifically (e.g., "150 Model XJ47 Whirlpool Washing Machines, 25 Gold L100 Dryers"). Specific listing is allowed, but of course could be quite cumbersome when lots of collateral is involved.

   b. The second example is "category." This means any kind of factual, categorical classification. For instance, Paula's World-of-Appliances might list the collateral as "all dryers, all washing machines, all stereos, all computers," etc.

   c. The third example is "a type of collateral defined in the Uniform Commercial Code." This simply means that the security agreement can use the collateral definitions we discussed in Chapter 13. Therefore, all Paula's World-of-Appliances's security agreement needs to say to describe the collateral is "inventory" (since "inventory" is a UCC type of collateral definition). As in, "Paula hereby grants a security interest in all inventory to First Bank."

But note: Under section 9–108(e)(2), a secured party is not allowed to use the term "consumer goods" in a secured transaction with a consumer for consumer purposes. This is a major instance in which using a UCC collateral type for the description will not be sufficient. The idea is that such clauses are undesirable from a public policy standpoint. We don't want banks scooping up a security interest on every single item in a consumer's home, such that if he defaults on the loan, the consumer is rendered completely without any personal property.

Which type of description above do you suppose is most commonly used by secured parties? Why do you think that is?

C) **Supergeneric description not sufficient.** You might think, since this is America and we have freedom of contract and everything, that Paula's World-of-Appliances (not being a consumer but rather a sophisticated business) could sign a security agreement giving First Bank a security interest in everything the business owned, besides land. For instance, "Paula's World-of-Appliances grants First Bank a security in all personal property." However, subsection (c) prohibits this kind of a so-called "supergeneric" collateral description. That is, as a matter of contractual specificity, the security agreement must be more specific than simply saying "all assets" or "all property." Note that Paula's World-of-Appliances could in effect agree to grant a security interest in all of the business's personal property assets. It's just that the security agreement would have to say something like: "Paula's World-of-Appliances grants First Bank a security in all inventory, equipment, accounts," etc.

APPLYING THE CODE

Problem 14-2: Attachment: Authenticated Agreement with Description of Collateral

A) Wayne's Widgets Company (Wayne) (which is in the business of selling you-know-what) borrows $100,000 from Second Bank. Wayne signs a security agreement, which states: "Wayne's Widgets Company hereby grants a security interest in all inventory and other assets."

Does Second Bank's security interest attach to the widgets currently owned by Wayne? Does it attach to the widget-making machine Wayne uses to manufacture the finished widgets?

B)   Same facts as A except that the security agreement describes the collateral as "all goods" owned by Wayne.

Before leaving attachment, an exception to the authentication/writing requirement needs to be mentioned. Section 9–203(b)(3)(B) provides that, in lieu of a written, authenticated security agreement, the third element of attachment can instead be satisfied when the debtor agrees to grant a security interest in collateral, and *transfers possession* of the collateral into the hands of a secured party. In other words, if possession of the collateral is transferred into the hands of a secured party, the security agreement can be *oral* instead of in writing and signed. This is in the nature of an exception to Article 9's statute of frauds.

APPLYING THE CODE

Problem 14-3: Attachment: Authentication Alternatives

A)   David needs $500 to pay bills. He takes his computer to Acme Pawn Shop, borrows $500, and leaves his computer as collateral. Does this transaction meet the requirements of attachment?

B)   What are the practical problems with using secured party's possession of the collateral instead of a written security agreement?

We have finished discussing the basic elements of attachment of the security interest under section 9–203. (One more time) those elements are: (1) the Secured Party must give value, (2) the Debtor must have sufficient rights in the collateral, and (3) the Debtor must authenticate a security agreement that sufficiently describes the collateral (or, an oral agreement will suffice if the Secured Party obtains possession of the collateral).

F. After-Acquired Property Clauses, Future Advance Clauses, and Proceeds

Now that we know how a security interest comes into existence, we need to know what the scope of the security interest is. That means we need to know about "after-acquired property" and "future advances" and "proceeds."

G. After-Acquired Collateral

Security agreements are executed and signed at a particular moment in time. They generally cover the collateral described in the agreement, as it exists at that point. Consider the following example.

> Say that on June 1, Wayne's Widget Company (in the business of selling you-know-what) signs a security agreement and grants a security interest to First Bank in "all equipment" in order to secure a $100,000 loan being made to Wayne by First Bank. As of June 1, Wayne owns 2 pieces of equipment used in his business—a John Deere Model 8900 forklift, and a Manitowoc 1400 industrial crane. On August 1, Wayne purchases an additional crane, the Broderson IC-200. But, the Broderson will not be part of First Bank's collateral, because it was not part of Wayne's equipment when the security agreement was signed on June 1. The security agreement, as drafted, only granted a security interest in all of Wayne's *existing* equipment. But, the Broderson was acquired *after* the security agreement was signed, so it isn't included.

Was there a way for First Bank to have drafted the security agreement with Wayne so that the Broderson crane *would* have been included in its collateral once acquired? Yes. See the following section.

READING THE CODE

> ### TEX. BCC SECTION 9.204: After-Acquired Property. . . .
>
> **(a)** Except as provided in Subsection (b), a security agreement may create or provide for a security interest in after-acquired collateral.

(b) A security interest does not attach under a term constituting an after-acquired property clause to . . . consumer goods . . . unless the debtor acquires rights in them within 10 days after the secured party gives value. . . .

Why would a secured party want an after-acquired property clause in its security agreement?

Section 9–204 authorizes the parties to include "after-acquired property clauses" in the security agreement (except for consumer goods—again, we don't want unsophisticated consumers doing this, just like we don't want them giving the bank everything all in one fell swoop). The way to do it is to include an express after-acquired clause. Therefore, in the above example, First Bank would have included the following: "Wayne's Widget Company grants a security interest to First Bank in all equipment, *now owned or hereafter acquired.*" And, *voilà*—now, once Wayne acquires rights in the Broderson crane, it will be included in First Bank's collateral because of the express after-acquired clause in the security agreement.

Normally, in order for property acquired after the execution of the security agreement to be included in the security interest, an express after-acquired clause like the above must be included. However, there are a couple of types of collateral where courts will normally assume, or imply the agreement to include, an after-acquired clause. These two types of collateral are *inventory and accounts*. The reason is actually the nature of inventory and accounts—they are constantly reducing and replenishing. So, Wayne's Widget Company is constantly selling widgets (hopefully), but also is constantly making new widgets for sale. Same is true for accounts (Wayne constantly sells widgets to customers, creating accounts receivable; but then they routinely pay what they owe, decreasing the amount of accounts receivable). As a result, if Wayne signs a security agreement that states: "Wayne hereby grants a security interest in all inventory," courts will generally interpret it to include after-acquired inventory, even though it doesn't say so expressly (of course, good lawyers such as what you all will be will likely take care to include an after-acquired clause to be safe). Do you now see why courts imply the existence of an after-acquired clause for inventory and accounts? Over time, what would be the effect on inventory and accounts collateral if the courts did not do so?

H. Future Advances

To continue the example of Wayne's Widget Company, remember that Wayne borrowed $100,000 on June 1, and let's say it granted First Bank a security interest in "all equipment, now owned or hereafter-acquired." So, when the Broderson crane comes in, the entire $100,000 debt is secured by all three pieces of equipment.

But what if First Bank loans Wayne another $100,000 on October 1? Can First Bank claim all the collateral to secure the whole $200,000 loan balance (plus interest), or just the $100,000 that was in existence at the time the loan and security agreement was executed? The answer is just the first $100,000 loan in existence, if the agreement says nothing otherwise. Can the agreement say otherwise? Yes. See (again) section 9–204.

READING THE CODE

TEX. BCC SECTION 9.204: After-Acquired Property; Future Advances

(c) A security agreement may provide that collateral secures . . . future advances or other value, whether or not the advances or value are given pursuant to commitment.

Basically, section 9–204 says that the parties can include a future advance clause, just like they can include an after-acquired clause. And, if included, in the above example the entire $200,000 loan balance would be secured by all the collateral. So, First Bank will want to include language along the following lines: "Wayne hereby grants a security interest in all equipment, now owned or hereafter acquired (the after-acquired clause), in order to secure payment of the $100,000 loan made on June 1, as well as any future advances that First Bank makes thereafter (the future advances clause)."

APPLYING THE CODE

Problem 14-4: After-Acquired Property and Future Advances

Paula's World-of-Appliances borrows $100,000 from First Bank on March 1. In order to secure the loan, Paula signs a security agreement, which states: "*Paula hereby grants First Bank a security interest in all inventory, equipment and accounts, in order to secure the $100,000 loan made on March 1, as well as all future advances which First Bank may make, from time to time, in its discretion.*" As of March 1, Paula's inventory consists of 100 red washing machines and 100 red dryers. Her equipment on that date consists of an Acme L100 forklift she uses in the warehouse area to move products around, and which she has owned for three years. As of March 1, Paula has outstanding accounts of $20,000 owed by 50 different commercial customers. Answer the following:

A) Does First Bank have an attached security interest in the 100 red washers and 100 red dryers? The Acme L100 forklift? The $20,000 in accounts?

B) On May 1, Paula purchases 300 blue washing machines and a new Acme L200 forklift to replace the L100. She also sells 50 red washing machines to a new commercial client, who agrees to pay $15,000 on or before July 1. As of May 1, does First Bank have an attached security interest in (1) the blue washing machines, (2) the L200, and (3) the new $15,000 account? Why or why not as to each?

C) On June 1, First Bank loans Paula an additional $50,000. Does First Bank's collateral secure the entire $150,000 combined balance, or just the original $100,000 loan made on March 1?

I. Proceeds of Collateral

So far, we have been talking about the secured party's security interest becoming attached to "original collateral"—that is, to the collateral that debtor granted a security interest in at the inception of the loan and security agreement. So, again, say that on March 1, Paula's World-of-Appliances borrows $100,000 from First Bank, and Paula signs a security agreement granting a security interest in her equipment (which then consists primarily of the Acme L100 forklift). As of March 1, First Bank's security interest in the Acme L100 forklift has attached. This forklift is the "original collateral."

What if Paula decides to sell the forklift? Say that Paula sells the Acme L100 to Wayne's Widget Company for $5,000. Wayne agrees to pay Paula within one year.

We will later learn in Chapter 19 that under section 9–201 (and also 9–315(a)(1)), a security interest generally continues in the original collateral notwithstanding sale (unless the secured party consents or waives it). Thus, Wayne has bought a forklift subject to a security interest. So, if Paula defaults on her loan, First Bank can repossess the forklift from (a very disappointed and disgruntled) Wayne.

But what about the $5,000 account obligation that Wayne owes Paula in exchange for the sale of the forklift? What do we call it? More important, does First Bank also have a security interest in this account?

READING THE CODE

◼ TEX. BCC SECTION 9.102(a)(65): Definitions

[note: this is subsection (a)(64) in the uniform act]

"Proceeds" . . . means the following property:

(A) whatever is acquired upon the sale, lease, license, exchange, or other disposition of collateral;

(B) whatever is collected on . . . account of collateral . . . . [or]

(E) . . . insurance payable by reason of the loss . . . of, defects . . . in, or damage to, the collateral.

Can you think of scenarios in which each of these categories of proceeds arise? Why does the UCC define proceeds?

The $5,000 account is proceeds of the forklift original collateral because it is what Paula acquired (from Wayne) upon the sale of the collateral. Note under subsection (E) that the same result would occur if the forklift was stolen and Paula's insurance company paid a claim on the policy—the money received from the insurance company would be proceeds. In general, just about anything of value arising from collateral is proceeds of the collateral.

And, very simply put, the Code provides that if the security interest is attached to the original collateral, its security interest attaches to the proceeds received on account of the collateral. (Go read sections 9–203(f) and 9–315(a)(2) if you don't trust us). So in the scenario above, First Bank now has a security interest in both the forklift in the hands of Wayne and the $5,000 account that is owed to Paula.

APPLYING THE CODE

Problem 14-5: Continuation of Security Interest and Proceeds

On August 1, Wayne's Widget Company (in the business of selling you-know-what) borrows $100,000 from First Bank and signs a security agreement granting a security interest in all of its inventory, equipment and accounts in order to secure the loan. Determine whether First Bank's security interest has attached to the following items:

A) The widgets on hand in Wayne's warehouse as of August 1?

B) An Acme L100 forklift that Wayne owned as of August 1?

C) The Acme L100 forklift that Wayne sold to Kevin's Laundromat on September 1, and which is in the possession of Kevin's Laundromat as of that date?

D) The $5,000 amount that Kevin agreed to pay Wayne for the forklift on or before October 1?

E) The $20,000 in cash collected from various in-store customers purchasing widgets during the month of August (and currently deposited and identified and traceable in Wayne's checking account)?

F) The $50,000 in amounts owed by Wayne's various commercial customers, as of August 1, who bought widgets from Wayne on credit during the month of July?

What if, instead of selling the Acme L100 forklift to Kevin for $5,000, Wayne had traded the forklift to Kevin in exchange for an industrial model XJ52 Whirlpool washing machine?

Test Your Knowledge

To assess your understanding of the material in this chapter, click here to take a quiz.

15

Perfection: Filing to Obtain Perfection

Key Concepts

- The general requirements for perfection: attachment plus applicable perfection method
- Filing as a perfection method
- The requirement to file in the correct office and in the correct state
- The importance of the location of the debtor (i.e., what state to file in, in order to perfect)
- The required contents of a financing statement
- The tolerance for errors in the financing statement generally, and in debtor's name specifically

In the last chapter, we defined the concept of attachment. Attachment is defined as the process by which a security interest becomes enforceable. That is, attachment is all about *creating* the security interest by *contract* (i.e., the security agreement) by and between the Debtor and the Secured Party. Debtor signing the security agreement, along with the secured party giving value and debtor having rights in the collateral, is enough to bring the security interest into existence.

In this chapter, we will introduce a new concept. Perfection. A secured party will not only want its security interest to attach, it will also want to *perfect* its security interest in some way. *Perfection* is an Article 9 concept, which is designed to give the world *notice* of the Secured Party's security interest in Debtor's collateral. The UCC wants the world to have notice of all security interests. Why? So future secured parties/lenders can make good, informed decisions about whether to make loans and agree to take security interests in stuff to secure those loans.

EXAMPLES AND EXPLANATIONS

To take an example—say David's Donut Shop borrows $25,000 from First Bank to help with his operating expenses in running the donut shop. David grants First Bank a security interest in all of his equipment in order to secure the loan. A few months later, David is short of cash (again) and decides to seek another loan. Being tapped out at First Bank, David applies for credit at Second Bank. Second Bank wants to know what kind of collateral David can offer to secure the loan. David offers to grant a security interest in his equipment to Second Bank in order to secure the new loan (yes, the same equipment that First Bank already has a security interest in). If you're Second Bank, it sure would be nice to know whether David had already granted a security interest in the equipment to someone else. If Second Bank knew, it probably would make a different decision about making the loan and taking a security interest in the equipment. For example, Second Bank could seek a security interest in different collateral, charge David a higher interest rate on the loan, or even decide against making the loan.

Perfection is the UCC's way to try to make sure that other parties (like Second Bank in the above example) usually have a way to find out about security interests that a Debtor has granted to other Secured Parties. Notice and perfection is what the UCC wants to happen (i.e., it's the underlying policy driving the UCC Article 9 rules on perfection). To look ahead in our materials (spoiler alert), the way the UCC incentivizes secured parties to perfect their security interests is to give them a good priority position if they do (priority being the concept that if two or more parties have an interest in collateral, we need priority rules to determine who has first dibs on the stuff). Getting perfected is the best way to ensure a good priority result in the event of conflicting claims in the collateral. We are going to talk about priority later in the course.

But we are getting ahead of ourselves. Let's back up, and discuss what perfection is under the Code, and how to get perfected. We'll start with the general definition and framework, and then go from there.

A. Perfection: General Rule and Overview

Perfection under Article 9 starts with section 9–308:

READING THE CODE

> ### TEX. BCC SECTION 9.308: When Security Interest . . . Is Perfected. . . .
>
> **(a)** . . . a security interest is perfected if it has attached and all of the applicable requirements for perfection in sections 9.310 through 9.316 have been satisfied. A security interest is perfected when it attaches if the applicable requirements are satisfied before the security interest attaches.

As you can see from section 9–308, there are two basic requirements for perfection: (1) attachment, plus (2) satisfaction of some other "applicable requirements" in some other UCC sections. We know what attachment is from our last chapter ((1) value, (2) debtor has rights in the collateral, and (3) debtor has signed a security agreement describing the collateral OR an alternative like the secured party's possession of the collateral), and now we know there is no perfection without attachment. But we need something more than attachment now in order to get perfected—we need "applicable requirements for perfection" to have been satisfied.

What are those "applicable requirements" referred to in sections 9–310 through 9–316? Well, actually, there are quite a few of them, several of which are very specialized and beyond the scope of this basic commercial concepts course. They are different kinds of "perfection methods" that can be utilized in different contexts. We will focus, for now, primarily on three primary perfection methods:

1. Filing

2. Possession

3. Automatic Perfection

Filing is the most common way to perfect a security interest (well, actually, attachment + filing is the most common way to perfect a security interest). A piece of paper (called a "financing statement") is filed in a public office (probably the Secretary of State), and a public, searchable database is thereby created with all of the important information about security interests in existence. Filing is the most common way to perfect, and it's the most important one to know about, so we will start with it first. First though, let's make sure we understand the basic components of perfection as set forth in Section 9–308.

APPLYING THE CODE

Problem 15-1: Perfection: Satisfying All Elements

Wayne Enterprises borrowed $150,000 from First Bank for general operating expenses. In order to secure the loan, Wayne agreed to grant a security interest in all accounts to First Bank. On March 1, First Bank gave Wayne a cashier's check for $150,000. Through a mishap that day, Wayne did not sign a security agreement. On March 2, First Bank filed a financing statement in the Secretary of State's office (which satisfied all of the requirements for filing under the UCC). On March 5, First Bank, realizing its error, called Wayne and demanded that he come into the Bank's offices to sign the security agreement. Wayne signed the security agreement later that day.

A) Is First Bank's security interest perfected? Why or why not? If it is perfected, when did it become perfected? March 1, March 2, or March 5?

B) What if the facts had been different, in that on March 1 the only thing that happened was that First Bank filed a financing statement in the Secretary of State's office (which satisfied all of the requirements for filing under the UCC). On March 2, Wayne signed the security agreement, but First Bank didn't tender the cashier's check to Wayne until March 5 (and there was no binding commitment to give credit beforehand). Is First Bank's security interest perfected? Why or why not? If it is perfected, when did it become perfected? March 1, March 2, or March 5?

B. Filing: The Default Perfection Method

As we just learned, filing is, by far, the most important perfection method. And, filing is, by far, the most commonly used method of perfection, especially in commercial (as opposed to consumer) transactions. And, filing is actually the default method for perfection under the UCC, as the next section demonstrates.

READING THE CODE

> **TEX. BCC SECTION 9.310: When Filing Required to Perfect Security Interest. . . ; Security Interests . . . to Which Filing Provisions Do Not Apply**
>
> **(a)** Except as otherwise provided in subsection (b) . . . , a financing statement must be filed to perfect all security interests . . . .

Notice a couple of things from section 9–310. First, filing is the *default* way to perfect a security interest, subject to exceptions. Second, the piece of paper that is filed is called a "financing statement."

We will next go through the basics of achieving proper perfection of a security interest by filing a financing statement. In doing so, we will focus primarily on three things: (1) where to file the financing statement, (2) what information the financing statement must contain, and (3) what happens if there are mistakes in that information.

One last thing to keep in mind before we begin discussing those three concepts: we will focus in this chapter on achieving perfection by filing *initially*. That is, stuff that has to be done to get perfected by filing from the outset. In the next chapter, we will follow up with stuff that happens *after* the initial filing, and how to keep the filing current (and thus, how to keep the security interest perfected).

C. Where to File

The first thing we need to know is *where* to file the financing statement. We have to figure out where to file so that we contact the right office for the right form, pay the right filing fees, know where to send the financing statement, and of course, file in the right office.

D. The Right Office

The government office that takes most financing statements for filing is the Secretary of State's office:

READING THE CODE

> ### ■ TEX. BCC SECTION 9.501: Filing Office
>
> **(a)** . . . if the local law of this state governs perfection of a security interest. . . , the office in which to file a financing statement to perfect the security interest . . . is:
>
> . . . .
>
> **(2)** the office of the Secretary of State. . . .

Notice that we left some stuff out of the above section (you've noticed we do that a lot, right?). There are exceptions to when the Secretary of State is the right filing office, as when there is a special type of security interest involving land or something,[1] but most of the time it is the Secretary of State's office. Why do you suppose that the drafters made the Secretary of State the office to file?

E. The Right State

Notice another thing about section 9–501 above. It starts out by saying "if the local law of this State governs perfection of a security interest. . . ." That is, if "this State's" law governs, then you perfect by filing in "this State's Secretary of State's office." So, that means we have to determine which State's law applies before we know what state to file in—i.e., which state's Secretary of State office. To answer this, we have to look at (you guessed it) another couple of Code sections.

---

1   The Code doesn't say "land or something," of course. What it says is that, instead of the Secretary of State, a secured party files in the same office for recording mortgages (i.e., usually the county real estate clerk where deeds and mortgages are filed), when there are certain types of collateral related to land or real estate. The types of collateral mentioned in section 9–501(a)(1) are "as-extracted collateral" (which is stuff like oil and gas immediately after it has been removed from underground), "timber to be cut" (which are trees which are slated to be cut down and sold shortly), and "fixtures" (which are goods that have been permanently affixed to real property—e.g., gas station pumps at a convenience store). For these very specific, real estate-related categories of collateral, the Code mandates filing in the county real estate records office, instead of the Secretary of State. Since we are not going to hold you responsible for this knowledge in this basic course on core commercial concepts, this little footnote is just for your future edification.

READING THE CODE

> ### ▪ TEX. BCC SECTION 9.301: Law Governing Perfection and Priority of Security Interests
>
> . . . the following rules determine the law governing perfection . . . of a security interest in collateral:
>
> **(1)** . . . while a debtor is located in a jurisdiction, the local law of that jurisdiction governs perfection . . . of a security interest in collateral.

From section 9–301, we find out that the law that applies to perfection is the *location of the debtor*. Not the location of the secured party, and not (usually) the location of the collateral, but rather the location of the debtor. The idea here is that debtors don't move nearly as often as collateral, and so it makes sense to base the rule on where the debtor is located.

But, we have another step. Where, actually, is the debtor located? It depends on what kind of debtor we are talking about. This is governed by section 9–307, and a couple definitions in section 9–102(a):

READING THE CODE

> ### ▪ TEX. BCC SECTION 9.307: Location of Debtor
>
> **(a)** In this section, "place of business" means a place where a debtor conducts its affairs.
>
> **(b)** Except as otherwise provided in this section, the following rules determine a debtor's location:
>
>   **(1)** A debtor who is an individual is located at the individual's principal residence.
>
>   **(2)** A debtor that is an organization and has only one place of business is located at its place of business.
>
>   **(3)** A debtor that is an organization and has more than one place of business is located at its chief executive office.
>
>   . . . .
>
> **(e)** A registered organization that is organized under the law of a State is located in that State.

TEX. BCC SECTION 9.102(a)(71)

"Registered organization" means an organization formed or organized solely under the law of a single state . . . by the filing of a public organic record with . . . the state . . . .

TEX. BCC SECTION 9.102(a)(68–a)

[note: this is subsection (a)(68) in the national uniform version]. "Public organic record" means a record that is available to the public for inspection and that is:

(A) a record consisting of the record . . . filed with . . . a State . . . to form or organize an organization . . . .

Based on these sections, we see different rules for where a debtor is located, based on what (or who) the debtor is. So, in a nutshell, we have the following:

A) **Individual debtors are located at their principal residence**—i.e., where they live. "Individual" debtors are human beings. They are not part of any organization, but rather are on their own (either as a consumer debtor, or as a business that is a sole proprietorship). So, if Paula runs an appliance store in the Bronx (New York), but lives in Newark, New Jersey, for Article 9 purposes she is "located" in New Jersey. If Paula then borrows $50,000 from First Bank, and grants the Bank a security interest in all her inventory, First Bank should file in the New Jersey Secretary of State's office.

B) **Organizations (Non-Registered) are located at the place of business (or chief executive one if there's more than one).** "Organizations" are collections of two or more people or entities. A partnership is probably the simplest kind. So, say now that Paula (who lives in Newark, New Jersey) and Kevin (who lives in Baltimore, Maryland) form a partnership, Paula and Kevin's World-of-Appliances, which has its store in the Bronx. The partnership is "located" in the Bronx. If the partnership then borrows $50,000 from First Bank, and grants the Bank a security interest in all partnership inventory, First Bank should file in the New York Secretary of State's office.

C) **Organizations (Registered) are located in their state of registration.** Registered organizations are organizations whose formation requires registration in their State of creation. The 9–102(a) definitions clarify that "registering" means filing a "public organic record" with a State in order to be formed or organized under that State's laws. In other words, you can't just form a registered organization on a handshake. The most common type of registered organization is a corporation, which is created by filing a record called articles of incorporation with the state (along with a filing fee). An LLC would be another common example. So, say that Paula and Kevin's World-of-Appliances is now a corporation, which was registered in Delaware. The store is still in the Bronx, and Paula still lives in New Jersey and Kevin still lives in Maryland. However, if the corporation then borrows $50,000 from First Bank, and grants the Bank a security interest in all of the corporation's inventory, First Bank should file in the Delaware Secretary of State's office. This is because the corporation is considered to be located where it is registered, in Delaware.

APPLYING THE CODE

Problem 15-2: Location of Debtor (and Where to File)

In each of the following situations, First Bank loans $50,000 to the named Debtor, and the Debtor signs a security agreement granting a security interest in all inventory. What state should First Bank file in to perfect, as for each of the following Debtors?

A) The Debtor granting the security interest is David, for his business David's Donut Shop that he owns solely himself in his own name, as sole proprietor. The donut shop is in Baltimore, Maryland. David lives in Alexandria, Virginia, and obtained the loan from the Washington, D.C. branch of First Bank.

B) The Debtor granting the security interest is Paula's World-of-Appliances, a general partnership between Paula and David. No partnership documents were required to be filed with any state authority. Paula lives in Newark, New Jersey and David lives in Alexandria, Virginia. The appliance store is located in Queens (New York).

C) The Debtor is (again) Paula's World-of-Appliances, again a general partnership between Paula and David. No partnership documents were required to be filed with any state authority. Paula lives in Newark, New Jersey and David lives in Alexandria, Virginia. They still have the Queens store, as well as one opened in Paula's hometown of Newark, and also one in Philadelphia. Invoices delivered by the partnership list the Queens address for payment remittance, and the partnership letterhead lists the Queens office on top, with the Newark and Philadelphia stores listed on the bottom in small print.

D)   Kevin's Laundromat is a small, mom and pop laundromat operating in Baltimore, Maryland. Kevin and his wife have operated the laundromat for 30 years. In fact, they had also resided in Baltimore their entire lives, and neither of them had ever left the state of Maryland. A few years ago (before their loan with First Bank), a fancy Washington, D.C. lawyer had advised them to form a Limited Liability Company (LLC), and that Nevada would be an advantageous state to use for forming the LLC (because of tax and other benefits). Kevin and his wife did so, filing the appropriate paperwork and fee.

F. Contents of Financing Statement

Now that we know where to file the financing statement, let's talk about the financing statement itself. First of all, you should know that it is a one-page, fill-in-the-blank worksheet type of form (usually called a "UCC-1" form). The form is fairly uniform across the states, and the exact form of it is reproduced in the text of section 9–521, and is shown on the following page for your reference.

UCC FINANCING STATEMENT
FOLLOW INSTRUCTIONS

A. NAME & PHONE OF CONTACT AT FILER (optional)

B. E-MAIL CONTACT AT FILER (optional)

C. SEND ACKNOWLEDGMENT TO: (Name and Address)

| Print | Reset |

THE ABOVE SPACE IS FOR FILING OFFICE USE ONLY

1. DEBTOR'S NAME: Provide only one Debtor name (1a or 1b) (use exact, full name; do not omit, modify, or abbreviate any part of the Debtor's name); if any part of the Individual Debtor's name will not fit in line 1b, leave all of item 1 blank, check here ☐ and provide the Individual Debtor information in item 10 of the Financing Statement Addendum (Form UCC1Ad)

1a. ORGANIZATION'S NAME

OR

1b. INDIVIDUAL'S SURNAME	FIRST PERSONAL NAME	ADDITIONAL NAME(S)/INITIAL(S)	SUFFIX

1c. MAILING ADDRESS	CITY	STATE	POSTAL CODE	COUNTRY

2. DEBTOR'S NAME: Provide only one Debtor name (2a or 2b) (use exact, full name; do not omit, modify, or abbreviate any part of the Debtor's name); if any part of the Individual Debtor's name will not fit in line 2b, leave all of item 2 blank, check here ☐ and provide the Individual Debtor information in item 10 of the Financing Statement Addendum (Form UCC1Ad)

2a. ORGANIZATION'S NAME

OR

2b. INDIVIDUAL'S SURNAME	FIRST PERSONAL NAME	ADDITIONAL NAME(S)/INITIAL(S)	SUFFIX

2c. MAILING ADDRESS	CITY	STATE	POSTAL CODE	COUNTRY

3. SECURED PARTY'S NAME (or NAME of ASSIGNEE of ASSIGNOR SECURED PARTY): Provide only one Secured Party name (3a or 3b)

3a. ORGANIZATION'S NAME

OR

3b. INDIVIDUAL'S SURNAME	FIRST PERSONAL NAME	ADDITIONAL NAME(S)/INITIAL(S)	SUFFIX

3c. MAILING ADDRESS	CITY	STATE	POSTAL CODE	COUNTRY

4. COLLATERAL: This financing statement covers the following collateral:

5. Check only if applicable and check only one box: Collateral is ☐ held in a Trust (see UCC1Ad, item 17 and Instructions) ☐ being administered by a Decedent's Personal Representative

6a. Check only if applicable and check only one box:
☐ Public-Finance Transaction ☐ Manufactured-Home Transaction ☐ A Debtor is a Transmitting Utility

6b. Check only if applicable and check only one box:
☐ Agricultural Lien ☐ Non-UCC Filing

7. ALTERNATIVE DESIGNATION (if applicable): ☐ Lessee/Lessor ☐ Consignee/Consignor ☐ Seller/Buyer ☐ Bailee/Bailor ☐ Licensee/Licensor

8. OPTIONAL FILER REFERENCE DATA:

FILING OFFICE COPY — UCC FINANCING STATEMENT (Form UCC1) (Rev. 04/20/11)

International Association of Commercial Administrators (IACA)

The required substantive content of the financing statement is governed by section 9–502:

READING THE CODE

> ### ■ TEX. BCC SECTION 9.502: Contents of Financing Statement. . . .
>
> **(a)** . . . a financing statement is sufficient only if it:
>
> **(1)** provides the name of the debtor;
>
> **(2)** provides the name of the secured party . . . ; and
>
> **(3)** indicates the collateral covered by the financing statement.

G. Name of Debtor

The first thing the financing statement must include is the name of the debtor. This makes sense. The financing statement is actually a data-entry form. The Secretary of State is going to take the information on the form and enter it into the database, so others can do searches later. And others will probably search by the debtor's name. Usually, that debtor is asking for a loan, and the lender will want to search the records to see if that debtor has any other outstanding security interests.

There are some specific rules in Article 9 about what name to use, but most of the time it's really simple—the financing statement should use the Debtor's "real" name. So, corporate debtors should use the "real" corporate name—i.e., the one on the articles of incorporation. Partnerships should use the "real" partnership name, if there is one (as recited in a partnership agreement); otherwise, the financing statement should just list the names of the individual partners. Note again that the formal name of the Debtor should be used. The Code, in section 9–503(c), makes a specific point of mentioning that a "trade name" (i.e., a "d/b/a" or "doing business as" name) should *not* be the only name given on financing statements.

EXAMPLES AND EXPLANATION

Example: If "Paula's World-of-Appliances" was actually a trade name for the corporation, which was "Paula Enterprises, Inc.," according to the articles of incorporation, then the name on the financing statement should be "Paula Enterprises, Inc."

Individuals, like organizations, should use their "real" name. The Code actually says to use the name used on their driver's license, if they have one. (all of these rules are in section 9–503).[2]

APPLYING THE CODE

Problem 15-3: Contents of Financing Statement (Name of Debtor)

Wayne was involved in several different businesses, both on his own and also with other people. In each situation listed below, the described business borrowed money from First Bank, and granted a security interest in inventory and accounts (in which Wayne, or his related entity, had sufficient rights). Answer the following questions with respect to each scenario.

A) Wayne Barnes and Paula Franzese agreed to go into law practice together. They rented an office, and informally agreed to split all profits and expenses 50-50. Nothing was in writing. What name(s) should First Bank use on the financing statement? Is there anything else you need to know?

B) Wayne Barnes and Kevin Tu operated a laundromat together. The sign on the store said "Kevin's Laundromat." Wayne had joined the business recently, and when he did, they formed a Limited Liability Company (LLC) in Maryland. The LLC was formed by articles of organization, naming Wayne and Kevin, and describing the LLC as "KevWay Enterprises, LLC." If they borrow money after joining together, what name(s) should First Bank use on the financing statement? Is there anything else you need to know?

---

2   We are simplifying here for this course in core commercial concepts. If you read section 9–503(a) and (b), you will see that the Code drafters provided for an "Alternative A" and "Alternative B" for individual debtor names. Alternative A, which the vast majority of states have adopted, requires mandatory use of the name on the driver's license if one is issued. Alternative B allows use of the driver's license name, but does not require it if a different name may be applicable (such as the name on the debtor's birth certificate). For our purposes, we will just say that the general rule is to use the driver's license name.

C) Wayne Barnes operated a cell phone repair business on the side. He had a website for the business, which website showed his business name as "Way Cool Phone Repair." Wayne had always operated the business on his own and had never filed any paper with the state regarding the business. What name(s) should First Bank use on the financing statement? Is there anything else you need to know?

H. Name of Secured Party

The second thing the financing statement must include is the name of the secured party. This requirement is straightforward. The full, formal name of the secured party, usually a retailer or lender, must be provided.

I. Indication of Collateral

The third thing that the financing statement must include is a description of the collateral that is covered. The financing statement collateral description is governed by section 9–504:

READING THE CODE

> **TEX. BCC SECTION 9.504: Indication of Collateral**
>
> A financing statement sufficiently indicates the collateral that it covers if the financing statement provides:
>
> **(1)** a description of the collateral pursuant to section 9.108; or
>
> **(2)** an indication that the financing statement covers all assets or all personal property.

Recall that we have discussed collateral descriptions and section 9–108 before—when we discussed attachment and the security agreement in Chapter 14. Both the security agreement, and now the financing statement, require a description of the collateral.

The first thing to note about section 9–504 is that it incorporates the section 9–108 requirements as sufficient for a financing statement. So, the same requirements that we discussed as being sufficient for the security agreement, are also sufficient for the financing statement. Remember that the general test is that the description must "reasonably identify the collateral." Remember also that section 9–108 provides that the financing statement can list the collateral specifically, but it can also generally use the "UCC types" or definitions (e.g., "inventory," "equipment," or "accounts"—but remember, not "consumer goods" if it's a consumer transaction).

Supergeneric descriptions are allowed in the financing statement. The second thing to note about section 9–504 is that a financing statement is sufficient if it provides that it "covers all assets or all personal property." If you remember, this is exactly the *opposite* of the rule for security agreements (where supergeneric descriptions made the security agreement unenforceable). What's the reason for the difference? Well, the security agreement is about the *contract* between the Debtor and the Secured Party, and it's important to ensure that the contract is precise and accurate, to identify the parties' rights and obligations. But, the financing statement, remember, is just for *notice* purposes. So, the UCC says that simply putting "all assets" in the financing statement is generally sufficient for filing and perfection purposes because it gives notice to subsequent creditors that a security interest exists. Subsequent creditors can then investigate further to determine the scope of that security interest. Of course, remember that the financing statement only "perfects" the actual security interest, i.e., only what the security agreement actually conveys a security interest in.

APPLYING THE CODE

Problem 15-4: Contents of Financing Statement (Description of Collateral)

Paula's World-of-Appliances uses the following in operating her business: (1) a forklift (a Wesco Battery Powered Lift Truck), and (2) a set of 10 iPads equipped with Square credit card readers, for use in ringing up customer sales. Paula also had, as of June 1, 1,812 washers, dryers and other home appliances in her inventory. She further had, as of June 1, $20,000 in open accounts receivable owing from various commercial customers. On June 1, Paula borrowed $100,000 from First Bank, and signed a security agreement that granted a security interest in her inventory and equipment.

Are the following collateral descriptions sufficient in First Bank's financing statement?

A) "Inventory and Equipment"

B) "Wesco forklift, 10 iPads, and all washers, dryers and other appliances held for sale"

C) "All collateral listed in Exhibit A" (but no Exhibit was attached)

D) "All Assets"

E) If the financing statement says "All Assets," what collateral is First Bank perfected in?

    1. None?

    2. The forklift and iPads?

    3. The washers and dryers?

    4. The accounts?

J. Mistakes in the Financing Statement

We now know that in order to properly perfect a security interest by filing, the financing statement must contain: (1) the name of the debtor, (2) the name of the secured party, and (3) an indication of the collateral. The Secured Party obviously wants to put the correct information in the financing statement so that it will be perfected.

But what if the Secured Party makes a mistake? What if the Secured Party is mistyped in the financing statement as "Dirst Bank" instead of "First Bank"? What if the collateral is described as a "Wasco" forklift instead of a "Wesco" forklift?

K. Minor Errors/Seriously Misleading Rule

Section 9–506(a) has a rule of some tolerance for financing statement mistakes:

READING THE CODE

■ TEX. BCC SECTION 9.506: Effect of Errors or Omissions

(a) A financing statement substantially satisfying the requirements of this subchapter is effective, even if it has minor errors or omissions, unless the errors or omissions make the financing statement seriously misleading.

Minor errors that are not seriously misleading are therefore not fatal to the financing statement. So, if the secured party is described as "First Vank" instead of "First Bank," the financing statement may still be effective to perfect. If the collateral is described as a "forest green" Wesco forklift, when in reality it's more of a Kelly green, then it's probably ok. Everyone can probably figure out what's going on. So, the security interest is still perfected if it's just a minor error.

L. Special Rules for Debtor's Name

Although the general rule for financing statement errors is the "minor errors/seriously misleading" rule, section 9–506 reads a little differently where the debtor's name is concerned (since it is arguably the most important piece of information in the financing statement). The rest of section 9–506 provides as follows:

READING THE CODE

■ TEX. BCC SECTION 9.506: Effect of Errors or Omissions. . . .

(b) Except as otherwise provided in Subsection (c), a financing statement that fails sufficiently to provide the name of the debtor . . . is seriously misleading.

(c) If a search of the records of the filing office under the debtor's correct name, using the filing office's standard search logic, if any, would disclose a financing statement that fails sufficiently to provide the name of the debtor . . . , the name provided does not make the financing statement seriously misleading.

Notice that we did not use examples of misspelling *debtor's* name above. That's because of this rule, which is much less forgiving. Subsection (b) basically says that *any* mistake in Debtor's name ruins the financing statement. Even one letter off—so, if it described the *Debtor's* name as "Wane Enterprises" instead of "Wayne Enterprises," then because it is the Debtor's name that is misspelled, the initial presumption is that the financing statement would not be effective.

However, before you decide for sure that a misspelled Debtor's name ruins the financing statement, you have to read subsection (c) along with subsection (b). Subsection (c) is what is known as the "search logic exception." It basically goes like this. Say that Wayne Enterprises, Inc., borrowed money from First Bank, and gave a security interest in certain collateral. First Bank filed a financing statement with the Secretary of State that inadvertently typed the name as "The Wayne Enterprises Co." At first glance, things might look bad for First Bank since this is not exactly right. However, say that Second Bank then performed a search query for "Wayne Enterprises, Inc." (spelled and specified exactly right) in the Secretary of State database (using the Secretary of State's own search system, i.e., their own "search logic"), and the mistyped financing statement pulled up in the search results. This "saves" First Bank's mistyped financing statement. After all, we got the result Article 9 wants—Second Bank got notice of First Bank's security interest in Wayne Enterprise's collateral (even though First Bank misstated the Debtor's name).

APPLYING THE CODE

Problem 15-5: Errors in the Financing Statement

David Epstein ran David's Donut Shop as a sole proprietorship. David was the sole owner, and had not filed any documents with the state to form his business. David borrowed $50,000 from First Bank for general operating funds. To secure the loan, David signed a security agreement granting a security interest in all his accounts to First Bank. Far and away David's biggest account was his ongoing relationship with Stately Law School ("Stately"), which regularly bought donuts on credit for student and staff meetings at the law school (faculty meetings being generally all-vegan affairs). Is there any problem with any of the following financing statement descriptions filed by First Bank to perfect this security interest (all financing statements listed the creditor as "First Bank")?

A) Debtor listed as "David's Donut Shop"?

B) Debtor listed as "Dave Epstein"? Is there anything else you need to know? Debtor listed as "Davoid Epstein"? Is there anything else you need to know?

C) Debtor listed as "David Epstein d/b/a David's Donut Shop"?

D) Debtor listed as "Carl Epstein"? Is there anything else you need to know?

E) Collateral listed as "All Accounts"?

F) Collateral listed as "Statly Law School Account"?

G) Collateral listed as "Rogers Law School Account"?

H) Collateral listed as "Inventory"?

How *should* the Debtor and Collateral be described here?

Test Your Knowledge

To assess your understanding of the material in this chapter, click here to take a quiz.

16

Perfection: Post-Filing Events

Key Concepts

- The duration of financing statements (and lapse)
- The continuation of financing statements
- The change of debtor's name and effect on perfection: 4-month rule
- The change of debtor's location and effect on perfection: 4-month rule
- Generation of proceeds and staying perfected in a security interest in proceeds

In the last chapter, we discussed the process of perfection by filing. Specifically, we discussed how a secured party gets perfected through filing a financing statement, *at the beginning* of the secured transaction. Now you know the three main things about that: 1) where to file (in the Secretary of State's office where debtor is located), 2) what to file (a financing statement with the name of debtor, name of secured party, and indication of collateral) and 3) whether mistakes are tolerated in the financing statement (minor errors are ok, except that no mistakes in debtor's name are allowed unless the search logic exception applies).

If there is attachment and these steps are followed, the secured party is perfected *initially*. But, things change. Stuff happens. Perfection (unlike diamonds or the Highlander) will not last forever. We need to figure out what things can happen to affect the secured party's perfection by filing. That is, what post-filing events can occur to cause the secured party's security interest to cease to be perfected?

In this chapter, we will focus on four basic post-filing events that can have this effect: 1) lapse of time, 2) change of debtor's name, 3) change of debtor's location and 4) sale or other disposition of collateral in exchange for proceeds.

A. Lapse of Time

Financing statements have a specific lifespan—five years. That's it. At five years, if nothing else is done, the financing statement lapses and the security interest is no longer perfected. But what if the loan is still not paid off at that time, and the secured party wants to remain perfected beyond five years? Section 9–515 has most of these answers:

READING THE CODE

> ### TEX. BCC SECTION 9.515: Duration and Effectiveness of Financing Statement; Effect of Lapsed Financing Statement
>
> **(a)** Except as otherwise provided in subsection . . . (e) . . . , a filed financing statement is effective for a period of five years after the date of filing.
>
> . . . .
>
> **(c)** The effectiveness of a filed financing statement lapses on the expiration of the period of its effectiveness unless before the lapse a continuation statement is filed pursuant to subsection (d). Upon lapse, a financing statement ceases to be effective and any security interest . . . that was perfected by the financing statement becomes unperfected, unless the security interest is perfected otherwise. . . . .
>
> **(d)** A continuation statement may be filed only within six months before the expiration of the five-year period specified in Subsection (a) . . . .
>
> **(e)** . . . upon timely filing of a continuation statement, the effectiveness of the initial financing statement continues for a period of five years commencing on the day on which the financing statement would have become ineffective in the absence of the filing. Upon the expiration of the five-year period, the financing statement lapses in the same manner as provided in subsection (c), unless, before the lapse, another continuation statement is filed pursuant to subsection (d). Succeeding continuation statements may be filed in the same manner to continue the effectiveness of the initial financing statement.
>
> . . . .

Section 9–515 provides the following basic rules for financing statements:

1. **Duration.** Financing statements last for five years. So, if First Bank files a financing statement to perfect a security interest granted to it by Kevin's Laundromat on January 10, 2023, at 2:00 p.m., the financing statement lapses, or expires, on January 10, 2028, at about 1:59 p.m. (the financing statements are date-stamped and time-stamped upon filing).

2. **Perfection ceases upon lapse.** Once the financing statement lapses, the security interest is not perfected anymore (unless the secured party did something else to get perfected). So, continuing the above example, when the clock strikes 2:00 p.m. on January 10, 2028, First Bank's security interest is no longer perfected.

3. **Continuation statement can be filed.** If the secured party wants its security interest to remain perfected, and keep the financing statement in effect, section 9–515 gives it a way to do so—the continuation statement. The continuation statement does what it sounds like—it "continues" the original financing statement in effect. If a continuation statement is filed correctly, the financing statement remains effective for an additional five years from the original five-year anniversary of the initial filing. So, if First Bank files a proper continuation statement, the financing statement will now last until January 10, 2033. Lapse will occur again at that point, unless another continuation statement is filed, and so on, and so on.

4. **Window to file continuation statements.** There's one catch with continuation statements. They can only be filed within a six-month window before the expiration of the financing statement. Not too early—not too late. If it's not filed in the six-month window, it has no effect at all. So, in order to continue the original financing statement, First Bank needs to file its continuation statement somewhere between July 10, 2027 and January 9, 2028, or so. And then, if First Bank wants to extend the effectiveness of the financing statement again, it would need to file another continuation statement somewhere between July 10, 2032 and January 9, 2033, or so. And so on and on, until the loan is paid off and First Bank doesn't care about extending it anymore.

APPLYING THE CODE

Problem 16-1: Financing Statement Duration

On March 1, 2022, Wayne Enterprises borrowed $100,000 from First Bank, and signed a security agreement granting First Bank a security interest in all inventory. The next day, March 2, First Bank filed a correctly prepared financing statement in the appropriate Secretary of State office. Answer the following questions:

A) As of March 1, 2027, Wayne still owed a sizable balance on the First Bank loan, so First Bank resolved to continue its perfection. It filed a continuation statement on March 15, 2027. Is First Bank still perfected? If so, what is the earliest date its current perfection started?

B) Say instead that First Bank filed a *new* financing statement, correctly prepared, on March 15, 2027. Is First Bank still perfected? If so, what is the earliest date its current perfection started?

C) What if, instead, First Bank filed a continuation statement on March 15, 2026? Does First Bank remain perfected beyond March 2, 2027?

D) What if First Bank filed a continuation statement on January 10, 2027?

B. Change of Debtor's Name

The next kind of change is something that could happen at any time. The Debtor could change its name. This is kind of a big deal, since we noted earlier that the debtor's name is the most important piece of information in the entire financing statement. It's the thing that everyone searches by when they search the Secretary of State's database.

So, say that Wayne Barnes borrows money from First Bank, and First Bank files a financing statement in Wayne's name. Then, a year later, Wayne changes his name to Ringo (he's always had a thing for the Beatles, but "Paul" seemed so ordinary). Wayne even changes his driver's license to say "Ringo Barnes." "Ringo" then seeks to borrow money from Second Bank. Second Bank checks the records for "Ringo"

Barnes, and doesn't find any (not knowing to search for Wayne because "Ringo" didn't tell Second Bank about his former life). This is a problem, obviously. And so the UCC has something to say about it:

READING THE CODE

TEX. BCC SECTION 9.507: Effect of Certain Events on Effectiveness of Financing Statement

. . . .

(c)   If the name that a filed financing statement provides for a debtor becomes insufficient as the name of the debtor . . . so that the financing statement becomes seriously misleading . . . :

(1)   the financing statement is effective to perfect a security interest in collateral acquired by the debtor before, or within four months after, the filed financing statement becomes seriously misleading; and

(2)   the financing statement is not effective to perfect a security interest in collateral acquired by the debtor more than four months after the filed financing statement becomes seriously misleading, unless an amendment to the financing statement which renders the financing statement not seriously misleading is filed within four months after that event.

Notice several things about section 9–507(c) and debtor name changes:

1.   **Four-month rule for name change.** Once a debtor changes its name, a four-month timer starts. It doesn't matter what kind of debtor it is. So, maybe Paula Franzese borrows money from First Bank, who files a financing statement; and later, Paula gets married and changes her name to Paula Hilfiger—the rule is triggered. Maybe Datsun changes its name to Nissan—the rule is triggered. Or maybe Cincinnati Bengals wide-receiver Chad Johnson changes his name to Ocho Cinco—the rule is triggered. Any debtor name change triggers the four-month rule.

Why do you suppose the Code creates a four-month rule here? Why not a shorter time frame, like thirty days?

2. **Secured party stays perfected in collateral acquired up until the four-month anniversary of name change, but not collateral acquired after that (if it doesn't amend the financing statement).** Section 9–507(c)(1) means that even if a debtor changes its name, the secured party doesn't have to do anything to stay perfected in the collateral the debtor *already owns*, and that debtor acquires in the four months after the name change. So, if "Ringo" acquired collateral three months after the name change, First Bank is still perfected in that collateral without amending the "Wayne Barnes" financing statement it previously filed. But First Bank would not be perfected in an item of collateral "Ringo" acquired five months after the name change, if it hadn't amended the financing statement.

Why do you suppose the Code lets the secured party remain perfected in the previously existing collateral, even if it doesn't update the financing statement?

3. **Secured party must amend the financing statement within four months in order to stay continuously perfected in collateral going forward past four months.** Section 9–507(c)(2) means that unless a secured party amends the financing statement to update the debtor's name (by filing an amendment with the Secretary of State) within four months of the name change, the secured party will not be perfected in any collateral acquired by the debtor starting four months and one day after the name change. So, if an amendment is filed within four months, First Bank will be perfected in the collateral that "Ringo" acquires in month five. But if no amendment is filed during that time, First Bank will not be perfected in that collateral acquired after the four-month anniversary of the name change. (Note, however, that First Bank could always file a financing statement *after* the four-month anniversary. If it did so, it would again be perfected in all the collateral. *But,* for reasons we will cover in the subsequent chapters on priority, First Bank's delay may cause it to lose a dispute with other creditors claiming the collateral.)

At this point, bright students like yourselves usually ask how the secured party is supposed to know if the debtor changes its name, and whose fault is it if secured party doesn't find out? The answer is, first of all, that the Code doesn't care. If the secured party does not amend the financing statement within four months, then the section 9–507(c) consequences happen regardless. As a practical and business matter, the secured party will probably contractually require that the debtor update secured party with any name changes, and may also communicate with the debtor from time to time to be sure this isn't the case. In short, it's the secured party that has every incentive to keep tabs on the debtor and his doings.

APPLYING THE CODE

Problem 16-2: Debtor's Name Change

Paula's World of Appliances, Inc. ("Paula") borrowed $50,000 from First Bank on March 1. The same day, Paula signed a security agreement granting First Bank a security interest in all inventory and equipment, now owned and hereafter acquired. As of that date, Paula owned one significant piece of equipment—a Wesco battery-powered forklift. She also held in inventory 200 Whirlpool washers and 150 Maytag dryers. On March 2, First Bank filed a financing statement, naming the debtor correctly as "Paula's World of Appliances, Inc.," and describing the collateral as "all assets." On May 1, by amendment of its articles of incorporation, Paula's World of Appliances, Inc., formally changed its corporate name to "Pro Appliance Emporium, Inc." ("Pro Appliance"). On July 1, Pro Appliance purchased an additional forklift to use in the warehouse, a Hyster S30. As of September 1, Pro Appliance still had 100 Whirlpool washers on hand, and 75 of the Maytag dryers. On October 1, it acquired 100 Samsung brand washers as a newer model to start selling as the Whirlpools were going out of style.

A) Assume that First Bank never filed an amendment to the financing statement. Is First Bank's security interest still perfected in anything? If so, in what? (The Whirlpool washers or Maytag dryers on hand, the Wesco, the Hyster S30, or the Samsungs?)

B) How does your answer to the above change if First Bank had filed an amendment to the financing statement, updating the debtor's name to "Pro Appliance Emporium, Inc.", on August 1? What if the amendment wasn't filed until October 15?

C) What if the August 1 financing statement was amended to change the debtor's name to "Paula's Appliance Superstore Co."?

C. Change of Debtor's Location

As we have just seen, if Debtor changes its name, it's a big deal. The database is indexed according to the Debtors' names, and so the names should be kept relatively up-to-date.

What if the Debtor moves? Not down the street, but to a different *state*? Recall from our discussion in the last chapter that the secured party must file in the state where the debtor is *located*. (Sections 9–301, 9–307). So, if a debtor moves to a different state, then they are not even in the right database anymore. And so (surprise), the UCC has something to say about this as well:

READING THE CODE

> ### TEX. BCC SECTION 9.316: Effect of Change in Governing Law
>
> (a) A security interest perfected pursuant to the law of the jurisdiction designated in section 9.301(1) . . . remains perfected until the earliest of:
>
>   (1) the time perfection would have ceased under the law of that jurisdiction; [or]
>
>   (2) the expiration of four months after a change of the debtor's location to another jurisdiction . . . .
>
> (b) If a security interest described in Subsection (a) becomes perfected under the law of the other jurisdiction before the earliest time or event described in that subsection, it remains perfected thereafter. If the security interest does not become perfected under the law of the other jurisdiction before the earliest time or event, it becomes unperfected and is deemed never to have been perfected . . . .
>
> . . . .
>
> (h) The following rules apply to collateral to which a security interest attaches within four months after the debtor changes its location to another jurisdiction:
>
>   (1) A financing statement filed before the change of the debtor's location pursuant to the law of the jurisdiction designated in section 9.301(1) . . . is effective to perfect a security interest in the collateral if the financing statement would

> have been effective to perfect a security interest in the collateral if the debtor had not changed its location. . . . .

Notice several things about section 9–316 and debtor state location changes:

1. **Four-month rule for location change.** Once a debtor changes its location to a different state, a four-month timer starts. It doesn't matter what kind of debtor it is. So, maybe Paula Franzese (an individual) moves her primary residence from New Jersey to New York—the rule is triggered. Maybe the partnership of Kevin and Wayne, which runs Kevin's Laundromat, changes the location of the laundromat facility from New Mexico to Maryland—the rule is triggered. Or maybe Kevin and Wayne's partnership (now a successful chain of multiple business locations) changes its partnership headquarters from Maryland to New York—the rule is triggered. Any section 9–307 debtor location change from one state to another triggers the four-month rule. (Remember also that financing statements are only good for five years to begin with, so the secured party doesn't get an "extension" if the debtor changes states less than four months before the expiration of the financing statement). Five years is five years.

   Akin to a question we asked a little earlier, why do you suppose that the Code gives the secured party four months to file in the new state, instead of a lesser time like twenty or thirty days?

2. **The secured party is temporarily perfected in any collateral acquired by the debtor during the four-month period, but. . . .** Because it wasn't really clear in the original section 9–316, the UCC drafters added subsection (h) to take care of collateral acquired during the four months after the debtor changes locations to a different state. In a word, the secured party's financing statement in the original state "covers" this collateral acquired during the four-month period, until we see how it ultimately works out. So, say that Paula's World-of-Appliances was a sole proprietorship of Paula, Paula originally resided in New Jersey, and First Bank filed in New Jersey in order to perfect a security interest granted to it by Paula. On March 1, Paula moves her residence to New York. In the interim, First Bank's New Jersey filing is perfection for any collateral acquired by Paula from March 1 through June 30, subject to the next point . . .

3. **The secured party must file in the new state within four months (or sooner if the first financing statement is less than four months away from its five-year lapse point), or it becomes unperfected in ALL of the collateral (old and new).** If the secured party files a financing statement in the new state within four months of debtor's move, then all is good. The security interest remains perfected continuously in all of the collateral—there is no "gap" or lapse of perfection. However, if the secured party does not file in the new state by the deadline, then it becomes COMPLETELY unperfected in ALL of the collateral (both that which debtor already owned, that which was acquired in the four-month period after the move, and that which is acquired subsequently to the four-month period while unperfected). Notice that this is a much harsher rule than when the secured party never filed an amendment updating the debtor's new name (where the secured party at least remained perfected in the collateral debtor already owned and which they acquired within four months of the name change). The idea is that if the secured party does not even get in the right database (i.e., file in the new state), then it will lose all perfection entirely.

APPLYING THE CODE

Problem 16-3: Debtor's Change of Location

Assume now that Paula Franzese owns and runs her appliance store herself, as an individual sole proprietor. The store's "trade name" (or dba) was "Paula's World of Appliances," but she took out the loan and granted all security interests described below in her own individual name. Paula was a New Jersey resident, and her store was located in Newark, New Jersey. Paula borrowed $50,000 from First Bank on March 1, 2021. The same day, Paula signed a security agreement granting First Bank a security interest in all inventory and equipment, now owned and hereafter acquired. As of that date, Paula owned one significant piece of equipment—a Wesco battery-powered forklift. Also on March 1, 2021, First Bank filed a financing statement in the New Jersey Secretary of State's office, naming the debtor correctly as "Paula Franzese" and describing the collateral as "all assets."

On March 1, 2023, Paula purchased a condo in the Upper West Side in Manhattan, New York. Although she still kept her New Jersey house for occasional weekend getaways, most of the time from then on she stayed at the condo. The store location, however, remained in Newark. As of the previous day, Paula held in inventory 200 Whirlpool washers and 150 Maytag dryers. On May 1, 2023, Paula purchased an additional forklift to use in the warehouse, a Hyster S30. As of July 1, 2023, Paula still had 100 Whirlpool washers on hand, and 75 of the Maytag dryers. On October 1, 2023, she acquired 100 Samsung brand washers, as a newer model to start selling as the Whirlpools were going out of style.

A) Assume that First Bank never filed anything after its March 1, 2021 financing statement. Is First Bank still perfected in anything? If so, in what? (the Whirlpool washers or Maytag dryers on hand, the Wesco, the Hyster S30, or the Samsungs?)

B) How does your answer to the above change if First Bank had filed a properly prepared financing statement in the New York Secretary of State's office on June 1, 2023? What difference does it make if First Bank did not file in New York until August 15, 2023?

C) Assume now that Paula's move to New York had occurred on February 1, 2026. What is the deadline for First Bank to file in New York if it wants to remain continuously perfected in all collateral?

D) Assume now that Paula never moved her primary residence from New Jersey to New York. Instead, she decided to move her store from Newark, NJ to Brooklyn, NY. What is the deadline, if any, for First Bank to refile in New York?

D. Staying Perfected in Proceeds

For this chapter, we have been focused somewhat on staying perfected in *original* collateral. That is, once the secured party is perfected in the debtor's original collateral to begin with, how does it stay perfected in that original collateral? So, when Paula's World-of-Appliances grants a security interest to First Bank in her inventory (the original collateral in this example), the rules discussed so far are about First Bank's getting—and then staying—perfected in the inventory.

But the last post-filing event we want to cover is how to get and stay perfected in *proceeds* of the original collateral. Recall from Chapter 14 that any time the Debtor sells, leases, or otherwise disposes of collateral (or collects on it, or collects insurance money on it), the stuff that Debtor gets in return is proceeds. So, when Paula sells a washing machine and receives a check, that check is proceeds.

We already know (also from Chapter 14), that if a security interest is attached in the original collateral, then it is automatically *attached* in whatever proceeds are generated. (*See* section 9–203(f)). We haven't yet talked about how the security interest gets *perfected* in proceeds. Let's do that now, by looking at parts of section 9–315:

READING THE CODE

TEX. BCC SECTION 9.315: Secured Party's Rights . . . in Proceeds

. . . .

(c) A security interest in proceeds is a perfected security interest if the interest in the original collateral was perfected.

(d) A perfected security interest in proceeds becomes unperfected on the 21st day after the security interest attaches to receipt of the proceeds unless:

  (1) the following conditions are satisfied:

   (A) a filed financing statement covers the original collateral;

   (B) the proceeds are collateral in which a security interest may be perfected by filing in the office in which the financing statement has been filed; and

   (C) the proceeds are not acquired with cash proceeds;

  (2) the proceeds are identifiable cash proceeds; or

  (3) the security interest in the proceeds is perfected other than under subsection (c) when the security interest attaches to the proceeds or within 20 days thereafter.

The first thing to note about section 9–515 is that if a security interest in original collateral is perfected, then a security interest in proceeds is *automatically* perfected, albeit only for 20 days. So, say that Paula's World-of-Appliances has granted a security interest in her inventory to First Bank, in order to secure a loan to First

Bank. Say further that First Bank has filed a financing statement in the Secretary of State's office, listing the collateral as "inventory". First Bank's security interest in inventory is perfected. Now say that Paula sells a washer and dryer to Kevin's Laundromat on credit, giving Kevin 60 days to pay (an account). The account is proceeds of the washer and dryer inventory. Under section 9–315(c), therefore, since First Bank's security interest in the inventory (original collateral) was perfected, its security interest in the Kevin's Laundromat account (proceeds) is also perfected. But the perfection of the security interest in proceeds is temporary—it's only perfected for 20 days, unless some other rule is satisfied.

Subsection (d) provides the rules for when a security interest in proceeds remains perfected *beyond* 20 days. At issue is whether First Bank's security interest will stay perfected in the Kevin account proceeds (which is good for First Bank), or whether the account proceeds will slip through its fingers because of lost perfection (which is bad for First Bank). Subsection (d) has three different scenarios for how a security interest in proceeds can stay perfected beyond the 20 days.

1. **First Proceeds Rule: Same financing office rule/no cash.** The most complicated rule is the first one, which is in subsection (d)(1). Subsection (d)(1) has three requirements. The first requirement is simply that a filed financing statement covers the original collateral. In our example, First Bank filed a financing statement for the inventory (the original collateral), so this one is satisfied. (Note, that if the secured party never filed a financing statement—for example if it's security interest was perfected in another way besides filing—Subsection (d)(1) would be inapplicable; i.e., it wouldn't work.)

   The second requirement is that the proceeds are collateral in which a security interest may be perfected by filing in the office in which the financing statement has been filed. This is much easier to satisfy than it may sound at first. In fact, it's almost always satisfied, if the security interest in original collateral was perfected by filing to begin with. What this rule requires is that you pretend that a brand new loan and secured transaction were entered into, where the original collateral was the proceeds that have been received. So, here, pretend that Paula borrowed money, and as original collateral granted First Bank a security interest in her accounts (since an account is the proceeds she received from the sale of the washer and dryer original collateral). If that alternative hypothetical security interest was entered into, where would First Bank file in order to perfect its security interest in accounts? Well, the same office where it did file—the Secretary of State's office. So, this rule is easily satisfied in our scenario (it almost always will be because filing is almost always an appropriate way to perfect—about the only time it wouldn't be is if Paula had swapped a washing machine for Kevin's car. Then we would be talking about First Bank's needing to be noted on the certificate of title, not filing. There are other examples, but for the moment, they are beyond the scope of this course in basic commercial concepts). So, the second requirement is satisfied.

The third requirement of this rule is probably the most important, since the first two will typically be satisfied. The third requirement is that the proceeds are not acquired with cash proceeds (there can be proceeds of proceeds). This means, no cash changed hands in between the sale or disposition of the original collateral and the proceeds we are talking about. So, in our example, this is satisfied. Paula sold original collateral (a washer and dryer in inventory) and received in exchange an account (Kevin's promise to pay for the goods sold). No cash has changed hands yet. Therefore, the third element of this rule would be satisfied, and that means that First Bank's security interest remains perfected in the Kevin's Laundromat account beyond 20 days.

Note that the result would be the same regardless of the type of proceeds received, as long as no cash changed hands. So, for instance, say that instead of selling on account, Paula had agreed to swap Kevin the washer and dryer in exchange for Kevin's prized life-size, solid gold statue of David Epstein. The same result would apply—First Bank's security interest in the original collateral was perfected by filing, you would file in same place if you were doing a brand new transaction with the statue as original collateral, and again note that no cash was exchanged. We went from a washer and dryer, straight to the Epstein statue. First Bank's security interest would remain perfected.

But, say instead that Wayne owned the Epstein statue. And that Paula sold the washer and dryer to Kevin for $10,000 cash, and *then* Paula used the money separately to purchase the statue from Wayne. The statue is still proceeds, but now the third requirement has not been satisfied. We can't say that the washer and dryer proceeds—i.e., the Epstein statue—was not acquired with cash proceeds, because in fact it *was* acquired with cash proceeds. And, under the rule when cash intervenes, things are messier and harder to trace, and therefore the Code says that First Bank's security interest will not automatically remain perfected in the Epstein statue beyond the 20 days (unless some other rule is satisfied).

2. **Second Proceeds Rule: Cash proceeds.** The rule of section 9–315(d)(2) is much, much simpler. If the proceeds *are* identifiable cash proceeds, then the secured party remains perfected in those proceeds beyond the 20 days. Simple. For purposes of this rule, "cash proceeds" means not only cash money, but also checks, and bank deposit accounts. (Section 9–102(a)(9)). So, when Paula sells the washer and dryer to Kevin, and Kevin gives Paula cash, or a check, then those cash proceeds are First Bank's proceeds. And as long as the cash stays put (and can be directly traced to the sale of the washer and dryer) and Paula doesn't spend it, First Bank's security interest remains perfected in such cash proceeds beyond the 20 days.

3. **Third Proceeds Rule: Otherwise perfected.** If neither the first rule (same office/no cash) nor the second rule (cash proceeds) is satisfied, then the secured party's only other way to remain perfected in the proceeds beyond the initial 20 days is the third rule, contained in section 9–315(d)(3). Subsection (d)(3) states that the security interest in the proceeds must be perfected "other than under subsection (c) when the security interest attaches to the proceeds or within 20 days thereafter." In a nutshell, subsection (d)(3) means this—either the secured party's financing statement collateral description already includes the proceeds, or it must be amended within 20 days to include the proceeds.

Go back to our example where Paula sold the washer and dryer to Kevin for cash, and Paula then used that cash to buy the life-sized Epstein statue. First Bank fails the first rule of subsection (d)(1) because the statue was obtained with cash proceeds. First Bank fails the second rule of subsection (d)(2) because a statue is not cash proceeds (it's non-cash proceeds). And, actually, at the moment, First Bank fails the third test, but maybe not for long. Remember that First Bank's financing statement described the collateral as "inventory." The Epstein statue is not inventory as to Paula because she is not in the business of selling statues. So, First Bank must amend the current financing statement within 20 days if it wants its security interest to stay perfected in the Epstein statue. First Bank could amend it to describe the collateral as "inventory and David Epstein statue." Or maybe the amendment says "all assets". Of course, if First Bank's financing statement had originally described the collateral as "all assets," then First Bank would have remained perfected in the statue under the third rule without taking any action—its financing statement would already cover the David Epstein statue proceeds. So, the third rule generally requires that the financing statement either already describe the proceeds received, or that it be amended so that it describes the proceeds received.

APPLYING THE CODE

Problem 16-4: Staying Perfected in Proceeds

Wayne's Widget Company (in the business of selling you-know-what) borrowed $25,000 from First Bank. On May 1, Wayne signed a security agreement granting First Bank a security interest in all of Wayne's inventory. Also on May 1, First Bank filed a financing statement in the correct Secretary of State's office, describing the collateral as "inventory." On May 10, Wayne entered into the following transactions. For each one, decide whether First Bank must take action in order to remain perfected beyond May 30:

A) Wayne traded 100 of his Model XJ widgets to Paula's Hardware in exchange for 25 Model ZY widgets.

B) Wayne traded 100 of his Model XJ widgets to Paula's World-of-Appliances in exchange for 10 iPads to use to ring up customer sales in Wayne's widget stores.

C) Wayne traded 100 of his Model XJ widgets to Kevin's Laundromat in exchange for Kevin's used 2016 Ford F-150 delivery pickup (which is subject to the state certificate of title laws).

D) Wayne sold 100 Model XJ widgets to Bobby Buyer. Bobby paid with a check, which Wayne deposited in a bank account.

E) Wayne sold 100 Model XJ widgets to Bobby Buyer, who agreed to pay for the widgets 45 days from the date of delivery.

Wayne sold 100 Model XJ widgets to Bobby Buyer. Bobby paid with cash. Wayne then used the cash to buy a new Wesco battery-powered forklift for use in his warehouse area.

Test Your Knowledge

To assess your understanding of the material in this chapter, click here to take a quiz.

17

Perfection (Possession and Automatic Perfection)

Key Concepts

- The method of perfection by direct possession
- The role of continuous perfection
- The role of third-party perfection
- Automatic perfection of purchase-money security interest in consumer goods
- Other categories of automatic perfection

In the last two chapters, we have gone over the basic rules of perfection by filing. Filing is the most important method of perfection and the most common by far. But, it's not the only method.

Before we move on to priority in the next chapter, let's discuss two other methods of perfection besides filing. One is possession, and the other is automatic perfection (which means the security interest is perfected automatically upon attachment—no need to file or do anything else).

A. Possession

Filing is the most common method used to perfect an attached security interest. And, it is the default way. But it is not the only way. Possession of the collateral by the Secured Party is another perfection method that works for lots of collateral types.[1]

---

1   There is another perfection method we are not really discussing in this course on core commercial concepts, which is a method called "control." "Control" is an Article 9 possession-type equivalent for certain types of collateral where ordinary "possession" isn't really feasible or legally effective by itself. The concept applies to investment property and deposit accounts (see sections 9–104 and 9–106)—two types of collateral we are not focusing on in this course. But now, we have planted the seed for when you study it for the bar exam.

You might wonder, as an initial matter, how possession of the collateral by the Secured Party accomplishes the notice policy of the UCC.

EXAMPLES AND EXPLANATIONS

Take an example. Wayne borrows money from First Bank for general living expenses, and Wayne agrees to grant First Bank a security interest in his prized (and dorky) stamp collection. Because the stamps are fragile (and also First Bank doesn't trust Wayne any further than it can throw him), First Bank insists on taking the stamp collection into its own possession while the loan is unpaid and outstanding, so Wayne can't touch it. Wayne brings the stamp collection up to First Bank, signs all the papers, gets the money, and First Bank puts the stamp collection in its vault. All is good (for now, assume First Bank is properly perfected by doing this).

Later, Wayne decides he needs more spending money (all those Beach Boys albums and memorabilia don't come cheap), and so he approaches Second Bank in order to get another loan. Second Bank asks what Wayne can offer as collateral for the loan. Wayne energetically replies about his sweet stamp collection, and, reluctantly, Second Bank asks to see it. Wayne responds that he can't show it right now, because it's currently in the vault at First Bank. Moreover, he tells Second Bank he's not allowed to retrieve the stamp collection while his loan at First Bank is outstanding and unpaid. Well, at that point, Second Bank has a pretty good idea now that First Bank must claim some type of interest in the stamp collection (why else would it be holding it until Wayne's debt is paid off?), and therefore Article 9's policy objectives of notice have been served by the possession.

B. Direct Possession

Perfection by possession is fairly straightforward under Article 9, and is provided by section 9–313:

READING THE CODE

> ### TEX. BCC SECTION 9.313: When Possession by . . .
> ### Secured Party Perfects Security Interest Without Filing
>
> **(a)** . . . a secured party may perfect a security interest in . . . goods . . . by taking possession of the collateral. . . .
>
> **(d)** If perfection of a security interest depends upon possession of the collateral by a secured party, perfection occurs no earlier than the time the secured party takes possession and continues only while the secured party retains possession.

Notice three things about sections 9–313(a) and (d). First, *perfection by possession.* The first thing is simple—the way a secured party perfects via possession is simply by taking physical possession of the collateral. That's it. Just like Wayne's stamp collection in the above example. First Bank took possession of the stamp collection from Wayne—that's enough for perfection by possession.

Second, *what can be perfected via possession?* The other thing to notice is what types of collateral can be perfected by possession. Of the ones we are discussing in this basic commercial concepts course, it's just one category—goods. Recall that there are four categories of goods (consumer goods, inventory, farm products and equipment). So, a security interest in any of these four categories of goods may be perfected by possession.

> Note: As an aside, there is one type of property, which is a good, that actually *cannot* usually be perfected via possession (the Code says this in parts of section 9–313 that we left out of the excerpt above). It's motor vehicles—mostly cars and trucks—which are covered by a system of laws in all 50 states for certificates of titles (a title is issued for the car, and then secured parties usually perfect by notating their security interest or lien directly on the face of the title). Since cars and trucks have their own system of doing things with certificates of title, section 9–313 says that you can't usually perfect a security interest in a car or truck, just by taking possession. Instead, you have to get on the certificate of title.[2]

---

2   As a side note, section 9–311(d) also says that if the debtor is in the business of selling cars—i.e., a car dealer—and grants a security interest in his entire inventory of cars, the security interest may be perfected by filing a financing statement instead of getting noted on each certificate of title.

The main type of collateral we have previously discussed, that cannot be perfected via possession, is accounts. A secured party can't "possess" an account receivable. It doesn't make sense—there's nothing to possess. Recall that an account is a contract right to be paid money for property sold or services rendered. An intangible right like that can't be "possessed;" in fact, there may or may not be any pieces of paper to possess, anyway. Therefore, there is no perfection of a security interest in accounts by possession. That won't work.

Third, *timing and duration of perfection via possession.* Under subsection (d), perfection by possession only commences when the secured party actually obtains possession. And it only lasts while the secured party has possession. In the example with Wayne and his stamp collection, say that Wayne decided after a couple of months that he just had to take his stamp collection home for a few days one long weekend. If First Bank relinquishes it to Wayne on a Friday, it stops being perfected (if it hasn't done anything else to keep perfected, like filing a financing statement). If Wayne brings the collection back to the Bank the following Tuesday, the Bank is perfected again but only from that point forward (we'll see why this might matter later when we talk about priority). Why do you think section 9–313(d) is structured this way?

One more thing—perfection by different methods. In the previous two chapters, we discussed perfection by filing. Now we are discussing perfection by possession. These are two different methods of perfection. It turns out that, either one of these methods can work for lots of different collateral (including goods). And, in fact, the Code envisions that over the life of a security interest, more than one perfection method might be used. Section 9–308(c) provides the rule:

READING THE CODE

TEX. BCC SECTION 9.308(c): [Continuous Perfection; Perfection by Different Methods]

A security interest . . . is perfected continuously if it is originally perfected by one method under this chapter and is later perfected by another method under this chapter, without an intermediate period when it was unperfected.

As long as there is no "gap" between methods, perfection of a security interest can be accomplished by different methods in sequence over its lifetime.

EXAMPLES AND EXPLANATIONS

So, for instance, if Kevin grants a security interest in a washing machine to State Bank, Bank could initially perfect the security interest by possessing the washing machine (method #1). But then, Bank could decide to file a financing statement (method #2). As long as there was no period in-between, where Bank was perfected by neither possession nor filing (nor any other method), Bank's security interest would be considered continuously perfected back to the beginning when it first took possession (which will be good for priority, as we will learn in subsequent chapters). If Bank waits a few days between relinquishing possession and filing, Bank is again perfected—but the gap in between methods means that the perfection will be deemed to "start over" with the filing (this could be bad for priority, as we will see later).

APPLYING THE CODE

Problem 17-1: Perfection by Possession (Direct)

Paula's World-of-Appliances borrowed $100,000 from First Bank for general operating expenses. In order to secure the loan, Paula agreed to grant First Bank a security interest in a solid gold, life-sized statue of Paula herself (with a bejeweled and dazzling store logo featured prominently on the statue). Paula had commissioned the statue to be made a couple of years ago, to be placed near the front door of her flagship store. On March 1, Paula signed the security agreement, and First Bank handed Paula a $100,000 cashier's check. The same day, Paula signed a document committing to deliver the statue within 48 hours. On March 2, Paula had the statue delivered to the Bank via courier. The Bank then placed the statue in its vault.

A) Does First Bank have a perfected security interest in the statue? If so, on what day was First Bank perfected—March 1 or March 2?

B) What if, due to Paula's being upset at relinquishing the statue, the Bank reluctantly agrees to let Paula keep the statue, as long as she agrees that she will be "possessing it for the Bank." Is Bank perfected?

C) Now assume that Paula delivered the statue on March 2 as previously stated. On April 1, Paula called the bank and said she was really missing her statue and wanted it back. The bank told her to come in the next day. At the end of the day on April 1, Bank filed a financing statement describing the statue. Paula retrieved the statue on April 2. Is Bank perfected? Does your answer change if Bank did not file until April 5?

D) Now assume that Paula delivered the statue on March 2 as previously stated. On April 1, missing her statute, Paula proposes to exchange the statue for a lesser, copper statue of Wayne (Wayne was once the Vice President of Paula's World-of-Appliances and quickly ordered a statue of himself, but was summarily fired for incompetence after less than a month on the job). The Bank agrees, and so on April 2, Paula retrieves the "Paula statue" from the Bank, and delivers the "Wayne statue" to the Bank. As of April 2, is Bank perfected in the "Paula statue"? The "Wayne statue"? Either? Why or why not?

E) What if, at Bank's insistence (after seeing the copper "Wayne statue" for too long), on May 1 Paula returns the "Paula statue" to the Bank and takes the "Wayne statue" back (and then trashes it). Is Bank perfected in the "Paula statue"? If so, as of what date is First Bank perfected in it?

Problem 17-2: Perfection by Possession (Direct)

Wayne Enterprises borrows $100,000 from First Bank for general operating expenses. To secure the loan, Wayne signs a security agreement granting a security interest in accounts. On May 1, Wayne signed the security agreement, and First Bank tendered the $100,000 to Wayne. On this same date, pursuant to the Bank's requirements, Wayne delivered copies of all invoices representing its outstanding accounts receivable, for money owed by customers for services performed, which amounts were due within the next 60–90 days. Thirty days later, on June 1, First Bank becomes concerned about whether its interests are sufficiently protected, and asks you for advice. Is First Bank's security interest in the accounts perfected? Why or why not?

C. Third-Party Possession

Normally, when the secured party wants to perfect by possession, it simply takes possession of the collateral itself. However, sometimes the secured party may not want to (or may not be able to) directly possess the collateral itself. Say that Kevin's Laundromat has a humongous, industrial washing machine, an Acme model XL500, which is approximately the size of a Ford Expedition, and that Kevin wants to use the washing machine as collateral for a loan with First Bank. First Bank (if it wants to perfect its security interest by possession) has no place to put the darn thing. What can First Bank do?

First Bank can use a third party to possess the collateral on its behalf, under section 9–313(c):

READING THE CODE

TEX. BCC SECTION 9.313(c)

. . . a secured party takes possession of collateral in the possession of a person other than the debtor, the secured party, or a lessee of the collateral from the debtor in the ordinary course of the debtor's business, when:

(1) the person in possession authenticates a record acknowledging that it holds possession of the collateral for the secured party's benefit; or

(2) the person takes possession of the collateral after having authenticated a record acknowledging that it will hold possession of the collateral for the secured party's benefit.

Note that, for third-party possession to work for perfection of a security interest, the third party must authenticate (i.e., sign) a written record (document) that it is possessing for the secured party. Why do you suppose section 9–313(c) has this writing requirement?

And, it has to be a legitimate, independent third party. So, not the debtor (or anyone substantially controlled by the debtor), and not the secured party (well, of course, the secured party can possess, but then it's not "third-party" possession under 9–313(c), it's "direct" possession under 9–313(a)).

APPLYING THE CODE

Problem 17-3: Third-Party Possession

David's Deluxe Hardware Store borrows $100,000 from First Bank. To secure the loan, David grants a security interest in a large forklift, an Acme model XL100 (David had two forklifts, and it decided it could get by for the time being with its other one). David was primarily in the business of retail sale of hardware items, although it also had a leasing department, which leased certain tools and machinery to consumers and businesses on a week-by-week or month-by-month basis. First Bank wanted to perfect its security interest in the Acme XL100 by possession, but it did not want to keep the forklift on its premises. Therefore, First Bank telephoned Wayne's Warehouse, to inquire whether Wayne was willing to take possession of it on First Bank's behalf. Wayne orally stated that he was, and thereafter First Bank had the forklift delivered to Wayne's Warehouse, where it currently remains.

A) Is First Bank's security interest in the Acme XL100 perfected? Why or why not?

B) Is your answer different if, upon delivery of the Acme XL100, Wayne signed a document, which stated: "Wayne Enterprises hereby acknowledges that it is holding the Acme XL100 forklift owned by David's Deluxe Hardware Store, on behalf of First Bank"? What if Wayne had signed the authorization *before* delivery of the forklift?

C) Assume now that, instead of using Wayne's Warehouse, First Bank asked Kevin, a Vice President of David's Deluxe Hardware Store, to take the forklift home with him. Kevin signed a document, which stated: "Kevin hereby acknowledges that it is holding the Acme XL100 forklift owned by David's Deluxe Hardware Store, on behalf of First Bank." Is First Bank perfected now? What if Kevin had signed the authorization *before* delivery of the forklift?

D) Assume now that, instead of equipment, David has granted a security interest in inventory. And, the Acme XL100 forklift is one of the items that David leases to customers on a month-to-month basis. In fact, the forklift is currently leased out on a month-to-month basis to Wayne's Warehouse, who is paying David a monthly rental amount for use of the forklift. In order to perfect its security interest in the forklift by possession, First Bank arranges for Wayne to sign a document, which stated: "Wayne hereby acknowledges that it is holding the Acme XL100 forklift owned by David's Deluxe Hardware Store, on behalf of First Bank." Is First Bank perfected now? Would it have mattered if Wayne had signed the acknowledgment *before* delivery of the forklift?

D. Automatic Perfection

The next type of perfection method is. . . . to do nothing. That is, sometimes the UCC provides that security interests are *automatically perfected* simply upon attachment. No need to take possession, and no need to file anything.

Allowing secured parties to be perfected when they haven't filed anything, or taken possession of the collateral, cuts against the UCC's policy of wanting to give notice to the world of these security interests. No notice to anyone if nothing has been filed or possessed. But, for various policy reasons, several specific categories of secured transactions are allowed to be automatically perfected.

E. PMSI in Consumer Goods

The categories of automatic perfection are contained in section 9–309. Far and away the most common and most important one for you to know is the first one on the list:

READING THE CODE

> ### TEX. BCC SECTION 9.309: Security Interests Perfected upon Attachment
>
> The following security interests are perfected when they attach:
>
> **(1)** a purchase-money security interest in consumer goods, except [for motor vehicles which must be perfected by notation on the certificate of title for most security interests where a single car or truck is the collateral].

Therefore, under section 9–309(1), a secured party with (1) a purchase-money security interest (PMSI) in (2) consumer goods, is perfected simply upon attachment (i.e., upon (a) giving value, (b) debtor having rights in the collateral, and (c) debtor signing a security agreement describing the collateral). No need to file. No need to possess. The idea for this automatic perfection rule is that it is expensive and burdensome to ask retailers and banks to file for every single small consumer transaction, since these are not large commercial transactions involving a whole lot of money. So, purely for convenience and logistics, Article 9 doesn't make secured parties do anything extra to perfect. Just attach, that's it.

The good news here is that we have already covered both of these components to this automatic perfection rule. You already know what a PMSI is—basically, a security interest in goods purchased, to secure the loan or credit that was given specifically to purchase the goods in the first place (remember that the purchase-money credit can be either the seller directly financing the purchase, or a third-party lender like a bank extending a loan specifically for the purchase of the item and the loan proceeds are then actually used for such purpose). And you already know what consumer goods are—goods used or bought for use primarily for personal, family, or household purposes (i.e., not for business purposes). Put those two concepts together, and you have the most common category of automatic perfection.

EXAMPLES AND EXPLANATIONS

So, to take an example, say that Kevin goes to Paula's World-of-Appliances, and buys a Whirlpool washing machine and a Maytag dryer, on credit, for use in Kevin's home for personal and family purposes. Paula extends the $1,500 credit to Kevin to cover the price of the washer and dryer, and Kevin then signs a security agreement granting a security interest in the washer and dryer in order to secure repayment of the $1,500 financed purchase price. Paula would be automatically perfected. Paula's security interest is a PMSI—Paula (the direct-financing seller) extended credit to enable Kevin to purchase the washer and dryer, and then he gave Paula a security interest in the purchased items to secure payment of the purchase price. And, the washer and dryer are consumer goods as to Kevin—he bought them for his personal use in his own home (not for a business). So, Paula has a PMSI in consumer goods, and therefore does not need to file or take possession of the washer and dryer in order to perfect. Once her security interest was attached, it also perfected.

Notice one thing in the section 9–309(1) excerpt above (which we edited and paraphrased quite a bit). The automatic perfection rule of PMSI in consumer goods does not apply to motor vehicles—cars and trucks. The reason, as we have talked about before, is that cars and trucks have certificates of title. And, under the laws of every state, the special perfection method when you grant a security interest in a car or truck you are purchasing (or even granting a security interest in a car you own free and clear—a so-called "title loan"), is for the secured party to make a notation of its security interest on the face of the title. So, secured parties financing the purchase of individual cars or trucks aren't automatically perfected. Instead, they have to notate the title with a description of their security interest.[3]

APPLYING THE CODE

Problem 17-4: Automatic Perfection—PMSI in Consumer Goods

Wayne went to David's Deluxe Hardware Store to buy a gas grill, to use in his backyard for entertaining guests at his home, and for general family use. Wayne decided to get the top of the line, so he wanted to purchase a Weber Summit S-670 Natural Gas Grill. The price was $2,500. David had in-store financing (3 years same-as-cash), which Wayne applied for and received. On April 10, Wayne signed a contract whereby: 1) Wayne agreed to pay David the price of the grill in 36 monthly installments (for 3 years) and 2) Wayne granted a security interest in the grill in order to secure payment of the $2,500 price.

A) Is David's Deluxe Hardware Store's security interest in the grill perfected? Why or why not?

B) Would your answer be the same if, instead, Wayne had bought the grill in his capacity as owner of Wayne's Western Restaurant and Grill? Why or why not?

C) What if, instead of a grill, Wayne's Western Restaurant and Grill had purchased a delivery truck from David's Deluxe Auto Lot, which

---

3   A quick reminder that, as we have mentioned before, section 9–311(d) also says that if the debtor is in the business of selling cars—i.e., a car dealer—and grants a security interest in his entire inventory of cars, the security interest may be perfected by filing a financing statement instead of getting noted on each certificate of title.

truck was a used 2016 Ford F-150 pickup (signing a contract agreeing to repay the purchase price over time in installments and agreeing to grant David's security interest in the truck). Is David perfected upon attachment? Is your answer different if Wayne had bought the truck for personal purposes?

D)   Assume now that we are back to Wayne buying the original Weber grill from David's Deluxe Hardware Store, for personal and family purposes. Wayne actually paid the loan off early, and so he then owned the grill free and clear. Six months later, however, Wayne needed another loan (surprise, surprise). He approached Kevin's Fast and Easy Money Lending, and arranged for a $1,000 cash loan from Kevin. Wayne signed a contract (1) agreeing to pay off the loan in 10 monthly installments, with 12% interest, and (2) granting Kevin a security interest in the Weber grill. Is Kevin perfected upon attachment? Why or why not?

F. Other Categories of Automatic Perfection

As discussed, a PMSI in consumer goods is the most important category of automatic perfection in section 9–309. Most of the other instances in which automatic perfection is applicable are highly technical and specific, and way beyond the scope of this course in basic commercial concepts. The following excerpt will list a couple of the other categories of automatic perfection in section 9–309, so you can have an idea of what else is in the section:

READING THE CODE

> ### TEX. BCC SECTION 9.309: Security Interests Perfected upon Attachment
>
> The following security are perfected when they attach:
>
> . . . .
>
> **(2)** an assignment of accounts . . . which does not by itself or in conjunction with other assignments to the same assignee transfer a significant part of the assignor's outstanding accounts . . . .; [and]

(5) a security interest created by the assignment of a health-care-insurance receivable to the provider of the health-care goods or services
. . . .

Subsection (2) is about assigning (which can include granting a security interest in) a small, "insignificant" amount of the debtor's accounts, in order to secure a loan. So far, we have just assumed that a debtor granting a security interest in accounts to secure a loan is granting a security in ALL of his accounts. All means 100%. All is always significant. So, there is no automatic perfection for a security interest in all accounts—filing is required. On the other hand, if a debtor only granted a security interest in 1 out of 1,000 accounts that would likely be insignificant (unless it was a really huge, disproportionate dollar amount). And so, section 9–309(2) basically says there is no need to file if it's only one out of a thousand accounts. Obviously, more than one could also still be insignificant, and so "how much" of the debtor's accounts before it becomes significant is a fact issue that would be handled by courts on a case-by-case basis (of course, if you're the secured party, when in doubt, you will file). But, for very small percentages of debtor's accounts, these are likely much smaller transactions, and so the UCC provides for automatic perfection—no need to file or do anything else to perfect.

Subsection (5) is about something we haven't really discussed—the "health-care-insurance receivable." It's what it sounds like. Say that David has health insurance with the AARP. When he goes to the doctor or the hospital, his contract with AARP provides that they will pay (or reimburse) a certain dollar amount for medical services received. Well, when David goes to the doctor and receives medical care, his doctor may not make David pay everything that might be owed that day. So, in a way, the doctor is extending credit to David—giving him time to pay. Of course, a big reason that the doctor will do this is that he knows that David has insurance that will probably pay a lot of the amount owed. And, in fact, the doctor may (they often do) have David sign something that signs over David's right to collect under his AARP health insurance so that the doctor can collect it directly from the insurance company. Section 9–309(5) recognizes that the doctor is a "secured creditor" here (extending credit to David for the medical services amounts, and also taking a security interest in the AARP health insurance which will eventually pay for them). But, what it also says is that doctors aren't banks, and so the UCC isn't going to make the doctors file or do anything in this situation to perfect their security interests in the health insurance.

APPLYING THE CODE

Problem 17-5: Automatic Perfection: Other Categories

Wayne Enterprises engaged in consulting services and billed its clients on a monthly basis. Payment for consulting services rendered was due within 30 days of service, and Wayne would regularly send out invoices reflecting the amounts owed. As of June 1, Wayne had over 500 clients, which owed him approximately $1 million. On that date, Wayne borrowed $100,000 from First Bank and signed a security agreement granting First Bank a security interest in all accounts. Also on June 1, Wayne borrowed $50,000 from his uncle Larry (a retired landscaper), and signed a security agreement in favor of Larry. The security agreement with Larry granted Larry a security interest in a single account owed by one of Wayne's customers, Paula's World-of-Appliances, in the amount of $45,000. Neither First Bank nor Larry filed a financing statement. Is either security interest perfected? Why or why not?

Test Your Knowledge

To assess your understanding of the material in this chapter, click here to take a quiz.

18

Priority: Basic Rules

Key Concepts

- The priority rule between two perfected Article 9 security interests (first-to-file-or-perfect)
- The priority rule between a perfected and unperfected security interest
- The priority rule between two unperfected security interests
- The priority rule between a security interest and a judicial lien

In the last few chapters, we have discussed the process of perfection of a security interest. If you recall, we said that perfection was the UCC's way to encourage secured parties to take steps—usually filing—that give the world notice of the secured party's security interest. By the secured party's filing (and thereby the security interest getting perfected), anyone can search the Secretary of State database and find the record of the secured party's security interest granted to it by the Debtor.

The way that the UCC "encourages" secured parties to perfect their security interests is through the rules on *priority*. Priority is about ranking security interests (and other types of interests) in order of preference.

State debtor-creditor law is not a "share and share alike" deal. There are winners and losers. Article 9 has rules of priority in order to sort out the winners and the losers when (1) two or more creditors try to collect their debts from the same property, or (2) when creditors try to collect debts from property that their debtor has sold to a third party.

For example, say that Kevin's Laundromat takes out two different loans, with First Bank and Second Bank. He borrows $50,000 from each bank, and grants each of them a security interest in all his equipment. If Kevin defaults on the loans, the two banks do not necessarily split up Kevin's equipment, sell it to the highest bidder and share equally in the net sale proceeds. Instead, one of them will have "first priority," and the other one will have "second priority" and that will affect their relative rights. As a practical matter, what this means is that if the value of Kevin's collateral is not enough to satisfy both loans in full then the bank without first priority will lose out. Suppose that Kevin's collateral is worth $50,000. The bank with first priority will get paid in full. The bank with second priority will get nothing. We will learn in Chapter 21 that, if First Bank is the one foreclosing on the collateral and it has first priority, First Bank gets paid first out of the money. And, we will learn in Chapter 21 that, if Second Bank is the one foreclosing and it has second priority, then First Bank's security interest will still be attached to the collateral after it's sold. Getting perfected is the best thing that a secured party can do to have a leg up in any future priority dispute, when two or more parties have contesting claims to collateral.

Now that we know the rules on how to get perfected, let's talk about the core commercial concepts of priority. We are going to start with the basic rules. In the next chapter, we will add in some special rules.

A. General Priority Rules: Secured Party vs. Secured Party

The most basic priority concept in Article 9 is one that you've probably heard before. First in time, first in right. When two or more secured parties both claim an interest in the same stuff owned by a debtor, the default rule is first-in-time, first-in-right. But, first to do what? Well, that depends a bit on exactly what situation we're talking about. Let's take a look at section 9–322(a) for the details:

READING THE CODE

> ### TEX. BCC SECTION 9.322: Priorities Among Conflicting Security Interests in . . . Same Collateral
>
> **(a)** Except as otherwise provided in this section, priority among conflicting security interests . . . in the same collateral is determined according to the following rules:
>
> **(1)** Conflicting perfected security interests . . . rank according to priority in time of filing or perfection. Priority dates from the earlier of the time a filing covering the collateral is first made or the security interest . . . is first perfected, if there is no period thereafter when there is neither filing nor perfection.

> **(2)** A perfected security interest . . . has priority over a conflicting unperfected security interest . . . .
>
> **(3)** The first security interest . . . to attach or become effective has priority if conflicting security interests . . . are unperfected.

Note that section 9–322(a) has three different rules, at least a couple of which are "first-in-time" type of rules. We will look at each of them in turn.

B. First-to-File-or-Perfect (Two Perfected Secured Parties)

Section 9–322(a)(1) is the most important rule in section 9–322(a), and the most commonly applicable one. This is the rule that applies when the priority dispute is between two or more perfected Article 9 security interests. Notice that the rule is that the security interests rank according to priority of time of filing *or* perfection. That is, the first secured creditor to do *either one* of those things. For purposes of this rule, it's important to note that the UCC actually allows a secured party to file *before* it has attached:

READING THE CODE

> ### TEX. BCC SECTION 9.502: Contents of Financing Statement; . . . Time of Filing Financing Statement
>
> . . . .
>
> **(d)** A financing statement may be filed before a security agreement is made or a security interest otherwise attaches.

Early filing is allowed for purposes of convenience, under section 9–502(d). The secured party might file several days before the debtor signs the security agreement or the loan is made, just to have everything in place by the time the loan transaction closes. But, as section 9–322(a) now makes clear, early filing can also have a very important effect on priority.

EXAMPLES AND EXPLANATIONS

To take an example, assume that David's Donut Shop borrowed money from both First Bank and Second Bank, granting each of them a security interest in accounts. First Bank loaned the money on January 1, 2023, and David signed a security agreement that same day. On January 2, 2023, First Bank filed. One month later, on February 1, 2023, Second Bank loaned the money to David, and David signed a security agreement that same day. On February 2, 2023, Second Bank filed. Clearly, First Bank has priority in the accounts, because it was the first to file or perfect (actually, it was the first to be both filed *and* perfected).

But remember that all that it takes is to be either the first to file, *or* be the first to perfect. Either one will do it. So, assume now that all First Bank did on January 1 and 2 was to file an authorized financing statement—that's it. No loan, no security agreement, no attachment in January. In February, Second Bank did everything listed—file, loan, attach, perfect. And then say that, in March sometime, First Bank finally got around to making the loan, getting a signed security agreement, and thereby getting an attached security interest in the first place. First Bank would still win—it was the first to file. All it takes is to be the first to file, or perfect. Since, in the changed facts, First Bank was still the first one to do either one of those things, it has priority (remember—early filing is therefore rewarded under Article 9).

Notice one more thing about section 9–322(a) and the "first-to-file-or-perfect" rule. It's not actually enough to be the first to file or perfect. The secured party has to be the first to file or perfect, be perfected, and stay continuously perfected. The secured party can't have "gaps" or lapses in perfection, but then try to claim the earliest date of original perfection before the lapse occurred.

EXAMPLES AND EXPLANATIONS

So, say that First Bank was fully perfected in a security interest in accounts granted by David's Donut Shop on January 1, 2022, and perfected on that date by filing. Second Bank was fully perfected in a security interest in David's accounts, by filing on January 1, 2025. At this point, First Bank clearly has priority. But, what if First Bank lets its financing statement lapse on January 1, 2027 (by not filing a continuation statement), and then gets re-perfected on February 1, 2027 by filing a new financing statement? Although First Bank was first to perfect—on January 1, 2022—it can't say, in the words of section 9–322(a), that there was "no period thereafter when there is neither filing nor perfection." Because, there was such a period—namely, the lapse from January 1, 2027 to February 1, 2027. So, guess who wins? Second Bank, because it was the secured party with the earliest time of filing or perfection (January 1, 2025), with "no period thereafter when there is neither filing nor perfection." That is, no gaps or lapses. First Bank had a gap, so the earliest date it can use in the priority conflict is February 1, 2027—the one that does not have any gaps afterwards.

With all this in mind, let's consider several problems to illustrate the first-to-file-or-perfect rule.

APPLYING THE CODE

Problem 18-1: Priority: First-to-File-or-Perfect (Filing First)

Wayne's Widget Store took out two different loans in order to help with general operating expenses. For both loans, Wayne planned to grant a security interest in his inventory. On May 1, First Bank loaned Wayne $50,000, and filed a financing statement describing the collateral as "all inventory." On May 10, Second Bank loaned Wayne $75,000. That same day, Wayne signed a security agreement granting Second Bank a security interest in all inventory. The next day, May 11, Second Bank filed a financing statement describing the collateral as "all assets." On the morning of May 20, the loan officer for First Bank realized (to his horror) that he had neglected to have Wayne sign a security agreement at all. Therefore, after calling Wayne and demanding that he stop by the First Bank offices that afternoon, Wayne signed a security agreement on May 20, granting a security interest in all his inventory.

A)   Which secured party, First Bank or Second Bank, was first to perfect? (Remember that perfection is attachment plus a perfection method like filing).

B)   Which secured party, First Bank or Second Bank, has priority? Is it the same as the first to perfect? Why or why not?

Problem 18-2: Priority: First-to-File-or-Perfect (Perfecting First)

Wayne's Widget Store borrowed money from First Bank and Second Bank, in order to help with general operating expenses. Wayne had a painting of widgets, known as "The Mystery and Wonder of the Widget," which he normally had hung prominently near the front entrance of his main headquarters. The painting was worth $1 million. Wayne decided to grant a security interest in the painting to both First Bank and Second Bank in order to secure the loans. On June 1, Second Bank made a loan of $50,000 to Wayne, and Wayne signed a security agreement granting a security interest in the painting. On this same day, First Bank made a loan of $25,000 to Wayne, and Wayne signed a security agreement granting a security interest in the painting.

On June 5, Second Bank took actual possession of the painting, and placed it in the vault at the main offices of Second Bank. On June 6, First Bank filed a financing statement describing the collateral as "painting—'The Mystery and Wonder of the Widget.' "

A) Which secured party, First Bank or Second Bank, was first to *file*?

B) Which secured party, First Bank or Second Bank, was first to *perfect*? (Remember that perfection is attachment plus a perfection method like filing).

C) Which secured party, First Bank or Second Bank, has priority?

Problem 18-3: Priority: First-to-File-or-Perfect (Continuous Perfection)

On August 1, 2022, Wayne's Widget Store, Inc., borrowed $100,000 from First Bank in order to assist with its general operating expenses. In order to secure the loan, Wayne signed a security agreement granting a security interest in all inventory to First Bank. First Bank filed a financing statement describing the debtor as "Wayne's Widget Store, Inc.," and the collateral as "inventory."

On July 1, 2024, after a couple of years of declining business, Wayne decided to change the corporation's name to "Wonderful Widget Emporium, Inc." On December 1, 2024, Wayne (in the new corporate name) borrowed more money, this time a $125,000 loan from Second Bank. In order to secure the loan, Wayne signed a security agreement granting a security interest in all inventory to Second Bank. Second Bank filed a financing statement describing the debtor as "Wonderful Widget Emporium, Inc." and the collateral as "all assets."

On December 18, 2024, barely in time for Christmas, Wayne received a shipment of a new inventory item, one that he had not carried before—the Widget XL1000. The initial shipment consisted of 1,000 units of the Widget XL1000, with more arriving daily. The item was Wayne's hottest seller, and very valuable.

Right before the end of the year, First Bank became aware for the first time of the name change. Therefore, on December 30, 2024, First Bank amended its financing statement, changing the debtor's name to "Wonderful Widget Emporium, Inc."

As of December 30, 2024, who has priority in the Widget XL1000s, and why?

C. Perfected Secured Interests Have Priority over Unperfected Secured Interests

The second rule of section 9–322(a) is hardly surprising. Between two security interests, if one is perfected and one is not, then the perfected security interest has priority over the unperfected security interest. Note that this is not really a "first-in-time" rule because only one security interest has been perfected—that security interest is not the "first" one to initially be perfected, it's the only one to perfect (or at least to currently *be* perfected). The rule, in short, is that perfection beats nonperfection.

APPLYING THE CODE

Problem 18-4: Perfection Beats Nonperfection

Kevin's Laundromat, Inc., a Delaware corporation, operated a laundromat in Baltimore, Maryland. Kevin, through the corporation, borrowed

$50,000 from First Bank in order to help with Kevin's operating expenses. To secure the loan, Kevin signed a security agreement granting First Bank a security interest in all Kevin's equipment, now owned or hereafter acquired. On March 1, First Bank filed a financing statement with the Maryland Secretary of State, describing the collateral as "all equipment." Subsequently, on May 1, Kevin again borrowed money, this time $75,000 from Second Bank. To secure the loan, Kevin signed a security agreement granting Second Bank a security interest in all Kevin's equipment, now owned or hereafter acquired. On May 1, Second Bank filed a financing statement with the Delaware Secretary of State, describing the collateral as "all equipment."

A) Which secured party, First Bank or Second Bank, has priority in Kevin's equipment? Why?

B) Is your answer different if First Bank had filed with the Delaware Secretary of State? If so, why?

D. First to Attach (Between Two Unperfected Security Interests)

Sometimes, although not often, there may be a priority dispute between two secured parties, and neither one of their security interests are perfected. This may be because both security interests have lapsed in perfection, or possibly because neither of them were ever perfected in the first place (or possibly some combination of the two). In this case, the third rule of section 9–322(a) comes into play: "[t]he first security interest . . . to attach or become effective has priority if conflicting security interests . . . are unperfected." Simply put, the first to attach has priority.

APPLYING THE CODE

Problem 18-5: First to Attach

Paula's World-of-Appliances, Inc. ("Paula") borrowed $50,000 from First Bank in order to help with operating expenses. A few days prior to the loan, in anticipation of the transaction, First Bank filed a financing statement, which inadvertently described the debtor as "Crazy Ray's Home Improvement Emporium" (the First Bank loan officer obviously got his files confused). At closing on February 1, First Bank delivered a cashier's check for $50,000 to Paula. Through another oversight, no security agreement was signed that day.

One month later, on March 1, Paula borrowed an additional $75,000, this time from Second Bank. In order to secure the loan, on March 1 Paula (in the correct corporate name) signed a security agreement granting Second Bank a security interest in all inventory and accounts. That same day, Second Bank wired the $75,000 directly into Paula's corporate checking account.

On March 5, in reviewing the paperwork, First Bank realized (to its horror) that it had never gotten a signed security agreement from Paula. Therefore, after demanding that she drop everything and come by the First Bank offices, on March 5, Paula (in the correct corporate name) signed a security agreement granting First Bank a security interest in all inventory and accounts.

A) Which security interest has priority, First Bank's or Second Bank's, in Paula's inventory and accounts? Why? Are you applying section 9–322(a)(1), (2) or (3)?

B) How would your answer be different if Paula had signed the First Bank security agreement on February 1? Are you applying section 9–322(a)(1), (2) or (3)?

C) How would your answer be different if First Bank's financing statement had described the debtor's name as "Paula's World-of-Appliances, Inc."? Are you applying section 9–322(a)(1), (2) or (3)?

E. First-in-Time, First-in-Right: Secured Party vs. Lien Creditor

Our first priority rule discussed above was section 9–322, which is a first-in-time, first-in-right rule. And it was a rule to address priority conflicts between two creditors, which each have security interests contractually granted under Article 9 of the UCC. But sometimes, an Article 9 secured party can come into conflict with someone besides another Article 9 secured party.

F. What's a Lien Creditor?

The next kind of priority conflict we will discuss is one between an Article 9 security interest and what's called a *lien creditor*. Lien creditor is a term that is defined in section 9–102(a):

READING THE CODE

> ### TEX. BCC SECTION 9.102: Definitions
>
> **(a)** In this Article:
>
> . . . .
>
> > **(52)** "Lien creditor" means . . . a creditor that has acquired a lien on the property involved by attachment, levy, or the like . . . .

So, a "lien creditor" is a creditor, we know that much. But, it's a particular kind of creditor—one that has acquired a lien on property "by attachment, levy, or the like." What may not be apparent to you from reading this—but we'll just tell you plainly—is that these methods referred to are mostly *judgment collection* methods.

So, a lien creditor is a creditor that originally obtained a money judgment in court, on either a debt or contract or tort. Really, it could be a judgment on any kind of cause of action, as long as the end result is a money judgment. But, it takes more than a mere judgment to make a judgment creditor a lien creditor. A money judgment is just a piece of paper—there's no property with a lien on it yet.

Recall from Chapter 12 that once a creditor has become a judgment creditor, then state law usually gives a variety of judgment collection methods to the judgment creditor, most of which are designed to compel the debtor to surrender some of his property or money in satisfaction of the judgment. These take many forms, and go by different names, like abstract, execution, levy, attachment, replevin, and garnishment, to name a few. What most of them require is for the judgment creditor to request a writ or other document from the court clerk, and then file it somewhere (such as the county real estate records office) or deliver it to a sheriff with a request to attempt to seize any of the debtor's available property (the sheriff's action in using the writ to then seize property is usually called "*levying*"). When the judgment creditor is successful in having the sheriff seize some of the judgment debtor's property—sometimes called a *levy* on such property—then the judgment creditor at that point obtains a judicial lien on such property in order to secure payment of the judgment debt (this lien or claim on such seized assets is sometimes called an *in rem* claim, or claims against property). Notice that the lien creditor only obtains a judicial lien to the extent of the property actually seized. It doesn't get a lien on anything not seized or taken by the sheriff through the writ process. Once such property is seized, however, this is the point at which the judgment creditor becomes a lien creditor. It becomes a judicial lien creditor.

EXAMPLES AND EXPLANATIONS

To take an example, say that Wayne has a Visa credit card, and owes $10,000 on the card. The Visa debt is "unsecured" debt. Visa did not get a security interest from Wayne. Now say that Wayne (unsurprisingly) defaults on his payments, and Visa sues Wayne for a judgment for the unpaid balance. Once Visa obtains a money judgment against Wayne, it is a judgment creditor (but not yet a lien creditor). Then, if Visa has the court clerk issue a writ of execution, delivers it to the sheriff, and the sheriff is able to successfully seize Wayne's speedboat (owned free and clear) in order to satisfy the judgment, Visa has obtained a judicial lien on Wayne's speedboat. Once the sheriff seized the speedboat pursuant to the writ—that is, once the sheriff "levied" on the speedboat—Visa became a lien creditor. It is owed a money judgment, and it now has a judicial lien on the speedboat in order to secure payment of the judgment.

G. First-in-Time, First-in-Right Rule: Secured Parties vs. Lien Creditors

What if both a lien creditor *and* an Article 9 secured party have an interest in the same stuff? That is, the lien creditor has a judicial lien on an item, but an Article 9 secured party has a contractually granted security interest in the same item. Section 9–317(a) addresses this type of priority dispute:

READING THE CODE

> **TEX. BCC SECTION 9.317: Interests That Take Priority over or Take Free of Security Interest . . .**
>
> **(a)** A security interest . . . is subordinate to the rights of:
>
> . . . .
>
> > **(2)** a person that becomes a lien creditor before the earlier of the time:
> >
> > > **(A)** the security interest . . . is perfected; or
> > >
> > > **(B)** one of the conditions specified in section 9.203(b)(3) is met and a financing statement covering the collateral is filed.

Section 9–317(a) is a first-in-time, first-in-right rule. It is a little bit of apples to oranges, though. On the lien creditor's side, what the lien creditor has to do is get the judicial lien—the moment the sheriff levies on, and takes possession of, property pursuant to a writ is the moment the lien creditor has done his part.

On the secured party's side, notice that there are two possibilities. One possibility, under section 9–317(a)(2)(A), is that the secured party's security interest is perfected before the lien creditor obtains a judicial lien by levy. This means what perfection generally means—the secured party's security interest has attached, plus has also been perfected via some perfection method (usually filing). If the secured party does this, gets perfected before the judicial lien arises by sheriff's levy, then the Article 9 secured party has priority in the property.

Notice that there is a second possibility for the secured party's security interest to take priority over the lien creditor. Under section 9–317(a)(2)(B), the secured party does not really have to get fully perfected before the judicial lien arises by levy. All it has to do is meet "one of the conditions specified in section 9–203(b)(3)" and file a financing statement. If you go back and look at section 9–203(b)(3), you will be reminded that it is the third element of attachment. And, the primary way to satisfy section 9–203(b)(3) is for the debtor to sign a security agreement with a reasonable description of the collateral. So, under this second possibility, all the secured party has to do to defeat a lien creditor in priority is to: (a) have debtor sign a proper security agreement granting a security interest in the property at issue, and (b) file a financing statement describing that property. Note that this could technically be before the secured party is perfected, since the loan may not have been made yet (no value). Nevertheless, if these two things are done before the lien creditor obtains a judicial lien by sheriff's levy, then the secured party has priority in the property.

APPLYING THE CODE

Problem 18-6: Secured Party vs. Lien Creditor

David's Donut Shop had a contract dispute with Kevin's Laundromat because Kevin had provided cleaning for David's work uniforms for his employees, and David had not paid Kevin for several months. As a result, Kevin initiated a lawsuit against David, and obtained a judgment on April 20 for breach of contract in the amount of $25,000. Part of the reason David was dragging his feet on paying Kevin was that business was slow, and he didn't have the cash to pay Kevin in full. Therefore, prior to the judgment being entered, on April 15, David borrowed $50,000 from First Bank in order to bolster his operating funds. In order to secure the loan, David signed a security agreement granting a security interest to First Bank in all his equipment. On May 1, Kevin obtained a writ of execution from the court clerk, and sent the writ to the local sheriff with instructions to seize any and all of David's property in order to satisfy the judgment. On May 5, the sheriff arrived at David's Donut Shop, and seized David's Star Max Twin Pot Commercial Countertop Deep Fryer, bringing it back to the sheriff's station. The next day, First Bank filed a proper financing statement, describing the collateral as "all equipment."

A)   Who has priority in the Star Max Deep Fryer, Kevin's Laundromat or First Bank? Why?

B)   Would your answer be any different if First Bank had filed on May 3? April 30?

C)   What if First Bank had filed on May 1, but had not loaned the money to David until May 10?

Would it have made any difference if Kevin's judgment had been entered on March 30? Why or why not?

Test Your Knowledge

To assess your understanding of the material in this chapter, click here to take a quiz.

19

Priority: Special Rules

Key Concepts

- The general rule of superpriority for purchase-money security interests
- The special rule of superpriority for purchase-money security interests in inventory
- The default rule of buyers taking subject to security interests
- The Buyer in Ordinary Course of Business rule
- Priority between buyer and unperfected security interest

In the last chapter, we began discussing the Article 9 rules on priority. Priority is the UCC's system of ranking security interests and other types of interests in a debtor's property. Whoever has first priority gets first dibs on the collateral and can use it to pay their debt off, before the next creditors get to do the same.

Last time, we started our priority discussion by looking at the basic rules. Those basic rules are that the creditor that is first in time is generally first in right. This plays out in different ways, depending on the circumstances and who the contesting creditors are. Between two or more creditors with perfected Article 9 security interests, the rule is that the secured party that is first to file or perfect has priority, so long as they have remained continuously perfected since such perfection. Of course, a perfected secured party always has priority over an unperfected secured party, and if both secured parties are unperfected then the rule is that the first secured party to attach has priority. Finally, if the secured party is in a priority contest with a lien creditor, then the secured party must generally be perfected (or, at least, file a financing statement and obtain a signed security agreement from debtor) before the lien creditor obtains its judicial lien by levy or the like. Otherwise the lien creditor has priority.

All of these rules so far are our "basic" rules—first-in-time, first-in-right (in various ways). But, now it is time to add some "special" rules. With these rules, the party who was first may not win. That's because there are other circumstances that dictate a different outcome; things that are more important to the outcome than just "coming first."

There are two main things that we will talk about here which dictate special rules. One is status as a purchase-money security interest (PMSI—a concept previously discussed in Chapter 13 and Chapter 15). And the other is status as a good faith buyer of certain goods and other items. So, we have some special rules on PMSI, and some special rules on buyers. Let's do PMSI first.

A. Purchase-Money Security Interest: Superpriority

Recall in Chapter 13 we defined the concept of purchase-money security interest, or PMSI. A PMSI combines the concepts of "purchase-money obligation" and "purchase-money collateral."

Remember that a purchase-money obligation is a loan or a debt that is incurred specifically to enable the purchaser to purchase the item. It's an "earmarked" loan for that specific purpose (as opposed to, say, a loan for general operating expenses). The purchase-money obligation could be credit extended either by a direct-financing seller of the good, or it could also be extended by a third-party lender like a bank (as long as the debtor actually used the loan proceeds to buy the goods).

The purchase-money collateral is the goods that were purchased with the purchase-money loan, and then granted as collateral to secure the very loan that enabled the debtor to purchase the goods. Tie these two concepts together and you have a purchase-money security interest (PMSI). That is, a loan or credit that specifically enabled the debtor to purchase something, and the debtor turned right around and granted a security interest in the purchased item to secure the purchase-money loan that enabled its purchase in the first place.

It turns out, PMSIs are given special treatment in a few instances. The basic reason is that the debtor wouldn't have owned the goods at all if the PMSI creditor hadn't enabled them to buy the goods. In a capitalistic society, we like debtors buying things. And we like the creditors who enable them to buy those things. And so the UCC gives special priority treatment to PMSI secured creditors who enable debtors to buy things like this. The PMSI creditors just have to follow certain steps, depending on the context and the circumstances.

In that vein, we'll look at two basic PMSI priority rules. The first one is the general rule for a PMSI secured party vs. a non-PMSI secured party. The second one is the rule for a PMSI in inventory vs. a non-PMSI security interest in inventory. In both rules, if the PMSI follows the steps, the result will be "superpriority"—that is, PMSI secured parties will enjoy priority in the collateral, even if they're not first. That is, they are "second-in-time, but first in right." They win not by being first, but by being PMSI (and following certain steps).

B. PMSI vs. Non-PMSI: General Rule

The first special PMSI rule, which provides for superpriority, even over earlier-perfected security interests in the same collateral, is section 9–324(a). That section provides as follows:

READING THE CODE

> ### TEX. BCC SECTION 9.324: Priority of Purchase-Money Security Interests
>
> **(a)**   . . . a perfected purchase-money security interest in goods other than inventory . . . has priority over a conflicting security interest in the same goods . . . if the purchase-money security interest is perfected when the debtor receives possession of the collateral or within 20 days thereafter.

Note a few things about section 9–324(a):

1. The first thing to note is that this rule applies to purchase-money security interests (PMSIs), of course. So, if the security interest is *not* PMSI—i.e., it's not specifically earmarked for the purpose of purchasing the goods in question—then you should apply the regular first-in-time rules discussed in the previous chapter. But, if it's PMSI, then this rule is in play.

2. The second thing to note is that this rule applies to *goods*, except for inventory. There is a special rule that applies if the PMSI goods are inventory.

We'll discuss that one in a minute. But, this is for non-inventory goods. So, as a practical matter, we are talking about either equipment or consumer goods (but mostly equipment). Stuff that a business uses in running its business, as opposed to stuff that it's in the business of selling (e.g., Best Buy's Wesco forklift in the back warehouse, not its TVs and computers).

3. The third thing to note is that under this rule the PMSI secured party has a deadline to perfect, which is no later than 20 days after the debtor obtains possession of the goods. If they have a PMSI in non-inventory goods, and they perfect within 20 days after debtor gets possession of the goods, they win the priority dispute. Even though their security interest came later. Superpriority (second-in-time, first-in-right). Why do you suppose that the UCC imposes this twenty-day requirement?

APPLYING THE CODE

Problem 19-1: PMSI vs. Non-PMSI (Default Rule)

On February 1, Wayne's Widget Warehouse (in the business of selling you-know-what) borrowed $100,000 from First Bank for general operating expenses. In order to secure the loan, Wayne signed a security agreement granting First Bank a security interest in all his equipment, now owned or thereafter acquired. First Bank filed a proper financing statement on February 2. On March 1, Wayne purchased a new Acme XL400 Widget-Making-Machine from Paula's World-of-Appliances, for a price of $50,000. Wayne planned to use the Acme XL400 to manufacture widgets for sale. Paula directly financed the purchase with Wayne. Wayne paid $10,000 down, and agreed to pay the remaining $40,000 over 3 years with interest. Wayne also signed a security agreement granting Paula a security interest in the Acme XL400 Widget-Making-Machine. The Acme XL400 was delivered to Wayne's place of business on March 5. Paula filed a proper financing statement on March 15.

A) Does First Bank have a security interest in the Acme XL400? Why or why not?

B) Who has priority in the Acme XL400, First Bank or Paula's World-of-Appliances? Why?

C)   What if Paula had filed on March 30? Does Paula even still have a perfected security interest if that is the case? If so, who has priority in the Acme XL400?

C. PMSI vs. Non-PMSI: Inventory Rule

The next PMSI rule of section 9–324 is one that deals with inventory. Under the default rule, we just saw that the only thing a PMSI in non-inventory goods has to do to obtain superpriority is perfect within 20 days after debtor gets possession of the goods. This is not the case with inventory. It's harder to get superpriority in a PMSI in inventory. Let's look at section 9–324(b) to see what more is required:

READING THE CODE

> **TEX. BCC SECTION 9.324: Priority of Purchase-Money Security Interests**
>
> . . . .
>
> **(b)** . . . a perfected purchase-money security interest in inventory has priority over a conflicting security interest in the same inventory . . . if:
>
> **(1)** the purchase-money security interest is perfected when the debtor receives possession of the inventory;
>
> **(2)** . . . the purchase-money secured party sends an authenticated notification to the holder of the conflicting security interest;
>
> **(3)** the holder of the conflicting security interest receives any required notification within five years before the debtor receives possession of the inventory; and
>
> **(4)** the notification states that the person sending the notification has or expects to acquire a purchase-money security interest in inventory of the debtor and describes the inventory.

The first thing to note about subsection (b) is that, unlike the default rule, there is no 20-day grace period to file after debtor gets possession of the goods. Instead, if the PMSI collateral is inventory, the PMSI secured party must be perfected *when the debtor receives possession* of the inventory. That is, by or before the time when debtor physically receives the inventory. No grace period—the PMSI secured party in inventory better be filed and perfected by the time debtor gets the goods.

The second thing to note about subsection (b) is that, in order to get superpriority over a prior perfected security interest in inventory, the PMSI secured party must also send an authenticated notification to any other conflicting security interests in the inventory. This requirement is spelled out in subsections (b)(2), (b)(3), and (b)(4). Note the following aspects of the authenticated notification requirement:

A) Subsection (b)(2) provides that it must be an *authenticated* notification. Remember that this usually means in writing, and signed. Not oral—a phone call won't do it. Of course, you also have to know who the conflicting secured parties are in order to know where to send the notice. We didn't include the UCC provision that says so, but obviously the prior, conflicting security interest must have filed a prior financing statement in order to require the PMSI secured party in inventory to send the notice (otherwise how would he know whom to send it to?)

B) Subsection (b)(3) covers a couple of things. First and foremost, it means that the notification must be sent *before* the debtor receives possession of the inventory. The notice is too late if it comes afterwards. So, note that two things must happen before the debtor gets possession of the inventory—the PMSI secured party must be perfected *and* it must have already sent the authenticated notice to the conflicting prior secured party. The second thing subsection (b)(3) covers is *how long* any sent notice is good for—and the answer is five years, as long as it fairly describes what is being financed. For the description, see the next point.

C) Subsection (b)(4) requires that the notification states that the person has or expects to have a PMSI in inventory, and that the notification describe the particular inventory in which a PMSI will be claimed. So, a notice to First Bank that a PMSI financer intended to do a purchase-money transaction in Model A widgets would be good for five years of subsequent Model A widget PMSI transactions. But the Model A notice obviously wouldn't be good for a subsequent Model

B widget PMSI transaction—a new notice for that type of inventory would be required.

Why does section 9–324(b) require such additional hurdles in order to obtain superpriority over a prior perfected security interest in inventory? Remember the nature of inventory—it is constantly depleting and replenishing. So, Paula's World-of-Appliances is constantly selling washers and dryers, and constantly getting new shipments of fresh inventory of washers and dryers. If First Bank has a security interest in all of Paula's inventory, now owned and hereafter acquired, then it assumes that anytime new washers and dryers come in the door they become part of its collateral. If a PMSI is going to come in and finance a batch of inventory and get superpriority in that batch over First Bank, it is only fair to give First Bank a heads-up so it can plan accordingly, and at least keep track of what collateral it can count on in the event of a default. This is why section 9–324(b) requires both perfection *and* notice to the prior perfected secured party, *both* of which must occur before the debtor obtains possession of the inventory.

APPLYING THE CODE

Problem 19-2: PMSI vs. Non-PMSI (Inventory Rule)

On March 1, Paula's World-of-Appliances borrowed $100,000 from First Bank for general operating expenses. To secure the loan, Paula signed a security agreement granting First Bank a security interest in all inventory. On March 2, First Bank filed a financing statement describing the collateral as "all assets." As of that date, Paula's inventory consisted of 1,000 washers and dryers consisting of the Whirlpool, Maytag and Samsung brands. On May 1, Paula responded to a solicitation from David's Dynamic Wholesalers to buy a set of 300 LG washers and dryers. David offered direct credit for Paula to purchase the LG washers and dryers at a price of $80,000. Paula paid $10,000 down and agreed to pay David the $70,000 balance in 2 years with interest. To secure the loan, Paula signed a security agreement granting David a security interest in the LG washers and dryers, as well as all of Paula's other inventory. On May 2, David called First Bank and informed it that he was taking a PMSI in the 300 LG washers and dryers. A day later, on May 3, David filed a financing statement describing the collateral as "inventory." The LG washers and dryers were delivered to Paula on May 5.

A) Who has priority in the Whirlpool, Maytag and Samsung inventory? Why? Are you applying section 9–322(a), 9–324(a), or 9–324(b)?

B) Who has priority in the LG inventory? Why? Are you applying 9–322(a), 9–324(a), or 9–324(b)?

C) What should David have done differently on May 2 in order to change the outcome?

D) Assume now that on May 2, David had sent a written, signed letter to First Bank, stating that David intended to acquire a PMSI in LG washers and dryers being sold to Paula. First Bank received the letter on May 6. Who has priority in the LG inventory? What if the letter was received on May 4?

Problem 19-3: PMSI vs. Non-PMSI (Identifying Proper Rule and Result)

Similar facts as Problem 19-2, with some differences. On March 1, Paula's World-of-Appliances borrowed $100,000 from First Bank for general operating expenses. To secure the loan, Paula signed a security agreement granting First Bank a security interest in all inventory and equipment, now owned and hereafter acquired. On March 2, First Bank filed a financing statement describing the collateral as "all assets." As of that date, Paula's inventory consisted of 1,000 washers and dryers consisting of the Whirlpool, Maytag and Samsung brands. She also owned a Wesco battery-powered Model A forklift for moving products around in the warehouse. On May 1, Paula responded to a solicitation from David's Dynamic Wholesalers to buy a set of 300 LG washers and dryers and also a bigger Wesco forklift (the Model B). David offered direct credit for Paula to purchase the LG washers and dryers and the Wesco Model B forklift, at a price of $95,000. Paula paid $10,000 down and agreed to pay David the $85,000 balance in 2 years with interest. To secure the loan, Paula signed a security agreement granting David a security interest in all Paula's inventory and equipment, including the financed items. The LG washers and dryers, and the forklift, were delivered to Paula on May 5. On May 24, David filed a financing statement describing the collateral as "all assets."

Who has priority, First Bank or David's Dynamic Wholesalers, in the following, and why? In each case, what could the creditor with inferior priority have done to have priority in the items?

A)   The Whirlpool, Maytag and Samsung items?

B)   The Wesco Model A forklift?

C)   The LG washers and dryers?

D)   The Wesco Model B forklift?

D. Buyers: To Take Free, or Not to Take Free? (That Is the Question)

At first glance, talking about buyers may not seem like a priority dispute, like with two or more creditors fighting over collateral. After all, a buyer is not usually a creditor. So, when Kevin's Laundromat sells a used washing machine to Wayne (and all of Kevin's equipment is collateral for a loan with First Bank), Wayne is a buyer of the washing machine. The conflict between Wayne vs. First Bank is not between two creditors, but there is nevertheless a potential dispute. The issue is—does Wayne take free and clear of First Bank's security interest when he buys the washing machine? If not, then whenever Kevin defaults on his loan, First Bank could come and repossess the washing machine from Wayne. On the other hand, if Wayne does take free, then Wayne doesn't care if Kevin defaults because First Bank no longer has a security interest in the washing machine. Wayne owns it "free and clear" of First Bank's former security interest.

E. Default Rule: Buyers Take Subject to Security Interest Unless Secured Party Consents

The default rule is bad news for Wayne. Because under the default rule, buyers do *not* take free of a security interest in the items sold. This is provided for most directly in section 9–315(a):

READING THE CODE

> ### TEX. BCC SECTION 9.315: Secured Party's Rights on Disposition of Collateral and in Proceeds
>
> **(a)** Except as otherwise provided in this chapter . . . :
>
>   **(1)** a security interest . . . continues in collateral notwithstanding sale, lease, license, exchange, or other disposition thereof unless the secured party authorized the disposition free of the security interest . . . ; and
>
>   **(2)** a security interest attaches to any identifiable proceeds of collateral.

Subsection (a) provides the default rule—a security interest *continues* in collateral notwithstanding sale or other type of disposition.

> So, again, say that Kevin has granted a security interest in all his equipment to First Bank to secure a loan. When Kevin sells a used washing machine (equipment) to Wayne, the default rule is that First Bank's security interest *continues* to attach to the washing machine after the sale. So, Wayne now owns a washing machine with a security interest still on it—he owns it *subject* to First Bank's security interest.

Why should the rule be as it is in section 9–315(a)(1), and what does it have to do with general property concepts?

Recall that the secured party also generally gets a claim in any *proceeds* of the sale under section 9–315(a)(2). So, as we have covered before, if Wayne paid Kevin $500 for the used washing machine, that $500 is proceeds of First Bank's collateral and First Bank's security interest attaches to the proceeds as well.

But, First Bank's security interest *also* remains attached to the original collateral, now in the hands of Wayne, the buyer. Such is the default rule. Absent some exception, a debtor like Kevin can't just sell a piece of collateral and magically remove the security interest from it. Again, this means that if Kevin defaults on his loan with First Bank, First Bank can come repossess the washing machine from Wayne. First Bank still has a security interest on it.

The only way provided by section 9–315(a)(1) for the collateral to be sold free of the security interest is for the secured party to *consent* for it to be sold free of its security interest. Such consent could be express—Kevin writes or calls First Bank and explicitly asks First Bank to allow the sale to Wayne free of the security interest (most likely in exchange for an assurance that the proceeds from the sale will be immediately delivered to First Bank). Or it could be implied over time—maybe Kevin has sold washing machines to various people regularly over a period of time without asking permission. First Bank was aware of these sales every time they happened, and yet never objected. At some point, most courts will hold that First Bank has impliedly consented to the sales free of the security interest, or has waived its security interest upon sale. Of course, this doesn't change the secured party's right to demand the proceeds received from such sale.

APPLYING THE CODE

Problem 19-4: Selling to a Buyer (Default Rule)

Wayne's Widget Warehouse borrowed $50,000 from First Bank for general operating expenses. In order to secure the loan, Wayne signed a security agreement granting First Bank a security interest in all equipment. On May 1, First Bank perfected its security interest by filing. On June 1, Wayne sold a used Acme XL400 widget-making-machine to David's Dynamic Wholesalers for a price of $5,000. Wayne's security agreement with First Bank was silent regarding sales of collateral. David delivered a $5,000 check to Wayne, which Wayne deposited, and Wayne delivered the Acme XL400 to David.

A) If Wayne defaults on his loan, can First Bank repossess the Acme XL400 from David? Why or why not?

B) What should David have asked Wayne to do before finalizing the sale?

C) If you represented David, what additional facts would you like to know?

F. Exception #1: Buyer in the Ordinary Course of Business

The first part of section 9–315(a) says "except as otherwise provided in this article. . . ." So, even though the default rule is that a security interest continues in collateral notwithstanding sale, the Code has some exceptions to that rule. And we are going to focus on a couple of those exceptions.

The first exception—and far and away the most important one—is called the "buyer in ordinary course of business rule." It is provided in section 9–320, with an important definition in section 1–201:

READING THE CODE

> ### ■ TEX. BCC SECTION 9.320: Buyers of Goods
>
> **(a)**   . . . a buyer in ordinary course of business . . . takes free of a security interest created by the buyer's seller, even if the security interest is perfected and the buyer knows of its existence.

> ### ■ TEX. BCC SECTION 1.201: General Definitions
>
> . . . .
>
> **(b)** Subject to definitions contained in other articles of the Uniform Commercial Code that apply to particular articles or parts thereof:
>
> . . . .
>
> **(9)** "Buyer in ordinary course of business" means a person that buys goods in good faith, without knowledge that the sale violates the rights of another person in the goods, and in the ordinary course from a person . . . in the business of selling goods of that kind. . . . . Only a buyer that takes possession of the goods . . . may be a buyer in ordinary course of business. "Buyer in ordinary course of business" does not include a person that acquires goods in a transfer in bulk . . . or in total or partial satisfaction of a money debt.

Section 9–320(a) provides the basic exception—if a buyer is a "buyer in the ordinary course," then such a buyer takes completely free of any security interest that the seller had granted to a secured party. It doesn't matter if the security interest is perfected, or if the buyer knows there is a security interest. Buyers in ordinary course of business take free.

But what is a buyer in ordinary course of business? Section 1–201(b)(9) answers this question. That section makes the following points about a buyer in the ordinary course of business:

- First and foremost, you must look at the seller's business. Buyers in the ordinary course of business buy from a seller *in the business of selling goods of that kind.* So in our prior example, Wayne would *not* be a buyer in the ordinary course of business when he buys a used washing machine from Kevin's Laundromat. Why? Kevin is in the business of letting people wash and dry their clothes at his laundromat—he is not in the business of selling washing machines. Now, if Wayne instead went into Paula's World-of-Appliances and bought a brand new washing machine from Paula, then he likely *would* be a buyer in the ordinary course of business. Almost always, buyers buying seller's *inventory* are buyers in the ordinary course, whereas buyers buying seller's *equipment* are not.

- Second, notice that the buyer must buy in *good faith.* "Good faith" is an amorphous concept—for our purposes, it basically means the buyer didn't have any reason to know something was wrong with the sale. So, for instance, if Wayne somehow knew that Paula wasn't supposed to sell a particular washing machine to him because her secured lender was required to pre-approve any sales, then Wayne won't be a buyer in the ordinary course. But such scenarios are rare. Note that this *doesn't* mean the buyer has to be unaware of the fact that there is a security interest—indeed, section 9–320(a) specifically says the buyer takes free, even if it knows of the security interest's existence. It has to be something more, some knowledge of the loan agreement or other contract being violated, or some other type of bad faith.

- Third, the buyer must generally take *possession* of the goods to be a buyer in the ordinary course of business. So, if Wayne contracts to buy the washing machine from Paula, but he hasn't taken possession yet, then he generally isn't yet a buyer in the ordinary course of business. "Ordinary" buyers buy their goods and take them home, or to their place of business where they intend to use them.

- Fourth, "transfers in bulk" are excluded from buyer in ordinary course status. This does not mean that someone bought 5–10 washing machines, and so they were really "bulky" to load onto the buyer's truck. It means, basically, that a buyer is buying substantially all of the assets of an entire business, including a bunch of inventory. So, if Paula's World-of-Appliances is going out of business, and sells her entire business—including all of her current inventory of washers and dryers—to Kevin's Kool Appliance World, then Kevin is not a buyer in the ordinary course. Bulk buyers are not ordinary buyers.

- Fifth, buyers who "pay" for goods by forgiving debt are excluded from buyer in ordinary course status. It's not "ordinary" for Wayne to pay for a washing machine from Paula's World-of-Appliances, by letting Paula off the hook for a personal debt Paula owed Wayne. Only regular sales where more ordinary consideration is received (so there will be proceeds at least for the bank to grab onto once the sale is made—no proceeds for Paula's secured lender if all Paula gets is off the hook on her debt to Wayne).

Before answering the problem below, ask yourself—why does the Code provide that buyers in ordinary course take free of security interests? What policy rationale is being advanced?

APPLYING THE CODE

Problem 19-5: Buyers in the Ordinary Course of Business

David's Dynamite Hardware store is a retail hardware store. Last year, David borrowed $100,000 from First Bank for general operating expenses. To secure the loan, David signed a security agreement granting First Bank a security interest in all inventory and equipment. First Bank was perfected by filing.

Decide whether each of the following buyers take their purchased items from David free and clear of First Bank's security interest:

A) Wayne bought a power drill for use in his business.

B) Kevin bought a belt sander for use in his home.

C)   Paula's World-of-Appliances bought the Wesco battery-powered forklift that David used in the back storage area to move products around. Is there anything else you need to know?

D)   Kevin's Laundromat bought a wet-dry vac for use in Kevin's business.

E)   Does it change your answer if Kevin was aware that David had granted a security interest in inventory and equipment to First Bank?

F)   Wayne, a C.P.A., bought a lawn mower in exchange for letting David off the hook for the tax preparation fees David still owed Wayne from last tax season.

G)   Kevin bought 10 lawn mowers for use in his landscaping business. Is your answer different if Kevin bought 95% of David's inventory as part of Kevin's startup of a new hardware store?

G. Exception #2: Buyer vs. an Unperfected Secured Party

The buyer in the ordinary course of business rule is the most important buyer rule. However, there are a few others. Most of them are beyond the scope of this course on core commercial concepts, but we will learn about one more.

If you recall from the last chapter on basic priority rules, we looked at the first-in-time, first-in-right rules for priority conflicts between an Article 9 secured party and a lien creditor. If you remember, those rules were in section 9–317, and they came down to the fact that if a lien creditor obtained a judicial lien on the property before the secured party was perfected (or at least before the secured party filed and obtained a signed security agreement from the debtor), then the lien creditor would prevail.

Section 9–317 has a similar rule for buyers of certain things, and whether the buyer takes free of a security interest in the things:

READING THE CODE

> **TEX. BCC SECTION 9.317: Interests That Take Priority over or Take Free of Security Interest . . . .**
>
> **(b)** . . . a buyer . . . of . . . goods . . . takes free of a security interest . . . if the buyer gives value and receives delivery of the collateral without knowledge of the security interest . . . and before it is perfected.

Under section 9–317(b), a buyer of goods will take free of a security interest if the buyer actually gives value for the goods (i.e., actually "buys" them for money or other consideration), and the buyer receives delivery or possession. Also, the buyer must receive possession of the purchased items with *no knowledge at all* of the existence of the security interest. Finally, all this must happen *before* the secured party is perfected.

In a sense, this rule is the cousin to the rule in section 9–317(a) that provides that lien creditors that obtain a judicial lien before the secured party is perfected have priority. Section 9–317(b) provides that genuine buyers who buy (without knowledge) before the secured party is perfected "have priority," or take free of the unperfected security interest. Either way, usually secured parties who are unperfected at the time a lien creditor obtains a lien, or a buyer buys the goods from the secured party's debtor, are in trouble. It pays, therefore, for a secured party to get perfected, and to get perfected quickly.

APPLYING THE CODE

Problem 19-6: Buyers vs. Unperfected Secured Parties

Kevin's Laundromat borrowed $50,000 from First Bank for general operating expenses. To secure the loan, Kevin signed a security agreement granting First Bank a security interest in all his equipment (mainly consisting of his washing machines and dryers). On June 1, the loan proceeds were delivered and the security agreement was signed. On June 19, First Bank filed a financing statement, perfecting its security interest.

Decide whether each of the following buyers take their purchased items from Kevin free and clear of First Bank's security interest (note that Kevin did not usually sell his equipment when he was finished using it, but rather normally donated it to his favorite charity):

A) Wayne bought one of Kevin's washing machines on June 5, and took it home that day. Wayne paid $500 cash, and was unaware of First Bank's security interest.

B) Paula bought one of Kevin's washing machines on June 10, and brought it to her store that day for resale in the used section of Paula's World-of-Appliances. Paula was unaware of First Bank's security interest. She agreed to pay $600 within 30 days of the sale.

C) Kevin's friend, David, had recently fallen on some hard times and needed a washing machine. Kevin, moved by compassion, decided to give a washing machine to David as a gift on June 15. David was unaware of First Bank's security interest, and took the machine home that day.

D) Wayne bought one of Kevin's washing machines on June 17, and took it home that day. Wayne paid $500 cash. Although Kevin said nothing about First Bank's security interest, Wayne was next-door neighbor to the First Bank president. The president told Wayne about First Bank's interest when he saw Wayne bringing the washing machine into his house.

Paula bought one of Kevin's washing machines on June 20, and brought it to her store that day for resale in the used section of Paula's World-of-Appliances. Paula was unaware of First Bank's security interest. She paid $600 cash for the machine.

Test Your Knowledge

To assess your understanding of the material in this chapter, click here to take a quiz.

20

Default: Part 1
(Before Foreclosure Sale)

Key Concepts

- The elements that constitute a default
- The secured party's rights upon default
- The secured party's right to self-help repossession and duty not to breach the peace
- The secured party's collection of account collateral upon default
- The right of redemption

Our final topic to discuss for Secured Transactions is the rules on default. Up until now, we have focused on how to create a security interest and how to perfect it. We also just finished discussing our rules on priority of conflicting security interests between two or more claims to the collateral. Now, we will talk about the Article 9 rules on default, which ultimately have to do with the secured party's *enforcement* rights against the collateral and against the debtor.

When a secured party makes a loan and takes a security interest in collateral, obviously the secured party hopes the loan will just be paid back according to its terms. That way, the secured party gets its money back, and hopefully some interest, and all is good. It doesn't really want the debtor to default on the loan.

But, remember that the whole reason it's called a "security" interest is because by having such an interest in collateral, secured parties are more "secure" in knowing they will likely get paid what they are owed. That is, either the debtor/obligor will pay back the loan according to the terms; or, instead as a fallback, the secured party will be able to enforce the security interest by repossessing the collateral, selling it, and using the money to pay the debt. This latter option is largely what Article 9 means when it talks about "default" rights, but there are a few other points that Article 9 covers as well.

A. What Is Default?

What is default, and why do we care? Well, as already alluded to above, it's only on default that a secured party can act to enforce the security interest, by repossessing the collateral or otherwise. Specifically, the first part of section 9–601 provides as follows:

READING THE CODE

> ### TEX. BCC SECTION 9.601: Rights After Default; Judicial Enforcement . . . .
>
> **(a)** After default, a secured party has the rights provided in this subchapter and . . . those provided by agreement of the parties.

Let's stop right there. Notice that section 9–601(a) says a secured party has various rights, but only *after default*. Why do you suppose that the secured party's enforcement rights do not arise until default? In any event, until there's a default, the secured party does *not* have those various rights. This raises the question—what *is* default?

The short answer is—default is whatever the contract or security agreement says it is. It is completely a matter of contract. Far and away the most important kind of default is always going to be missing a payment on the loan or credit obligation. But the debtor and the secured party could name any number of other events as conditions of default, like:

- Loss or damage to the collateral

- Failing to keep insurance on the collateral

- Failing to keep the collateral in good condition and repair

- Failing to inform the secured party of any name change or change of debtor's location

- Death, dissolution or bankruptcy of the debtor

If any of these contractually-specified events occur, then, as far as Article 9 is concerned the debtor is in default and then, and *only* then, can the secured party take enforcement steps with respect to the credit obligation or the collateral.

APPLYING THE CODE

Problem 20-1: Default

David's Donut Shop owed $100,000 on a loan with First Bank. First Bank had a security agreement, whereby David had granted First Bank a security interest in all his equipment and accounts in order to secure the loan. The security agreement was very short, and section 5 of the contract simply read in full as follows:

> Section 5: Events of Default. It shall be a condition of default if debtor fails to make, when due, any payment on the primary credit obligation secured hereby.

The payments on David's loan to First Bank were due in the amount of $3,000 per month for 36 months. David was very diligent in timely making all payments on the loan. However, a year after the loan was made, David failed a city health inspection, and his donut shop was shut down pending the required remedial action to bring his shop back into compliance. First Bank, upon hearing about this development, wants to take enforcement action against David, including suing on the debt and possibly repossessing all of David's donut shop equipment.

A)   Is First Bank allowed to take such action, as a result of the failed city inspection? If not, what should First Bank have done differently in order to have allowed it to do so?

B)   What if, instead of David's failing a city health inspection, First Bank found out that David had no insurance for his equipment or his business? Would this allow First Bank to take enforcement steps? If not, what should First Bank have done differently in order to have allowed it to do so?

C)   What if David had missed a loan payment on March 1?

B. Rights upon Default: Judicial Enforcement

Now that we have established what a default is, let's talk next about what rights a secured party has upon debtor's default. For this, we will start with section 9–601 again:

READING THE CODE

> ### TEX. BCC SECTION 9.601: Rights After Default; Judicial Enforcement . . .
>
> **(a)** After default, a secured party has the rights provided in this part and . . . those provided by agreement of the parties. A secured party:
>
> > **(1)** may reduce a claim to judgment, foreclose, or otherwise enforce the claim [or] security interest . . . by any available judicial procedure . . .
> >
> > . . . .
>
> **(c)** The rights under Subsection. . . (a) . . . are cumulative and may be exercised simultaneously.

From section 9–601(a), we learn that upon default, the secured party has basically two avenues of judicial enforcement rights. One avenue is something that all creditors have, whether they have a security interest or not. This is the right to *reduce a claim to judgment*. That is, upon default a secured party can usually sue the debtor in court, and get a money judgment for the amount of the debt. Because a secured transaction involves a debt, this is an option. So, say that Paula's World-of-Appliances has a $100,000 loan with First Bank, and First Bank also has a security interest in all of Paula's inventory. If Paula defaults, one option would be for First Bank to just go ahead and sue Paula and get a $100,000 money judgment. The judgment would be for "Paula's" (the company's) *personal liability* on the debt—it says Paula's World-of-Appliances is supposed to get out its checkbook and give First Bank the money. Secured parties can take this step upon default.

The second avenue available to secured parties upon debtor's default is to *foreclose* the claim, or otherwise *judicially enforce it*. This remedy has to do not with getting the money judgment, but with getting the *collateral* with court help. So, in our example, if First Bank wants to, it can put the money judgment on hold and instead go right to court and get judicial assistance with taking possession of Paula's inventory—that is, to get the court to *repossess* it for First Bank. This would usually be accomplished by a court action, accompanied with some kind of request for pre-judgment remedy like an order to the sheriff to go and collect the property. Once the property is collected by the sheriff, then it can be noticed for a sale, and the money from the sale can be used to pay off the debt.

Notice that section 9–601(c) provides that these rights are cumulative and can be exercised simultaneously. There is no prescribed sequence in which they must be exercised. The secured party can sue on the debt first, or it can seek court assistance with taking possession of the collateral first or it could do both simultaneously.

APPLYING THE CODE

Problem 20-2: Judicial Enforcement

Kevin's Laundromat had a $50,000 loan with First Bank, and First Bank had an enforceable security interest in all of Kevin's equipment to secure the loan. On February 1, Kevin defaulted on the loan and security agreement by missing a payment. Answer the following questions about First Bank's enforcement options:

A) May First Bank sue immediately for a money judgment for the balance of the loan? Are there any other facts you need to know?

B) May First Bank immediately seek judicial foreclosure and court-assisted repossession of Kevin's equipment? Without having first obtained a money judgment?

C) What order should First Bank proceed in and why? Are there any other facts you would like to know before deciding?

C. Rights upon Default: Self-Help Repossession and Duty Not to Breach the Peace

We now know that after default, a secured party has two basic avenues of remedy: (1) sue and obtain a money judgment for the debt, and (2) proceed to foreclose on the collateral—i.e., take possession of it and sell it.

If the secured party wants to proceed by foreclosure and physically taking and selling the collateral, it turns out that the secured party has another possible choice to make. We already know that the secured party can proceed with a judicial foreclosure, which involves invoking the powers of the court to obtain an order which directs the sheriff to go get the collateral and set up a court-supervised sale of it to help pay off the debt. But, section 9–609 provides another way to go for the secured party:

READING THE CODE

> **TEX. BCC SECTION 9.609: Secured Party's Right to Take Possession After Default**
>
> **(a)** After default, a secured party . . . may take possession of the collateral . . . .
>
> **(b)** A secured party may proceed under subsection (a):
>
> **(1)** pursuant to judicial process; or
>
> **(2)** without judicial process, if it proceeds without breach of the peace.

Section 9–609 provides that the secured party has *two* possible routes for taking possession of the collateral. The first one is judicial process. This is the process we have just discussed—invoking the powers of the court and the sheriff to obtain possession of the debtor's collateral.

The second route provided by section 9–609 is to proceed without judicial process. That is, the secured party can use so-called "self-help" and just go repossess the collateral on its own, without invoking the court process. Banks and secured lenders do this all the time, of course, and often either have employees do it or hire independent contractors to do it. Section 9–609 specifically authorizes the use of these "repo men" and their tow trucks to go repossess debtor's collateral, without using the court or the sheriff.

There's just one big caveat. If the secured party chooses to use self-help, it cannot *breach the peace*. We are, after all, running a society here, and so section 9–609 says that secured parties cannot breach the peace when attempting to repossess their collateral when the debtor defaults.

Section 9–609 does not define breach of the peace. There are a lot of cases that are litigated based on this. In general, here are some recurring themes:

Things that probably breach the peace:

- Physical violence, or threats of physical violence, by either debtor or secured party (needless to say, if First Bank's repo agent breaks Wayne's kneecaps, or threatens to do so, there is a breach of the peace)

- "Noisy protests" by debtor or family member

- Entry into enclosed area like garage or home

- Breaking locks to enclosed areas or structures for entry

Things that probably don't breach the peace:

- Peaceable persuasion of debtor to turn collateral over

- Taking from open garage without incident

- Breaking the collateral itself in order to take it

- Taking from street or parking lot or driveway without incident

- Using some amount of trickery or sneakiness

Two other things should be noted about self-help repossession. First, obviously the secured party has the right to take possession of the collateral upon default, so the taking of possession is not wrongful as against the debtor if default has occurred—i.e., it's not *conversion* under tort law. However, secured parties have to be careful about whether they take anything else when they repossess the collateral. For instance, if there is a computer in the car when the secured party repossesses the car, taking the computer is technically wrongful and not authorized. The secured party could be liable for conversion if the inadvertently-taken item is not promptly returned.

Second, courts have held that the duty to refrain from breaching the peace when engaging in self-help repossession is *non-delegable*. That basically means that a secured party is responsible and liable for the breach of the peace, even when the secured party has engaged an independent contractor to perform the repossession. So, if First Bank uses its own employee to repossess Wayne's collateral, then clearly First Bank is responsible if the employee breaches the peace. However, First Bank will also be responsible if it hires an independent contractor, Randy's Repossessors, to perform the repossession and Randy breaches the peace. Although under tort law principals are not generally vicariously liable for the torts of their independent contractors (as opposed to employees), in this case the rule goes the other way and the principals (secured parties) *are* liable, for reasons of public policy and the likelihood of non-peaceful things happening when people's stuff gets forcibly taken away.

APPLYING THE CODE

Problem 20-3: Self-Help and Breach of the Peace

Wayne has a two-year old Honda Civic, which he purchased with a loan from First Bank. First Bank also has a perfected security interest in the Civic. Wayne has recently defaulted on his loan, and First Bank has hired Kevin's Kourageous Repo service to repossess the Civic. Determine whether First Bank or Kevin breached the peace in obtaining, or attempting to obtain, possession of the Civic.

A) Kevin went to Wayne's driveway and began to take steps to connect the car to Kevin's tow truck. When Wayne appeared, Kevin said he was taking the Civic. When Wayne objected, Kevin flashed a Glock 9 mm pistol.

B) What if Kevin called Wayne, and told him that First Bank just needed him to drive to the First Bank offices to sign some paperwork needed for the title? Wayne showed up, parked the Civic, and went inside the bank office, whereupon Kevin towed the Civic from the Bank parking lot. The First Bank officer told Wayne, "Surprise, it's repossession day!"

C) What if Kevin went to Wayne's house and brought his brother-in-law, David, who was a part-time sheriff? Even though he was off-duty, Kevin asked David to show up with him, wearing his sheriff's uniform and county-issued gun.

D) What if, when Wayne went outside to ask what Kevin was doing, Wayne's wife also came out? Wayne was fairly calm, but his wife began shouting obscenities at Kevin, telling him (in much saltier language than we can print here) that he "better not" take the Civic?

E) What if Kevin knew that Wayne was attending a funeral for his grandmother on a Saturday afternoon, and, while Wayne was inside for the funeral, Kevin towed the Civic?

F) What if Kevin showed up at Wayne's address in the middle of the night where the Civic was parked on the street? Kevin broke the glass to the driver-side window, hot-wired the car and drove it away.

G) What if First Bank says it didn't tell Kevin to do any of these things, and it shouldn't be liable for Kevin's bad conduct in conducting the repossession?

D. Collecting Account Collateral

The above principles have focused, for the moment, on the process of a secured party seeking possession of physical, tangible collateral—goods, specifically (whether consumer goods, inventory or equipment). What if the collateral for the secured debt is not tangible, but is instead accounts held by the debtor and granted as collateral to secure a loan? There is no "repossession" of accounts—there is nothing to repossess. No physical force needed, no breach of the peace implicated.

So, what to do when a debtor has granted accounts as collateral (money that customers owe the debtor for goods sold or services rendered), and then that debtor defaults? Let's take a look at section 9–607 of the Code:

READING THE CODE

TEX. BCC SECTION 9.607: Collection and Enforcement by Secured Party

(a) If so agreed, and in any event after default, a secured party . . . may notify an account debtor or other person obligated on collateral to make payment . . . to . . . the secured party . . . .

Notice that this right is generally applicable "after default," which is also when the right to repossess physical collateral arises. Although sometimes the agreement between the debtor and the secured party allows collection of accounts aside from default, we will continue to focus on the situation where a debtor defaults, and then the secured party seeks to collect on the underlying accounts (the equivalent to "repossessing" the accounts . . .). So, as before, the debtor generally must have defaulted before the secured party can proceed.

Once the debtor defaults, however, the secured party can take the steps in section 9–607(a). And those steps are simply to tell the underlying "account debtor" to make payment to the secured party.[1] That is, pay the secured party instead of the debtor. Remember that accounts are defined as money owed for property sold or services rendered. So, these are usually business customers of the debtor who owe the debtor.

APPLYING THE CODE

Problem 20-4: Collecting Account Collateral

Kevin's Laundromat had a $50,000 loan with First Bank, which was secured by all Kevin's accounts. Kevin opened his laundromat to the public, but he also had several commercial accounts, where he provided laundry services for businesses. One of these customers was The David Hotel,

---

1   The Code has details about such demands for the account debtor to pay the amount owed to the secured party instead of the debtor. For instance, any such demand is generally required to be authenticated and in writing, not oral. Further, the account debtor is entitled to demand proof of the actual assignment/grant of security interest in the account being demanded to pay. These provisions are contained in section 9.406 of the Code, but we are not focusing on these specifics for purposes of this course in core commercial concepts.

owned by guess who. As of May 1, The David Hotel owed Kevin $25,000 for outstanding bills owed for laundry of bed linens at the hotel. On May 1, Kevin defaulted on the First Bank loan.

A) May First Bank demand that The David Hotel pay the $25,000 balance directly to First Bank?

B) If you represent The David Hotel, what do you suggest?

C) Is there anything Kevin can do? (See next section below)

E. Redemption

After the collateral has been repossessed, or the secured party has made collection demand on accounts, the secured party is going to want to take steps to sell it at foreclosure sale (or actually collect the account monies). We will talk about that in a bit.

But first, after repossession or demand on accounts, the debtor might want to try to get possession or dominion of the collateral back, before it is sold or collected. Of course, the secured party is not going to just have a change of heart and hand it back to the debtor out of pure benevolence. But, there are scenarios in which the secured party might let the debtor have the collateral back—indeed, might be required to give it back.

Article 9 calls this process *redemption*. As in, debtor has the ability to "redeem" the collateral—to get it back. And section 9–623 of the Code provides the rules on redemption:

READING THE CODE

> ### TEX. BCC SECTION 9.623: Right to Redeem Collateral
>
> **(a)** A debtor . . . or any other secured party or lienholder may redeem collateral.
>
> **(b)** To redeem collateral, a person shall tender:

> **(1)** fulfillment of all obligations secured by the collateral; and
>
> **(2)** the reasonable expenses and attorney's fees [incurred by secured party].
>
> **(c)** A redemption may occur at any time before a secured party:
>
> **(1)** has collected collateral under section 9.607; [or]
>
> **(2)** has disposed of collateral or entered into a contract for its disposition under section 9.610 . . . .

As you can see, section 9–623 provides the *who, how, and when* of redemption under Article 9:

- **Who.** Under subsection (a), it is primarily the debtor who can redeem the collateral. But note that another secured party or lienholder might want to redeem it.

> So, say that First Bank has repossessed all of Kevin's washing machines and dryers from his laundromat. Kevin could redeem his equipment back. But, what if Kevin also owed money to Second Bank, who had a security interest that was second in priority to First Bank? In that case, Second Bank could choose to redeem the equipment (by paying First Bank, of course— see below)

- **How.** Under subsection (b), the price of redemption is revealed to be "fulfillment of all obligations," as well as payment of reasonable expenses and attorneys' fees. In short, pay everything that's owed plus expenses. In theory, when a debtor misses one monthly payment, all that is "owed" is that one monthly payment. In reality, once default occurs, the secured party will almost always have successfully "accelerated" the debt, so that the entire balance is owed at the point of debtor trying to redeem (and some expenses and attorneys' fees have been incurred by then as well). So, as a practical matter, to redeem the collateral the debtor generally has to pay the entire balance, with interest, expenses and attorneys' fees. Since the debtor doesn't usually have that much cash lying around, this generally means taking out a loan somewhere else to pay the debt off and redeem the collateral.

- **When.** Redemption can occur beginning anytime after the secured party has repossessed the collateral, but there's a deadline when it becomes too late. Under subsection (c)(2), that deadline is once the secured has "disposed of [the] collateral." That is, once the secured party has already conducted the foreclosure sale and sold it to a buyer (about which more in the next chapter). At that point, it's too late to redeem. If the collateral is accounts which the secured party has begun demanding be paid to it directly, then subsection (c)(1) provides that the deadline is once the secured party has "collected [the] collateral." That is, once the debtor's customers have responded to the secured party's demand and sent the money to the secured party, the account is collected—too late for debtor to redeem the account and keep the collections to itself.

APPLYING THE CODE

Problem 20-5: Redemption

Paula's World-of-Appliances borrowed $100,000 from First Bank. To secure the loan, Paula signed a security agreement granting a security interest in all inventory, equipment and accounts to First Bank. First Bank's security interest was perfected by a financing statement filed on March 1. Paula had also borrowed money subsequently from Second Bank, which also held a perfected security interest in all of Paula's inventory, equipment and accounts. Second Bank's security interest was perfected by a financing statement filed on April 1. Further, Paula had recently been sued by Wayne, an ex-employee, for wrongful discrimination. On May 1, Wayne had recovered a $50,000 money judgment against Paula, but had not yet taken any steps to collect on the judgment.

Paula defaulted on her loan payments to First Bank, having missed the June 1 monthly payment due of $5,000. Second Bank's loan agreement with Paula provided that Paula's default on any other loans would also constitute a condition of default on her Second Bank loan. When Paula missed the June 1 payment, First Bank hired a repo agent and an attorney to protect its interests. The repo agent repossessed a sizable portion of Paula's inventory (without breaching the peace), which inventory had a fair market value of $25,000. Paula went to First Bank's office the next morning, and tendered the late $5,000 payment and also requested the immediate return of the seized inventory. First Bank refused to take Paula's money. First Bank reminded Paula of the acceleration clause in the security agreement, which provided that the entire balance of the loan became immediately due and owing if any payment was missed. Accordingly, First Bank demanded the total unpaid balance of $90,000, plus the repo fee of $500, and incurred attorneys' fees of $2,000.

A)   What does Paula have to pay in order to redeem the inventory?

B)   Can Second Bank redeem the inventory instead of Paula? If so, what must it pay in order to do so?

C)   Can Wayne redeem the inventory instead of Paula? If so, what must he pay in order to do so?

Is it too late for anyone to redeem the collateral if an auction sale has been scheduled? What if the sale has already occurred?

Test Your Knowledge

To assess your understanding of the material in this chapter, click here to take a quiz.

21

Default: Part 2
(From Foreclosure Sale to the End)

Key Concepts

- The obligation of secured party to proceed in a commercially reasonable manner
- The rules regarding public versus private foreclosure sales
- The elements of notice obligations prior to foreclosure sale
- The application of sales proceeds to debt balance and determination of deficiency or surplus
- The foreclosure sale transfer of title and discharge of security interests
- Strict Foreclosure Rules (Acceptance of Collateral in Full or Partial Satisfaction of Collateral)
- The available remedies for Article 9 violations
- The rebuttable presumption rule regarding deficiency

In the last chapter, we began discussing default. We covered what a default is (usually a missed payment), and what rights arise upon default. Basically, the rights are to sue on the debt obligation, but also to proceed against the collateral (either through judicial assistance or by self-help as long as there is no breach of the peace). These two rights can be pursued in any order, or simultaneously. Then, we learned that, after the secured party has taken possession of the collateral (or demanded that accounts be paid to it), the debtor has the ability to redeem the collateral back by paying the amount owed, plus reasonable expenses and attorneys' fees.

Now, we will complete our discussion of Secured Transactions by following the scenario all the way until the end. We will assume debtor has defaulted, and the secured party has lawfully taken possession of the collateral. And, we will assume that the debtor is not going to be redeeming it back by paying what's owed. Instead, the secured party is going to now proceed to do what it bargained for the power to do by taking a security interest in the first place—the secured party is going to take and sell the collateral, and use the money to pay off the debt (or, perhaps, the secured party may strike a deal to accept the collateral in full or partial satisfaction of the collateral).

A. General Commercial Reasonableness Standard

Like pursuing a money judgment and taking possession of the collateral, the secured party's right to sell the collateral at foreclosure sale is conditioned upon default by the debtor. However, other requirements also apply. Section 9–610 provides the following in pertinent part:

READING THE CODE

> ### TEX. BCC SECTION 9.610: Disposition of Collateral After Default
>
> **(a)** After default, a secured party may sell . . . the collateral in its present condition or following any commercially reasonable preparation or processing.
>
> **(b)** Every aspect of a disposition of collateral, including the method, manner, time, place, and other terms, must be commercially reasonable. If commercially reasonable, a secured party may dispose of collateral by public or private proceedings, by one or more contracts, as a unit or in parcels, and at any time and place and on any terms.

Subsection (a) states that once there is a default, the secured party is entitled to sell the collateral. Since there likely already was a default before the secured party took possession of the collateral, this is not a huge reveal at this point. After all, the secured party repossessed the collateral in order to sell it. Notice also that the secured party is entitled to sell the collateral either "in its present condition or following any commercially reasonable preparation or processing." In general, the secured party is entitled to a great bit of leeway as to whether it needs to do anything to the collateral before selling it. But, there are outside limits where it would be "commercially reasonable" to prepare the collateral for sale and perhaps "commercially unreasonable" not to do so.

EXAMPLES AND EXPLANATIONS

Say for example that Kevin's Laundromat defaulted on his secured loan with First Bank, and First Bank had a perfected security interest in Kevin's equipment. After First Bank repossessed Kevin's equipment, First Bank realized that one of the washing machines, a Whirlpool Front Load Commercial Washer normally worth $2,500 in good condition, had malfunctioned because of the failure of a small, inexpensive part. If repair of the machine would cost $50, but not doing the repair might result in at least $500 less in foreclosure sale proceeds, then it is feasible that a court might decide that failure to repair the washing machine before attempting to sell it was not commercially reasonable.

Subsection (b) provides the overarching standard of commercial reasonableness for all aspects of the Article 9 sale process. It provides that "*every aspect* of a disposition of collateral, including the method, manner, time, place, and other terms, must be *commercially reasonable*." This is a broad standard, and "commercial reasonableness" is not defined in the Code. In general, the goal of the Code is to generate the best price possible for the collateral, so as to pay off the most debt possible (since—spoiler alert—debtor will still owe whatever balance is not paid off). All aspects of the secured party's process are scrutinized under this broad standard.

One area that has been the subject of some litigation under this standard is advertising. Nothing in Article 9 strictly requires advertising the repossessed collateral for sale. However, most courts would find that it was commercially unreasonable not to advertise—otherwise, how will very many people find out about the sale? Section 9–610(b) also mentions that the "method, manner, time [and] place" of the sale will be scrutinized. Nothing in the Code requires that the sale be held during business hours, in good weather, and at a safe location. But, most courts would likely frown on a sale held at 2:00 a.m. in the middle of a snowstorm. Far fewer (if any) people would be likely to come to such a sale, and thus it would not be very commercially reasonable to conduct the sale in such a way.

The last thing mentioned in subsection (b) is that the secured party may proceed to sell the collateral by either a *public or private* sale. These terms are not defined in the Code, either, although the comments to section 9–610 provide some guidance: "Although the term is not defined, . . . a 'public disposition' is one at which the price is determined after the public has had a meaningful opportunity for competitive bidding. Meaningful opportunity is meant to imply that some form of advertisement or public notice must precede the sale . . . and that the public must have access to the sale."

In a word, a *public* sale is basically a live, public auction. It's held on an exact date, time, and place (e.g., Tuesday, May 2, at 2:00 p.m., at First Bank's offices at 101 Main Street, Dallas, Texas). The public is invited, and usually there will be an auctioneer of some type. All members of the public will be invited to bid at the live auction, and of course typically the goods will be sold at the end to the highest bidder.

A *private* sale, therefore, is anything besides a live, public auction. It could be an auction where only a select group is invited (like an auction for car dealers only). Or, it could simply be where the secured party tries to sell the goods in an informal manner—perhaps by word of mouth, or by advertising in the paper (or Craigslist or eBay), or by parking a car in the bank parking lot with a "for sale" sign on it and a phone number.

APPLYING THE CODE

Problem 21-1: Acting in a Commercially Reasonable Manner

Paula's World-of-Appliances owed $100,000 to First Bank. First Bank held a security interest in all of Paula's inventory in order to secure the loan. After Paula defaulted on the loan, First Bank went to Paula's store and peaceably repossessed all of Paula's current inventory of appliances. Answer the following questions about First Bank's foreclosure sale options:

A) Does First Bank have to sell all of the inventory at once, or can it sell the items a few at a time?

B) Should it examine the items to determine whether they are in good working order? Why or why not? Are there any additional facts you need to know?

C) Assume that First Bank wants to hold a live auction to sell the inventory. Should it advertise the auction? If so, where and in what publications or media?

D) What if First Bank has scheduled a live outdoor auction for August 1, and at the time it is scheduled to start a torrential thunderstorm breaks out? Must it cancel the sale, or can it proceed?

E) Assume that First Bank does *not* want to hold a live auction. Should it advertise the items for sale? If so, where and in what publications or media?

F) What if First Bank learns, before making any specific plans, that Kevin's Laundromat is willing to buy the entire inventory for $25,000, as is and on the spot. Can/should First Bank take the deal without doing anything else? Is there anything else you need to know?

B. Pre-Sale Notice Requirements

The requirement to use commercial reasonableness is a broad, non-defined standard that applies to the Article 9 foreclosure sale process. One specific requirement that *is* statutorily defined is the requirement to give *notice* before any sale of the collateral. We have already noted that courts will often require some amount of advertising of the sale in order to be considered commercially reasonable, but that is not the kind of notice we mean for this next section. The notice that is specifically required is a particular kind of notice, to a particular group of people. These requirements are spelled out, in part, in sections 9–611 and 9–612.

READING THE CODE

TEX. BCC SECTION 9.611: Notification Before Disposition of Collateral

. . . .

(b) Except as otherwise provided in subsection (d), a secured party that disposes of collateral under section 9.610 shall send to the persons specified in subsection (c) a reasonable authenticated notification of disposition.

(c) To comply with subsection (b), the secured party shall send an authenticated notification of disposition to:

(1) the debtor;

(2) any secondary obligor; and

(3) if the collateral is other than consumer goods:

(A) any other person from which the secured party has received, before the notification date, an authenticated notification of a claim of an interest in the collateral;

(B) any other secured party or lienholder that . . . held a security interest in or other lien on the collateral perfected by the filing of a financing statement that:

(i) identified the collateral; [and]

(ii) was indexed under the debtor's name as of that date; . . . . [and]

(C) any other secured party that . . . held a security interest in the collateral perfected by compliance with a [certificate of title statute requiring lien notations].

(d) subsection (b) does not apply if the collateral is perishable or threatens to decline speedily in value . . . .

TEX. BCC SECTION 9.612: Timeliness of Notification Before Disposition of Collateral

(a) Except as otherwise provided in subsection (b), whether a notification is sent within a reasonable time is a question of fact.

(b) In a transaction other than a consumer transaction, a notification of disposition sent after default and 10 days or more before the earliest time of disposition set forth in the notification is sent within a reasonable time before the disposition.

From sections 9–611 and 9–612, several principles about the required foreclosure sale notice emerge:

- **Form:** Section 9–611(b) requires that the "notice of disposition (i.e., notice of the planned foreclosure sale of the collateral) must be *authenticated.*

That is, it must be in writing and signed by the secured party. Oral notices are not sufficient under the rule (and certainly, of course, generally *no* notice is not sufficient under the rule, either).

- **Required Recipients:** Section 9–611(c) states who the foreclosing secured party has to send the notice to. There are three categories of required recipients—debtor, secondary obligors (if any), and other secured parties (if any). First, the *debtor*, for obvious reasons. Second, any *"secondary obligors."* Recall that sometimes there can be other obligors besides the debtor. Sometimes there may be a guarantor of the debtor's obligation—say that Kevin's Laundromat owed the debt and granted a security interest in equipment to First Bank, but that Kevin's father had guaranteed the debt (had agreed to pay First Bank if Kevin didn't pay). Thus, not only Kevin, but also Kevin's father would have to be sent a notice of sale. Third, *other secured parties* with an interest in the collateral (other than consumer goods). Section 9–611(c)(3) provides three categories of such required notice recipients: (1) those who have sent an authenticated notice of a claim of an interest in the collateral, (2) those that have filed a financing statement identifying the debtor and the collateral being sold, and (3) those that are listed on the certificate of title of a car or truck (if that's what the collateral is).

- **Exception to Notice Requirement:** Section 9–611(d) provides that in a couple of instances, the secured party doesn't have to send any notices before selling the collateral. This is the case when the collateral is perishable or otherwise threatens to decline speedily in value.

So, for instance, if the Debtor was Wayne's Fruit and Produce, and the re-possessed collateral was fresh fruit and vegetables (in Fort Worth, Texas in the middle of August when the temperature stays at about 105 for several weeks in a row), then the secured party would not need to stop everything, and send out several days' notice before proceeding with sale of the produce. Otherwise, obviously, the collateral would spoil and be ruined, not helping either the secured party or the debtor.

- **How much notice must be given (how many days):** Section 9–612 addresses this issue, first in subsection (a) by simply providing that whether notice is sent within a reasonable time is generally a question of fact.

Subsection (b), however, provides a safe harbor for *commercial* transactions, such that notice sent after default and *10 days or more* before the earliest time of sale in the notice is deemed to be a reasonable time. In other words, a business debtor like Paula's World-of-Appliances will not be able to claim that it was commercially unreasonable for the secured party to not send her a sale notice 15 days before the sale. Ten days is always enough for commercial debtors. The Code does not expressly state what is a reasonable time for *consumer* transactions.

As for what the notice must *say*, the Code also provides specific rules on that. It is just the basic informational components you might expect—identify the debtor and the secured party, the collateral being sold, how it's going to be sold and when. Information about the amount of the debt generally must be provided as well. You can go read sections 9–613 and 9–614 in your spare time if you want to know more, but that level of detail will be handled by form books in practice, and so is beyond the scope of this course in core commercial concepts.

APPLYING THE CODE

Problem 21-2: Notice Requirements

David's Donut Shop owed $100,000 to First Bank on a loan secured by David's inventory and equipment. First Bank perfected by filing on January 15. First Bank also required David to get someone to guarantee or co-sign on the debt. David was able to persuade his friend Kevin to do so. David had also borrowed $50,000 from Second Bank on a loan secured by David's inventory and equipment. Second Bank perfected by filing on February 15. More recently, out of desperation, David had borrowed from two more friends. He borrowed $10,000 from Paula, and $5,000 from Wayne. To secure both loans, David signed two separate security agreements, granting both Wayne and Paula a security interest in David's inventory and equipment. Neither Wayne nor Paula ever filed a financing statement to perfect their security interests.

Finally, David's ability to pay all his loan payments ran out, and he defaulted on all his obligations to all creditors (First Bank, Second Bank, Paula and Wayne). On April 1, First Bank promptly and peaceably repossessed all of David's donut-making equipment (which was worth approximately $115,000), and also seized all of David's inventory of baked donuts and other items (which David normally threw out within a day or two). The baked goods had an approximate menu value (when fresh) of $2,000. First Bank sold the donuts and baked goods for $500 within 4 hours of repossessing them, to a rival cross-town donut shop, without advertising or taking any action besides contacting the rival donut shop. First Bank hired an auctioneer and planned a public auction at the offices of First Bank for May 1, at 10:00 a.m. Kevin, Second Bank, Wayne and Paula have all heard about what happened. Paula wrote a letter to First Bank, demanding notices of all subsequent actions and claiming an interest in the repossessed inventory and equipment. Wayne, who knew the First Bank president personally, called the president on the phone and told him to keep Wayne apprised of the goings-on with the sale of Kevin's collateral. Neither Second Bank nor Kevin contacted First Bank.

A)   Is First Bank *required* to send notice of the planned sale to each of the following? Why or why not?

1) David?

2) Second Bank?

3) Kevin?

4) Paula?

5) Wayne?

B)   If First Bank telephoned each person entitled to notice, on the afternoon of April 15, would such notice be sufficient under the Code? Why or why not?

C)   If First Bank mailed a written, signed notice to David, Kevin, Second Bank, and Paula on April 22, would this be sufficient under the Code? Is your answer different if the notice was sent on April 18? Why or why not?

D)   Did First Bank violate the Code by not sending notice to anyone of its plans for disposing of the donuts?

E)   Oh, by the way—was First Bank required to give notice to David (or anyone else) *before* repossessing the collateral that it was planning on repossessing? Why or why not? (Hint—we didn't read any code section that required it . . .)

C. Effects of the Foreclosure Sale

Once the foreclosure sale has actually occurred, what then? Hopefully, the secured party has peaceably repossessed the collateral, has acted in a commercially reasonable manner, and has given all required notices of the sale. And then, the sale actually happens. A buyer actually shows up and purchases the collateral, for real money. What do we do with that money, and what happens to everyone's interest in the aftermath of the foreclosure sale?

D. Application of Sale Proceeds/Deficiency or Surplus

The first order of business is to discuss what happens to the money received from the buyer at the foreclosure sale. This is addressed by section 9–615 of the Code:

READING THE CODE

> **TEX. BCC SECTION 9.615: Application of Proceeds of Disposition; Liability for Deficiency and Right to Surplus**
>
> **(a)** A secured party shall apply or pay over for application the cash proceeds of disposition under section 9.610 in the following order to:
>
> **(1)** the reasonable expenses of retaking, holding, preparing for disposition, processing, and disposing, and, to the extent provided for by agreement and not prohibited by law, reasonable attorney's fees and legal expenses incurred by the secured party;
>
> **(2)** the satisfaction of obligations secured by the security interest . . . under which the disposition is made;
>
> **(3)** the satisfaction of obligations secured by any subordinate security interest in or other subordinate lien on the collateral if:
>
> **(A)** the secured party receives from the holder of the subordinate security interest or other lien an authenticated demand for proceeds before distribution of the proceeds is completed . . . .
>
> **(d)** . . . after making the payments and applications required by Subsection (a) . . .:

> **(1)** . . . the secured party shall account to and pay a debtor for any surplus; and
>
> **(2)** the obligor is liable for any deficiency.

Looking at sections 9–615(a) and (d), here are the basics:

1. **Expenses come off the top.** Under subsection (a)(1), the foreclosing secured party first can use the money to pay any repossession and foreclosure-related expenses incurred, such as paying the repo fees, preparing the collateral for sale, advertising, etc. Attorneys' fees and legal expenses are also included here, presuming they are provided for by the parties' loan and security agreement.

2. **Next comes the foreclosing secured party's debt.** Once expenses have been paid off the top, subsection (a)(2) provides for "the satisfaction of obligations secured by the security interest . . . under which the disposition is made." In other words, the secured party running the foreclosure sale (usually the first priority secured party but not always) gets to apply the money to its debt next.

   Sometimes, the money stops here because it's not enough to pay off the foreclosing secured party's debt, and that's it. However, in the event that this is enough to pay off the foreclosing secured party's debt in full, then we move to the next step, which is . . .

3. **Next comes payment of lower priority secured claims (if notice has been sent to the foreclosing secured party).** After the foreclosing secured party's debt has been paid in full, subsection (a)(3) provides that the money is next allocated for "the satisfaction of obligations secured by any subordinate security interest in or other subordinate lien on the collateral." That is, secured claims that are lower in priority to the foreclosing secured party get paid next (if there's more than one of them, then they should be paid in order of their priority under the priority rules we learned previously). There is one big caveat here—in order to hold their place in line for such a distribution, the junior secured parties have to send written, authenticated demand for such proceeds to the foreclosing secured party, and they have to do it *before* the foreclosing secured party has finished distributing the proceeds. This is why the UCC requires the

foreclosing secured party to send its notice before the sale. If the junior secured parties have sent their demand, they get paid next.

Almost always, the money runs out here before all the junior secured parties can get paid. But sometimes, the collateral was so valuable and brought so much money at foreclosure sale (or, the debtor had enough equity in it because the debts were paid down pretty low at the time of default), that there will *still* be money left over. Either way, then we get to the final step . . . .

4. **Debtor gets surplus/or Debtor owes deficiency.** Under subsection (d)(1), if there is money left over after paying the expenses, foreclosing secured party's debt, and all junior secured parties' debts, then that money is called the *surplus*. It is what's left over, and it belongs to the debtor. This was debtor's property after all, and once all the secured claims have been satisfied, the leftover money is rightfully the debtor's. On the other hand, if one or more secured claims are not paid in full, then debtor still owes the remaining debt still outstanding—this is called a *deficiency* (i.e., the sales proceeds were deficient; not enough to pay off all the debt). Don't forget that the debtor signed a loan agreement, so debtor is still contractually obligated to pay whatever is still owed after applying all available foreclosure sales proceeds.

APPLYING THE CODE

Problem 21-3: Application of Sale Proceeds

Paula's World-of-Appliances owed $100,000 to First Bank, which loan was secured by a security interest in Paula's inventory. First Bank perfected by filing a financing statement on January 1. Paula also owed $50,000 to Second Bank, which loan was also secured by a security interest in Paula's inventory. Second Bank perfected by filing a financing statement on February 1. Neither loan was purchase money. Finally, Paula owed $40,000 to Third Bank, which loan was also secured by a security interest in Paula's inventory. Third Bank never perfected, by filing or otherwise. Paula subsequently defaulted on all loans, and First Bank peaceably repossessed all of Paula's inventory. First Bank paid the repo agent $1,000, and its attorney $2,500 for legal work in making demand for payment and arranging the foreclosure sale. Although Paula, Second Bank and Third Bank were all notified of the sale, none of them participated. Third Bank sent a signed letter to First Bank demanding its share of any sales proceeds. Second Bank's president played golf with First Bank's president the weekend before the sale, and told him on the 12th hole that he wanted to be sure to receive any proceeds from the Paula's World-of-Appliances foreclosure sale, since they were second in priority. The sale was properly held on June 1, and Paula's inventory was purchased at foreclosure sale by Kevin's Laundromat (who planned to use the machines in a chain of laundromats he was planning on opening throughout the East Coast). Kevin's winning bid for the inventory was $175,000, and he delivered a check for this amount to First Bank at the conclusion of the sale.

A) How should the sale proceeds be distributed? Specifically:

   1) How much, if any, should First Bank receive?

   2) How much, if any, should Second Bank receive?

   3) How much if any, should Third Bank receive?

   4) How much, if any, should Paula receive?

B) Will Paula's World-of-Appliances still owe any debt to First Bank, Second Bank, or Third Bank, after the distribution of foreclosure sale proceeds?

C) Would the outcome in (A) and (B) have been different if Second Bank's president had put his request in writing? In what ways?

D) Would the outcome in (A) and (B) have been different if Second Bank had done the foreclosure sale, instead of First Bank? Particularly, would First Bank receive any money from the sale?

E. Title Conveyance and Discharge of Security Interests

Now we know what happens to the money received at a foreclosure sale, but what about the collateral that got sold? When a buyer purchases collateral at a foreclosure sale, he expects to walk away owning it free and clear. But is that what happens? That is, what happens to the security interests on the collateral when it is sold under an Article 9 foreclosure sale? These answers are provided by section

9–617, and they are somewhat symmetrical with the rules of proceeds distribution we just covered:

READING THE CODE

> ### TEX. BCC SECTION 9.617: Rights of Transferee of Collateral
>
> **(a)** A secured party's disposition of collateral after default:
>
>   **(1)** transfers to a transferee for value all of the debtor's rights in the collateral;
>
>   **(2)** discharges the security interest under which the disposition is made; and
>
>   **(3)** discharges any subordinate security interest or other subordinate lien . . . .
>
> **(b)** A transferee that acts in good faith takes free of the rights and interests described in subsection (a), even if the secured party fails to comply with this chapter or the requirements of any judicial proceeding.

The provisions of section 9–617 quoted above basically provide the following:

A) **Title transfers from debtor to buyer.** Subsections (a)(1) and (b) make clear that the buyer (or "transferee" in the language of the provision) takes over all of debtor's rights. That is, before the sale the collateral was debtor's property, and after the sale the collateral is now buyer's property. Notice that as long as buyer is acting in good faith, this result applies even if the foreclosing secured party violates some part of Article 9 (such as by failing to send proper notices, or failing in some way to have a commercially reasonable sale). Buyer now owns the collateral.

B) **The foreclosing secured party's security interest is discharged.** Under subsection (a)(2), the sale of the collateral to the buyer at a foreclosure sale discharges—or, eliminates—the foreclosing secured party's security interest. That is, the buyer takes the property free and clear of the foreclosing secured party's security interest.

C) **Junior parties' security interests are discharged, too.** Finally, under section (a)(3), the sale of the collateral to the buyer at a foreclosure sale discharges—i.e., eliminates—all of the security interests that are junior in priority to the foreclosing secured party's security interest. So, a buyer at a foreclosure sale buys the collateral free of all security interests of the foreclosing secured party, and below. You should note that, although in the real world it is almost always the senior secured party that is doing the foreclosure sale, in theory, if a second-priority secured party conducted the sale, the sale would *not* discharge the senior security interest (nor would the senior secured party receive any proceeds from the sale). As a practical matter, if a feisty second-priority secured party starts the foreclosure process, the senior secured party generally declares a default and takes the process over.

APPLYING THE CODE

Problem 21-4: Transferee Rights and Discharge of Security Interests

Same facts as Problem 21-3. Answer the following:

A) Does Kevin take the collateral subject to any security interests held by First Bank, Second Bank, or Third Bank?

B) Is your answer any different, as to Kevin, if First Bank had only given all of the parties 48-hours' notice before conducting the sale on June 1?

C) Is your answer any different if it had been *Second Bank*, instead of First Bank, conducting the foreclosure sale?

F. Acceptance of Collateral in Full or Partial Satisfaction of Obligation

We have just discussed the full process and implications of a formal foreclosure sale process conducted by an Article 9 secured party, where the outcome is very much in doubt and may often be dependent on how many third party prospective buyers attend and bid on the collateral. That is, once this foreclosure sale process is commenced, the outcome is unpredictable and outside the control of either the foreclosing secured party or the debtor.

However, Article 9 actually provides a way for the secured party and the debtor to strike a deal—the secured party will just keep the collateral (to eventually resell it in its own time) and the debtor, in turn, will be let off the hook on some (or maybe even all) of the debt. That is, the parties can just skip planning and holding the foreclosure sale altogether and instead simply work out how much of a credit the secured party will give the debtor to reduce or eliminate the debt (instead of letting that reduction be determined by how much the collateral actually sells for at the formal foreclosure sale).

This process is sometimes referred to as "strict foreclosure," at least when the end result is complete elimination of debtor's obligation. Article 9—and sections 9–620 through 9–622 specifically—more exactly refers to it as "acceptance of collateral in full or partial satisfaction of obligation." The basic idea is simple. Instead of going through with the risk and uncertainty of a foreclosure sale, the secured party and debtor simply agree on how much the debtor's obligation on the debt will be reduced in exchange for surrendering the collateral to the secured party (who can then sell it or do whatever it wants with it). So, for instance, say Debtor owed $100,000 on a loan to Bank, which loan was secured by a security interest in equipment. After Bank repossessed the equipment (upon default by the Debtor), Bank could propose that it would forgive the entire debt in exchange for Debtor giving up any rights to the equipment – basically, call it even. Afterward, the parties would agree that Debtor would not owe any deficiency at all (this would be Bank accepting the collateral in *full satisfaction* of the obligation). Or, if Bank thought the equipment was worth less than that, Bank could instead propose to forgive only $80,000 of the debt in exchange for Debtor giving up any rights to the collateral. Afterward, the parties would agree that Debtor would still owe a $20,000 deficiency balance (this would be Bank accepting the collateral in *partial satisfaction* of the obligation).

Article 9 allows this process, with several safeguards and procedural limitations. Specifically, section 9–320 provides in relevant part:

READING THE CODE

> ### TEX. BCC SECTION 9.620: Acceptance of Collateral in Full or Partial Satisfaction of Obligation; Compulsory Disposition of Collateral
>
> **(a)** . . . a secured party may accept collateral in full or partial satisfaction of the obligation of the obligation it secured only if:
>
> **(1)** The debtor consents to the acceptance . . .
>
> **(2)** The secured party does not receive . . . notification of objection to the proposal authenticated by [(i) anyone that the secured party notified of the proposal as required by section 9.621, or (ii) anyone holding a subordinate interest in the collateral], [and]
>
> **(3)** If the collateral is consumer goods, the collateral is not in the possession of the debtor when the debtor consents to the acceptance.

Thus, section 9.620(a) requires first of all that debtor consents to the proposal. This is, essentially, an agreement between debtor and secured party. Notice, also, that if the collateral is *consumer goods*, this deal generally has to be proposed *after* the secured party has repossessed the collateral—if the collateral is still in debtor's possession when the fine print gets proposed (e.g., say the expensive TV is still hanging on Debtor's living room wall at the time), there is too much of a chance that debtor won't realize the true nature of what's happening and his consent will thus not be valid under 9–620(a)(3). Instead, the collateral has to be already out of debtor's hands, so that debtor is much more likely to realize that a final workout deal is being proposed.

Second, section 9.620(a) requires that no objections are received from certain other parties, who the secured party is required to notify of the proposal under section 9.621. The parties required to receive notice of the proposal—and who thus have veto power over it—are those parties known to have an interest in the collateral, including: (1) anyone that has sent the secured party authenticated notice of a claim of interest, (2) any secured party that has filed a financing statement of record covering the relevant collateral, and (3) any secured party that has perfected a security interest by being noted on the certificate of title (in the case of a car or truck). Additionally—only if the secured party is proposing a partial satisfaction (such that a deficiency will still be owed afterward)—the proposing secured party must also notify any secondary obligor (i.e., usually a guarantor), since such guarantee on the debt will still be "live" after any such partial satisfaction is executed.

So, to summarize and recap, a secured party that wants to propose acceptance of collateral in satisfaction of the debt (full or partial) basically just has to make a proposal, get debtor to validly consent to it, and get no authenticated (i.e., written and signed) objections within 20 days from the above parties after having sent them notice of the proposal. Assuming debtor consent and zero objections, the acceptance of collateral proposal will be finalized. (Of course, if debtor does not consent and/or one or more creditors object, the secured party will be required to proceed instead with a formal foreclosure sale process as described in the previous sections). The effect of such a completed acceptance of collateral in satisfaction, under section 9–622, is that: (1) the debtor's debt will be discharged to the extent consented to (full or partial), (2) secured party will now own all of debtor's rights in the collateral, and (much like section 9–617 with regular foreclosure sales) the proposing secured party's interest will be terminated, as well as all subordinate interests. The collateral will then belong to the proposing/accepting secured party, to sell it or do whatever it wants with it.

Ah, but we're not quite done. Section 9–620 contains several protections and limitations on the process, which can be briefly summarized as follows:

- There are no implied acceptances by the secured party of collateral in satisfaction. Section 9–620(b) makes clear that the secured party has not simply accepted the collateral in satisfaction unless it has *expressly* agreed to do so (either by sending a proposal or otherwise agreeing in an authenticated writing to do so). This was added to eliminate any argument that, by a secured party waiting too long to hold a foreclosure sale, it had just impliedly agreed to accept the collateral and let debtor off the hook. The debtor (or other secured parties) can always argue that such delay was a commercially unreasonable process under section 9–610 and seek damages caused by the delay, but there will be no argument that secured party has impliedly accepted the collateral in satisfaction of the obligation.

- Debtor's silence can only be consent to acceptance in full satisfaction, not partial. Section 9–620(c) provides that Debtor is deemed to consent to a proposal for acceptance in full satisfaction (i.e., Debtor will owe zero deficiency afterwards) by either expressly agreeing in an authenticated writing or by failing to object via an authenticated writing within 20 days after the proposal was sent. In a word, Debtor's silence will be deemed consent if the proposal is to let Debtor off the hook altogether. But not so if the secured party's proposal is only to let Debtor partially off the hook, such that the proposal is for Debtor to still owe money after the acceptance of collateral. In that case, silence (i.e., failure to object within 20 days) will not be consent, but rather Debtor only consents if he does so via an express, authenticated agreement. This is to keep Debtor from unwittingly agreeing to a large deficiency.

• Mandatory Disposition of Consumer Goods (the 60% rule). Section 9–620(e)–(f) provides a special protection of the equity in consumer goods, which will generally be for consumer debtors (i.e., non-business-es). It provides that if 60% of the cash price has been paid in the case of a PMSI in consumer goods (or, less likely, 60% of the loan has been paid if it's a non-PMSI), the secured party is not allowed to propose an acceptance in satisfaction. Rather, the secured party is actually required to hold a regular section 9–610 foreclosure sale. The reason for the rule is to keep the secured party from trying to capture a lot of built-up equity that should belong to the consumer. So, for instance, say that Debtor financed a car with Car Lot. The cash price was $10,000. Debtor paid $2,000 down, and agreed to pay the remaining $8,000 over time, and granted a PMSI in the car to Car Lot to secure the loan. A couple of years later, Debtor defaults, at which point the balance on the loan is down to $3,500. Consumer has paid now paid $6,500 of the original $10,000 cash price—i.e., 65%. That means (roughly speaking and ignoring depreciation) that Debtor owes $3,500, but that Debtor has $6,500 equity in the car (since we're assuming it's still worth $10,000 for simplicity's sake). We don't want Car Lot proposing to take the car and just "let Debtor off the hook." That's too good a deal for Car Lot, and is taking advantage of Consumer. Rather, we require Car Lot to actually formally do a foreclosure sale of the car, and then hopefully get close to $10,000, so that Car Lot pays the debt off and hands Debtor a check for $6,500 (this is the money that Car Lot was hoping to keep for itself but is prohibited from doing so by the mandatory disposition rule of sections 9–620(e)–(f). Subsection (f) clarifies that when the 60% rule requires formal foreclosure sale, such sale must either occur within 90 days or any longer period that debtor ad any secondary obligors have agreed to in a post-default signed writing.

- No Partial Satisfaction in Consumer Transactions. Section 9–620(g) provides one further consumer protection rule, i.e., for debtors who are consumers and not businesses or merchants. A secured party may not accept collateral in mere partial satisfaction of debtor's obligation, period. Consumers are often not sophisticated, and so they may not realize that liability on a deficiency may be contemplated. So, the rule is simple—if a consumer is involved, the only proposal allowed is to let the debtor totally off the hook in exchange for accepting the collateral. That is, only full satisfactions are allowed with consumer debtors. Not partial satisfactions, where a deficiency is still proposed to be owing after the acceptance.

Problem 21-5: Acceptance in Full or Partial Satisfaction of Obligation

Wayne's Western Wear ("Wayne") borrowed $50,000 from First Bank for general operating expenses. To secure the loan, Wayne granted a security interest to First Bank in all its inventory of western-themed clothing. First Bank's security interest was properly perfected by filing. A month later, Wayne also borrowed money from Second Bank and granted Second Bank a security interest in inventory. Second Bank's security interest was perfected by filing, which filing was one month after First Bank's filing. After a few months, Wayne defaulted on both loans and First Bank peaceably repossessed all the inventory. First Bank estimates that the inventory is worth approximately $45,000. Meanwhile, the balance on the loan is still $50,000. Answer the questions below about First Bank's options:

A) If First Bank wants to propose to accept the inventory in satisfaction of Wayne's debt obligation, who must it notify of the proposal?

B) Assume First Bank sends a proposal to all required parties, such that all receive it by May 10. If Second Bank calls First Bank on May 20 and objects to the proposal, will this be sufficient to require First Bank to conduct a full foreclosure sale?

C) If Wayne fails to object at all to the proposal, does that mean that Wayne has consented and First Bank can proceed with the acceptance in satisfaction? Is there anything else you need to know?

D) If the balance on the First Bank loan had been reduced to $15,000 at the time of First Bank's proposal, would this affect First Bank's options? Why or why not, and how if so?

E) Say now instead that we were dealing with Wayne's personal secured purchase-money debt obligation on an exercise machine purchased and financed from Kevin's Sporting Goods store, the original cash price of which was $5,000, and on which the current balance of the debt was still $4,500. Could Kevin propose to accept the exercise machine in full satisfaction of the debt? In partial satisfaction? Would it matter if the exercise machine had already been repossessed at the time of Kevin's proposal to accept the machine in satisfaction of the debt?

G. Remedies for Article 9 Violations

Our final topic is remedies. We have covered several requirements for secured parties to comply with when conducting the foreclosure sale process (or, as seen immediately above, the strict foreclosure process). What remedies are available to a debtor when the secured party fails to comply, such as failing to send proper notice of sale, or failing to have a commercially reasonably sale? Or, stating it a little differently, what are the consequences for the secured party's Article 9 violations?

For this final point, we will look at a couple of Code provisions, sections 9–625 and 9–626:

READING THE CODE

TEX. BCC SECTION 9.625: Remedies for Secured Party's Failure to Comply with Article

. . . .

(b) Subject to subsection . . . (d), . . . a person is liable for damages in the amount of any loss caused by a failure to comply with this chapter. . . .

(d) A debtor whose deficiency is eliminated under section 9.626 may recover damages for the loss of any surplus. However, a debtor . . . whose deficiency is eliminated or reduced under section 9.626 may not otherwise recover under subsection (b) for noncompliance with the provisions of this part relating to collection, enforcement, disposition, or acceptance.

> **■ TEX. BCC SECTION 9.626: Action in Which Deficiency or Surplus Is in Issue**
>
> **(a)** In an action arising from a transaction, other than a consumer transaction, in which the amount of a deficiency or surplus is in issue, the following rules apply:
>
> . . . .
>
> > **(3)** . . . if a secured party fails to prove that the collection, enforcement [or] disposition . . . was conducted in accordance with the provisions of this subchapter relating to collection, enforcement [or] disposition, . . . the liability of a debtor . . . for a deficiency is limited to an amount by which the sum of the secured obligation, expenses, and attorney's fees exceeds the greater of:
> >
> > > **(A)** the proceeds of the collection, enforcement [or] disposition . . .; or
> > >
> > > **(B)** the amount of proceeds that would have been realized had the noncomplying secured party proceeded in accordance with the provisions of this subchapter relating to collection, enforcement [or] disposition. . . .
> >
> > **(4)** For purposes of Subdivision (3)(B), the amount of proceeds that would have been realized is equal to the sum of the secured obligation, expenses, and attorney's fees unless the secured party proves that the amount is less than that sum. . . .
>
> **(b)** The limitation of the rules in subsection (a) to transactions other than consumer transactions is intended to leave to the court the determination of the proper rules in consumer transactions. The court may not infer from that limitation the nature of the proper rule in consumer transactions and may continue to apply established approaches.

Section 9–625 provides that a debtor can recover any actual damages for a secured party's violation of any provision of Article 9. This seems broad, and at first glance it is. So, for instance, if a secured party breached the peace in a repossession, such as by assaulting the debtor, this provision would allow the debtor to recover any actual damages for injuries sustained as a result.

But what if the main complaint is financial? So, for instance, what if the complaint is that the secured party didn't give any notice of the sale to anyone, or didn't advertise it so it was not a commercially reasonable sale, and in fact the sale brought much less in proceeds than debtor thinks it should have? In that instance, we have the provisions of section 9–626 to look to, and what is known as the *rebuttable presumption rule.* And, as section 9–625(b) suggests, if the rebuttable presumption rule of section 9–626 is implicated, most of the time that becomes the entire amount of relief allowed to the debtor.

Section 9–626 is rather clunky in its wording, but here's what it is doing. It presumes that, if a secured party had followed all the rules of Article 9 on collection and enforcement of the security interest, it would have received *exactly the amount of the debt,* plus expenses and attorneys' fees incurred. And, for a violating secured party, the recovery of the deficiency judgment is limited to this hypothetical, presumed amount. The long and short of this is that, if a secured party violates Article 9 in conducting the foreclosure sale, it *loses any right to a deficiency against the debtor!* It gets zero—that's the extent of the debtor's remedy against the secured party. Actually, if you go back to section 9–625(b), you'll see that the debtor can also recover "lost surplus" if it proves that the collateral should have sold for even *more* than the debt.

The presumption is rebuttable, however. Therefore, if the secured party can prove it wouldn't have made any difference—that is, that the collateral sold for what it was going to bring, and better notice or better advertising would not have changed the result, then the secured party has rebutted the presumption of no deficiency, and can then recover the deficiency owed (the debt minus the foreclosure sale proceeds received). The secured party generally does this by proving the market value of the collateral.

One last thing—under section 9–626, the rebuttable presumption rule only applies to non-consumer transactions. Section 9–626(b) states that the remedy in consumer transactions is left to the courts or individual states. Some states apply the same rebuttable presumption rule to consumer transactions. Some states actually impose a stricter standard with consumers by making the presumption *conclusive,* not rebuttable. Why do you think some states impose a stricter standard when consumer debtors are involved?

APPLYING THE CODE

Problem 21-6: Remedies for Article 9 Violations

Kevin's Laundromat owed First Bank $100,000 on a loan, which was se-
cured by all of Kevin's equipment. Kevin defaulted on the loan on May
1, and First Bank peaceably repossessed all of Kevin's laundromat equipment. First Bank planned a public auction sale for June 1, at the First
Bank offices, at 10:00 a.m. First Bank, however, failed to send out any
notice of the sale to Kevin or anyone else, and also failed to advertise the
sale beyond a few word of mouth communications. The sale, attended by
only 3 people, brought $15,000 from the high bidder for the equipment.
First Bank's expenses and attorneys' fees for the sale were $1,500. Kevin's
debt balance to First Bank as of this date was $90,000.

A)   How much of a deficiency judgment does First Bank wish it could
      obtain, ignoring its Article 9 violations?

B)   What is the problem faced by First Bank in its attempt to obtain
      a deficiency, given the provisions of section 9–626? That is, what
      deficiency judgment is the court more likely to presumptively award
      to First Bank?

C)   If instead First Bank can prove that the equipment only had a fair
      market value of $30,000 at the time of the sale, would First Bank be
      able to recover a deficiency against Kevin? If so, how much?

D)   What additional remedy, if any, can Kevin have if he can prove that
      the equipment had a fair market value of $110,000 at the time of sale?

Test Your Knowledge

To assess your understanding of the material in this chapter,
click here to take a quiz.

PART III

Negotiable Instruments:
Articles 3 and 4

22

Introduction to Negotiable Instruments

Key Concepts

- The development of negotiable instruments as a cash substitute
- The definition of negotiable instrument in Article 3 and each of its component requirements
- The difference between a promise to pay and an order to pay
- The breadth of the signed writing requirement
- The tests for determining whether a promise or order is unconditional
- The requirement of a fixed principal amount
- The distinction between a negotiable instrument that is "payable to order" and a negotiable instrument that is "payable to bearer"
- The limited exceptions to the requirement that there be no undertakings other than the promise to pay

What is a negotiable instrument? Negotiable instruments may seem like a foreign concept, but if you have written or cashed a check then you already have firsthand experience with them. This is because a check is one of many types of negotiable instruments governed by Articles 3 and 4 of the UCC. Other familiar examples of negotiable instruments include bank checks (such as cashier's checks, teller's checks or certified checks), traveler's checks, **some** promissory notes[1] and **some** certificates of deposit.[2]

---

1 Some but not all promissory notes will meet the requirements for negotiability in Section 3–104(a).

2 Article 3 does not apply to money, documents of title and investment securities. *See* section 3–102. Some certificates of deposit are investment securities and therefore outside of the scope of Article 3.

The bulk of this Chapter focuses on unpacking section 3–104 (and related provisions), which provide the framework for determining whether a particular writing satisfies the statutory requirements to constitute a negotiable instrument. For now, you can think of negotiable instruments as generally merging two basic concepts—a contractual obligation and monetary value. At its core, a negotiable instrument simply evidences a person's promise to pay or a person's order that someone else pay on their behalf (the contractual obligation) a specified amount of money (the monetary value). Now apply this working understanding of negotiable instruments to the everyday check. It is easy to see why a check is a negotiable instrument. When you write a check, you are ordering that someone else (your bank) pay a specified amount of money to the recipient of the check.

It is important to remember, however, that a negotiable instrument is much more than a simple contract to pay. As you will learn in subsequent Chapters, a host of important legal consequences distinguish negotiable instruments under the UCC from simple contracts to pay. For example, a holder in due course (don't worry, more to come on what exactly that is later) of a negotiable instrument obtains substantially greater rights and protections than the assignee of a simple contract to pay. Given the legal consequences, the proper identification of a negotiable instrument is extremely important. As a result, that subject forms the bulk of this first Chapter.

A. The Role of Negotiable Instruments

It may be useful to start by providing some context. Historically, negotiable instruments addressed a very real need for a method of safely and efficiently moving or transferring money (especially larger amounts) from one owner to another over long distances.

Imagine a time before credit cards, Internet payment, mobile payments and cryptocurrency. Even before the existence of electronic funds transfers and wire transfers. If cash were the only method of payment and you wanted to make a large purchase from overseas, you have limited options. Can you see why? You could mail the cash in a large envelope or box and entrust a courier to deliver it safely. Alternatively, you could put the cash in a duffle bag and travel abroad to personally deliver it. Neither option is particularly appealing or efficient.

The obvious solution is to develop a system for transferring wealth that does not rely on physically carrying and delivering cash. However, to be truly viable, the system would need to allow for payments to be quickly and reliably convertible into cash. If this were not the case, few people would be comfortable accepting it in lieu of cash.

Negotiable instruments were created as an early cash substitute. The system depends on the physical possession and delivery of pieces of paper that evidence an obligation to pay. These pieces of paper function as an effective cash substitute because they are easily sold for cash. This is because a prospective purchaser can independently verify whether a seller has the power to transfer an enforceable interest without looking beyond the information found on the paper itself. In addition, the purchaser can obtain the ability to enforce the payment obligation free from virtually all defenses, which provides added (and much needed) assurances of payment.

With the rise of electronic payment systems, the paper-based system of negotiable instruments may seem obsolete. However, negotiable instruments retain relevance in modern commerce. Despite the availability of new payment methods, negotiable instruments are still used to facilitate business deals. In addition, the purchase and sale of negotiable instruments continues to figure prominently in the banking industry and play a role in international trade.[3] Finally, the law applicable to negotiable instruments remains in many ways the foundation upon which modern payments law is built.

B. Requirements for Negotiability

The UCC defines the term "negotiable instrument" in section 3–104(a), which is excerpted below. Section 3–104(a) is a complex provision. Take a moment to read it carefully. Can you identify the requirements that must be satisfied before something qualifies as a negotiable instrument? How many are there?

---

3   Businesses and banks continue to use bills of exchange (a type of negotiable instrument that functions like an invoice of sorts) to facilitate international trade. Because international trade can involve parties located across the globe, it presents unique challenges and risks. For example, international trade often involves long-term arrangements, long-distance transportation lines, multiple legal jurisdictions (which may complicate or increase uncertainty in the event of a dispute) and the need for currency exchanges (which may make transactions more susceptible to exchange-rate fluctuations). As a result, the exporter (or seller) of goods may rightfully desire greater assurances of payment from the importer (or buyer) of goods before shipping. Bills of exchange provide that assurance and help to mitigate some of the risk. Typically, the exporter's bank issues the bill of exchange. By signing the bill of exchange, the importer becomes unconditionally obligated to pay. The importer's bank is also involved and provides a guarantee of payment. A bill of exchange, therefore, provides greater certainty. As such, businesses and banks continue to rely on bills of exchange to support commerce, especially in the context of international trade.

READING THE CODE

Maryland Commercial Law Code Section 3–104

(a) Except as provided in subsections (c) and (d), "negotiable instrument" means an unconditional promise or order to pay a fixed amount of money, with or without interest or other charges described in the promise or order, if it:

  (1) Is payable to bearer or to order at the time it is issued or first comes into possession of a holder;

  (2) Is payable on demand or at a definite time; and

  (3) Does not state any other undertaking or instruction by the person promising or ordering payment to do any act in addition to the payment of money, but the promise or order may contain (i) an undertaking or power to give, maintain, or protect collateral to secure payment, (ii) an authorization or power to the holder to confess judgment or realize on or dispose of collateral, or (iii) a waiver of the benefit of any law intended for the advantage or protection of an obligor.

Depending on how you parse the statute, section 3–104(a) encompasses no less than seven distinct requirements. The introductory clause of section 3–104(a) contains four requirements. Three additional requirements appear in section 3–104(a)(1)–(3). As a general rule, all seven requirements must be satisfied to achieve the status of a negotiable instrument. The failure to satisfy any one of the requirements is enough to defeat negotiability. Simply put, it cannot be a negotiable instrument unless all the requirements are met. Each of the requirements is explored in turn below.

1. Requirement 1: Promise or Order

The first sentence of section 3–104(a) expressly limits the definition of "negotiable instrument" to obligations that constitute either a "promise" or an "order." Because of this, a negotiable instrument must contain either a "promise" or an "order." If the obligation in question does not fall within one of these two definitions, it cannot qualify as a "negotiable instrument." Read the definitions below. What is the difference between an instruction to pay and an undertaking to pay?

READING THE CODE

> ### Maryland Commercial Law Code Section 3–103(a)
>
> **(a)** In this title:
>
> . . . .
>
> > **(6)** "Order" means a written instruction to pay money signed by the person giving the instruction. The instruction may be addressed to any person, including the person giving the instruction, or to one or more persons jointly or in the alternative but not in succession. An authorization to pay is not an order unless the person authorized to pay is also instructed to pay.
> >
> > . . . .
> >
> > **(9)** "Promise" means a written undertaking to pay money signed by the person undertaking to pay. An acknowledgment of an obligation by the obligor is not a promise unless the obligor also undertakes to pay the obligation.

The UCC defines a "promise" as an "undertaking to pay money." The person that makes a "promise" is called a "maker." To qualify as a "promise," a person must directly undertake an obligation to pay. That is to say, a maker must actually make a commitment to pay. Merely acknowledging the existence of a debt is not enough. As a result, it is important to pay close attention to the language used to determine whether it sets forth a sufficient commitment to pay.

Consider the words "I owe you $5,000." A person writing these words has not undertaken the obligation to pay $5,000. There is no promise or commitment to pay. Instead, these words are merely an acknowledgment that a debt is owed. It is not a "promise" and cannot qualify as a negotiable instrument.

Now consider the words "I will pay you $5,000 in 3 days" or the words "I promise to pay you $5,000 in 3 days." In both cases, the words evidence a direct commitment to pay. Even when the word "will" is used instead of "promise," the language is clearly promissory in nature. Both examples constitute a "promise" and may qualify as a negotiable instrument if the writing satisfies all the other requirements for negotiability.

EXAMPLES AND EXPLANATIONS

Wayne's Gaming, Inc. ("Wayne") manufactures and sells video game consoles around the globe. Kevin's Power Supply Co. ("Kevin") supplies the batteries that Wayne uses in its video game consoles. Wayne recently agreed to purchase batteries on credit with full payment due in 3 months. Given their long business relationship, the parties did not execute a formal written contract. However, Wayne did sign a short document that included the following: "This document evidences a debt of $100,000 owed by Wayne to Kevin for the purchase of batteries. Wayne shall pay Kevin $100,000 within 3 months after the date of this document.—Wayne."

The first sentence is nothing more than Wayne's acknowledgement of the existence of a debt in the amount of $100,000. If the signed document only included the first sentence, there would be no promise or undertaking by Wayne to actually pay Kevin. The second sentence, however, contains the requisite level of commitment to pay. Specifically, the word "shall" creates an obligation on the part of Wayne to actually pay Kevin. The inclusion of a specific timeframe for when the obligation to pay is due (3 months) further underscores Wayne's commitment or undertaking to pay. As such, the signed document contains a valid promise.

An order is distinct from a promise. The UCC defines an "order" as an "instruction to pay money." Accordingly, an "order" typically involves three parties—the person who orders the payment, the person who is instructed to pay, and the person who will receive payment. The person who orders the payment is called the "drawer." The person who is instructed to make the payment is called the "drawee." The person that the drawer instructs the drawee to pay is called the "payee."

So to qualify as an "order," one person must instruct another person to pay. The drawer must direct or demand that the drawee make the payment to the payee. Merely authorizing another person to make a payment is insufficient. As with the definition of "promise," the words used are critical to the determination. It is also important to recognize the drawee does not need to agree or even know about the order. Can you see why? Look at the definition of "order" and consider whether any part of it requires that the drawee be aware of the order to pay.

EXAMPLES AND EXPLANATIONS

David owes Paula $500. Unfortunately, David does not currently have the funds to pay the debt. When Paula presses David for payment, David tells her that he has just completed some landscaping work for Kevin. David writes the following on a post-it note: "Kevin, you may pay Paula $500 out of the amount that you owe me for the landscaping work that I just completed at your house. I hereby grant you permission to pay Paula according to the terms of this note.—David." David hands Paula the post-it note and tells her to go get payment from Kevin.

The post-it note does not contain an order. Under Article 3, an order is an instruction to pay money. While David may have intended that the post-it note serve as an instruction to Kevin to pay Paula $500, it does not actually direct or demand that Kevin make the payment. Instead, the word "may" is discretionary—that is Kevin has the option to pay. In addition, the second sentence only purports to grant Kevin permission to pay. This is merely an authorization to pay—not an instruction or demand to pay. Compare the language in the post-it note with the following—"I hereby instruct you to pay Paula $500" or "I demand that you pay Paula $500" or "I order you to pay Paula $500." Instead of authorizing or granting permission to pay, the foregoing more clearly include a directive to pay.

APPLYING THE CODE

Problem 22-1: Identifying Promises and Orders

Evaluate each of the following and determine whether the words qualify as a promise, an order or neither. As you do so, try to articulate the specific reason or reasons why.

A) Wayne buys Kevin a drink at happy hour. As they leave, Kevin hands Wayne a napkin on which he has written, "*I owe you a drink the next time we go out.—Kevin.*" If the napkin instead reads, "*I owe you $10 for the drink.—Kevin,*" would your answer change?

B) Kevin is opening a new coffee shop called The Supreme Cup. Kevin decides to buy custom t-shirts and travel mugs from David (a local entrepreneur with a printing business) to sell at the shop. The terms of their agreement were memorialized in a letter, which contained the following provision: "Kevin shall purchase and David shall sell 100 t-shirts and 200 travel mugs bearing The Supreme Cup logo (the "Custom Products"). The total purchase price is $1,000. Kevin has paid $200 to David in cash and acknowledges that $800 of the purchase price remains outstanding. Kevin promises to pay David the balance of $800 upon delivery of the Custom Products."

C) Kevin agrees to purchase a used car from Paula for $5,000. Kevin decides to pay Paula from money that he maintains in his checking account with First Bank. Kevin gets his checkbook out and gives Paula a personal check as payment. The complete personal check appears below.

KEVIN
222 Sunflower Lane
Seattle, WA

101

Date: _____

Pay to the order of: ___Paula_____ $ 5,000.00

___Five thousand and 00/100_____ DOLLARS

FIRST BANK
123 MAIN STREET
NEW YORK, NY

MEMO: __Car purchase_____   ____Kevin_____

D) Assume that Paula is unwilling to accept a personal check from Kevin for the car. Paula is worried that Kevin may not have sufficient funds in his account and does not want to wait for a personal check to clear before delivering the car. As a result, Kevin goes to his bank (First Bank) to obtain a cashier's check. First Bank immediately debits $5,000 from Kevin's account to guarantee payment and issues the cashier's check. The completed cashier's check appears below.

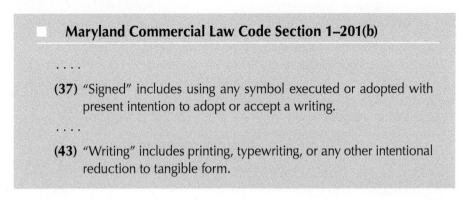

2. Requirement 2: Signed Writing

As you analyzed the definitions of "promise" and "order" in the preceding section, you probably noticed that both a "promise" and an "order" must be made pursuant to a signed writing. By incorporating the terms "promise" and "order" into the definition of "negotiable instrument," Article 3 also limits "negotiable instruments" to signed writings—specifically signed writings that promise or order the payment of money. *See* section 3–104, cmt. 1.

READING THE CODE

> ### ■ Maryland Commercial Law Code Section 1–201(b)
>
> . . . .
>
> **(37)** "Signed" includes using any symbol executed or adopted with present intention to adopt or accept a writing.
>
> . . . .
>
> **(43)** "Writing" includes printing, typewriting, or any other intentional reduction to tangible form.

The defined term "writing" includes "printing, typewriting, or any other intentional reduction to *tangible form*." *See* section 1–201(b)(43) (emphasis added). The term is broadly defined in a sense because it does not mandate a specific medium so long as it has a tangible form. As such, a promise or order on a piece of paper or any similar material would suffice. On the other hand, the requirement of a tangible form plainly excludes promises and orders that are only evidenced in an audio recording or any wholly electronic form. This may seem dated. But the writing requirement reflects the current system, which was developed for more traditional "written" instruments. This is because the system contemplated by Article 3 relies heavily on physical possession of the negotiable instrument and the ability of parties to independently verify a person's ability to transfer an enforceable interest by only looking at the four corners of the negotiable instrument. As such, the writing requirement means that negotiable instruments are limited to tangible things.

Finally, the "writing" must be signed by: (1) the person undertaking the promise to pay (i.e., the maker); or (2) the person giving the instruction to pay (i.e., the drawer). The UCC defines the term "signed" broadly and permits the use of "any symbol executed or adopted with present intention to adopt or accept a writing." *See* section 1–201(b)(37). Therefore, a valid signature may come in any form. It may be printed, stamped or written. Partial names, fictitious names, trade names, initials or even a thumbprint may suffice. In addition, a valid signature may appear on any part of the writing. In all cases, the essential inquiry is whether the circumstances indicate that the maker or drawer (as applicable) executed the symbol with present intent to adopt or accept the writing. If so, then the signature requirement is satisfied.

EXAMPLES AND EXPLANATIONS

Consider the following example.

Kevin was recently in a horrendous bicycle crash. Luckily, the doctors expect that he will make a full recovery. With that said, Kevin is currently confined to his hospital bed. In addition, Kevin does not have much use of his arms because they are currently in casts. Kevin, however, needs to get a rent check to his landlord today in order to avoid a late fee. Wayne offers to help. Wayne finds Kevin's checkbook and brings it to the hospital. At Kevin's direction, Wayne fills out the check and holds it by Kevin's hand. After some difficulty, Kevin manages to "sign" by marking a squiggly line (with no identifiable letters or words) on the check instead of his usual signature.

This requirement involves two distinct inquiries. First that there is a writing, and second, that Kevin has signed. There is little doubt that the check qualifies as a writing. The checkbook and the checks in it are tangible pieces of paper brought to Kevin by Wayne. The second inquiry depends entirely on Kevin's intent. Here, it seems clear that Kevin intended to execute and deliver a valid rent check to his landlord. It does not matter that the squiggly line is not Kevin's usual signature. It does not matter that the squiggly line is not legible. The squiggly line is a symbol, which Kevin executed with the present intent of adopting/accepting the check.

APPLYING THE CODE

Problem 22-2: The Signed Writing Requirement

A) Kevin's new business venture is a restaurant called Forage. Kevin agrees to purchase all of his produce for opening night from Wayne. To memorialize their conversation, Wayne sends Kevin the following email: *"This is Wayne. I just wanted to confirm that you, Kevin, promise to pay me $1,000 by Friday for the produce listed below."* Wayne includes an itemized list of the produce Kevin ordered. Wayne does not sign his name at the end of the message, but Wayne's email address is located at the top of the message in the "From" field. The email accurately reflects the agreed-upon terms. Does Wayne's email satisfy the signed writing requirement?

B) Instead of Wayne's email, assume that Kevin gave Wayne a written confirmation on printed letterhead containing Forage's logo along with Kevin's name and address. Kevin hand-wrote the following message on the letterhead: *"I, Kevin, promise to pay Wayne $1,000 by Friday for the produce listed below."* However, Kevin did not sign his name. Does Kevin's written confirmation satisfy the signed writing requirement?

3. Requirement 3: Promise or Order Must Be Unconditional

To qualify as a negotiable instrument, the promise or order to pay must be absolute and unconditional. Few people would be willing to accept a negotiable instrument in lieu of cash if this were not the case. Imagine if a person needed to investigate each condition to payment before accepting it and bear the risk of nonpayment where a condition is unsatisfied. This would run afoul of the fundamental purpose of negotiable instruments—to provide a cash substitute that is easily transferred from one person to another. Do you see why? Limiting negotiable instruments to unconditional obligations to pay eliminates any need to look beyond the face of the writing itself. This makes it possible to quickly evaluate the right to payment, which in turn, enhances the ability of negotiable instruments to function as a cash substitute. Section 3–106 governs when a promise or order is unconditional.

READING THE CODE

Maryland Commercial Law Code Section 3–106

(a) Except as provided in this section, for the purposes of section 3–104(a), a promise or order is unconditional unless it states (i) an express condition to payment, (ii) that the promise or order is subject to or governed by another record, or (iii) that rights or obligations with respect to the promise or order are stated in another writing. A reference to another record does not of itself make the promise or order conditional.

(b) A promise or order is not made conditional (i) by a reference to another writing for a statement of rights with respect to collateral, prepayment, or acceleration, or (ii) because payment is limited to resort to a particular fund or source.

As a general matter, a promise or order is deemed unconditional unless one of the following two tests makes the promise or order conditional.

1. **Test 1: Express Condition.** If the promise or order to pay is expressly conditioned on the occurrence of a specified event then it fails the unconditional requirement. An express condition to payment must be stated clearly and definitely. An unwritten or unstated condition to payment that is understood by the parties will not suffice.

   Article 3, therefore, distinguishes between express conditions and implied conditions. An express condition to payment defeats negotiability, but an implied condition will not. The determination hinges on the language of the promise or order. If the payment obligation is not subject to an express condition, the writing may still qualify as a negotiable instrument if it meets all the other requirements of negotiability.

2. **Test 2: Subject to, Governed by or Stated in Another Writing.** If the promise or order to pay indicates that it is controlled by the terms of another record,[4] then it fails the unconditional requirement. This occurs when the promise or order states that it is "subject to" or "governed by" another record, or that any "rights or obligations with respect to the promise or order are stated in another record." *See* section 3–106(a)(iii). Merely referencing or acknowledging the existence of another record, however, is not enough.

   Whether the referenced record contains a term that affects the right to payment is irrelevant. *See* section 3–106, cmt. 1. The determination again hinges on the language of the promise or order. If the language indicates that any rights or obligations with respect to the payment obligation are in another record then it cannot be a negotiable instrument. If this is not the case, the writing may still qualify as a negotiable instrument if it meets all the other requirements of negotiability.

   Why do you suppose that a written promise or order controlled by, subject to or governed by another record cannot qualify as a negotiable instrument? Can you articulate how this contravenes the foundational purpose of the negotiable instruments system?

3. **Exceptions:** A promise or order is not conditional if it only references another record for a statement of rights with respect to collateral, prepayment or acceleration. *See* section 3–106(b)(i).

   In addition, section 3–106(b) and section 3–106(c) clarify that two common practices will not make a promise or order conditional.

   First, a promise or order is not conditional merely because the payment is to be made from a particular fund or source. *See* section 3–106(b)(ii). In these instances, the payment obligation is viewed as unconditional and may still qualify as a negotiable instrument. This result is justified on the basis that potential purchasers can readily evaluate the payment source and decide whether to purchase the negotiable instrument (or not).

   Second, a promise or order is not conditional merely because payment requires a countersignature by the person whose specimen signature appears

---

4   A "record" is broadly defined as "information that is inscribed on a tangible medium or that is stored in an electronic or other medium and is retrievable in perceivable form." *See* section 3–103(a)(14).

on the promise or order. *See* section 3–106(c). The condition of requiring a countersignature does not defeat negotiability. This result is necessary to accommodate the use of traveler's checks (which are commonly viewed as cash substitutes appropriately governed by Article 3).[5]

APPLYING THE CODE

Problem 22-3: Exploring the Unconditional Requirement

David has agreed to purchase a used Honda Accord from Wayne for $4,000. To conclude the deal, they executed a Purchase Agreement on August 12, 2018. David paid $1,000 in cash and signed a promissory note for the remaining $3,000. Analyze each of the following provisions from the promissory note. Which of the provisions (if any) make the promissory note fail the unconditional requirement?

A) "I promise to pay $3,000 to Wayne if he conveys title to the car to me and delivers the car to me by September 22, 2022."

B) "In consideration of Wayne's promise to convey title to the car, I promise to pay $3,000 to Wayne."

C) "This Promissory Note is payable only out of the proceeds of David's book sales during the 2025 calendar year."

D) "This Promissory Note is made pursuant to the Purchase Agreement between David and Wayne dated August 12, 2022."

E) "This Promissory Note and any rights or obligations hereunder are subject to the Purchase Agreement between David and Wayne dated August 12, 2022."

F) "This Promissory Note is secured by the Security Agreement between David and Wayne dated August 12, 2022."

4. Requirement 4: Payment of a Fixed Amount of Money

The next requirement for negotiability in section 3–104(a) is that the promise or order must be for the payment of a fixed amount of money. In reality, this consists of two separate components. First, the promise or order must be for the payment of money. Second, the amount of the payment obligation must be fixed. We will look at each of these requirements in turn.

The first component requires that the promise or order be for the payment of money. This eliminates any obligation not payable in money from qualifying as a negotiable instrument. The UCC defines "money" broadly as "any medium of exchange currently authorized or adopted by a domestic or foreign government." *See* section 1–201(b)(24). The test for whether something constitutes "money" under the UCC is whether a government has sanctioned it as part of the official currency of that government. Therefore, both domestic and foreign currency falls within the definition of "money." But an obligation to "pay with" assets or commodities (other than money) is excluded.

The second component requires a fixed principal amount. This is because the amount payable under a negotiable instrument must be readily determinable from the face of the writing if it is to function as a freely transferable cash substitute. As a general rule, a promise or order is not payable in a fixed amount if the principal is uncertain, unspecified or can only be determined by reference to an outside source.

Although the principal amount must be fixed, "interest" and "other charges" are not subject to the fixed-amount requirement. *See* section 3–112, cmt. 1. As such, interest provisions can be expressed in any way that you can dream up, including a fixed rate, variable rate or by reference to an outside source. Other charges include things like attorneys' fees, collection costs, pre-payment penalties and late fees. Because the fixed amount requirement does not apply to other charges, a promise or order is payable in a fixed amount even if the amount of other charges is uncertain, unspecified or requires reference to an outside source to determine.

EXAMPLES AND EXPLANATIONS

Wayne is an inventor who has developed proprietary technology that improves the speed and efficiency of laptop computers. David's Computer, Inc. ("David") is a manufacturer of laptop computers, which incorporates Wayne's technology. David and Wayne are parties to a royalty agreement whereby David has promised to pay Wayne $1.00 for every laptop sold by David during the term of the agreement.

The royalty payments do not meet the fixed requirement. While "interest" and "other charges" do not need to be fixed, the principal amount of the payment obligation—here the royalty—must be a fixed amount of money. To be fixed, the amount must be ascertainable from the face of the agreement itself without reference to any outside source. Here, the method for calculating the payment amount is clearly specified in the agreement—$1.00 per laptop sold. However, the amount is uncertain because the number of laptops sold is an unknown quantity. As such, the amount of the royalty cannot be determined without referencing sales figures for the period in question.

APPLYING THE CODE

Problem 22-4: Exploring the Fixed Amount Requirement

A)   Kevin obtains a $10,000 loan from David. Kevin then signs a writing acknowledging the debt and promising to repay the loan by giving David a diamond valued at $10,000. Does this writing provide for the payment of a fixed amount of money? What if Kevin promised to repay the loan by giving David $10,000 worth of Microsoft stock? $10,000 worth of bitcoins?

B)   During an international commercial law conference in Vietnam, Paula borrowed 100,000 Vietnamese Dong (the official currency of the country of Vietnam) from Kevin. Kevin requested that Paula repay the loan after they returned to the United States. In response, Paula executed a promissory note (below). Does this promissory note provide for payment of a fixed amount of money?

PROMISSORY NOTE

I promise to pay 100,000 Vietnamese Dong with interest to Kevin
30 days from the date of executing this note (the "<u>Maturity Date</u>");
provided that the payment under this note shall not exceed the
balance in my First Bank Savings Account on the Maturity Date.
Paula
April 2, 2022

C) Assume that the promissory note signed by Paula in part (B) (above)
included a provision explaining that interest would be charged at the
Prime Rate published in the Money Rates section of the Wall Street
Journal and that the interest rate would be adjusted to reflect the
then current Prime Rate on the first day of each calendar year. Does
this promissory note satisfy the fixed amount of money requirement?

D) Assume that the promissory note signed by Paula in part (B) (above)
also provided for Paula to pay reasonable attorneys' fees and collection
costs incurred by Kevin in connection with any default by Paula. Does
this promissory note satisfy the fixed amount of money requirement?

5. Requirement 5: Payable to Bearer or Order

Per section 3–104(a)(1), a negotiable instrument must be "payable to bearer" or
"payable to order."

This terminology may be foreign, but the concepts are simple. A negotiable instrument made "payable to bearer" is payable to whomever has possession of it. These
types of negotiable instruments are also referred to as bearer paper. In contrast,
a negotiable instrument made "payable to order" is payable to a specified person
who is identified by the instrument. These types of negotiable instruments are
also referred to as order paper.

To determine whether a negotiable instrument meets the requirement of being
"payable to bearer" or "payable to order," you must apply the tests set forth in
section 3–109. Section 3–109(a) governs when a negotiable instrument is "payable
to bearer." Section 3–109(b) governs when a negotiable instrument is "payable
to order."

To determine whether a negotiable instrument is "payable to bearer" or "payable to order," examine the specific words used in the promise or order. The words must exactly match those permitted by section 3–109. This is a rigid requirement and the failure to use the correct words will prevent the writing from qualifying as a negotiable instrument. Look at section 3–109(a)–(b). Can you articulate what words will make a negotiable instrument payable to order? What words will make a negotiable instrument payable to bearer?

READING THE CODE

> ### ■ Maryland Commercial Law Code Section 3–109
>
> **(a)** A promise or order is payable to bearer if it:
>
>   **(1)** States that it is payable to bearer or to the order of bearer or otherwise indicates that the person in possession of the promise or order is entitled to payment;
>
>   **(2)** Does not state a payee; or
>
>   **(3)** States that it is payable to or to the order of cash or otherwise indicates that it is not payable to an identified person.
>
> **(b)** A promise or order that is not payable to bearer is payable to order if it is payable (i) to the order of an identified person or (ii) to an identified person or order. A promise or order that is payable to order is payable to the identified person.

According to section 3–109, a negotiable instrument can be made "payable to bearer" in one of three ways:

1. A negotiable instrument is "payable to bearer" if it states "pay to bearer" or "pay to the order of bearer." Alternatively, a negotiable instrument can use any other language that has the effect of clearly indicating that the person in possession of it is entitled to payment. This last part allows for a little less rigidity in form without substantively changing anything.

2. A negotiable instrument that does not state a payee is treated as "payable to bearer." For example, a negotiable instrument is "payable to bearer" if the payee is left blank as follows: "Pay to the order of _____."

3.   A negotiable instrument is "payable to bearer" if it states "pay to cash" or "pay to the order of cash." Alternatively, the negotiable instrument can use other language to indicate that it is not payable to an identified person.

In contrast, a negotiable instrument can only be made "payable to order" in one of two ways:

1.   A negotiable instrument is "payable to order" if it states that it is "payable to the order of [an identified person]." For example, "pay to the order of Wayne."

2.   A negotiable instrument is also "payable to order" if it states that it is "payable to [an identified person] or order." For example, "pay to Wayne or order."

It is also important to note that a negotiable instrument cannot be both "payable to bearer" and "payable to order." The terms are mutually exclusive under Article 3. If a negotiable instrument purports to be "payable to bearer" and "payable to order," then it is "payable to bearer."

APPLYING THE CODE

Problem 22-5: Exploring the Payable to Order or Bearer Requirement

A)   Wayne signs a promissory note that states in relevant part "*I promise to pay $5,000 to David.*" Is this promissory note payable to order or bearer under Section 3–109? If so, which one?

B)   Wayne signs a promissory note that states in relevant part "I *promise to pay $5,000 to the holder of this promissory note.*" Is this promissory note payable to order or bearer under section 3–109? If so, which one?

---

6. Requirement 6: Payable on Demand or at a Definite Time

Per section 3–104(a)(2), a negotiable instrument must be "payable on demand" or "payable at a definite time." Section 3–108 defines both of these terms. Like section 3–109, section 3–108 contains rigid and precise requirements, so it is again important to pay careful attention to the specific words used in the promise or order.

READING THE CODE

> ### ■ Maryland Commercial Law Code Section 3–108
>
> **(a)**   A promise or order is "payable on demand" if it (i) states that it is payable on demand or at sight, or otherwise indicates that it is payable at the will of the holder, or (ii) does not state any time of payment.
>
> **(b)**   A promise or order is "payable at a definite time" if it is payable on elapse of a definite period of time after sight or acceptance or at a fixed date or dates or at a time or times readily ascertainable at the time the promise or order is issued, subject to rights of (i) prepayment, (ii) acceleration, (iii) extension at the option of the holder, or (iv) extension to a further definite time at the option of the maker or acceptor or automatically upon or after a specified act or event.

In general, a negotiable instrument is "payable at a definite time" if the promise or order is payable at a time (or more than one time) that is "readily ascertainable at the time the promise or order is issued." *See* section 3–108(b). For example, a negotiable instrument is "payable at a definite time" if it specifies a fixed date or dates (e.g., "payable on February 2, 2022" or "payable on the first day of each month in 2022"), or states that it is payable on elapse of a definite period of time after sight or acceptance (e.g., "payable 60 days after acceptance.").[6] Given the broad definition in section 3–108(b), a variety of other provisions setting forth the time for payment could also qualify as being "payable at a definite time."

Section 3–108(b) also makes it clear that a number of provisions commonly found in negotiable instruments do not impact the determination of whether a negotiable instrument is "payable at a definite time." Section 3–108(b) permits

---

6   "After sight" and "after acceptance" are terms of art that generally provide for payment a specified number of days after a negotiable instrument has been presented, reviewed and accepted for payment.

provisions that accelerate the time for payment, extend the time for payment, or allow for prepayment of the obligation. If a negotiable instrument is otherwise "payable at a definite time," the existence of any one of these provisions will not change that determination.

In general, a negotiable instrument is "payable on demand" if the promise or order states that the holder has the ability to unilaterally determine when the payment is due. Specifically, section 3–108(a) provides that a negotiable instrument is "payable on demand" if it meets one of the two tests.

1. A negotiable instrument is "payable on demand" if it states that it is "payable on demand," or "payable at sight." Alternatively, a negotiable instrument may use other language to indicate that it is payable at the will of the holder.

2. A negotiable instrument is "payable on demand" if it does not state any time for payment.

APPLYING THE CODE

Problem 22-6: Exploring the Demand or Definite Time Requirement

Evaluate each of the following and determine whether it is payable on demand, payable at a definite time, or neither.

A) A promissory note that states "I promise to pay to the order of David $5,000 on my next birthday."

B) A promissory note that states "I promise to pay to the order of David $5,000 when I have funds available."

C) A promissory note that states "I promise to pay to the order of David $5,000 six months after the date of this promissory note."

D) A promissory note that states "I promise to pay to the order of David $5,000 on August 12, 2025 (the "Maturity Date"). All amounts owed under this promissory note will become immediately due and payable upon any default. This promissory note may be paid at any time in advance of the Maturity Date without any penalty."

E)   A check that states "Pay to the order of David $5,000." Assume that no date for payment is specified.

---

7. Requirement 7: No Other Undertakings or Instructions

The last requirement of a negotiable instrument is in section 3–104(a)(3). Per section 3–104(a)(3), a negotiable instrument cannot contain "any undertaking or instruction by the [maker or drawer] to do any act in addition to the payment of money. This simply means that a negotiable instrument is generally limited to the payment obligation and nothing more. This has sometimes been referred to by the courts as the "courier without luggage" rule. So subject to a few exceptions, the inclusion of any additional undertakings and instructions by the maker or drawer prevents a promise or order from qualifying as a negotiable instrument. The UCC recognizes three exceptions to the prohibition against additional undertakings or instruction.

1.   The maker or drawer may "give, maintain, or protect collateral to secure payment." As a practical matter, this exception facilitates the practice of granting a security interest in collateral to secure the payment obligation evidenced by a negotiable instrument.

2.   The maker or drawer may "authorize or empower the holder to confess judgment or realize on or dispose of collateral." This exception validates provisions that authorize the holder to quickly and efficiently obtain a default judgment if there is a default on the negotiable instrument.

3.   The maker or drawer may waive the benefit of any law intended for the advantage or protection of an obligor. This exception generally allows for the inclusion of a number of relatively common provisions that provide for the waiver of different statutory and common law protections that may complicate a holder's attempt to collect on the negotiable instrument. This includes the waiver of benefits granted by the Code (such as presentment and notice of dishonor) and protections under other non-Code law (such as suretyship defenses, homestead exemptions and any applicable statute of limitations). Accordingly, a note could provide that the maker waives the benefit of every statute conferring upon the maker any right or privilege of exemption, stay

of execution, or other relief from enforcement of a judgment. Such a provision would not constitute an additional undertaking. As such, its inclusion in an instrument would not defeat negotiability. It is important to note, however, that this does not necessarily mean that the waiver provision itself will ultimately be enforceable—for example if other law prohibits the waiver.

EXAMPLES AND EXPLANATIONS

Kevin promises to pay Paula $1,000 in 90 days. Kevin also grants Paula a security interest in his prized (and very valuable) sports memorabilia collection. Specifically, if Kevin defaults, Paula has the right to sell the memorabilia and apply the proceeds to any outstanding amount owed by Kevin. In addition, Kevin agrees that: (1) he will not sell or otherwise dispose of any of the memorabilia without first getting Paula's written consent, and (2) he will maintain insurance to protect the memorabilia against any loss. Kevin and Paula ultimately sign a written document that reflects the above terms.

The writing signed by Kevin and Paula satisfies the no other undertakings requirement. The writing does include promises in addition to the foundational promise to pay—the grant of a security interest, the promise to obtain Paula's consent prior to disposing of any memorabilia, and the promise to maintain insurance. However, all the additional promises fall within the exception for giving a security interest and protecting collateral.

APPLYING THE CODE

Problem 22-7: Exploring the No Other Undertakings Requirement

Paula has agreed to purchase a struggling business from David. Paula and David sign a writing stating that Paula promises to pay David $250,000 and assume all of the current liabilities of David's business, including payment of overdue taxes and repayment of a line of credit. Paula also agrees to grant David a security interest in the business and all of its assets as collateral to secure her obligation to pay the $250,000. Does this writing satisfy the no-additional undertakings or instructions requirement?

C. Types of Negotiable Instruments

In working through the requirements for negotiability, you may have realized that "negotiable instrument" is an umbrella term. Anything that meets the requirements is a negotiable instrument. As a result, there are many different types of negotiable instruments.

Article 3 classifies negotiable instruments into one of two general categories—drafts or notes. Article 3 distinguishes these categories by looking to the foundational payment obligation. If the negotiable instrument is based on an order to pay then it is a "draft." If the negotiable instrument is based on a promise to pay then it is a "note." Within these two categories, Article 3 recognizes several different types of negotiable instruments. *See* section 3–104(f)–(j). At this time, you may want to take a look at the different types of negotiable instruments listed in section 3–104. An in depth review of each type is beyond the scope of the core commercial law concepts covered in this book. However, it may be useful to get a feel for the things that qualify as negotiable instruments. Some of these are likely to be more familiar to you than others.

Moving forward, pay close attention to the language used in the excerpted Code provisions. In some instances, the Code may refer to "negotiable instruments" broadly. Other provisions may apply more narrowly to a specific category or type of negotiable instrument. These distinctions can have a material impact on how the Code applies.

Test Your Knowledge

To assess your understanding of the material in this chapter, click here to take a quiz.

23

Transferring and Enforcing Negotiable Instruments

Key Concepts

- The distinction between issuance of a negotiable instrument, transfer of a negotiable instrument, negotiation of a negotiable instrument, and presentment of a negotiable instrument
- The requirements for becoming a "holder" of a negotiable instrument
- How to identify who has the right to enforce a negotiable instrument
- The effect of indorsements (both special indorsements and blank indorsements) on the character of a negotiable instrument
- How to identify who is liable for payment on a negotiable instrument
- The distinction between acceptor liability, issuer liability and drawer liability

In the previous Chapter, we discussed the requirements of a negotiable instrument. By satisfying each of these requirements, a writing can transcend from simple contract to negotiable instrument. But the creation of a negotiable instrument is just the beginning. For a negotiable instrument to accomplish its intended purpose, it must be put into action.

Recall that the core of a negotiable instrument is a payment obligation. Before the obligation is actually paid, the negotiable instrument must change hands. That is to say, it will travel. In the normal course of events, the instrument will move from one person to the next until it is ultimately presented for payment. The act of payment on the instrument results in conversion of the obligation into cash—ending the life cycle of the negotiable instrument. Only through this series of events will the negotiable instrument be able to accomplish its purpose—moving money or wealth efficiently without the use of cash.

This Chapter focuses on the process by which negotiable instruments move and looks at two related questions. Who is entitled to enforce a negotiable instrument? And who is liable to pay on a negotiable instrument?

A. Issuance of a Negotiable Instrument

The maker of a note or the drawer of a draft starts the process of moving the negotiable instrument from one person to the next. This first delivery of the negotiable instrument is called the issuance, which is defined in section 3–105.

READING THE CODE

> **Maryland Commercial Law Code Section 3–105**
>
> **(a)** "Issue" means the first delivery of an instrument by the maker or drawer, whether to a holder or nonholder, for the purpose of giving rights on the instrument to any person.

Section 3–105 is relatively straightforward. The maker or drawer must take some action that can be fairly categorized as delivery of the instrument. An instrument is properly issued regardless of whom receives the delivery. Section 3–105 makes this clear by specifying that delivery can be to a person with the status of a "holder" or not.

Ultimately, the intent of the maker or drawer is what matters. In fact, it is paramount. The maker or drawer must deliver the negotiable instrument "for the purpose of giving rights on the instrument to any person." Note that issuance occurs if the maker or drawer intends to give rights to any person. The maker or drawer need not intend to give rights to the person who receives delivery. So long as the maker or drawer intends to give rights to someone, the instrument has been issued.

In short, issuance boils down to two requirements: (1) the maker or drawer must have delivered the instrument, and (2) the maker or drawer must have intended to grant rights on the instrument to someone. To anyone. It does not matter who.

APPLYING THE CODE

Problem 23-1: When Is an Instrument Issued?

A) Paula writes a personal check that is payable to the order of Wayne. Before Paula can give it to Wayne, a thief steals the check. Has the check been issued? Why or why not?

B) Paula writes a personal check that is payable to the order of Wayne. Paula plans to mail the check to Wayne, but she has not had a chance to get to the post office yet. Has the check been issued? Why or why not?

C) David signed a promissory note acknowledging a debt and promising to pay Wayne $10,000. After signing the promissory note, David left it on his desk and stepped out to grab lunch. Assume that the promissory note is a negotiable instrument. Has the promissory note been issued? Why or why not?

D) Wayne spontaneously decides to stop by David's office to ask about the status of the promissory note. While David was out to lunch, Wayne popped his head into the office and saw the signed promissory note on David's desk. Wayne decided to take the promissory note to save himself a trip back to David's office. Has the promissory note been issued? Why or why not?

E) Kevin writes out a check that is payable to the order of Wayne. Kevin gives the check to his assistant before leaving for the day and asks his assistant to give the check to Wayne who will be stopping by later. Has the check been issued? Why or why not?

B. Transfer of a Negotiable Instrument

In some cases, the maker or drawer will issue the instrument directly to the person that will ultimately enforce it. That person simply holds the instrument until they present it to the maker or drawer for payment. However, the main function of negotiable instruments is to facilitate the movement of wealth with physical delivery of the negotiable instrument acting as a substitute for the physical delivery of cash. Therefore, it is quite common for negotiable instruments to change hands (often many times) after being issued—moving from person to next until the instrument is finally presented to the maker or drawer for payment.

Because negotiable instruments frequently move, the transfer of negotiable instruments under Article 3 is foundational a concept. Outside of Article 3, the term "transfer" is commonly used to encompass any act of moving something to another person or place. However, under Article 3, the term "transfer" has a very particular meaning. Not every move of a negotiable instrument to a new person will constitute a "transfer" under Article 3. The UCC covers the transfer of negotiable instruments in Section 3–203.

READING THE CODE

Maryland Commercial Law Code Section 3–203

(a) An instrument is transferred when it is delivered by a person other than its issuer for the purpose of giving to the person receiving delivery the right to enforce the instrument.

Section 3–203 is relatively straightforward. It should be clear that a transfer only occurs when two elements exist.

1. **Delivery.** Someone other than the issuer must deliver the instrument to another person. The instrument must change hands, but the issuance of an instrument by its maker or drawer does not qualify as a transfer.

2. **Intent.** The state of mind of the person who delivers the instrument is key. The person who delivers the instrument must do so for the purpose of giving the right to enforce the instrument. Note that the requisite intent to transfer an instrument differs from the intent needed to issue an instrument. To issue an instrument, the maker or drawer must intend to grant rights to any person. To transfer an instrument, the intent required is more exacting. A transfer requires intent to grant the person receiving delivery of the instrument (not any person) the right to enforce it. This requirement plainly excludes any delivery that is involuntary or otherwise lacks the requisite state of mind.

EXAMPLES AND EXPLANATIONS

Consider the following examples.

Example 1: Wayne owes David $1,000. Wayne signs a note promising to pay $1,000 to the order of David in 3 months. Wayne then delivers the note to David. David stores the note in his safe until payment is due (3 months later). David then presents the note to Wayne and demands payment on the note.

When Wayne delivers the note to David, it has been issued. That is the first delivery of note by the maker of the note (Wayne). In signing and delivering the note, Wayne presumably intends to grant David (who qualifies as "any person") rights in the instrument—specifically the right to enforce/collect payment of the $1,000 debt when due. Thus, the note has been issued because Wayne has the requisite intent when delivering the note to David. But, in this scenario, the note has never been transferred. As noted above, the note is issued when Wayne first delivers the note to David. Therefore, Wayne is the issuer of the note and section 3–203 expressly limits transfers to delivery by a person other than the issuer. This leaves David's act of presenting the note to Wayne for payment as the only other potential delivery to assess. David is a person other than the issuer so his delivery of note to another person could potentially fit within the Section 3–203 meaning of transfer. Initially, David's demand for payment from Wayne is only a delivery if David gives up possession of the note to Wayne. Even if the note changes hands, David lacks the necessary intent for a transfer. David's purpose is to obtain payment on the note himself (not to give Wayne the right to enforce the note). As such, no transfer has occurred.

Example 2: In contrast, assume that after 1 month, David's furnace breaks down. In need of some quick cash to buy a replacement, David sells the $1,000 promissory note to Kevin, assigning the right to collect payment from Wayne when due. Upon finalizing the sale of the note, David removes the note from his safe and hands it to Kevin.

David has now transferred the note to Kevin. As discussed in Example 1 above, David is not the issuer. Accordingly, his delivery of the instrument to another person (Kevin) can constitute a transfer if he has the necessary state of mind. David has voluntarily given possession of the note to Kevin and the assignment further evidences David's intent to grant Kevin (the person receiving delivery) the right to enforce payment. Accordingly, David's sale of the note to Kevin constitutes a transfer of the note under section 3–203. At this point, Kevin could hold the note and present it to Wayne for payment when due. Alternatively, Kevin could decide to transfer the note to yet another person.

You should see now that the meaning of "transfer" under Article 3 does not encompass every instance of a negotiable instrument changing hands or coming into the possession of a new person. A transfer only occurs if a person other than an issuer delivers the instrument. In addition, an instrument is only transferred if it is delivered with intent to give the recipient rights to enforce it. As such, each transfer involves a new party who could potentially seek payment. Even so, you should recognize that Section 3–203(a) only deals with whether a transfer has occurred. We will examine the question of who is entitled to enforce an instrument later in this Chapter.

C. The Process of Negotiation and Becoming a Holder

Article 3 also recognizes a special type of transfer (which can be voluntary or involuntary) called a negotiation.

READING THE CODE

Maryland Commercial Law Code Section 3–201

(a) "Negotiation" means a transfer of possession, whether voluntary or involuntary, of an instrument by a person other than the issuer to a person who thereby becomes its holder.

(b) . . . if an instrument is payable to an identified person, negotiation requires transfer of possession of the instrument and its indorsement by the holder. If an instrument is payable to bearer, it may be negotiated by transfer of possession alone.

Maryland Commercial Law Code Section 1–201(b)

(21) "Holder" means:

(i) The person in possession of a negotiable instrument that is payable either to bearer or to an identified person that is the person in possession . . .

Some, but not all, transfers will be a negotiation as defined in section 3–201(a). Whether an instrument has been negotiated turns on the status of the transferee.

If an instrument is transferred to a person who is a "holder," it has been negotiated. Conversely, an instrument has not been negotiated if it is transferred to a person who is not a "holder."

The definition of "holder" involves two components. A "holder" must have possession of the negotiable instrument—you must "hold" it to be a "holder." In addition, the person in possession of the negotiable instrument must have the right to enforce it.

1. **Possession:** This requirement is relatively straightforward. A person cannot be a "holder" without actually having possession of the negotiable instrument. The requirement focuses on physical possession alone. It does not consider how possession was obtained or even whether the possession is lawful.

   For example, a thief who steals an instrument from its rightful owner now has possession. The theft also results in the loss of possession by the rightful owner. In this situation, the rightful owner of the instrument can no longer qualify as a "holder." However, as we will see below, the thief may still obtain the status of a "holder" if the remaining requirement is met.

2. **Right to Enforce:** This requirement is a little more convoluted. In general, this requirement means that an examination of the instrument itself should indicate that the person in possession has the right to enforce the payment obligation that the instrument evidences.

   The definition of "holder" in section 1–201(b)(21)(i), however, does not refer explicitly to the right to enforce. Instead, it states that the negotiable instrument must be payable "either to bearer or to an identified person that is the person in possession." This requirement essentially distinguishes between bearer paper and order paper. Luckily, these are concepts that we explored in the previous Chapter!

   Verifying the right to enforce bearer paper is simple. Bearer paper is an instrument payable to whoever is in possession of it. If the face of an instrument indicates that it is payable to whoever has possession, then possession alone grants the right to enforce. Nothing more is needed. Whoever has possession of bearer paper is the "holder." Accordingly, bearer paper may be negotiated (i.e., transferred to a new "holder") by the transfer of possession alone. *See* section 3–201(b).

In contrast, the right to enforce order paper requires more than mere possession. Order paper is an instrument payable to an identified person. Because of this, the identified person (and no one else) has the right to enforce. Therefore, the "holder" of order paper must (1) have possession and (2) be the person identified on the instrument as the payee. Simply stated, verifying the right to enforce order paper requires confirmation that the person identified on the instrument as the payee is the person in possession. Because of this, the negotiation of order paper involves an additional step. The current "holder" must transfer possession of the instrument. In addition, the current holder must properly indorse the instrument. An indorsement indicates that the instrument is now payable to the transferee (making the transferee the person identified on the instrument as having the right to payment). This is the only way to negotiate order paper along with the status of "holder" to another person. *See* section 3–201(b).

EXAMPLES AND EXPLANATIONS

The following example highlights the differing requirements for becoming a holder of an instrument that constitutes bearer paper versus an instrument that constitutes order paper.

Assume that Kevin steals two instruments from David. The first instrument is a check that is payable to the order of bearer (or cash)—that is to say, it is payable to whoever has possession of the check. The second instrument is a check that is payable to the order of a specifically identified person—David.

Whether Kevin (a thief) is a holder depends on the type of instrument in question. The first check is bearer paper. As such, it is payable to whoever has possession. Since Kevin stole the check he has possession. An examination of the first check would confirm that Kevin has the right to payment on the check because it is payable to whoever has possession and Kevin has possession. He has both possession and the right to enforce payment of the first check. This makes Kevin the holder of the bearer paper. The result is different for the second check. The second check is order paper that is payable to David. Kevin has possession of the second check. However, Kevin does not have the right to enforce payment. An examination of the second check would confirm that Kevin is not the rightful payee. David (not Kevin) is the identified payee. David has not indorsed the instrument to Kevin so nothing on the face of the second check indicates that Kevin now has the right to enforce payment. As a result, Kevin has possession, but Kevin is not a holder because he does not have the right to enforce. In addition, David is no longer a "holder." As the identified payee, David has the right to enforce. As such, David was the holder when he had possession of the instrument. However, David no longer has possession so he no longer qualifies as a holder.

In the end, determining whether the person in possession of an instrument is a holder is relatively straightforward. If the instrument is bearer paper, the person with possession is a holder. But, if the instrument is order paper, the person in possession is only a holder if: (1) the instrument originally identifies them as the payee or (2) the instrument contains a subsequent indorsement that identifies them as the payee.

At this point, you may be asking yourself what happens if the instrument is order paper and it identifies more than one payee? Who is entitled to enforce then? This, of course, is not an uncommon occurrence. Checks are often payable to two more persons—either jointly or in the alternative. For example, a check payable to "David and Wayne" is payable jointly to both of them. On the other hand, a check payable to "David or Wayne" is payable in the alternative to either of them. In some cases, it may be unclear whether the instrument is payable jointly or in the alternative. For example, a check payable to "David and/or Wayne."

Luckily, the UCC provides a solution in section 3–110(d), which provides the rules that govern in these situations. Take this opportunity to practice parsing code provisions. Read section 3–110(d) (excerpted below), and try to articulate who has the right to enforce if an instrument is payable to two or more persons jointly? What if the instrument is payable in the alternative to two or more persons? What if there are two or more payees but the instrument is ambiguous as to whether it is payable jointly or in the alternative?

READING THE CODE

Maryland Commercial Law Code Section 3–110(d)

(d) If an instrument is payable to two or more persons alternatively, it is payable to any of them and may be negotiated, discharged, or enforced by any or all of them in possession of the instrument. If an instrument is payable to two or more persons not alternatively, it is payable to all of them and may be negotiated,

> discharged, or enforced only by all of them. If an instrument payable to two or more persons is ambiguous as to whether it is payable to the persons alternatively, the instrument is payable to the persons alternatively.

APPLYING THE CODE

Problem 23-2: Determining the Person(s) Entitled to Enforce

Paula goes to a garage sale that is being held jointly by David, Kevin and Wayne. Paula finds a number of items to buy, including some vintage law books. To pay for the items, Paula writes a check.

A) Assume that Paula's check is "payable to the order of David, Kevin and Wayne." David is the most responsible of the sellers so he hangs onto the check. Is David a holder? Can David negotiate the check to another person? Can David go to the bank and cash the check? If not, what is required?

B) What if Paula's check was "payable to the order of David or Kevin or Wayne"? Again, assume that David has possession of the check. Is David a holder? Can David negotiate the check to another person? Can David go to the bank and cash the check? If not what is required?

C) What if Paula's check was "payable to the order of David, Kevin and/ or Wayne"? Again assume that David has possession of the check. Is David a holder? Can David negotiate the check to another person? Can David go to the bank and cash the check? If not what is required?

D. Indorsements

As we have seen, indorsements are used primarily in connection with negotiating instruments. The UCC defines the term indorsement in section 3–204(a).

READING THE CODE

Maryland Commercial Law Code Section 3–204

(a) "Indorsement" means a signature, other than that of a signer as maker, drawer, or acceptor, that alone or accompanied by other words is made on an instrument for the purpose of (i) negotiating the instrument, (ii) restricting payment of the instrument, or (iii) incurring indorser's liability on the instrument, but regardless of the intent of the signer, a signature and its accompanying words is an indorsement unless the accompanying words, terms of the instrument, place of the signature, or other circumstances un-ambiguously indicate that the signature was made for a purpose other than indorsement . . .

An indorsement can be nothing more than a signature, but the person signing must not be signing: (1) as the maker of a note, (2) as the drawer of a draft or (3) to accept a draft for payment. Section 3–204(a) further requires that the signature appear on the instrument itself or on a separate piece of paper affixed to the instrument. Finally, the signature must be made for one of the three identified reasons listed in section 3–204(a)(i)–(iii).

Article 3, however, takes a liberal approach indorsements. Article 3 treats every signature that appears on an instrument (no matter its location) as an indorsement unless there is unambiguous evidence that the person signed for another purpose. Evidence of contrary intent can take the form of words accompanying the signature. The terms of the instrument or the location of the signature can also make it clear that a signature was not intended as an indorsement. For example, the terms of a promissory note may unambiguously indicate that a person is signing as the maker of the note (i.e., the person who is directly undertaking the obligation to pay). Similarly, the location of a signature on the bottom right corner of a personal check may unambiguously indicate that a person is signing as the drawer (i.e., the person ordering another to make payment).

In negotiating an instrument to a new holder, the current holder of an instrument most commonly uses one of two types of indorsements—a special indorsement or a blank indorsement.[1] Section 3–205 describes both types of indorsements.

READING THE CODE

Maryland Commercial Law Code Section 3–205

(a) If an indorsement is made by the holder of an instrument, whether payable to an identified person or payable to bearer, and the indorsement identifies a person to whom it makes the instrument payable, it is a "special indorsement". When specially indorsed, an instrument becomes payable to the identified person and may be negotiated only by the indorsement of that person . . .

(b) If an indorsement is made by the holder of an instrument and it is not a special indorsement, it is a "blank indorsement". When indorsed in blank, an instrument becomes payable to bearer and may be negotiated by transfer of possession alone until specially indorsed.

(c) The holder may convert a blank indorsement that consists only of a signature into a special indorsement by writing, above the signature of the indorser, words identifying the person to whom the instrument is made payable.

- **Special Indorsement:** A special indorsement is an indorsement by the holder of the instrument that identifies a person to whom the instrument is payable. *See* section 3–205(a).

  For example, if David is the holder, he could specially indorse the instrument to Kevin by writing "pay to Kevin" and signing his name.

  The effect of a special indorsement is that the instrument becomes payable to the identified person. Thereafter, the instrument can only be negotiated

---

1   Article 3 of the UCC also recognizes a third type of indorsement called an "anomalous indorsement," which is an indorsement made by a person who is not the holder of the instrument. This type of indorsement does not affect the manner in which the instrument may be negotiated. This type of indorsement is beyond the scope the core commercial law concepts covered in this textbook. But feel free to take a look at section 3–205(d) if it piques your interest.

via transfer of possession and the indorsement of the identified person unless a subsequent holder indorses it in blank.

- **Blank Indorsement:** A blank indorsement is an indorsement by the holder of the instrument that does not identify a person to whom the instrument is payable. Any indorsement that is not a special indorsement is a blank indorsement. *See* section 3–205(b).

  Examples of blank indorsements include the signature of the holder alone, or with words such as "pay to order," "pay to bearer" or "pay to cash."

  The effect of a blank indorsement is that the instrument becomes payable to bearer—whoever has physical possession of the instrument. The instrument can now be negotiated via transfer of possession alone unless it becomes specially indorsed by a subsequent holder.

It is important to note that only the holder of an instrument can make a valid indorsement—whether a special indorsement or a blank indorsement. An indorsement by anyone other than the holder will be ineffective for the purpose of negotiating the instrument. Any person who obtains possession of an instrument without a proper indorsement will not qualify as a "holder." For the same reason, any indorsement to a subsequent transferee would also be defective.

You should also see that indorsements can change the character of an instrument. *See* section 3–109(c). A holder can change bearer paper to order paper via a special indorsement. Similarly, a holder can change order paper to bearer paper via a blank indorsement. Because the most recent indorsement controls, an instrument can change type back and forth, as it changes hands.

APPLYING THE CODE

Problem 23-3: Blank Indorsements

A) Paula writes a $100 check that is payable to the order of Wayne and hands it to him. Wayne signs his name on the back of the check with nothing more and heads off to the bank to deposit it. When Wayne arrives at the bank, he realizes that the check is nowhere to be found. As Kevin is walking by, he sees the check and picks it up. Is Kevin a holder?

B) Assume that Kevin then gives the check to David as payment for a lost bet. Kevin does not sign the check before giving it to David. Is David a holder?

Problem 23-4: Following the Chain of Title

A) Wayne writes a $500 check that is payable to the order of Kevin and hands it to him. Kevin writes, "pay to bearer" on the back of the check and signs his name below the words. He then places the check in his briefcase. At this point, is Kevin a holder?

B) Kevin then walks over to David's garage sale. After browsing for a bit, Kevin finds a bicycle that he wants to purchase. Kevin hands the $500 check to David in exchange for the bicycle. David writes, "pay to Paula" below Kevin's signature and then signs his own name. David then places the check in his safe. At this point, is David a holder?

C) Later that night, a thief breaks into the safe and takes the $500 check. The thief then writes, "pay to cash" and forges Paula's signature. The thief brings the $500 check to a nearby gas station and offers to sell it to the owner for cash. The owner inspects the $500 check and sees that it has been most recently indorsed as payable to cash. If the owner agrees to purchase the check, will the owner be a holder?

E. Obtaining Payment on a Negotiable Instrument

The journey of a negotiable instrument ends when a person entitled to enforce seeks to collect payment on it. The process of collecting payment begins with presentment of the instrument for payment.

F. Presentment

READING THE CODE

Maryland Commercial Law Code Section 3–501

(a) "Presentment" means a demand made by or on behalf of a person entitled to enforce an instrument (i) to pay the instrument made to the drawee or a party obliged to pay the instrument or, in the case of a note or accepted draft payable at a bank, to the bank, or (ii) to accept a draft made to the drawee.

(b) The following rules are subject to. . .agreement of the parties. . .

(1) Presentment may be made at the place of payment of the instrument and must be made at the place of payment if the instrument is payable at a bank in the United States; may be made by any commercially reasonable means, including an oral, written, or electronic communication; is effective when the demand for payment or acceptance is received by the person to whom presentment is made; and is effective if made to any one of two or more makers, acceptors, drawees, or other payors.

(2) Upon demand of the person to whom presentment is made, the person making presentment must (i) exhibit the instrument, (ii) give reasonable identification and, if presentment is made on behalf of another person, reasonable evidence of authority to do so, and (iii) sign a receipt on the instrument for any payment made or surrender the instrument if full payment is made.

(3) . . . the party to whom presentment is made may (i) return the instrument for lack of a necessary indorsement, or (ii) refuse payment or acceptance for failure of the presentment to comply with the terms of the instrument, an agreement of the parties, or other applicable law or rule.

Presentment is simply a demand for payment. The demand for payment is typically made on the maker of a note or the drawee of a draft. Article 3's default rule is that presentment can be made in any way that is commercially reasonable. Unless the instrument provides otherwise, an effective presentment can be made via oral, written or electronic communication.

Upon presentment, the recipient of the demand can require that the presenter provide enough information to allow for evaluation of the presenter's right to receive payment. This ordinarily means that the presenter must produce the instrument along with reasonable identification. If presenting an instrument on behalf of another person, then reasonable evidence of authority must also be provided.

This allows the recipient of the demand to confirm that the presenter has possession of the instrument. In addition, the recipient of the demand can examine the instrument along with the chain of indorsements to: (1) evaluate whether the instrument has been properly negotiated and (2) determine who is entitled to enforce. The recipient of the demand can then check to presenter's identification to help ensure that they are paying the correct person.

This process again highlights one of the primary advantages of negotiable instruments—the ability to verify the right to payment without looking much beyond the four corners of the instrument. As we have seen before, this hallmark of negotiable instruments allows for ease of transfer and facilitates the use of instruments as a cash substitute.

G. Honor or Dishonor

After an instrument is properly presented for payment, there are basically two options. The recipient of the demand can either pay or refuse to pay.

The act of paying or accepting an instrument for payment is called honoring the instrument. If any payment is made, the recipient of the demand can require that the presenter sign a receipt on the instrument for any amount paid. *See* section 3–501(b)(2)(iii). If the instrument is paid in full, the recipient of the demand can require that the presenter surrender the instrument. *Id.* Upon payment in full and surrender of the instrument, the life of the instrument effectively ceases.

In general, the recipient of a proper presentment dishonors the instrument by failing to pay or refusing to accept the instrument for payment. Section 3–502 contains detailed rules governing dishonor. In most cases, an instrument that is payable at the time of presentment is dishonored if it is not paid on that day.

The most obvious example is a draft or note that is payable on demand. Since the instrument is payable on demand, it is dishonored if payment is not made on the day of presentment. *See* section 3–502(a)(1), (b)(2), (d)(1).

The same is generally true for a draft or note that is not payable on demand—for example those that are payable on a specified date. When the instrument is presented on or after the date that it becomes payable, it is dishonored if not paid on the day of presentment. If presentment occurs before the date that the instrument becomes payable then it is dishonored if not paid on the day it becomes payable. *See* section 3–502(a)(2), (b)(3)(i), (d)(2).

There are some notable exceptions to this general rule:

- **Notes Not Payable on Demand and Not Payable at or through a Bank.** This exception only applies to notes that are not payable on demand. In addition, the note cannot be payable at or through a bank. This type of note is dishonored if it is not paid on the day that it becomes payable. Presentment is not even required as a precondition. *See* section 3–502(a)(3).

  For example, Kevin executes a note that contains a promise to pay Wayne $1,000 on September 22, 2050. It is now September 23, 2050. Kevin has not paid the $1,000 because Wayne has not asked him for it. This note meets each requirement of the section 3–502(a)(3) exception. The note is not payable on demand. It is payable on a specific date—September 22, 2050. In addition, the note is not payable at or through a bank. Instead, it is payable through an individual—Kevin. Thus, the note is dishonored if it is not paid on September 22, 2050, regardless of presentment (or lack of presentment) by Wayne.

- **Checks Presented to Payor Bank other than for Immediate Payment.** This exception applies to checks that are not presented for immediate payment over the counter. Upon presentment to the payor bank (i.e., the drawee bank), this type of check is dishonored if the bank returns the check in a timely manner or sends timely notice of dishonor or nonpayment. The bank also dishonors the check if it becomes "accountable" for the check, which occurs if the bank fails to either pay or send timely notice of dishonor (or promptly return the check). *See* section 3–502(b)(1).

  For example, Kevin maintains a checking account at First Bank. Kevin writes a $1,000 check drawn on his account at First Bank that is payable to the order of Wayne. Wayne goes to Second Bank where he maintains a savings account and deposits the check. Second Bank presents the check to First Bank for payment. First Bank dishonors the check by returning it to Second Bank and indicating First Bank's refusal to pay.

APPLYING THE CODE

Problem 23-5: Presentment and Dishonor

A) On September 22, Paula issues and delivers a $10,000 negotiable promissory note to David. The note is payable upon demand. On September 23, David hires a same-day courier service to send a letter demanding payment in full. Paula reads the letter later that day, but feels that it is unreasonable for David to be demanding payment so soon. One week later, David has not heard a peep from Paula and has not received payment. Has the negotiable promissory note been dishonored?

B) Kevin loans Paula $5,000. In exchange, Paula issues and delivers a $5,000 negotiable promissory note to Kevin. The note is payable with interest on Kevin's 50th birthday. On February 2, 2031 (Kevin's 50th birthday), Kevin attempts to send Paula an email demanding payment, but types in the wrong email address. Paula never receives the email and does not pay Kevin. Has the negotiable promissory note been dishonored?

C) Kevin is planning to remodel his kitchen. As an avid fan of home improvement television shows, Kevin is certain that he can finish the job in a week. Kevin enlists his friend Wayne to help hang cabinets and install a new tile back splash. Kevin wants to thank Wayne for his hard work. Short on cash, Kevin writes a draft, ordering a company named On Trend to pay Wayne $500. Kevin is an investor in On Trend, which designs and manufactures bow ties. Kevin receives $1 for every bow tie that is sold during the calendar year. Kevin tells Wayne that he has arranged for Wayne to receive the $500 from the amounts owed to him by On Trend. The draft is payable on April 2. The draft also states that presentment must be made in person at On Trend's corporate headquarters in Baltimore. Unable to travel to Baltimore, Wayne sends a certified letter demanding payment. On

Trend received the letter at its corporate headquarters on March 15. It is now April 5 and On Trend has not paid. Has the draft been dishonored? Would your answer be different if On Trend received the certified letter on April 3?

H. Enforcement and Liability

Until now, this Chapter has focused primarily on examining the life cycle of an instrument from issuance to presentment. We have seen how instruments function as a cash substitute. Instruments represent an obligation to pay that is freely transferable. As a result, they can move from one person to the next with relative ease and frequency.

For an instrument to serve its ultimate purpose, payment must be made to the person who is entitled to receive it. In many cases, the process operates seamlessly. The instrument is honored when presented for payment. The maker of a note keeps its promise to pay, or the drawee of a draft accepts it for payment as instructed. All is well.

In other cases, the instrument is dishonored when it is presented. The presenter is left with a piece of paper instead of the money it represents. To get paid, the presenter may need to convince the recipient of the demand of its right to payment. If this fails, the presenter may need to pursue a lawsuit seeking enforcement of the instrument.

Now that we have an understanding of an instrument's life cycle, we have the context to tackle the essential issues of enforcement and liability.

With all the people who may come into contact with a negotiable instrument during the course of its life, who has the right to enforce it? In addition, who is liable for making the payment? The remainder of this Chapter deals with answering these questions.

I. Who Has the Right to Enforce an Instrument?

Who has the right to enforce an instrument? Article 3 provides a straightforward answer to this question by defining exactly who is "a person entitled to enforce" an instrument.

READING THE CODE

> #### Maryland Commercial Law Code Section 3–301
>
> "Person entitled to enforce" an instrument means (i) the holder of the instrument, (ii) a nonholder in possession of the instrument who has the rights of a holder, or (iii) a person not in possession of the instrument who is entitled to enforce the instrument pursuant to section 3–309 or section 3–418(d). A person may be a person entitled to enforce the instrument even though the person is not the owner of the instrument or is in wrongful possession of the instrument.

Section 3–301 basically identifies three categories of "persons entitled to enforce" an instrument:

1. **Holders.** Having learned about the process of properly negotiating an instrument, it should come as no surprise that a "holder" of an instrument is a "person entitled to enforce" it. *See* section 3–301(i).

2. **Nonholder in Possession with Rights of a Holder.** Under section 3–301(ii), a person without the status of a "holder" may still enforce the instrument if they have both: (a) possession of the instrument and (b) the rights of a holder.

   You may be wondering how a person can have the rights of a holder without actually being a holder. Recall the definition of holder in section 1–201(b)(21). A holder must have possession of an instrument that is payable to bearer or that specifically names them as the payee. Therefore, a person cannot be a holder if they have possession of an instrument that names another person as the payee. Section 3–203(b) provides the rest of the answer. Under section 3–203(b), the transfer of an instrument (whether or not it is a negotiation) "vests in the transferee any right of the transferor to enforce the instrument." This means that if the person transferring an instrument is a person entitled to enforce it then the recipient of the transfer gets the same right to enforce. Thus, a person who is not a holder (because they have possession of an instrument that specifically names another payee) might still have the right to enforce payment of the instrument if they received transfer of the instrument from a holder who had the right to enforce it.

With that in mind, section 3–301(ii) basically accommodates the following scenario:

EXAMPLES AND EXPLANATIONS

David writes a check that is payable to the order of Kevin and delivers it to him. Kevin sells the check to Wayne for cash. Kevin delivers the check to Wayne but never indorses it. Wayne now has possession of the check, but the check is still payable to the order of Kevin.

Wayne is not the identified payee of the check and cannot qualify as the "holder" of the instrument. Wayne has possession, but he is not entitled to enforce because the identified payee is still Kevin. However, under Section 3–203(b), Wayne acquired all of Kevin's rights upon transfer. Kevin was a "holder" of the check with right to enforce. Wayne acquired Kevin's rights in the check, including Kevin's rights to enforce. Accordingly, Wayne is a "person entitled to enforce" even though he is not a "holder."

3. **Person Without Possession who is Entitled to Possession.** Without possession of an instrument, a person cannot qualify as a holder. However, section 3–301(iii) recognizes two situations where a person without possession is actually entitled to it. In these cases, the person without possession of the instrument has the right to enforce it.

First, a person may be entitled to enforce a lost, stolen or destroyed instrument by complying with section 3–309.

Second, a person may be entitled to enforce an instrument that was paid or accepted by mistake if the payor recovers the payment or the person who mistakenly accepts the instrument for payment revokes the acceptance in accordance with section 3–418.

After identifying the three categories of "person entitled to enforce," the last sentence of section 3–301 provides important interpretive guidance.

Section 3–301 acknowledges that the right to enforce does not require either lawful ownership or rightful possession of the instrument. All that matters is qualifying as a "holder" or fitting into one of the categories of non-holders entitled to enforce.

The consequence of this should be clear. To facilitate the use of negotiable instruments as a cash substitute, Article 3 favors added certainty in the right to enforce payment. This comes at the expense of accepting some unjust results. For example, a thief that steals bearer paper is a holder. As a result, the thief is a person entitled to enforce the stolen instrument.

At this point, it is probably worth noting that having the right to enforce an instrument does not equate to success in doing so. The right to enforce an instrument is subject to defenses, which we will learn about in a subsequent chapter.

J. Who Is Liable for Payment on an Instrument?

Having defined the "persons entitled to enforce an instrument," the next question is who is liable for payment? The answer involves two steps.

The threshold requirement is a signature. No one can be held liable for payment on an instrument unless they (or an agent) sign the instrument. *See* section 3–401(a) (below). The rationale is simple. The signature exhibits the person's assent to be bound by the obligation to pay.

READING THE CODE

> #### Maryland Commercial Law Code Section 3–401
>
> **(a)** A person is not liable on an instrument unless (i) the person signed the instrument, or (ii) the person is represented by an agent or representative who signed the instrument and the signature is binding on the represented person under section 3–402.
>
> **(b)** A signature may be made (i) manually or by means of a device or machine, and (ii) by the use of any name, including a trade or assumed name, or by a word, mark, or symbol executed or adopted by a person with present intention to authenticate a writing.

The next step is determining the basis of the liability incurred. This depends on whether the person signed the instrument as an issuer, drawee, drawer or indorser.

- **Issuer Liability.** The maker of a note and the issuing bank of a cashier's check[2] both incur liability as an issuer. *See* section 3–412 (below). The issuer promises to pay according to the terms of the instrument. When payment becomes due, the issuer is obligated to pay it. The terms of the instrument at the time of issuance govern.

READING THE CODE

Maryland Commercial Law Code Section 3–412

The issuer of a note or cashier's check or other draft drawn on the drawer is obliged to pay the instrument (i) according to its terms at the time it was issued or, if not issued, at the time it first came into possession of a holder, or (ii) if the issuer signed an incomplete instrument, according to its terms when completed, to the extent stated in sections 3–115 and 3–407. The obligation is owed to a person entitled to enforce the instrument or to an indorser who paid the instrument under section 3–415.

- **Acceptor Liability.** The drawee of a draft must accept the draft to incur liability to a person entitled to enforce it—hence the term acceptor liability. See section 3–413 (below). Acceptance is a condition to liability. As such, a drawee is not liable on an instrument until the drawee accepts it. *See* section 3–408. To accept a draft, the drawee must agree to pay by signing on the instrument. *See* section 3–409(a). Upon acceptance, the drawee is obligated to pay the instrument. The terms at the time of acceptance govern.

READING THE CODE

Maryland Commercial Law Code Section 3–413

(a) The acceptor of a draft is obliged to pay the draft (i) according to its terms at the time it was accepted, even though the accep-

---

2   A cashier's check is a particular type of check. Specifically, it is a check where the bank is both the drawer and the drawee. As a result, the bank is effectively in the same position as the maker of a note. The bank issues the cashier's check as the drawer and then receives the demand for payment as the drawee.

tance states that the draft is payable "as originally drawn" or equivalent terms, (ii) if the acceptance varies the terms of the draft, according to the terms of the draft as varied, or (iii) if the acceptance is of a draft that is an incomplete instrument, according to its terms when completed, to the extent stated in sections 3–115 and 3–407. The obligation is owed to a person entitled to enforce the draft or to the drawer or an indorser who paid the draft under section 3–414 or section 3–415.

- **Drawer Liability.** The drawer of a draft (other than a cashier's check) becomes liable if an ***unaccepted*** draft is dishonored. *See* section 3–414(b) (below). Dishonor is a condition to the drawer's liability. Dishonor typically occurs when the drawee refuses the drawer's order to pay. After dishonor, the drawer is obligated to pay according to the terms of the instrument. The terms at the time of issuance govern.

  The scope of drawer liability is different for an ***accepted draft***. If a bank accepts the draft, the drawer is no longer liable. *See* section 3–414(c) (below). If anyone other than a bank accepts the draft, the drawer incurs the same liability as an indorser (discussed below). *See* section 3–414(d) (below).

READING THE CODE

Maryland Commercial Law Code Section 3–414

(b) If an unaccepted draft is dishonored, the drawer is obliged to pay the draft (i) according to its terms at the time it was issued or, if not issued, at the time it first came into possession of a holder, or (ii) if the drawer signed an incomplete instrument, according to its terms when completed, to the extent stated in sections 3–115 and 3–407. The obligation is owed to a person entitled to enforce the draft or to an indorser who paid the draft under section 3–415.

(c) If a draft is accepted by a bank, the drawer is discharged, regardless of when or by whom acceptance was obtained.

(d) If a draft is accepted and the acceptor is not a bank, the obligation of the drawer to pay the draft if the draft is dishonored by the acceptor is the same as the obligation of an indorser under section 3–415(a) and (c).

- **Indorser Liability.** Any person that signs (other than as a maker, acceptor, or drawer) may incur liability as an indorser. We have seen that Article 3 treats any signature on an instrument as an indorsement unless there is unambiguous evidence of contrary intent.

  An indorser becomes liable if the instrument is dishonored. *See* section 3–415(a) (below). Dishonor is a condition to the indorser's liability. After dishonor, the indorser is obligated to pay according to the terms of the instrument. The terms at the time of indorsement govern.

  An indorser's obligation to pay extends beyond the person who is entitled to enforce. Indorser liability also runs to any subsequent indorser that pays the instrument. To limit liability, an indorser may indorse an instrument with the words "without recourse." *See* section 3–415(b) (below). In addition, indorser liability is discharged if any of the events in section 3–415(c)–(e) occur.

READING THE CODE

Maryland Commercial Law Code Section 3–415

(a) Subject to subsections (b), (c), (d), and (e) and to section 3–419(d), if an instrument is dishonored, an indorser is obliged to pay the amount due on the instrument (i) according to the terms of the instrument at the time it was indorsed, or (ii) if the indorser indorsed an incomplete instrument, according to its terms when completed, to the extent stated in sections 3–115 and 3–407. The obligation of the indorser is owed to a person entitled to enforce the instrument or to a subsequent indorser who paid the instrument under this section.

(b) If an indorsement states that it is made "without recourse" or otherwise disclaims liability of the indorser, the indorser is not liable under subsection (a) to pay the instrument.

(c) If notice of dishonor of an instrument is required by section 3–503 and notice of dishonor complying with that section is not given to an indorser, the liability of the indorser under subsection (a) is discharged.

(d) If a draft is accepted by a bank after an indorsement is made, the liability of the indorser under subsection (a) is discharged.

> **(e)** If an indorser of a check is liable under subsection (a) and the check is not presented for payment, or given to a depositary bank for collection, within 30 days after the day the indorsement was made, the liability of the indorser under subsection (a) is discharged.

Again, it is important to remember that the ultimate determination of whether a person who is liable must actually pay is subject to potential defenses. Rest assured that defenses are discussed in a subsequent chapter. At this point, our discussion of liability is solely for the purpose of identifying whom to seek enforcement against.

APPLYING THE CODE

Problem 23-6: Enforcement

David issues and delivers a negotiable promissory note payable to the order of Kevin. The note is for $1,000 payable on February 2. Kevin wants to get the money sooner so he can buy a nice birthday gift for his wife. Wayne offers Kevin $800 in cash for the note. Kevin agrees. Before handing the note to Wayne, Kevin writes "Pay to Wayne" on the top and signs his name. Is Kevin a person entitled to enforce the note? Is Wayne?

Problem 23-7: Liability of Issuers and Indorsers

A) David executes a negotiable promissory note and delivers it to Kevin. The note is payable to the order of Kevin. Kevin sells the note to Paula. Before delivering the note to Paula, Kevin signs his name on the back. Paula then sells the note to Wayne. Before handing the note to Wayne, Paula writes "pay to Wayne" and signs her name on the back. Upon presentment, David refuses to pay. Who can Wayne seek recovery against?

B) Adding to part (A), assume that Kevin is liable to Wayne as an indorser and ultimately pays on the note. Can Kevin seek recovery against Paula or David?

Problem 23-8: Limits on Indorser Liability

On March 15, David writes a check drawn on his account at First Bank and delivers it to Kevin. The check is payable to the order of Kevin. Kevin then agrees to sell the check to Paula. On April 1, Kevin signs his name on the back and writes "without recourse." Kevin delivers the check to Paula later that day. Paula then agrees to sell the check to Wayne. On May 1, Paula writes "pay to Wayne" on the back of the check and signs her name. Paula delivers the check to Wayne later that day. On May 29, Wayne deposits the check in his account at Second Bank. On June 3, Second Bank presents the check to First Bank for payment. First Bank dishonors the check. Is Kevin liable to Wayne as an indorser? Is Paula?

Problem 23-9: Drawer and Acceptor Liability

A) Kevin is in desperate need of coffee beans for his coffee shop—The Supreme Cup. Kevin identifies Paula (a local roaster) with supply on hand. Paula does not require immediate payment from Kevin. In exchange for the coffee beans, Kevin gives Paula a letter. In the letter, Kevin instructs David to pay $1,000 to Paula on demand. Kevin explains that David owes him $1,000 and is "definitely good for it." Kevin also promises that he will let David know that Paula would be coming. When Paula presents the letter, David refuses to pay. David denies owing Kevin any money. David also says that he "doesn't know a thing about this" and "hasn't heard from Kevin in months." Can Paula seek recovery against either David or Kevin?

B) Kevin wants to purchase more coffee beans from Paula. Having learned from her first experience with Kevin, Paula requests payment in the form of a certified check. Kevin goes to First Bank (where he maintains his accounts) and asks the cashier for a certified check. The cashier confirms that Kevin has sufficient funds in his account and prepares a certified check that is payable to the order of Paula. If First Bank dishonors the certified check can Paula seek recovery against Kevin? Consider section 3–409(d) when answering this question.

Test Your Knowledge

To assess your understanding of the material in this chapter, <u>click here</u> to take a quiz.

24

Holder in Due Course

Key Concepts

- How holder in due course status allows negotiable instruments to function as a cash substitute by providing greater assurance of payment
- Holders in due course take free of many of the defenses that can be raised to escape or reduce the obligation to pay on a negotiable instrument
- The requirements that must be satisfied to establish holder in due course status under Article 3

Holder in due course status (HDC status) is one of the most distinctive features of the system of negotiable instruments. Unlike a transferee or even a holder, the holder in due course enjoys favored treatment. The most significant legal consequence of this preferred status is immunity from many of the defenses that can be raised to escape or reduce the obligation to pay on the instrument. Because of this, a holder in due course enjoys significantly increased certainty in enforcement and collection.

This Chapter begins with a brief discussion of the function of the holder in due course within the system of negotiable instruments. However, the bulk of the Chapter examines the requirements that a person must satisfy to qualify as a holder in due course. The question of what claims and defenses can be asserted against a holder in due course will be more fully explored in the next Chapter.

A. The Function of the Holder in Due Course in the System of Negotiable Instruments

The fact that a holder in due course takes free of most defenses to payment is not some trivial thing. It means that a holder in due course is insulated from a host of defenses that would otherwise prevent collection. As such, the enhanced protections enjoyed by the holder in due course come at the expense of others who may be forced to pay despite having a compelling defense.

Why then does this preferred status exist? The special treatment of holders in due course reflects the central purpose of negotiable instruments—to facilitate the movement of money without the risks and impracticability of transferring large amounts of cash. Using a negotiable instrument instead of cash only accomplishes this objective if ease of transfer is coupled with assurances of collecting payment. Otherwise, a negotiable instrument is little more than a piece of paper.

HDC status functions as Article 3's mechanism for improving the ability of transferees to enforce the instrument. Those that qualify can rest assured because most defenses will not render the payment obligation uncollectable. With this preferred treatment, a holder in due course can treat a negotiable instrument as the functional equivalent of cash.

Even though HDC status prioritizes ease of transfer and certainty in collection, the law still seeks to limit potential injustices. Article 3 sets forth a number of strict requirements for HDC status. Consequently, only a subset of all transferees will qualify for preferential treatment. The full range of defenses remain available to assert against those that do not qualify as a holder in due course.

B. Requirements of Holder in Due Course Status

Article 3 defines the term "holder in due course" in section 3–302(a). To put it mildly, there is a lot going on. The bulk of the definition is split between section 3–302(a)(1) and section 3–302(a)(2). Section 3–302(a)(1) contains one requirement. Section 3–302(a)(2) enumerates six additional requirements.

READING THE CODE

Maryland Commercial Law Code Section 3–302

(a) ... "holder in due course" means the holder of an instrument if:

(1) The instrument when issued or negotiated to the holder does not bear such apparent evidence of forgery or alteration or is not otherwise so irregular or incomplete as to call into question its authenticity; and

> **(2)** The holder took the instrument (i) for value, (ii) in good faith, (iii) without notice that the instrument is overdue or has been dishonored or that there is an uncured default with respect to payment of another instrument issued as part of the same series, (iv) without notice that the instrument contains an unauthorized signature or has been altered, (v) without notice of any claim to the instrument described in section 3–306, and (vi) without notice that any party has a defense or claim in recoupment described in section 3–305(a).

Before we get to the requirements in section 3–302(a)(1)–(2), it is important to take note of the introductory language in section 3–302(a). This part of the definition incorporates two foundational requirements. Luckily, these two requirements are things that we have already explored in previous Chapters. First, a "holder in due course" must establish that the thing they possess is actually a negotiable instrument. We know from Chapter 22 that a negotiable instrument is a special type of undertaking to pay that meets all of the requirements in section 3–104. Second, a "holder in due course" must establish that they are a "holder" of the negotiable instrument. We know from Chapter 23 that only some transferees qualify as a "holder" under section 1–201(b)(21).

If both the foundational elements are met, a transferee must still satisfy each of requirements in section 3–302(a)(1) and section 3–302(a)(2) to achieve HDC status. Each of these requirements is discussed below.

C. No Evidence of Inauthenticity

A holder in due course must show that the instrument does not contain any obvious defect that would cause its authenticity to be questioned. Section 3–302(a)(1) is only concerned with defects that are apparent on the face of the instrument at the time it is issued or negotiated to the person seeking HDC status. Why do you suppose that this is the case?

Section 3–302(a)(1) reflects a straightforward policy choice. Preferred treatment should not extend to those that choose to take an instrument with an obvious problem. Stated simply, if you choose to take an instrument with an obvious problem, it's on you.

Specifically, section 3–302(a)(1) contains two tests. First, the instrument must not show any "apparent evidence of forgery or alteration." Second, even if there is no evidence of forgery or alteration, the instrument cannot be "so irregular or incomplete" that it calls into questions the instrument's authenticity. If an instrument fails to satisfy either of these tests, then HDC-status is defeated.

APPLYING THE CODE

Problem 24-1: Defects and Authenticity

A) Paula uses word processing software on her computer to prepare a draft that instructs David to pay Kevin $500. After printing the draft, Paula signed it using blue ink and delivered it to Kevin. Kevin replicated Paula's draft using his own computer and word processing software. The draft was identical to Paula's original draft except the amount of $500 was changed to $1,500. After printing the replicated draft, Kevin carefully traced Paula's signature from the original draft using blue ink. Kevin then sold the draft to Wayne for cash. Can Wayne establish that the check was obtained without any reason to question its authenticity under section 3–302(a)(1)?

B) Paula writes a check for $500 that is made out to Kevin. After receiving the check from Paula, Kevin adds the number 1 between the dollar sign and the number 5 so that the check is now in the amount of $1500. Kevin also adds the words "One Thousand" in front of the words "Five Hundred Dollars" on the line where the amount of the check is written out in words. Kevin's additions appear to be in a darker blue ink than all of the other writing on the check. The words "One Thousand" are also compressed and appear much smaller than the words "Five Hundred Dollars." Kevin persuades Wayne to purchase the check and indorses it to Wayne. Can Wayne establish that the check was obtained without any reason to question its authenticity under section 3–302(a)(1)?

C) On August 12, Paula stopped by Kevin's office and wrote him a check for $500. Paula completed the check with the exception of the memo line, which was left blank. Paula also signed the check before realizing that she had written the wrong date on the check. Due to the mistake, Paula tore the check into six pieces and threw it into the trash. Paula then wrote a new check for Kevin. After Paula left, Kevin rummaged through the trash and retrieved the pieces of the first check. Kevin then taped the pieces back together. Kevin convinced Wayne to purchase the check by explaining that he accidentally tore up the check while cleaning out his wallet. Kevin then indorsed the check to Wayne. Can Wayne establish that the check was obtained without any reason to question its authenticity under section 3–302(a)(1)?

D. Issued or Transferred for Value

A holder in due course must give value for the instrument. *See* section 3–302(a)(2)(i). The concept of "value" appears throughout the UCC. However, the Article 3 definition of value (defined in section 3–303(a)) is distinct from the general definition of value (defined in section 1–204) that applies to other Articles.

As used in Article 3, the term "value" is related to the concept of consideration. However, value is not the same as consideration. What then qualifies as value?

In many cases, the requirement of value is easily met. When an instrument is sold, there is little doubt that the buyer's payment qualifies as value. Value, however, extends beyond the payment of money. Section 3–303(a) clarifies that an instrument is issued or transferred for value in each of the three situations that follow.

Promise of Future Performance. Value is present if an instrument is issued or transferred for a promise of future performance. However, a transferee's promise of future performance only qualifies as value to the extent that the promise has been performed. *See* section 3–303(a)(1).

Here, Article 3's definition of value is much narrower than the concept of consideration. A promise of future performance alone is typically sufficient consideration to support a simple contract. In contrast, an instrument is only issued or transferred for value if performance has occurred. Therefore, a promise to perform a service in the future typically constitutes consideration. However, a promise to perform a service in the future is not value until the service is performed.

In some cases, a promise is only partially performed. If so, value exists only to the extent of the performance. As a result, transferees may still qualify as a holder in due course by meeting all of the requirements. However, they will only receive the benefit of holder in due course status for a ratable portion of the amount payable under the instrument. Section 3–302(d) provides the following formula:

(Value of Partial Performance/Value of Promised Performance) x Amount Payable under the Instrument

EXAMPLES AND EXPLANATIONS

The following example illustrates how the formula works.

Assume that Paula issues a $2,000 note to Kevin as payment for a large delivery of his locally roasted coffee beans. Kevin sells the $2,000 note to David who agrees to pay $1,000 for it in two installments of $500. After paying the first installment, David learns that Kevin has not delivered the coffee beans to Paula.

David's payment of the first installment is partial performance of his promise. David has given value. If David obtains HDC status, he can only assert rights as a holder in due course to a portion of the $2,000 due under the note. David promised to pay $1,000 but only paid $500. David has only performed 50% of what was promised (500 / 1000 = .5). As a result, David can only assert the rights of a holder in due course with respect to 50% of the amount of the note or $1,000 (.5 x 2,000 = 1,000).

As you no doubt know by now, for every general rule there is bound to be an exception or two. Here, there are two exceptions to the general rule that a promise of future performance must be performed to qualify as value. The first exception applies when a negotiable instrument is issued or transferred in exchange for another negotiable instrument. A negotiable instrument includes a promise to pay in the future (either on demand or at a specified time). Applying the general rule from section 3–303(a)(1), a negotiable instrument would only constitute value to the extent that the promise to pay has been performed. Section 3–304(a)(4) creates an exception so that a negotiable instrument is value even though no payment has been made on the instrument.

The second exception most commonly applies when a bank issues a letter of credit to a third party in exchange for a negotiable instrument. By issuing a letter of credit, a bank guarantees that the third party will receive payment. The guarantee is effectively a promise to pay in the future. Under section 3–303(a)(1), the letter of credit would only constitute value to the extent that the bank had paid. Section 3–303(a)(5) creates an exception so that any irrevocable commitment to a third party is value even though performance has not occurred. Because a bank's guarantee of payment under a letter of credit cannot be rescinded, it falls within this exception.

Security Interest or Lien. Value is present if an instrument is issued or transferred and the transferee obtains a security interest or nonjudicial lien in the instrument. *See* section 3–303(a)(2). The transferee's acquisition of either a security interest or nonjudicial lien qualifies as value.

The term "security interest" most commonly covers Article 9 security interests where an instrument is given by a debtor as collateral. However, a security interest may also arise in bank collection cases under section 4–210.

Non-judicial liens generally refer to common law liens or statutory banker's liens. Article 3 expressly excludes liens obtained by judicial process. This means that liens obtained in connection with a judgment in a lawsuit do not constitute value.

Payment of or Security for a Pre-existing Claim. Value is present if an instrument is issued or transferred as payment (or security) for a pre-existing claim against any person whether or not the claim is due. *See* section 3–303(a)(3).

The scope of section 3–303(a)(3) is relatively broad. It applies to any claim against any person. The transferee's claim can arise out of a contract or otherwise. In addition, the transferee's claim can be against the issuer, transferor of the instrument or any other person. This means that value is present even when an instrument is given in payment of (or as security for) a third person's obligation or debt.

Finally, the transferee is not required to give or promise anything new in return. The simple fact that the instrument is given to pay or secure a pre-existing claim owed to the transferee is enough to establish value. Here, Article 3's definition of "value" again diverges from the concept of consideration. Generally speaking, a benefit received in the past will not suffice as consideration for a contract. Something new must typically be given.

EXAMPLES AND EXPLANATIONS

The following scenario illustrates the distinction.

David borrows $500 from Wayne. David and Wayne do not sign a note to evidence the debt, but David promises to pay Wayne back in one year. Six months later, Wayne asks David to issue a note for the debt. David says that he will do so if Wayne agrees to extend the time for repayment. Wayne refuses to make any concessions or give anything new in return. David relents and issues the note.

Value is present because the note was issued as payment or security for Wayne's pre-existing claim against David for repayment of the $500 loan. The fact that David has one year to pay, and it has only been six months, does not matter. Under section 3–303(a), value is present even though Wayne's claim is not yet due. In addition, Wayne takes the instrument for value whether or not Wayne has given consideration for the note under contract law. Here, Wayne did not provide any new consideration for the note. Wayne did not agree to extend the time for repayment, or make any other concessions. The lack of consideration, however, does not alter the outcome. Section 3–303(a) simply does not require the existence of consideration.

APPLYING THE CODE

Problem 24-2: What Qualifies as Value?

A) Wayne is attending Paula's birthday party next week. After spending the week looking for the perfect gift, Wayne ultimately decides to write Paula a check. Wayne puts the check in a birthday card and gives it to Paula at the party. Has Paula taken the check for value?

B) Kevin is searching for someone to paint the exterior of his 1920s craftsman house. After getting several bids, Kevin decides to hire Paula because she is willing to accept payment over time. Kevin agrees to pay Paula 10% of the total cost upfront in cash and to execute a note for the remainder. Later that day, Paula stops by to pick up the cash and the note. As Paula is leaving, she tells Kevin that she will probably get started next week after she finishes work on another job. Has Paula taken the note for value?

C) On January 1, David loaned $5,000 to a friend. The debt was evidenced by a note that provided for repayment on December 31. On February 1, the furnace in David's house unexpectedly broke. In need of cash to buy a replacement, David sold the note to Wayne for $4,000. Wayne agreed to pay the $4,000 in two installments—$3,000 on February 2 and $1,000 on March 2. Wayne paid the first installment as agreed. It is now February 15. Has Wayne taken the note for value?

D) On August 1, Kevin played in a "friendly" poker game. Kevin hit a run of bad luck and ultimately lost $500 to Paula. Kevin did not have the money, so he gave Paula an I.O.U. promising to pay her by the end of the year. In November, Paula started hearing rumors that Kevin had been losing significant amounts of money in poker games around town. Justifiably concerned that Kevin would not be able to pay the $500 when due, Paula asked Kevin for collateral. Kevin pulled out a $1,000 note that had been issued to him for some recently completed legal work and said, "This is all I've got." Kevin gave Paula the note and signed a security agreement granting her a security interest in the note. Has Paula taken the note for value?

E) Assume that Kevin (from part (D)) had no assets of value when Paula asked him for collateral. To help Kevin out of a jam, Wayne issued a check for $500 to Paula on Kevin's behalf. Has Paula taken the check for value?

E. Good Faith

A holder in due course must take an instrument in good faith. Article 3 defines good faith as "honesty in fact and the observance of reasonable commercial standards of fair dealing." *See* section 1–201(b)(20). This definition includes two components—the first is subjective and the second is objective. Failing to meet either component prevents the establishment of holder in due course status.

The subjective component of good faith requires "honesty in fact." As a purely subjective standard, the conduct of persons seeking HDC status is judged by what they actually believed or knew. What a reasonable person would do under the circumstances plays no role. In fact, what any other person would do is irrelevant.

A person lacks good faith only if it can be shown that they acted with willful dishonestly in light of the facts that were actually known at the time of taking the instrument.

It has been said that the subjective standard allows conduct taken with a "pure heart and empty head." This means that subjective good faith can exist even in extremely suspicious circumstances. Consider the following scenario.

EXAMPLES AND EXPLANATIONS

Imagine that you receive an email from a stranger. The email explains that the stranger's brother has been taken hostage by a violent street gang in a foreign country. The stranger is in need of money to pay ransom and offers to sell you a note for pennies on the dollar. You believe the stranger's tale, so you agree to buy the note. The stranger asks you to meet in a secluded location to get the note. When you arrive, a shady looking character steps out from the shadows and hands you a crumpled up note. You have always been extremely trusting, so it never crosses your mind to ask any questions. You are simply happy to help out.

In this case, you have acted with "honesty in fact" in purchasing the note. You actually believed the stranger's story and never questioned it. It does not matter that another person would have inquired further or even refused to purchase the note under the same circumstances. What another person would do is irrelevant. What a reasonable person would do is also irrelevant. The subjective component of good faith is met because you were acting with a "pure heart." That is, you were not acting with willful dishonesty.

The objective component of good faith is a relatively new development. Prior to the adoption of the definition now found in section 3–103(a)(6), the presence of good faith was judged by the subjective standard alone. The addition of an objective component reflects a policy decision to curb the scope of subjective good faith. Specifically, grossly negligent or even reckless conduct taken with a "pure heart" may no longer meet the requirement of good faith.

The objective component of good faith requires compliance with "reasonable commercial standards of fair dealing." Some courts have interpreted this requirement as involving two steps. First, the conduct of the person asserting HDC status must comport with industry or commercial standards applicable to the transaction. Second, the commercial standards must be reasonably intended to achieve fair dealing.

Take for example a bank that purchases instruments as part of its business. The bank's acquisitions of instruments must be consistent with standard practices within the banking industry. As such, the bank's conduct is judged against an objective third-party standard—industry practice. So the first step in the good faith analysis is determining whether the bank has complied with prevailing commercial practices in the banking industry. But that is not the end of the inquiry. Good faith also requires a determination that those industry practices are designed to result in fair dealing. This prevents the bank in our example from using practices designed to achieve an unfair advantage and then satisfying the good faith requirement by simply saying, "But everyone else was doing the same thing!"

In sum, the requirement of good faith now requires more than just subjective good faith. That is, having a pure heart is not enough. You must also observe reasonable standards of fair dealing that are designed to result in fair dealing.

APPLYING THE CODE

Problem 24-3: Evaluating Good Faith

Kevin is an entrepreneur who has launched several start-up companies. A few years back, two investors alleged that Kevin defrauded them. The claims were ultimately settled out of court.

Kevin has been seeking investors for a new venture—a mobile app of some sort. Wayne agreed to invest in Kevin's mobile app, giving Kevin a note for $120,000. The note is payable in 12 monthly installments of $10,000.

Kevin immediately took the note to David at First Bank, whom Kevin has been working with for years. Kevin offered to sell the note to First Bank for $20,000. David was stunned when Kevin offered to sell the note at such a steep discount. Kevin explained that the cash was needed to cover some unexpected operating expenses. Kevin also mentioned that he wanted to give First Bank the first shot in light of their longstanding banking relationship. Knowing that First Bank was unlikely to get an offer like this again, David jumped on the opportunity. David did not investigate Kevin's background or inquire about the nature of Kevin's business venture before agreeing to buy the note.

368 • Learning Commercial Law: Core Concepts •

Assume that David was aware of the allegations of fraud that had been leveled against Kevin in the past. Does First Bank's conduct in acquiring the note satisfy the requirement of good faith?

Problem 24-4: Good Faith and Industry Practice

As Kevin is walking down the street, he spots Wayne's checkbook on the ground. Kevin writes a check in the amount of $12,000 that is payable to himself and forges Wayne's signature. Kevin walks into a nearby check-cashing business, Fast Cash, where David is a new employee. Kevin asks David to cash the check. In accordance with Fast Cash's policies, David inspected the check to confirm that it was complete on its face. David also requested Kevin's ID to confirm that Kevin was indeed the payee of the check. Seeing nothing suspicious, David cashed the check and charged Kevin Fast Cash's customary service fee.

Assume that most check-cashing businesses follow the same procedure as Fast Cash when cashing checks for $1,500 or less. However, large checks—those for more than $1,500—are typically subject to additional requirements. At a minimum, supervisor approval is required for large checks. A few check-cashing companies even require that a supervisor contact the drawer to confirm the legitimacy of the check. Fast Cash typically cashes small checks of less than $500 and does not have a separate policy for large checks.

Assume further that David did not have any knowledge or reason to know that Kevin forged the check. Does Fast Cash's conduct in acquiring the check satisfy the requirement of good faith? Does your answer change if Fast Cash's policy requires supervisor approval before cashing large checks and David is a supervisor?

F. No Notice of Certain Defects

A person seeking HDC status cannot have notice of any of the problems listed in section 3–302(a)(2)(iii)–(vi). The rationale for this requirement is based on justice. A person with notice of defects in the note itself or the underlying transaction should not be able to use HDC status as a shield. As a result, notice of any of the listed problems defeats HDC status.

The notice requirement involves two inquires. Did the person seeking HDC status have notice? If so, was it notice of one of the four listed problems?

As defined in the UCC, notice includes actual knowledge of a fact. *See* section 1–202(a)(1). But notice extends beyond actual knowledge. A person also has notice of a fact if they have "received a notice or notification of it." *See* section 1–202(a)(2)). A notice is received when it comes to that person's attention or it is duly delivered. *See* section 1–202(e)(2). As such, a person may receive a notice even if it is never read. In addition, a person has notice when they have reason to know that a fact exists. *See* section 1–202(a)(3). Accordingly, notice exists when a person should know of a fact based on all of the facts and circumstances.

It is important to note that whether a person seeking HDC status has notice is judged at the time of taking the instrument. This time limitation is significant. It means that a notice is effective (to defeat HDC status) only if it is "received at a time and in a manner that gives a reasonable opportunity to act on it." *See* section 3–302(f). Therefore, notices received after the fact will not defeat HDC status.

There is one last limitation. Even if receipt of notice is timely, HDC status is defeated only if it provides notice of one of the following defects:

1. The instrument has been dishonored or is overdue.

2. The instrument contains an unauthorized signature or has been altered.

3. Another person has a claim to the instrument of the type described in section 3–306.

4. A person obligated to pay the instrument has a defense or claim in recoupment of the type described in section 3–305.

Each of these four defects is examined in turn below:

Defect 1: Notice of Dishonored or Overdue Instrument

A person that takes an instrument with notice that it has been dishonored or is overdue cannot establish HDC status. The concept of dishonor should be familiar to you from Chapter 23. In general, an instrument is dishonored if it is properly presented and the person receiving present-ment refuses to pay or accept it for payment. Section 3–304 contains the rules for determining when an instrument becomes overdue. These rules are summarized in the chart below.

Type of Instrument	When Overdue
Check	Earlier of: (1) the day after demand for payment; or (2) 90 days after the check's date
Instrument Payable on Demand (other than a Check)	Earlier of: (1) the day after demand for payment; or (2) a period of time after the instrument's date which is unusually long under the circum-stances
Instrument Payable at a Definite Time (if principal is paid in install-ments)	Typically, upon nonpayment of an installment But, if the due date has been accel-erated, the day after the accelerated due date
Instrument Payable at a Definite Time (if principal not paid in install-ments)	Typically, the day after the due date But, if the due date has been accel-erated, the day after the accelerated due date

Defect 2: Notice of Unauthorized Signature or Altered Instru-ment

The focus of the second defect is clear-cut. A person cannot qualify for HDC status if they take an instrument with notice that the instrument contains an unauthorized signature or has been altered.

As a practical matter, many signatures can appear on an instrument. The original issuer of an instrument signs as the maker of a note or the drawer of draft. An instrument is also signed by indorsers as it is transferred and negotiated to new holders. An unauthorized or forged signature by any of these parties reflects a serious defect in the process.

An instrument is altered if there is any unauthorized change that purports to modify any obligation of one of the parties. An instrument is also altered if anything relating to an obligation of one of the parties is added to an incomplete agreement without authorization. Some changes to an instrument will not pose a problem. Others will raise a real question as to the legitimacy of the instrument. For example, the drawer of a check could legitimately cross out the name of the payee to correct a misspelling. In contrast, a sinister payee could cross out the due date of a note to replace it with an earlier date. Alternatively, they could add some zeros to the dollar amount, fraudulently increasing the amount payable. The key is that an alteration is both unauthorized and impacts a party's obligation.

Defect 3: Notice of a Claim to the Instrument

A holder in due course must take the instrument without notice of any person having a claim of the type described in section 3–306. *See* section 3–302(a)(2)(v). Section 3–306 will be discussed more fully in Chapter 25. For now, a general understanding of the types of claims covered is sufficient for the purposes of evaluating notice.

Section 3–306 governs what Article 3 calls claims to the instrument. A claim to the instrument exists when a third party claims to have some sort of "property or possessory right" to the instrument. State property law governs whether a third party has a claim to the instrument. The simplest examples are ownership, security interests and liens.

However, claims to the instrument also include claims that a person in rightful possession of an instrument was wrongfully deprived of it. Accordingly, section 3–306 generally covers instances where a third party asserts that an instrument should be returned to them because: (1) it is their property or (2) they have some other right to possession.

A person that takes an instrument with notice of a third-party claim to the instrument cannot establish HDC status.

Defect 4: Notice of a Defense or Claim in Recoupment

A holder in due course must take the instrument without notice of any person obligated to pay on the instrument having a defense or claim of the type described in section 3–305. *See* section 3–302(a)(2)(v). The extent and applicability of the defenses and claims in section 3–305 (like the claims to the instrument in section 3–306) are more fully explored in Chapter 25. A brief overview of section 3–305 appears below to provide some context for the analysis of whether or not notice of a defense or claim exists.

Broadly speaking, section 3–305 sets forth various affirmative defenses that could be asserted by a person obligated to pay on the instrument against a person seeking to enforce it. These defenses generally relate to an alleged defect in: (1) the way that the person became obligated to pay on the instrument; (2) the underlying contract that gave rise to the instrument; or (3) the issuance of the instrument. In each case, the defense is asserted in order to escape liability on the obligation to pay.

Section 3–305 also identifies a particular group of claims—what Article 3 calls claims in recoupment. A claim in recoupment is basically a claim of offset. A claim in recoupment does not eliminate the obligation to pay. Instead, a claim in recoupment may allow for a reduction in the amount payable on the instrument.

A person that takes an instrument with notice of a defense against payment (or a claim in recoupment that may reduce the obligation to pay) cannot qualify as a holder in due course.

Try the following problems to practice identifying potential defects that may prevent establishment of HDC status.

APPLYING THE CODE

Problem 24-5: Notice of Dishonor or Overdue Payment

David issued a note to Paula promising to pay $10,000 on September 22. On September 22, Paula tried to find David to collect but learned that David had skipped town. Three days later, Paula negotiated the note to Wayne for cash. Wayne did not ask any questions about the note. Paula did not volunteer any information and was just happy to have sold the note. Can Wayne qualify as a holder in due course of the note?

Problem 24-6: Claims of Ownership

Wayne is the owner of a small business that manufactures and sells bow ties. Wayne's business is not set up for e-commerce yet, so customers must mail in a paper order form that is available on Wayne's website. Kevin filled out an order form for 5 bow ties at a price of $50 per bow tie. On April 1, Kevin mailed the completed order form back with a $250 check payable to Wayne.

Wayne received Kevin's order and check in the mail on April 10. On May 15, Wayne indorsed the check by signing his name on the back. Wayne put the check back in the envelope with Kevin's order form and went to the bank to deposit the check. Unfortunately, Wayne lost the envelope on the way. David happened to be walking by a few minutes later and spotted the envelope on the ground. David picked it up. Upon opening the envelope, David found Kevin's order form and the check.

Assume that Wayne would have a claim to the instrument under section 3–306. Can David qualify as a holder in due course of the check?

Problem 24-7: Notice of Defenses

Paula's car has been giving her endless problems since she purchased it from the prior owner. After the car failed to start (for what seemed like the millionth time), Paula asked a mechanic to conduct a thorough inspection. The mechanic informed Paula that someone turned the odometer back. The odometer reads 20,000 miles instead of 100,000 miles. As a result, many of the car's parts were worn out and in desperate need of replacement.

Instead of replacing the parts, Paula contracted to sell the car to Kevin. Paula did not disclose any of the information that she learned from the mechanic. In fact, Paula represented that the odometer reading was accurate. Kevin issued a note to Paula for the agreed-upon purchase price of $10,000.

Assume that Paula's misrepresentation about the accuracy of the odometer reading would provide Kevin with a defense to payment under section 3–305.

A)   After selling the car, Paula offers to sell the note to her friend Wayne for $8,500 in cash (which reflects a typical discount for the risk and delay in payment). Wayne had nothing to do with Paula's misrepresentations to Kevin. Can Wayne qualify as a holder in due course? Does your answer change if Paula offers to sell the note to her friend Wayne for $1,000 in cash?

B)   Assume that Wayne has been with Paula on several occasions when the car has broken down. Can Wayne qualify as a holder in due course? Does your answer change if Paula also complained to Wayne of being scammed after the mechanic informed her of the odometer issue?

Problem 24-8: Notice of Defect and Holder in Due Course Status

A)   Kevin is working as a summer intern in the legal department of a small start-up technology company. Kevin received his first paycheck on June 1. Kevin misplaced the check, but found it a couple months later when he was cleaning out his office. On September 15, Kevin negotiates the check to Wayne as payment for an outstanding debt. Can Wayne qualify for HDC status?

B)   Kevin is fired after a dispute with his boss. Kevin decides to get his revenge by forging a promissory note in the amount of $25,000. Kevin uses a promissory note that he helped to draft earlier in the summer as a template. Kevin inserts his name as the payee. With one exception, the promissory note is identical to the other notes that the start-up has previously issued. David, the CFO, is the only person authorized to sign the notes on behalf the start-up. David typically signs his name using blue ink. Kevin's forged note contains an electronic copy of David's signature printed in black ink.

Kevin takes the note to his local bank branch and sells the note for cash. Assume that Kevin is a regular customer of the bank. Kevin deposits his paycheck (about $800) every two weeks. As a result, Kevin has often talked to the bankers about his internship and how much he has enjoyed the work. Can the bank qualify for HDC status?

G. Summary of Requirements for HDC Status

In conclusion, the requirements of HDC status can be summarized as follows:

1. The person seeking HDC status must be a holder of an instrument.

2. The face of the instrument must not have any apparent evidence of forgery or alteration or be so irregular or incomplete that its legitimacy is called into question.

3. The person seeking HDC status must take the instrument for value.

4. The person seeking HDC status must have acted in good faith in taking the instrument.

5. The person seeking HDC status must take the instrument without notice of any of the following problems:

   a. The instrument has been dishonored or is overdue.

   b. The instrument has been altered or contains an unauthorized signature.

   c. A third party has a claim to the instrument.

   d. A person obligated to pay on the instrument has a defense to payment or a claim in recoupment.

Test Your Knowledge

To assess your understanding of the material in this chapter, click here to take a quiz.

25

The Legal Effect of Holder
in Due Course Status

Key Concepts

- The different types of defenses and claims that can be asserted to avoid or reduce liability for payment on an instrument
- A holder in due course takes subject to the real defenses in Article 3
- A holder in due course takes free from the personal defenses in Article 3, claims in recoupment and claims to the instrument
- A discharge of the obligation to pay an instrument is not effective against a holder in due course who acquires the instrument without notice of the discharge
- The role of the Shelter Rule in protecting transferees that do not qualify as holders in due course

The preferred status of a holder in due course has been mentioned on occasion in prior Chapters. To this point, we have simply said that a holder in due course takes an instrument free from the most significant defenses to payment. The time has now come to explore more fully the legal rights of a holder in due course.

This Chapter starts with an overview of the various types of defenses and claims that could be asserted by a person obligated to pay an instrument. The remainder of the Chapter deals primarily with the availability of those defenses and claims against a holder in due course as compared to a holder without that preferred status.

A. Types of Defenses and Claims

As we saw in Chapter 23, a person entitled to enforce can collect payment from any number of parties who have signed the instrument. By signing the instrument, a person may incur liability as a maker, drawee, drawer or indorser. *See* sections 3–412 through 3–415. But persons obligated to pay an instrument may still try to avoid or reduce their liability by asserting a valid defense or claim. Article 3 recognizes the following categories of defenses and claims—real defenses, personal defenses, claims in recoupment, claims to the instrument and discharges.

B. Real Defenses

READING THE CODE

> ### Maryland Commercial Law Code Section 3–305
>
> **(a)** Except as stated in subsection (b), the right to enforce the obligation of a party to pay an instrument is subject to the following:
>
>   **(1)** A defense of the obligor based on
>
>   **(i)** infancy of the obligor to the extent it is a defense to a simple contract,
>
>   **(ii)** duress, lack of legal capacity, or illegality of the transaction which, under other law, nullifies the obligation of the obligor,
>
>   **(iii)** fraud that induced the obligor to sign the instrument with neither knowledge nor reasonable opportunity to learn of its character or its essential terms, or
>
>   **(iv)** discharge of the obligor in insolvency proceedings . . .

A person obligated to pay an instrument may assert one of the defenses listed in section 3–305(a)(1). These defenses are commonly referred to as "real defenses." The real defenses only arise in specific circumstances, which are outlined below.

1. Infancy (Section 3–305(a)(1)(i))

Minors may be able to avoid payment on the grounds that they lack the legal capacity to enter into a contract. Article 3 makes it clear that the defense of infancy is only available "to the extent that it is a defense to a simple contract." As a result, the availability of the defense depends entirely on the law of the applicable jurisdiction. If a particular state allows minors to defend against contractual liability because they are under the age of majority, the minors may assert the same defense against any obligation to pay on an instrument. Because the defense is jurisdiction specific, the exact scope of the defense and conditions under which the defense is available will vary from state to state.

2. Duress, Incapacity or Illegality (Section 3–305(a)(1)(ii))

A person obligated to pay may assert a defense based on: (1) duress; (2) lack of legal capacity or (3) illegality of the transaction. Each of the defenses is evaluated under the law of the applicable jurisdiction. As a result, the requirements of each defense will inevitably differ from state to state. Even so, the core concepts should be familiar.

- *Duress.* Generally, duress involves an unlawful threat that induces the person threatened into an action that they would not otherwise have taken. That is, the person threatened would not have taken the action in the absence of the threat. This most commonly comes from threats of physical violence and economic harm. It is important to also note that the threat need not be limited to a direct threat against the person coerced into acting. Duress can also occur when the threat is made against another person (for example, a loved one or relative).

  In the context of Article 3, duress might be raised as a defense to payment if the obligor's liability on an instrument was incurred because of an unlawful threat. For example, when a threat induces the obligor's agreement to issue or negotiate an instrument.

- *Incapacity.* Incapacity covers situations where a person lacks legal capacity for any reason other than infancy (which is covered by section 3–305(a)(1)(i)). This includes incapacity that stems from "mental incompetence, guardianship, ultra vires acts or lack of corporate capacity to do business." *See* Official Comment 1, section 3–305.

  Accordingly, the obligor on an instrument may have a defense based on incapacity or fitness if the obligor lacks the mental competency or fitness to sign the instrument. In addition, a corporate obligor may have a defense if the issuance or negotiation of an instrument extends beyond the powers listed in its charter or articles of incorporation.

- *Illegality.* The defense of illegality is generally limited to situations where an instrument is issued or negotiated in connection with a transaction that violates a statute. In these cases, the illegality of the underlying transaction may provide the basis for a defense against payment.

The official comments note that the defense of illegality comes up most frequently in connection with gambling or usury. Think of a note issued to pay off an illegal gambling debt. Or a check issued to repay a loan with an illegally high interest rate. However, the defense may arise under a variety of other state statutes.

At first glance, these defenses may appear extremely broad. Article 3, however, requires more than just the existence of duress, incapacity or illegality. Not all instances of duress, incapacity or illegality will rise to the level of a real defense. Real defenses are limited to situations where "other law nullifies the obligation of the obligor." This means that a statute or common law must actually void the instrument due to the alleged duress, incapacity or illegality. If applicable state law merely makes the obligation to pay voidable, it falls outside the scope of the real defenses. An in-depth analysis of each instance where state law voids an instrument due to a real defense is far beyond the scope of this course. The general principal, however, is relatively straightforward. Even so, the drafters of the UCC provide a useful example.

The Official Comments to section 3–305 note that whether an obligation is void or voidable due to duress is a matter of degree. An instrument signed at gunpoint is void. But an instrument signed under threat of prosecuting a relative may only be voidable. The same is generally true with respect to instruments signed under the wrongful threat to breach a contract—i.e., economic duress. Therefore, the first example can be the grounds for a real defense. The second and third examples cannot.

3. Fraud in Factum (Section 3–305(a)(1)(iii))

A person obligated to pay may attempt to defend on the grounds of fraudulent inducement. However, the real defense is extremely limited. The obligor must be induced by fraud to sign the instrument without knowledge or the opportunity to learn of the instrument's character or its essential terms.

Section 3–305(a)(1)(iii) applies when the fraud is designed to mislead the obligor in one of two ways. First, when the obligor is tricked into signing without knowing that the thing they are signing is an instrument. Second, when the obligor is defrauded into signing without knowing the instrument's terms.

In itself, the obligor's ignorance of these facts is not sufficient to satisfy the requirements of section 3–305(a)(1)(iii). The obligor must also have had no reasonable opportunity to learn that they are signing an instrument or the essential terms of the instrument. Because of this, an obligor's reckless or negligent behavior in signing an instrument will not be excused.

To determine whether there is a reasonable opportunity to obtain knowledge, Article 3 instructs us to take all relevant factors into account. *See* section 3–305, Official Comment 1. Relevant factors include:

- The obligor's intelligence, education, business experience, and ability to read or understand English;

- The nature of any representations made to the obligor and whether the obligor had good reason to rely on the representations;

- The possibility of obtaining independent information; and

- The need for acting without delay

4. Discharge in Insolvency Proceeding (Section 3–305(a)(1)(iv))

A person obligated to pay may assert a defense if the instrument has been discharged in an insolvency proceeding. The term insolvency proceeding most commonly refers to bankruptcy. But the definition is broad enough to include any proceeding intended to liquidate or rehabilitate the estate of the person involved. *See* section 1–201(b)(22).

Under federal bankruptcy laws, a debtor may have certain types of debts discharged. When a debt is discharged, the debtor is released from personal liability. Attempts to enforce that liability are barred because the debtor is no longer legally obligated to pay. This is intended to allow the debtor to start fresh.

Section 3–305(a)(1)(iv) simply incorporates this concept into the system of negotiable instruments. If the debt represented by an instrument is discharged in bankruptcy (or another insolvency proceeding), the obligor can raise it as a defense against the person seeking to collect payment.

C. Personal Defenses

READING THE CODE

> **Maryland Commercial Law Code Section 3–305**
>
> **(a)** Except as stated in subsection (b), the right to enforce the obligation of a party to pay an instrument is subject to the following: . . .
>
> > **(2)** A defense of the obligor stated in another section of this title or a defense of the obligor that would be available if the person entitled to enforce the instrument were enforcing a right to payment under a simple contract . . .

The defenses in section 3–305(a)(2) are commonly referred to as the "personal defenses." The personal defenses fall into two broad categories—defenses specifically stated in Article 3 and defenses based on common law contract principles.

1. **Article 3 Defenses:** A number of defenses are sprinkled throughout the provisions of Article 3. Any defense stated in Article 3 falls under the umbrella of section 3–305(a)(2). The most common of these defenses relate to the issuance of the instrument.

   For example, section 3–105(b) provides the drawer or maker with a defense if the instrument was never issued. Recall that issuance is the first delivery of an instrument for the purpose of giving rights to any person. Accordingly, nonissuance may be a defense where the instrument was never delivered—for example if the instrument was lost or stolen before delivery by a would be issuer. Nonissuance may also be a defense where the instrument is delivered but for a reason other than to give rights in it.

   Section 3–105(b) also provides the drawer or maker with a defense if: (1) the instrument is conditionally issued and the condition fails; or (2) the instrument is issued for a special purpose and the special purpose is not fulfilled.

   Section 3–303(b) is another example of a defense specifically stated in Article 3. Section 3–303(b) provides the drawer or maker with a defense if "the instrument is issued without consideration." Similarly, the issuer has a defense if the instrument is issued for a promise of performance and the promise has not been performed when due.

The defenses in section 3–105(b) and section 3–303(b) are illustrative. Other sections of Article 3 specify defenses that may apply in other situations.[1] However, a detailed exploration of the nuances of each of these defenses is beyond the scope of this book. Instead, the focus should be on understanding that the personal defenses in section 3–305(a)(2) encompass each and every defense specified in another provision of Article 3.

2. **Common Law Contract Defenses:** Exploring all of the possible common law contract defenses is well beyond the scope of core commercial law concepts covered by this book. For our purposes, it suffices to say that the personal defenses include "any defense of the obligor that would be available if the person entitled to enforce the instrument were enforcing a right to payment under a simple contract." Stated plainly, the personal defenses encompass any common law contract defense. The Official Comments note that the most prevalent of these defenses are fraud, misrepresentation, or mistake in the issuance of the instrument. But other familiar contract defenses include: (1) lack of or failure of consideration, (2) non-occurrence of a condition precedent, and (3) unconscionability.

D. Claims in Recoupment

READING THE CODE

Maryland Commercial Law Code Section 3–305

(a) Except as stated in subsection (b), the right to enforce the obligation of a party to pay an instrument is subject to the following: . . .

(3) A claim in recoupment of the obligor against the original payee of the instrument if the claim arose from the transaction that gave rise to the instrument; but the claim

---

1   In addition to the defenses in section 3–105(b) and section 3–303(b), Article 3 defenses can be found in section 3–106(c) (failure to countersign a traveler's check); section 3–117 (modification by a separate agreement); section 3–206(f) (payment in violation of a restrictive indorsement); and section 3–417(b) (breach of warranty when a draft is accepted).

> of the obligor may be asserted against a transferee of the instrument only to reduce the amount owing on the instrument at the time the action is brought.

Claims in recoupment were introduced briefly in Chapter 24. At that time, it was explained that a claim in recoupment is essentially a claim of offset. More specifically, a claim in recoupment is Article 3 terminology for a legally recognized claim that the obligor has against the original payee of the instrument. The obligor essentially argues that the amount owed under the instrument should be reduced by the amount of the offsetting claim against the original payee.

Section 3–305(a)(3) does not apply to every claim that an obligor may have against the original payee. The claim must arise from the **same transaction** that gave rise to the instrument. As a result, a claim of the obligor that is wholly unrelated to the instrument falls outside of section 3–305(a)(3).

EXAMPLES AND EXPLANATIONS

The following examples illustrate the "same transaction" requirement in section 3–305(a)(3).

Example 1: Assume that David issues an $8,000 note to Wayne for the purchase of a new jet ski. Shortly thereafter, David learns that the engine is defective and spends $1,000 on repairs.

David (the obligor on the note) may have a breach of warranty claim against Wayne (the original payee). The breach of warranty also arises from the same transaction as the note. This is a classic claim in recoupment.

Example 2: Assume that David also purchased a Winnebago from Wayne 3 months prior to buying the jet ski. Wayne negligently caused damage to David's property when delivering the Winnebago. In addition, the Winnebago's brakes were recently found to be defective.

On these facts, David may have a negligence claim and another breach of warranty claim against Wayne. But neither claim could be asserted by David to reduce the amount owed on the $8,000 note issued for the jet ski. Both are claims of the obligor (David) against the original payee of the note (Wayne). Unfortunately, the claims are unrelated to the jet ski purchase, which is the transaction that gave rise to the note. These are not claims of recoupment of the type described in section 3–305(a)(3).

By now, it should be clear that the basis of a claim in recoupment is a claim that the obligor has against the original payee. But the true function of section 3–305(a)(3) is to let the obligor assert claims in recoupment against subsequent holders of the instrument. A claim in recoupment can only be asserted against a subsequent holder "to reduce the amount owing on the instrument at the time the action is brought." This means that the obligor can never recover any money from a subsequent holder based on a claim in recoupment. This is true even if the amount of the claim exceeds the amount owed on the instrument. The obligor can only reduce what they owe on the instrument to zero and seek the remainder from the original payee. Consider the following example:

EXAMPLES AND EXPLANATIONS

Kevin issues a note to Paula as payment for a car. Paula immediately transfers the note to Wayne. The note is payable in 12 monthly installments of $1,000. Kevin has paid Wayne a total of $8,000 on the note (8 monthly installments) when he learns that the car's electrical systems are defective. Kevin pays a mechanic $5,000 to fix the problem. Assume that the defect gives Kevin a breach of warranty claim against Paula.

Kevin's claim of $5,000 exceeds the $4,000 remaining on the note by $1,000. Kevin is only entitled to an offset on the amounts then owing on the note. If Wayne tries to enforce the note, Kevin can assert the claim in recoupment (breach of warranty) to avoid the obligation to pay the remaining $4,000. Kevin, however, has no affirmative right of recovery against Wayne. Kevin cannot recover any of the amounts previously paid to Wayne. Kevin would have to sue Paula to recover the remaining $1,000 for breach of warranty.

E. Claims to the Instrument

READING THE CODE

Maryland Commercial Law Code Section 3–306

A person taking an instrument, other than a person having rights of a holder in due course, is subject to a claim of a property or possessory right in the instrument or its proceeds, including a claim to rescind a negotiation and to recover the instrument or its proceeds. A person having rights of a holder in due course takes free of the claim to the instrument.

Claims to the instrument were also introduced briefly in Chapter 24. You should recall that the term generally refers to a third-party claim of a property or possessory right in the instrument. *See* section 3–302. This basically boils down to a claim that another person's right to possess the instrument trumps that of the person who currently has physical possession of the instrument. It is essentially a claim to recover the instrument or its proceeds.

The claims covered by section 3–306 typically arise when a prior holder of the instrument asserts that they were wrongfully deprived of possession. This includes claims of ownership and other rights to possession (such as security interests and liens). For example, the legal owner of an instrument may claim ownership of a lost or stolen instrument. Similarly, a secured party may claim the right to possess a lost or stolen instrument that serves as collateral for a debt.

Section 3–306 also covers claims to rescind the negotiation of an instrument based on other state law. This type of claim arises when a prior holder voluntarily negotiates the instrument to another person, but later claims the right to rescind the negotiation and recover the instrument. The grounds for rescission may differ from state to state, but generally include infancy, exceeding corporate powers, incapacity, fraud, duress, mistake, breach of duty, or illegality. *See* section 3–302.

Claims to the instrument are personal. To assert one as a defense to payment, the obligor on an instrument must personally have a claim to the instrument. Alternatively, the obligor may use another person's claim to the instrument as a defense if the other person is: (1) joined in the action and (2) personally asserts the claim against the person entitled to enforce. *See* section 3–305(c).

F. Discharge of Obligation to Pay

An obligor may defend on the grounds that he or she has been discharged either fully or partially from the obligation to pay. Like a discharge in bankruptcy (discussed above), Article 3 recognizes that an obligor may have been released from personal liability for a number of other reasons. Discharge under Article 3 is governed by sections 3–601, 3–602, 3–603, 3–604 and 3–605. The most common grounds for discharge under Article 3 are if: (1) payment is made on the instrument, or (2) the person entitled to enforce agrees to release liability.

1. Discharge by Payment

Payment is a ground for discharge under Article 3. *See* section 3–602(a). This merely reflects common sense. If an instrument is paid, there is no longer an obligation to pay it. Under section 3–602(a), an instrument is discharged to the extent that a payment is made. So partial payment discharges liability for the amount paid.

The only requirements are that payment must be made "by or on behalf of the person obligated to pay the instrument, and to a person entitled to enforce the instrument." *See* section 3–602(a). Note that there is no requirement that the obligor ascertain the rightful owner of an instrument. The obligor is generally discharged so long as payment is made to a person that qualifies as a person entitled to enforce.

Recall that: 1) a person entitled to enforce must have possession of the instrument and 2) the instrument must indicate that the person in possession has the right to payment. This means that in some cases, payment to a thief can discharge the obligation to pay. Accordingly, a thief that steals bearer paper is a person entitled to enforce.

In fact, payment discharges the obligor even if the obligor knows that the rights of the person entitled to enforce are being contested. *See* section 3–602(c). The fact that a third party is asserting a claim to the instrument is of no consequence. Subject to very limited exceptions, the obligor is discharged by paying the person entitled to enforce. You are probably wondering, what are these exceptions? Here is one just to give you an idea—an obligor is not discharged if the third party obtains an injunction against payment and payment is made with knowledge of the injunction.

In limited circumstances, payment to a person that formerly was entitled to enforce an instrument will even discharge the obligation to pay. *See* section 3–602(b). Discharges of this type are limited in two ways. First, the obligor must not have received adequate notice of the transfer. Second, the instrument must be a note.

2. Discharge by Agreement

A person entitled to enforce can also agree to discharge the obligation to pay an instrument. This is reflected in different ways under section 3–601 and section 3–604.

Under section 3–601(a), liability can be discharged by an act or agreement with the person obligated to pay, which would discharge the obligation to pay money under a simple contract. Stated more simply, a person entitled to enforce can agree to discharge liability via a contract supported by consideration.

The requirement of consideration generally excludes an agreement to discharge liability for less than full payment unless the obligor gives something new. For example, the person entitled to enforce might accept less than full payment before the due date. Alternatively, the person entitled to enforce could accept something other than money—like goods or services—in satisfaction of the obligation to pay.

Under section 3–604, liability can be discharged with or without new consideration. This is accomplished by cancellation or renunciation of the instrument.

A person entitled to enforce cancels an instrument by taking an intentional voluntary act indicating discharge. All of the following qualify as such an act: (1) surrendering the instrument to the person obligated to pay; (2) destroying the instrument; (3) striking out the signature of the person obligated to pay; and (4) adding words to the instrument indicating discharge—for example "discharged" or "released" or "void" or the amount of a partial payment.

Renunciation requires a signed record. The person entitled to enforce must renounce his or her rights in the signed record. For example, a person entitled to enforce could renounce by writing, "I agree not to sue Obligor on the note dated September 22, 2009" or "I discharge Obligor from liability on the note dated April 1, 2003."

G. Rights of a Holder in Due Course

The legal effect of holder in due course status is significant. As discussed above, defenses to payment are plentiful under Article 3 and other state law. However, a holder in due course is not subject to most of these defenses. With fewer barriers to payment, a holder in due course can enforce an instrument with much greater certainty.

Consider the following excerpt from the section 3–305. This is the same provision that we just examined relating to real defenses, personal defenses and claims in recoupment. Can you determine whether real defenses can be asserted against someone with holder in due course status? What about personal defenses? Claims in recoupment? Discharges?

READING THE CODE

Maryland Commercial Law Code Section 3–305

(a) Except as stated in subsection (b), the right to enforce the obligation of a party to pay an instrument is subject to the following:

    (1) A defense of the obligor based on (i) infancy of the obligor to the extent it is a defense to a simple contract, (ii) duress, lack of legal capacity, or illegality of the transaction which, under other law, nullifies the obligation of the obligor, (iii) fraud that induced the obligor to sign the instrument with neither knowledge nor reasonable opportunity to learn of its character or its essential terms, or (iv) discharge of the obligor in insolvency proceedings;

    (2) A defense of the obligor stated in another section of this title or a defense of the obligor that would be available if the person entitled to enforce the instrument were enforcing a right to payment under a simple contract; and

    (3) A claim in recoupment of the obligor against the original payee of the instrument if the claim arose from the transaction that gave rise to the instrument; but the claim of the obligor may be asserted against a transferee of the instrument only to reduce the amount owing on the instrument at the time the action is brought.

(b) The right of a holder in due course to enforce the obligation of a party to pay the instrument is subject to defenses of the obligor stated in subsection (a)(1), but is not subject to defenses of the obligor stated in subsection (a)(2) or claims in recoupment stated in subsection (a)(3) against a person other than the holder.

After analyzing the excerpt from section 3–305 above, it should be clear that the action is in section 3–305(b). Section 3–305(a) establishes the real defenses, personal defenses and claims in recoupment, but section 3–305(b) governs the extent to which they can be asserted against a holder in due course. In short, a holder in due course takes subject to real defenses, but free of personal defenses and claims in recoupment.

The rationale is relatively simple. The real defenses protect such significant interests that they can always be asserted. Accordingly, the right of a holder in due course to enforce the obligation to pay is always subject to the real defenses in section 3–305(a)(1). *See* section 3–305(b). Consider the defense of infancy as an example. There is little reason to enforce an instrument against a minor without the legal capacity to contract. Similarly, no legitimate purpose is served by enforcing an instrument that arises from duress, incapacity, illegality or fraud. The interests protected by the real defenses are so important that they trump any need for transferability and certainty of payment in the system of negotiable instruments.

In contrast, the ability to assert a defense or claim (other than a real defense) is largely cut off by achieving HDC status. A holder in due course is not subject to a personal defense or a claim in recoupment that the obligor has against another person. *See* section 3–305(b). The practical impact is substantial. Article 3 defenses, contract defenses and claims in recoupment against prior holders of the instrument will not prevent a holder in due course that currently possess the instrument from enforcing it. Section 3–305(b) insulates the holder in due course.

Now let's turn to section 3–306 and claims to the instrument. A person having the rights of a holder in due course also takes free of any claims to the instrument. This is because section 3–306 specifically excludes holders in due course. Recall that section 3–306 states that, "a person taking an instrument, *other than a person having rights of a holder in due course*, is subject to a claim of a property or possessory right in the instrument or its proceeds." Thus, third party attempts to recover the instrument based on a claim of ownership or rightful possession cannot be asserted against a holder in due course.

Finally, discharge of the obligation to pay is not effective against a holder in due course who acquires the instrument without notice of the discharge. *See* section 3–601(b). This may seem counterintuitive. If a discharge is a release from liability, why then does a person that has been discharged from the obligation to pay an instrument remain liable for payment to a holder in due course who acquires the instrument without notice of the discharge? Here, Article 3 prioritizes the right of a holder in due course to collect payment. Article 3 places the onus on those who have been discharged. They are incentivized to ensure that notice is provided—for example by taking possession of the instrument, destroying the instrument or requiring that the discharge be reflected on the instrument. Any person (including a holder in due course) with such notice should not acquire the instrument and expect payment. The discharged party, however, is in the best position to ensure that this occurs. So as between the discharged party and a holder in due course, it is the discharged party who more appropriately bears responsibility when there is no notice of discharge.

It should now be abundantly clear that holders in due course enjoy significant benefits under Article 3. Holders in due course basically take subject only to the real defenses. Because the most common defenses to payment are eliminated, holders in due course can be relatively certain of collecting payment. This is consistent with the purpose of the system of negotiable instruments—promoting the use of instruments as a substitute for cash and a mechanism for efficiently moving money.

APPLYING THE CODE

Problem 25-1: Fraud and the Holder in Due Course

A) Kevin spent the last year building a prototype for a new kitchen gadget and is now ready to make it available to the public. Kevin contracts with Wayne to manufacture the kitchen gadget. Wayne assured Kevin that he was capable of manufacturing the gadget and that he had years of experience. Wayne also provided Kevin with positive reviews from entrepreneurs that he worked with previously and data showing that less than .01% of the products he manufactured failed to meet quality standards. Kevin issued a note to Wayne as payment. After issuing the note, Kevin learned that Wayne's manufacturing facility was incapable of producing the volume needed. In addition, Wayne had falsified the reviews and data. Does Kevin have a defense if Wayne seeks to enforce the note when due? Does your answer change if Wayne negotiates the note to a bank that qualifies as a holder in due course and the bank tries to enforce the note?

B) David has been employed by Paula as a personal assistant for the last 5 years. David often drafts letters for Paula to sign as part of the job. Recently, David handed Paula a stack of letters and asked her to sign at the bottom. When Paula took the letters, David said: "It's nothing important. Mostly marketing letters. Just the usual." Paula quickly signed each of the letters as requested. Unbeknownst to Paula, one of the "letters" was actually a note payable to David. Does Paula have a defense if David tries to enforce the note? Does your answer change if David negotiates the note to a bank that qualifies as a holder in due course and the bank tries to enforce the note?

Problem 25-2: Theft and the Holder in Due Course

A) Paula has been negotiating with Kevin to purchase a piece of land that he owns in the mountains. In anticipation of finalizing the deal, Paula prepared and signed a note payable to Kevin in the amount of $20,000 (the agreed-upon purchase price). The note was on Paula's desk when Kevin came over to discuss the few remaining issues. Paula and Kevin got into a heated exchange. Paula told Kevin that the deal was off. Before leaving the room to take a quick phone call, Paula put the note into an envelope and placed it in a desk drawer. While Paula was out of the room, Kevin took the note. After leaving, Kevin sells the note to a bank for cash. Assume that the bank has no reason to know of Kevin's theft and qualifies as a holder in due course. Can Paula assert any defenses if the Bank seeks to enforce the note?

B) Paula issues a $500 check to Kevin as payment for a new bike. Kevin signs the back of the check and places it in his wallet. On the way to the bank, Wayne mugs Kevin. Wayne negotiates the check to David to satisfy an outstanding debt. Assume that David has no reason to know of Wayne's theft and qualifies as a holder in due course. Can Kevin recover the check from David?

Problem 25-3: Failure of Consideration

Kevin owns a start-up that has designed a new video game console. David owns a company that sells eco-friendly commercial-grade batteries that Kevin would like to use as a component in his video game console. David agrees to sell Kevin 10 cases of batteries for $8,000 with delivery by September 22. Kevin issues a note payable to David in the amount of $8,000. The note is due one month later on October 22. Assume that David never delivers the batteries. If David attempts to enforce the note, does Kevin have a defense to payment? Does your answer change if David negotiates the note to a bank that qualifies as a holder in due course and the bank tries to enforce the note?

Problem 25-4: Defenses and the Holder in Due Course

The same facts as Problem 25-3 above. But assume that David actually delivers the batteries on September 22 as agreed. After accepting delivery of the batteries, Wayne discovers that half of the batteries are defective.

Wayne is forced to purchase replacements from another seller at a cost of $5,000. Assume that the defective batteries failed to meet the specifications of the contract and that this would be a breach of warranty.

A)   If David attempts to enforce the note, does Kevin have a defense to payment? Does your answer change if David negotiates the note to a bank that qualifies as a holder in due course and the bank tries to enforce the note?

B)   Assume that Kevin had already paid the $8,000 note. Could Kevin recover any of the money paid to David?

C)   Assume that Kevin entered into a second contract with David. Kevin issued another note for $8,000. David delivered the batteries under the second contract on time and there were no defects. Could Kevin raise the defective batteries from the first contract as a defense against David's attempts to enforce the second note? Assume that David also damaged Kevin's loading dock when delivering the defective batteries under the first contract. Could Kevin raise the property damage from the delivery as a defense against David's attempt to enforce the second note?

H. Rights of a Person Entitled to Enforce Without HDC Status

Those without HDC status take the instrument subject to all of the defenses and claims described above. Thus, a person obligated to pay on the instrument can assert any real defense, personal defense, claim in recoupment, claim to the instrument and discharge against a person seeking to enforce that does not have HDC status.

Without HDC status, there are simply more ways for the obligor to avoid or reduce the obligation to pay. Compared to the rights of an HDC, the biggest difference is exposure to defenses that could be asserted against a prior holder. As a result, a person without HDC status is less certain of enforcing the note and collecting payment.

This does not mean that a person without HDC status will never collect on the instrument. In many cases, payment is made without incident following demand. Even if a viable defense exists, Article 3 provides protection under what is called the "Shelter Rule." The Shelter Rule appears in section 3–203(b), which deals with the transfer of instruments.

READING THE CODE

Maryland Commercial Law Code Section 3–203

(b) Transfer of an instrument, whether or not the transfer is a negotiation, vests in the transferee any right of the transferor to enforce the instrument, including any right as a holder in due course, but the transferee cannot acquire rights of a holder in due course by a transfer, directly or indirectly, from a holder in due course if the transferee engaged in fraud or illegality affecting the instrument.

Section 3–203(b) clarifies that a transfer vests in the transferee "any right of the transferor to enforce the instrument, including any rights as a holder in due course." *See* section 3–203(b). The transferee effectively steps into the shoes of the transferor.

To be clear, the transferee is not a holder in due course. To be a holder in due course, the transferee must directly satisfy all of the applicable requirements. Section 3–203(b) allows a person who fails to obtain holder in due course status to assert the rights of the transferor who is an HDC. This may seem like a fine distinction. But it has practical ramifications.

Under section 3–203(b), the rights of a transferee are derived from the transferor. If the transferor is a holder in due course, the transferee obtains all the transferor's rights, including immunity from most defenses to payment. But the transferee is also subject to any defenses that could be asserted against the transferor. Do you see how this is different than actually having HDC status? If the transferee qualified directly as a holder in due course, they would only take subject to real defenses. All other defenses and claims against the transferor would be cut off. But if the transferee gets their rights via the Shelter Rule, they take subject to any defenses and claims that could be asserted against the transferor.

There is one final point worth mentioning. The Shelter Rule does not apply "if the transferee engaged in fraud or illegality affecting the instrument." If the transferee engages in this type of misconduct, the transferee will not obtain the rights of a holder in due course upon transfer from a holder in due course.

APPLYING THE CODE

Problem 25-5: Right to Enforce Without HDC Status

Kevin is a fashion designer who is in the process of creating his new spring collection. Kevin agrees to purchase 30 bolts of fabric from Paula. Kevin issues a note for the purchase price. Later that day, Paula gives the note to Wayne as a gift. Wayne presents the note to Kevin for payment. If Paula fails to deliver the fabric, does Kevin have a defense against Wayne?

Problem 25-6: Shelter Rule

Kevin, the fashion designer form Problem 25-5 above is back. Kevin is in the process of creating his new winter collection. Kevin again agrees to purchase 30 bolts of fabric from Paula. Kevin issues a note for the purchase price. Later that day, Paula negotiates the note to David who then gives the note to Wayne as a gift. Wayne presents the note to Kevin for payment. If Paula fails to deliver the fabric, does Kevin have a defense against Wayne? Assume that David is a holder in due course and has no notice of any defenses, including Paula's failure to deliver the fabric.

Problem 25-7: Scope of the Shelter Rule

Wayne contracted with David for the purchase of equipment. Wayne issued a note to David for the purchase price. The note is due 1 year after delivery of the equipment. Six months after accepting delivery of the equipment, some of the equipment broke down. Wayne discovered that the equipment had defective wiring and paid out of pocket to repair the problem. David was shocked when Wayne informed him of the defect. David immediately contacted the manufacturer of the equipment. Assume that the defective wiring constitutes a breach of warranty under the contract.

A)   If David is still in possession of the note, does Wayne have a defense against enforcement of the obligation to pay when due?

B)   After learning of the defective wiring from Wayne, David sells the note to Paula, who knows about Wayne's breach of warranty claim. If Paula attempts to enforce the note, does Wayne have a defense?

Test Your Knowledge

To assess your understanding of the material in this chapter, click here to take a quiz.

26

Checking Accounts and the Relationship Between Banks and Customers

Key Concepts

- The "properly payable" standard for when banks can charge a customer account
- The scope of bank liability for wrongful dishonor of a properly payable item
- Those who have the right to stop payment in accordance with Article 4
- The liability imposed on Banks for payments in violation of a valid stop payment order
- The customer's duty to examine the statement of account for unauthorized payments

In this Chapter, the focus shifts from the transfer and enforcement of instruments generally, to the checking system specifically. The checking system requires special attention because banks are involved.

Consider the relationship that you have with your bank. You open a checking account and deposit money with the bank. The bank agrees to hold your money and follow your instructions on how to dispose of money from the account. This is the defining feature of the checking relationship. It gives you the ability to direct the bank to pay out money from your account to specified third parties.

You have likely written, cashed or deposited many checks during your lifetime. However, it is unlikely that you have expended much thought considering the rules that govern: (1) the bank's obligation to pay a check, (2) what happens if the bank wrongfully refuses to pay, (3) the extent to which you can stop a bank from paying a check, and (4) the duties that you may owe to the bank. This chapter explores these foundational aspects of the bank-customer relationship.

A. Terms Governing the Bank-Customer Relationship

The checking relationship is contractual in nature. A contract is formed when the customer submits an application to open a checking account and the bank accepts it. The terms are generally comprised of whatever the bank and customer agree upon. This typically includes the standard terms and conditions provided by the bank in the application and other documents.

The bank-customer relationship, however, is not wholly a matter of private contract. The agreed upon terms are supplemented by Article 4 of the UCC, Federal Reserve regulations, and clearinghouse rules. *See* section 4–103(b).

The rest of this Chapter explores the default rules of the bank-customer relationship under Article 4. The provisions of Article 4 apply unless the parties have agreed otherwise. *See* section 4–103(b). The ability to vary the effect of Article 4 by agreement is subject to two limits. First, the parties cannot agree to disclaim the bank's responsibility for its lack of good faith or failure to exercise ordinary care. Second, the parties cannot agree to limit the measure of damages for the bank's lack of good faith or failure to exercise ordinary care. The ability to otherwise vary the effect of Article 4 reflects the opinion that "it would be unwise to freeze present methods to operation by mandatory statutory rules." *See* section 4–103, cmt. 1. Among other things, this recognizes the reality of changing conditions and the possibility for improved methods in the future.

B. Charging a Customer Account

From the customer's perspective, there may be nothing more important than the rules that specify when the bank can charge the customer's account. To that end, Article 4 begins with a foundational rule that describes when something is properly payable by the bank. This is supplemented by additional provisions that specify the right of the bank to charge a customer account (or decline to pay) in very specific circumstances.

C. The "Properly Payable" Standard

READING THE CODE

> **Maryland Commercial Law Code Section 4–401**
>
> **(a)** A bank may charge against the account of a customer an item that is properly payable from that account even though the charge creates an overdraft. Any item is properly payable if it is authorized by the customer and is in accordance with any agreement between the customer and bank.

Article 4 allows a bank to charge a customer account for any item that is properly payable. *See* section 4–401(a). According to section 4–401(a), "[a]n item is properly payable if it is authorized by the customer and is in accordance with any agreement between the customer and bank." The Official Comments explain that this standard is comprised of two requirements. First, the customer must have authorized the payment. Second, the payment must not violate the bank-customer agreement.

The UCC provides little guidance regarding the application of these requirements. However, one thing is clear. A check is not properly payable if the drawer's signature is forged or an indorsement is forged. *See* section 4–401(a), cmt. 1. Consider the following examples:

EXAMPLES AND EXPLANATIONS

Example 1: A thief steals a blank check from Paula. The thief forges Paula's signature and fills out the rest of the check, making it payable to himself.

The check is not properly payable if the thief presents it to the bank for payment. Paula has not authorized the bank to pay anyone, let alone the thief.

Example 2: Paula issues a check to David. The check is payable to the order of David. A thief steals the check from David. The thief forges David's signature on the back of the check.

This is a forged blank indorsement that purports to make the check payable to bearer. The check is not properly payable if the thief presents it to the bank for payment. Paula has authorized the bank to pay David, or David's order, not the thief.

Outside of forgeries, Article 4's guidance is much less definitive. However, the bank and its customer may agree that a check is not properly payable in other circumstances. Any payment in violation of the agreement would be improper.

For example, a joint checking account may require the signature of both customers who own the joint account. A check signed by one customer would not be properly payable. Similarly, a corporate checking account may require the signature of a specific named officer. A check signed by another officer would not be properly payable. Finally, a checking account may prohibit payment if there are insufficient funds. A check in an amount causing an overdraft would not be properly payable. In each of these examples, the check is not properly payable because it violates the agreement of the bank and its customer.

D. Other Provisions on Charging Customer Accounts

Even if a check is properly payable, a number of problems could complicate the right of banks to pay. The most common issues—overdrafts, postdating, stale checks and death/incompetence—are discussed below. Fortunately, Article 4 contains provisions that govern the right of banks to pay or refuse to pay in these specific situations.

1. Overdrafts

READING THE CODE

> #### Maryland Commercial Law Code Section 4–401
>
> **(b)** A customer is not liable for the amount of an overdraft if the customer neither signed the item nor benefited from the proceeds of the item.

An overdraft occurs when a customer authorizes a check, but does not have sufficient funds in the account to cover it. Charging the account would result in a negative balance. Overdrafts raise questions about the bank's entitlement to pay. Even though the check is properly payable, can the bank refuse to pay? Alternatively, because the check is properly payable, can the bank proceed with charging the customer's account?

Article 4 provides a definitive answer. The bank may charge a customer account for a check that is properly payable, even though it creates an overdraft. *See* section 4–401(a). However, the bank is not required to do so. The bank can refuse to pay if the check would create an overdraft. *See* section 4–402(a).

If the bank elects to pay a properly payable check that would create an overdraft, the customer is liable. The only exception is in section 4–401(b). The text of section 4–401(b) is somewhat unhelpful. However, it is intended to apply where there is more than one customer who can draw on an account. If so, a customer who does not sign is not liable for the overdraft unless the customer benefits from the proceeds of the check. *See* section 4–401, cmt. 2.

2. Postdated Checks

READING THE CODE

> ### ■ Maryland Commercial Law Code Section 4–401
>
> **(c)** A bank may charge against the account of a customer a check that is otherwise properly payable from the account, even though payment was made before the date of the check, unless the customer has given notice to the bank of the postdating describing the check with reasonable certainty. The notice is effective for the period stated in section 4–403(b) for stop-payment orders, and must be received at such time and in such manner as to afford the bank a reasonable opportunity to act on it before the bank takes any action with respect to the check described in section 4–303. If a bank charges against the account of a customer a check before the date stated in the notice of postdating, the bank is liable for damages for the loss resulting from its act. The loss may include damages for dishonor of subsequent items under section 4–402.

A postdated check is one presented to the bank for payment before the date of the check. Because the check contains a future date, it raises the issue of whether the bank can pay the check and charge the customer's account before the date of the check.

Article 4 again provides a definitive answer. In general, the bank may charge the customer's account for a postdated check so long as it is otherwise properly payable.

See section 4–401(c). Payment before the date of the check is permitted *unless* the customer has: (1) notified the bank of the postdating, and (2) described the check with reasonable certainty.

To be effective, the customer's notice must give the bank a reasonable opportunity to act before the bank has committed itself to paying the postdated check. As such, the notice must be given with sufficient time for the bank to act. In addition, the description of the check must be sufficient to allow the bank to identify the check at issue. Such a description might include items such as the check number, the amount of the check and the name of the payee.

An effective notice makes it improper for the bank to pay the postdated check before the date of the check. The bank is liable to the customer for damages for any losses resulting from the bank's wrongful payment of a postdated check. For example, the customer might suffer damages if payment of the postdated check resulted in insufficient funds in the account to cover other checks. These damages could include overdraft fees or losses if the bank decides not to pay the other checks.

A notice of a postdated check remains effective for 6 months unless the notice is provided orally. Oral notices lapse after 14 days unless the customer confirms the notice in a record. The notice can also be renewed for an additional six months if the customer delivers a record to the bank while the original notice is in effect. This is the same as the period of effectiveness for a stop-payment order (discussed below).

3. Stale Checks

READING THE CODE

Maryland Commercial Law Code Section 4–404

A bank is under no obligation to a customer having a checking account to pay a check, other than a certified check, which is presented more than six months after its date, but it may charge its customer's account for a payment made thereafter in good faith.

Stale checks are the opposite of postdated checks. Instead of presenting a check for payment before the date of the check, the check is presented to the bank long after the date of the check. Even if an old check is otherwise properly payable, the length of time that the check has been outstanding may indicate a problem. For example, the check may have been lost and another issued in its place. In other cases, the customer may still want the check paid. This again raises the issue of whether a bank can pay (or refuse to pay) when confronted with an old check.

Under Article 4, the bank has no obligation to pay a check that is presented more than six months after its date. *See* section 4–404. However, the bank has the option to charge the customer's account as long as the bank acts in good faith.

4. Death or Incompetence of Customer

READING THE CODE

Maryland Commercial Law Code Section 4–405

(a) A payor or collecting bank's authority to accept, pay, or collect an item or to account for proceeds of its collection, if otherwise effective, is not rendered ineffective by incompetence of a customer of either bank existing at the time the item is issued or its collection is undertaken if the bank does not know of an adjudication of incompetence. Neither death nor incompetence of a customer revokes the authority to accept, pay, collect, or account until the bank knows of the fact of death or of an adjudication of incompetence and has reasonable opportunity to act on it.

(b) Even with knowledge, a bank may for ten days after the date of death pay or certify checks drawn on or before that date unless ordered to stop payment by a person claiming an interest in the account.

A check is a customer's demand that the bank pay the identified payee. What then is the effect of the customer's death or incompetence on the banks' ability to act on behalf of the customer as directed?

Article 4's position is that the bank continues to have the right to pay or collect a check after the customer's death or incompetency. The bank's authority to act is not revoked until: (1) the bank knows of the death or an adjudication of incompetence; and (2) has a reasonable opportunity to act. *See* section 4–405(a). Accordingly, the bank is not liable to its customer for payments made without knowledge of the customer's death or incompetence.

Even if the bank has knowledge of the customer's death, the bank can pay an otherwise properly payable check for 10 days after the date of death. *See* section 4–405(b). This allows payees to cash recently issued checks without having to collect from the estate of the deceased via probate. Note that this limited period for payment only applies in the case of the customer's death. It is not available in the event of incompetence.

The need for section 4–405 is practical in nature. Given the sheer number of customers and transactions, it would be impracticable to require that banks confirm the continued life and competency of its customers. This would quite literally bring the system to a standstill.

APPLYING THE CODE

Problem 26-1: When Is a Check Properly Payable?

David has a checking account with FirstBank. On April 1, David writes a check for $80 payable to Paula. Paula places the check in her briefcase and promptly forgets about it. About a year later, the briefcase is donated to a charity. Kevin purchases the briefcase at a second-hand store and finds the check. Kevin signs Paula's name on the back of the check and deposits it into his own bank account. David only has $20 in his checking account when the check is presented for payment. Can FirstBank pay the check and charge David's account? Can FirstBank refuse to pay the check?

Problem 26-2: Postdated Checks

Kevin has a checking account with SecondBank. On February 1, Kevin writes a check for $1,000 payable to Wayne. Kevin dates the check March 1 because he will not have enough money until he deposits his next paycheck at the end of February. Wayne waits for a few weeks before depositing the check. The check is presented to SecondBank for payment on February 22.

A) Can SecondBank pay the check and charge Kevin's account?

B) Does your answer change if Kevin called SecondBank on February 1 and told the bank not to pay the check until March 1 at the earliest? Assume that Kevin provided SecondBank with the check number and all other information that the bank needed to identify the check in question.

Problem 26-3: Authorized Signers and the Bank-Customer Agreement

Paula, Inc. has a corporate checking account with ThirdBank. Paula, Inc. has authorized the President and the Treasurer to sign checks on behalf of the company. For checks under $100,000, the President and the Treasurer can each sign individually. But Paula, Inc. requires the signatures of both the President and the Treasurer for checks of $100,000 or more. Third-Bank was also provided with specimen signatures for Paula (the current President) and Wayne (the current Treasurer).

A)   Paula, Inc. just finished negotiating a $150,000 purchase order with David Corp., a supplier of important materials used in manufacturing Paula Inc.'s best-selling products. Since Wayne was on a 1-month safari in Africa, Paula signed a check for $150,000 payable to David Corp. David Corp. then deposited the check into its own bank account. Can ThirdBank pay the check and charge Paula, Inc.'s corporate account?

B)   Shortly after returning from Africa, Wayne was forced out of his position as Treasurer. Unhappy with the decision, Wayne hatched a plan to steal funds from Paula, Inc. Immediately after Wayne's removal, he wrote a check for $99,999.99 drawn on Paula, Inc.'s account at ThirdBank. The check was payable to Kevin, an accomplice in the scheme. Kevin deposited the check into his own bank account later that same day. Can ThirdBank pay the check and charge Paula, Inc.'s corporate account?

E. When Banks Refuse to Pay a Properly Payable Check

A check is generally dishonored if it is presented for payment and the bank refuses to pay. Typically, the bank dishonors a check by returning the check unpaid or sending a notice of nonpayment. As discussed above, a bank may have a valid reason for dishonoring a check. For example, banks commonly refuse to pay checks when the account contains insufficient funds. However, a bank may also act wrongfully by intentionally or mistakenly deciding to dishonor an item that should be paid.

The bank's wrongful dishonor of a check can have real consequences for the customer—both criminal and civil. Many states have criminalized the writing of bad checks—checks that are refused for payment. Under these statutes, the customer is potentially subject to monetary penalties and imprisonment.

In addition, the payee of a bounced check does not know whether the bank's dishonor was justified or wrongful. The payee only knows that they have not been paid. Based on non-payment, the payee might pursue civil penalties or contractual remedies against the customer (e.g., late fees, penalty payments). Equally important is the likelihood that nonpayment will negatively impact the ongoing relationship between the bank's customer and the payee. For example, the payee could decide to terminate a valuable business relationship with the bank's customer.

The implications of dishonor are potentially wide-ranging. The customer can suffer financially and mentally. As a result, Article 4 provides rules governing wrongful dishonor and the extent of bank liability for such acts.

F. Wrongful Dishonor

READING THE CODE

> **Maryland Commercial Law Code Section 4–402**
>
> **(a)** Except as otherwise provided in this title, a payor bank wrongfully dishonors an item if it dishonors an item that is properly payable, but a bank may dishonor an item that would create an overdraft unless it has agreed to pay the overdraft.

Absent a valid reason to refuse payment, the bank is liable if it dishonors any item that is properly payable—called wrongful dishonor. See section 4–402(a). The effect of this is that the bank is required to pay any check that is properly payable. Otherwise, the bank will be held liable.

The extent of bank liability for wrongful dishonor is limited. The bank is only liable to its customer. See section 4–402(b). No one else has a legal claim against the bank for wrongful dishonor. This means that the payee of the check (or the person entitled to enforce) cannot force the bank to pay.

EXAMPLES AND EXPLANATIONS

David, Inc. issues a check to Kevin Co. as payment for inventory. Kevin Co. presents the check for payment and Bank dishonors because it would create an overdraft. Bank returns the check unpaid. David, Inc. actually had enough money in its account so the Bank's actions constitute wrongful dishonor.

On these facts, David, Inc. has a cause of action against the Bank for wrongful dishonor. But Kevin Co. does not. Under section 4–402(b), the Bank's liability is limited to its customer—David, Inc.

G. Damages for Wrongful Dishonor

The extent of the bank's liability for wrongful dishonor is primarily a factual question. Under section 4–402(b), the bank is liable to its customer for any damages that are proximately caused by the wrongful dishonor, including consequential damages. Consequential damages might include damages for arrest or prosecution, lost profits, emotional distress or reputational harm. Whether any consequential damages are proximately caused by wrongful dishonor must be determined on the facts of each case.

Article 4 does not expressly provide for punitive damages in a cause of action for wrongful dishonor. The availability of punitive damages is left to other law. *See* section 4–402, cmt. 1. Accordingly, an aggrieved customer may also have the ability to seek punitive damages, especially if the bank acts intentionally and maliciously.

APPLYING THE CODE

Problem 26-4: Damages Proximately Caused

A)   Kevin owns a small coffee shop. He leases the space from David. Under the terms of the lease, Kevin agreed to pay $2,500 per month with rent due on the first day of each month. The lease allows David to charge Kevin interest on any late payments and a late fee of $100. Last month, Kevin's bank refused to pay the rent check that Kevin issued to David. When David sent Kevin a notice of non-payment, Kevin called the bank and learned that the bank had mistakenly dishonored the check due to a glitch in its system. Kevin wrote David a new check, but was forced to pay interest and the late fee. The next month the same thing happened. Sick of dealing with a deadbeat tenant, David commenced eviction proceedings against Kevin. Kevin hired an attorney to advise him during the process, but was ultimately evicted with 6 months remaining on the lease with David. Kevin ultimately found a new space for $3,000 per month and reopened 2 months later. Can Kevin hold the bank liable for damages? If so, what losses will the bank be liable for?

B)   Wayne Co. manufactures bicycle frames that are sold to independent retailers across the country. Wayne Co.'s bicycles are made from carbon fiber, which has been supplied by Kevin, Inc. for the last 10 years. The practice has been for Wayne Co. to pay for each shipment of carbon fiber by check within 30 days of delivery. When Kevin, Inc. deposited the most recent check, it was returned unpaid by the bank. Wayne Co. later learned that the bank mistakenly dishonored the check for insufficient funds. Wayne Co. eventually paid for the carbon fiber. But the relationship was ruined. The next time Wayne Co. tried to purchase carbon fiber, Kevin, Inc. refused to sell. Kevin, Inc. said it had plenty of demand from customers who would pay on time. Wayne Co. scrambled to find a new supplier and ultimately purchased carbon fiber at an increased cost. Wayne Co.'s manufacturing was disrupted, which delayed shipments to Wayne Co.'s retailers. After learning of the likely delay, 10 of Wayne Co.'s retailers cancelled their orders. Wayne Co. was only able to appease the remaining retailers by offering an 8% discount on the price of its bicycle frames. Can Wayne Co. hold the bank liable for the increased cost of carbon fiber? The cancelled orders? The lost revenue from the discounted sales?

H. The Customer's Right to Stop Payment of a Check

Up until now, this Chapter has explored the rights and obligations of the bank in the checking relationship. Starting now, the focus shifts to the rights and obligations of the customer.

The ability to stop payment of a check is one of the most significant legal rights provided to customers under Article 4. After writing a check, the customer may have any number of reasons to stop payment before it is paid out of their account. The customer may learn that the check was lost or stolen. The check may contain an error. The customer may wish to prevent an overdraft. If the check was issued as payment, the payee may not have performed satisfactorily. The list of reasons goes on and on.

From the perspective of the bank, stopping payment can be difficult, inconvenient and costly. The bank is being asked to identify a single check among all of its daily transactions without knowing if or when it will be presented for payment. Even so, Article 4 takes the position that stopping payment is a service that customers rightfully expect and are entitled to receive from banks. *See* section 4–403, cmt. 1.

I. Scope of the Right to Stop Payment

READING THE CODE

Maryland Commercial Law Code Section 4–403

(a) Any person authorized to draw on the account, if there is more than one person, may stop payment of any item drawn on the customer's account or close the account by an order to the bank describing the item or account with reasonable certainty received at a time and in a manner that affords the bank a reasonable opportunity to act on it before any action by the bank with

> respect to the item described in section 4–303. If the signature of more than one person is required to draw on an account, any of these persons may stop payment or close the account.

Under section 4–403(a), the "customer or any person authorized to draw on the account may stop payment of any item drawn on the customer's account." Note that this provision contains two important limitations. It limits both who can stop payment *and* the type of item that can be stopped.

Under section 4–403(a), only the customer or a person authorized to draw on the account has the right to stop payment. The customer is defined as any person who has the account with the bank. *See* section 4–104(a)(5). Accordingly, there may be more than one customer for a particular account (e.g., a joint checking account). The customer can also authorize others to write checks drawn on the account (e.g., via a power of attorney).

Where more than one person can draw on the account, any one of them can stop payment of any check. *See* section 4–403(a), cmt. 5. This includes the ability to stop payment of a check written by another authorized person. For example, if Kevin and Wayne open a joint account, they both individually have the right to stop payment. Assume that Kevin and Wayne are individually authorized to write checks on the account. If Kevin writes a check on the account, Wayne can stop payment of it. The reverse is also true. Kevin can stop payment of a check written by Wayne.

Similarly, any one of the authorized signers can stop payment of a check that requires multiple signatures. For example, if a corporate bank account requires the signature of both the President and the Treasurer, either one of them can stop payment.

Finally, the right to stop payment is limited to items that are payable from the customer's own account. For many checks this is a non-issue. However, cashier's checks and teller's checks are another story. *See* section 4–403, cmt. 4. Cashier's checks and teller's checks are purchased from the bank. The bank itself guarantees payment and the payment is made from the bank's own funds. Because cashier's checks and teller's checks are not drawn from the customer's account, there is no right to stop payment.

APPLYING THE CODE

Problem 26-5: Who Can Stop Payment of a Check?

A)   David and Kevin are officers of a corporation that is in the process of seeking bids for an office renovation. David's friend Wayne is one of many contractors who have submitted a bid. Before a final decision is made, David tells Wayne that he has been awarded the job. David then writes a check to Wayne in the amount of $10,000 for start-up costs. The check is drawn on the company's account at FirstBank. When Kevin learns of this, he immediately calls FirstBank to request that a stop-payment order be placed on the corporate account. Kevin informs FirstBank that the check in question is: 1) numbered 10111, 2) payable to Wayne, and 3) in the amount of $10,000. The next day, Kevin sends the bank an email to memorialize the conversation. The corporate checking account authorizes both David and Kevin to sign checks on behalf of the company. Does Kevin have the right to stop payment of the check? If so, has Kevin complied with the requirements for ordering a valid and effective stop-payment order?

B)   Assume that Wayne (from part (A) above) has not deposited the $10,000 check. After getting the check from David, Wayne indorsed it by signing on the back. Unfortunately, Wayne was pick-pocketed while on his way to the bank. Wayne wants to prevent the pick-pocket from getting paid on the check. Can he contact FirstBank to issue a stop-payment order?

J. The Process of Stopping Payment

The process for stopping payment is relatively straightforward. The customer or a person authorized to draw on the account simply issues a stop-payment order to the bank. The order can be made orally or in writing. However, the order must be timely and include statutorily required content.

1. Timeliness

To be timely, the bank must receive the stop-payment order at a time and in a manner that gives the bank a reasonable opportunity to act on it. This depends entirely on where the Bank is in processing the check. The order arrives too late if the bank has already: (1) accepted or certified the check, (2) paid the check in cash, (3) settled for the check, or (4) become accountable for the amount of the check. *See* section 4–303(a). If the bank has done any of the foregoing it has already incurred liability on the check so it is too late for the bank to act on a stop payment order.

Article 4 also allows banks to implement a cut-off time for receipt of stop-payment orders. The cut-off time cannot be any earlier than 1 hour after opening on the day after the bank receives the check. *See* section 4–303(a)(5). Assume that a bank opens at 9:30 AM. For any check that the bank receives on Tuesday, the cut-off can be no earlier than Wednesday at 10:30 AM.

2. Sufficiency of Description

In addition to the requirement of timeliness, a stop-payment order must describe the item or account with reasonable certainty. *See* section 4–403(a). The standard for judging the sufficiency of a description is not fixed. It depends on the current technological capabilities of the bank's system for processing checks. Article 4 explains it like this:

In describing the item, the customer, "in the absence of a contrary agreement, must meet the standard of what information allows the bank under the technology then existing to identify the item with reasonable certainty." Section 4–403, cmt. 5.

Given the sheer volume of daily checking transactions, banks rely on automated systems to determine whether a check is properly payable. Because of this, the description in a stop-payment order must include information that can be programmed into the bank's system so that the check is flagged and will not be paid when it comes through.

The technology used in the banking industry has and continues to depend primarily on three key pieces of information: (1) the customer's account number, (2) the precise check number, and (3) the exact amount of the check. The automated system can then decline payment of any item drawn on the customer's account if it matches the identified check number or the amount of the check.

Other descriptive information cannot be input into most bank systems under existing technology. Accordingly, information such as the payee's name or the date of the check will be insufficient unless it is accompanied by the customer's account number and either the check number or amount of the check. The exception is if the bank in question has upgraded capabilities that allow it to process more sophisticated inquiries or search using other inputs. Over time, the banking industry may adopt more advanced technology. If this occurs, what qualifies as a sufficient description will evolve. However, at present, the banking industry evinces very little incentive to implement upgrades.

3. Period of Effectiveness

READING THE CODE

Maryland Commercial Law Code Section 4–403

(b) A stop-payment order is effective for 6 months, but it lapses after 14 calendar days if the original order was oral and was not confirmed in writing within that period. A stop-payment order may be renewed for additional 6-month periods by a writing given to the bank within a period during which the stop-payment order is effective.

As discussed above, a stop-payment order can be valid if it is timely and contains a sufficient description. However, the order does not remain effective indefinitely. Stop-payment orders are generally effective for 6 months. But a stop-payment order that is given orally lapses after 14 days unless it is confirmed in a record during the 14-day period. *See* section 4–403(b).

A stop-payment order can be renewed for any number of additional 6 months periods by giving the bank written notice while the stop-payment order is still in effect. *See* section 4–403(b), cmt. 6. If a stop-payment order lapses for any reason it is like the stop payment order was never in effect. A new stop-payment order must be given. Unless and until this is done, the bank can pay the check in good faith even though the stop-payment order was previously in effect.

4. Stop-Payment Orders and Liability

As you might expect, the bank does not incur liability to the customer for paying a check when a stop-payment order is neither valid nor effective. The bank has the right to pay if the stop-payment order is not timely. The bank has the right to pay if the stop payment order lacks a sufficient description. The bank has the right to pay if the stop-payment order has lapsed.

The foregoing notwithstanding, stop-payment orders do raise questions about the potential liability of both customers and banks. If the bank complies with a stop payment order, the disappointed payee will likely be looking for a remedy. In these cases, what is the liability of the customer or the bank? On the other hand, if the bank pays a check in violation of a stop payment order, the customer may suffer harm. What then is the liability of the bank?

- **Liability for Compliance with a Stop-Payment Order.** A stop-payment order does not change the underlying obligation of the customer to pay on the check. It is merely an order to the bank not to pay. The payee can still attempt to enforce the instrument against the customer. The customer remains liable for the obligation to pay on the check if the customer does not have a valid defense, claim or discharge.

   The bank's liability is a different story. Banks are not liable to the customer for complying with a stop-payment order. The customer has ordered the Bank not to pay. The customer, therefore, has no basis for holding the bank responsible for any resulting losses. In addition, the payee has no legal right to force payment by the bank. The payee's only recourse is to pursue a legal action directly against the customer.

- **Liability for Payment in Violation of Stop-Payment Order.** After delivery of a valid a stop-payment order, the bank must comply. It is improper for the bank to pay in violation of a valid stop-payment order while it remains effective. *See* section 4–403, cmt. 7. The bank, therefore, will be liable to the customer for the loss resulting from payment of the check. *See* section 4–403(c).

   Note that the bank is liable for any payment in violation of a stop-payment order. There is no requirement that the bank act maliciously or even intentionally. An inadvertent or mistaken payment contrary to a stop-payment order is still improper.

APPLYING THE CODE

Problem 26-6: Stop-Payment Orders and the Holder in Due Course

David hires Wayne to do some plumbing work at his house. David writes Wayne a check for $800 as payment for the work. After Wayne leaves, the pipes start to leak and the basement floods. Once the water is under control, David contacts his bank and places an effective stop-payment order on the check.

A) Assume that Wayne deposits the check and David's bank refuses to pay. Is the bank liable to Wayne for nonpayment of the check? Is David liable?

B) Assume that Wayne instead sells the check to a check-cashing company that qualifies as a holder in due course. The check-cashing company tries to collect payment and the bank refuses to pay. Is the bank liable to the check-cashing company for nonpayment of the check? Is David liable?

K. Customer's Duty to Discover and Report Unauthorized Signatures

READING THE CODE

Maryland Commercial Law Code Section 4–406

(c) If a bank sends or makes available a statement of account or items . . . the customer must exercise reasonable promptness in examining the statement or the items to determine whether any payment was not authorized because of an alteration of an item or because a purported signature by or on behalf of the customer was not authorized. If, based on the statement or items provided, the customer should reasonably have discovered the unauthorized payment, the customer must promptly notify the bank of the relevant facts.

Customers have relatively few obligations in the checking relationship. However, Article 4 does place some responsibility on customers to assist in identifying forgeries, alterations and other unauthorized checks.

If you have a checking account, your bank probably provides you with a monthly statement. You may also recall a time when the bank would return the paid checks to you in the mail. These days, it is much more common for banks to provide you with access to an electronic copy of your paid checks. It is possible that you never gave any of this much thought. But in providing you with this information, the bank was complying with Article 4. Under section 4–406, a bank is not required to provide a statement of account. Nevertheless, if a bank decides to do so, it must also: 1) return or make available the items paid or 2) provide sufficient information in the statement to allow the customer to identify the items paid. As you might expect, virtually all banks do in fact provide customers with a statement of account.

The purpose of requiring banks to provide customers with this information is to facilitate an affirmative duty owed by customers. Under section 4–406(c), customers must exercise reasonable promptness to examine the provided items and statement of account. The customer is also charged with notifying the bank of any unauthorized signatures or alterations that should have been reasonably discovered.

The consequences of failing to comply with these duties are potentially significant. If the bank proves that the customer failed to comply, then the customer is generally precluded from asserting that the bank improperly paid the check due to the unauthorized signature or alteration. *See* section 4–406(d). This places the onus on customers to be vigilant. Customers must do their part to identify and prevent unauthorized payments or endure the consequences.

Test Your Knowledge

To assess your understanding of the material in this chapter, click here to take a quiz.

27

Check Collection

Key Concepts

- The check collection process relies on banks
- The distinct roles of Collecting Banks, Depositary Banks, Intermediary Banks, Payor Banks, and Presenting Banks in the check collection process
- Collecting Banks have a duty to exercise due care
- Payor Banks have a duty to either: (1) pay the check, (2) return the check unpaid or send a notice of nonpayment or (3) settle
- The effect of final payment under Article 4

All instruments eventually come into the hands of someone who wants to collect payment. Theoretically, the steps for obtaining payment are relatively straightforward. A note is presented directly to the maker for payment. A draft is presented directly to the person who has been instructed to pay. However, the process of converting a check into cash is complicated by the fact that payment is drawn on a customer's bank account. As a result, the check must be processed through the banking system before it is paid.

You are no doubt familiar with writing, cashing and depositing checks. But these mundane banking transactions are just a small part of the check-collection process. Important steps occur behind the scenes before the bank actually debits a customer's account to finally pay a check. This Chapter examines each of the steps in the check-collection process and the laws that govern it.

A. Terminology

Understanding the correct terminology is especially important because the check-collection process can involve a big cast of characters, including a variety of banks. Luckily, you are already acquainted with two of the key participants.

1. **Customer/Drawer.** In the context of check collection, the terms "customer" and "drawer" are often used interchangeably. This is because checks are drawn on (or paid from) funds in a bank account. As a result, the person who orders the bank to pay by writing the check (the "drawer") must typically have an account with the bank (making them a "customer" of the bank). *See* section 3–103(a)(5); section 4–104(a)(5).

2. **Payee/Person Entitled to Enforce.** Again, the terms "payee" and "person entitled to enforce" are sometimes used interchangeably. The person entitled to enforce a check is the holder of a check if it is payable to them as an identified person or payable to bearer. *See* section 3–301, section 1–201(b)(21). This encompasses the original payee of the check and subsequent transferees.

As noted above, the check-collection process relies upon banks. Article 4 defines a "bank" broadly as any person who is engaged in the business of banking. *See* section 4–105(1). The definition covers different types of financial institutions, including regional banks, state banks, national banks, savings and loan associations, credit unions and trust companies. Article 4 further categorizes banks into five different types based on the bank's role in the check-collection process. The categories are not mutually exclusive because a single bank commonly plays more than one role in the process.

1. **Depositary Bank.** The Depositary Bank is the first bank to take a check (even if it also qualifies as a Payor Bank) unless the check is presented for immediate payment over the counter. *See* section 4–105(2). Most commonly, the Depositary Bank is exactly what it sounds like. It is the bank where the person entitled to enforce has an account and deposits the check for collection.

EXAMPLES AND EXPLANATIONS

David and Kevin both have checking accounts at FirstBank. David writes Kevin a check drawn on his account at FirstBank. Kevin deposits the check into his account at FirstBank. FirstBank is the first bank to take the check. The check was not presented for immediate payment over the counter because Kevin deposited it into his account. So, FirstBank is the Depositary Bank. In this scenario, FirstBank would also be the Payor Bank (see below).

2. **Payor Bank/Drawee.** The Payor Bank is the bank that is the drawee of the check. *See* section 4–105(3); section 4–104(a)(8). Accordingly, the Payor Bank is the bank that is ordered or instructed to pay on a check.

EXAMPLES AND EXPLANATIONS

Kevin has a checking account at FirstBank. Kevin writes a check to Wayne that is drawn on the account at FirstBank. Wayne has an account at SecondBank and deposits the check there. In this scenario, FirstBank is the Payor Bank because Kevin is instructing FirstBank to pay Wayne on the check. SecondBank is the Depositary Bank.

3. **Intermediary Bank.** An Intermediary Bank is any bank to which a check is transferred during the collection process except for the Depositary Bank or Payor Bank. *See* section 4–105(4). This includes any Bank in the collection process that is not a Depositary Bank or Payor Bank.

   An Intermediary Bank is not always involved in check collection. The Depositary Bank can present the check directly to the Payor Bank for payment. However, it is not always possible or efficient to do so—for example when the two Banks are not set up for direct presentment. In these situations, the Depositary Bank may transfer the check to an Intermediary Bank that has the means to present the check. The function of the Intermediary Bank then is to facilitate presentment and payment.

EXAMPLES AND EXPLANATIONS

David has a checking account at FirstBank in the United States. David writes Paula a check drawn on his account at FirstBank. Paula lives abroad and deposits the check into her account at Local Bank. Local Bank transfers the check to International Bank who is in a better position to present the check because it has an arrangement with FirstBank.

International Bank is not the Depositary Bank because they were not the first bank to take the check. The Depositary Bank is Local Bank. In addition, International Bank is not the Payor Bank because they are not being instructed to pay the check. FirstBank is the Payor Bank because they are being instructed by David to pay the check. Thus, International Bank falls squarely within the definition of an Intermediary Bank. The check was transferred to International Bank during check collection. In addition, International Bank is neither a Depositary Bank, nor a Payor Bank. Note, that International Bank is also a Collecting Bank and a Presenting Bank (see below).

4. **Collecting Bank.** A Collecting Bank is any bank that handles the check during the check-collection process except for a Payor Bank. *See* section 4–105(5). By definition, this includes Intermediary Banks and Depositary Banks.

EXAMPLES AND EXPLANATIONS

David has a checking account with FirstBank. David writes Wayne a check drawn on his account at FirstBank. Wayne deposits the check into his account at SecondBank. SecondBank transfers the check to the Federal Reserve Bank that acts as a central clearinghouse for checking transactions.

Here, the Payor Bank is First Bank who is being instructed to pay by David. A Collecting Bank is any bank (other than the Payor Bank) that handles the check during check-collection. In this scenario, both SecondBank and the FederalReserve Bank are Collecting Banks. Both handled the check because it was transferred to them during check-collection, and neither one is the Payor Bank. Note that SecondBank is also a Depositary Bank. In addition, The Federal Reserve is also an Intermediary Bank.

5. **Presenting Bank.** The Presenting Bank is the bank that presents the check and demands payment. *See* section 4–105(6). This is the bank that submits the check to the Payor Bank for payment.

EXAMPLES AND EXPLANATIONS

David has a checking account with FirstBank. David writes Wayne a check drawn on his account at FirstBank. Wayne deposits the check into his account at SecondBank. The check is presented for payment directly by

SecondBank to FirstBank. In this scenario, SecondBank is the Presenting Bank because they are demanding payment on the check from FirstBank. SecondBank is also the Depositary Bank in this instance.

B. Overview of the Check-Collection Process

The check-collection process really begins when a check comes into the possession of a person who wants to enforce it. To collect payment, the check must be presented to the Payor Bank—the bank where the drawer of the check has an account. The Payor Bank can now verify that the check is properly payable. For example, the Payor Bank may confirm that: (1) the check is authorized and unaltered, (2) the drawer has an account with the Payor Bank, and (3) the drawer's account contains sufficient funds. Based on this, the Payor Bank can decide to pay the check or return it unpaid.

There are two ways to initiate the collection process. If it is feasible, the person trying to collect can go directly to a branch of the Payor Bank. Once there, they can present the check by handing it to a teller. Alternatively, the person trying to collect can deposit the check in the bank where they have an account. That bank (now a Depositary Bank) will act on behalf of its customer to facilitate collection through the appropriate banking channels. Generally speaking, the Depositary Bank will either itself present the check to the Payor Bank or arrange for the check to be presented to the Payor Bank by an Intermediary Bank.

The steps that must occur before final payment and the duties of the various banks in the process depend on the method of check-collection. An overview of the core components of the different check-collection methods follows.

C. Presentment over the Counter

Presentment of a check for immediate payment over the counter is the simplest method of check collection because it only involves one bank (diagramed below). The person entitled to enforce simply walks into the Payor Bank and hands the check to a teller. Of course, this is only practical if a branch of the Payor Bank is located in a place that is readily accessible.

Look at the diagram below.[1] It shows the basic transaction basic flow for check-collection when presentment is made over the counter.

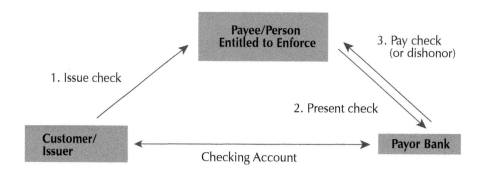

So, after issuance, the person entitled to enforce presents the check directly to the Payor Bank's teller. The Payor Bank now has a decision to make—pay the check in cash over the counter or refuse the demand for payment. Although the UCC refers to this as presenting a check for immediate payment, the language is somewhat misleading. The Payor Bank does not have to make an immediate decision. Section 3–502(b)(2) gives the Payor Bank until the end of the day to decide. The Payor Bank can decide at any time on the day that the check is presented to it. This gives the Payor Bank a short timeframe for determining whether it is obligated to pay the check.

The steps taken to verify a check will depend on the Payor Bank's policies and its agreement with the customer. Even so, the Payor Bank will surely check its system to verify: (1) the existence of the customer's account, (2) that the check is not subject to a stop-payment order, and (3) that customer has sufficient funds. It is likely that the Payor Bank will examine the check to determine its authenticity. In making a decision, the Payor Bank may also request ID or other information to confirm that the person presenting the check is entitled to payment.

If all is well, the Payor Bank will charge the customer's account and pay the check in cash. If there is a problem, the Payor Bank may refuse payment and dishonor the check. The check is also dishonored if the Payor Bank does not decide by the end of the day and fails to pay the check. As discussed in Chapter 26, the Payor Bank will be liable to its customer for damages arising from wrongful dishonor.

---

1   The black arrows depict the bank customer relationship. The numbered blue arrows depict the transaction flow.

D. Depositing for Presentment

Although over the counter presentment is an option, it is much more common to initiate the collection process by depositing the check in a bank. The person entitled to enforce simply deposits the check in a bank where they have an account. That bank is now in the role of a Depositary Bank. Before the account of the person entitled to enforce is finally credited, the check must first make its way through various banking channels to the Payor Bank. The Depositary Bank acts as an agent for its customer in facilitating presentment to and collection from the Payor Bank. *See* section 4–201.

Take a moment to consider the context in which a Depositary Bank provides this service. In any given day, a Depositary Bank will receive a huge number of checks for deposit. These checks will be drawn on accounts at different banks across the country and abroad. Some of the checks will be drawn on accounts at the Depositary Bank itself. Others will be drawn on accounts at banks that the Depositary Bank deals with frequently—for example large national banks or banks located in the same region as the Depositary Bank. For these banks, there may be an established mechanism or arrangement for directly presenting checks. But the Depositary Bank will inevitably receive some checks drawn on accounts at banks that the Depositary Bank deals with very rarely—for example small local or regional banks. In these instances, a direct arrangement may not exist. Even so, the Depositary Bank must still ensure that the check gets presented and that payment is collected. To do so, the Depositary Bank may need to rely on one or more Intermediary Banks, forwarding the check until it gets to an Intermediary Bank that is in a position to present the check to the Payor Bank.

It should be clear now that depositing the check is just the start. Once a check has been deposited, it begins its journey through the banking system. The Depositary Bank must sort all of the checks that it receives and determine the appropriate banking channel for collecting payment.

E. On-Us Items

Sometimes a Depositary Bank will receive a check for deposit that is written on another account at the Depositary Bank. Here is an example. Kevin and Paula both have checking accounts at FirstBank. Kevin writes Paula a check drawn on his account at FirstBank and Paula deposits the check into her account at FirstBank.

Look at the diagram below.[2] It shows the basic transaction flow for check-collection of on-us items using the example of Kevin and Paula's exchange.

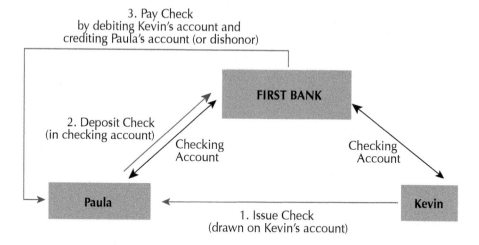

These are called "on-us items" because the Depositary Bank does not need to present the check to another bank for payment. Deposit and payment both occur at the same bank—the Depositary Bank. After the check is deposited, the Depositary Bank can determine whether the check is properly payable. If it decides to honor the check, the Depositary Bank debits the account of the drawer and credits the account of the person that deposited the check. The bank is acting as both the Depositary Bank and the Payor Bank.

F. Direct Presentment

When a check is not an "on-us item," the Depositary Bank must decide how to proceed with collecting from the Payor Bank. This is easiest if the Depositary Bank already has a relationship with the Payor Bank and has an established process for directly presenting checks. In these situations, the process looks something like this:[3]

---

2   The black arrows depict the bank customer relationship. The numbered blue arrows depict the transaction flow.

3   The black arrows depict the bank customer relationship. The numbered blue arrows depict the transaction flow.

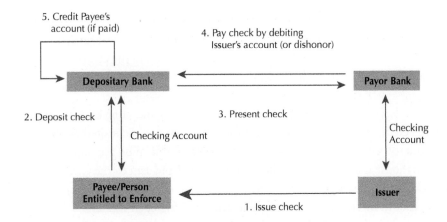

Banks typically establish direct presentment relationships via a Check-Clearing Agreement, which generally sets forth the process for sending checks and exchanging payment between the two banks. No bank has an agreement with every other bank. Two banks will typically enter into a Check-Clearing Agreement only if they frequently interact for the purposes of check collection. That is to say, a Check Clearing Agreement makes sense if two banks discover that a large number of checks deposited each day are drawn on the other bank. This makes it worthwhile to enter into a direct-send relationship that bypasses the cost and time of processing checks through an intermediary.

The Check-Clearing Agreement governs the process. But generally speaking, each bank sorts through its daily deposits and pulls all the checks that are drawn on the other bank. The amount of these checks is aggregated and each bank is given a provisional credit for the day. The checks are then sent as a bundle to the other bank. Each bank can now run the checks through their system to determine whether they should be paid. This is where checks might be dishonored for insufficient funds or if a valid stop-payment order exists. For any honored checks, the bank credits the customer's account and the provisional credit becomes final. For any dishonored checks, the bank sends notices of nonpayment or returns the check unpaid and the provisional credit is revoked.

G. Clearinghouse Transactions

A Clearinghouse is an association of banks (and sometimes nonbanks) that regularly engages in clearing checks. *See* section 4–104(a)(4). Unlike a Check-Clearing Agreement, a Clearinghouse can establish a relationship between more than two banks. It is basically an agreement between each of the participating members on the process—specifically the process for exchanging checks and settlement on a net basis. This allows all the banks in the same area to use the clearinghouse as a central office for clearing checks drawn on each of the other members.

Check collection via a Clearinghouse looks something like this. Each bank provisionally credits its customers' accounts for the amounts of deposited checks. Then the bank sorts its daily deposits to pull all the checks drawn on accounts with other Clearinghouse members. These checks are bundled and sent to the Clearinghouse. The Clearinghouse aggregates all the checks—crediting each member for the total amount of checks that it sends in and debiting each member for the total amount of checks sent in by other members that are drawn on it. So on the day, each member's account gets a credit (if there is a net positive) or a debit (if there is a net negative). Each member bank then receives all the checks drawn on it each day. They can then determine whether the check should be paid. Again, this is where a check might be dishonored for insufficient funds or if a valid stop-payment order exists. If the check is honored, the customer's provisional credit becomes final. If the check is dishonored, the customer's provisional credit is revoked. The Clearinghouse then balances the member's account in accordance with its rules.

H. Presentment Through Intermediaries

If the Depositary Bank does not have an agreement for directly presenting checks with the Payor Bank, then the Depositary Bank must forward the check to an intermediary who is in a better position to collect from the Payor Bank. Most commonly, other banks or the Federal Reserve act as intermediaries in the check collection process. In fact, a check may travel to more than one intermediary until it finally reaches one that can present the check to the Payor Bank.

- **Other Banks.** Other banks can serve as intermediaries in the check-collection process. If the Depositary Bank does not have a direct agreement or participate in a Clearinghouse with the Payor Bank, it can leverage the established arrangements/relationships of other banks. For example, the Depositary Bank may have a direct agreement with a bank that has a relationship with the Payor Bank. The direct agreement may provide for the Bank to act as an intermediary on behalf of others (such as the Depositary Bank) in collecting from the Payor Bank. Even if that is not the case, that bank may have a relationship with another Bank that does have an arrangement with the Payor Bank. The check can continue moving in this way until it reaches a bank that is able to present the check to the Payor Bank.

- **Federal Reserve.** The Federal Reserve Bank has also established a nation-wide check-clearing system. This gives just about every bank in the United States a method for collecting (or clearing) checks regardless of what bank the check happens to be drawn on.

  Federal Reserve Banks are located across the country in different regions. To use the Federal Reserve Bank as an intermediary, the Depositary Bank simply sends the check to the Federal Reserve Bank who will present the check to the Payor Bank. Generally, the Depositary Bank sends the check to the Federal Reserve Bank in its own region. The check will then be forwarded to the Federal Reserve Bank in the Payor's region, who will present the check to the Payor Bank for payment. There is also a streamlined process for banks that deal with a large number of checks. These banks can simply send the check to the Federal Reserve Bank in the Payor Bank's region.

Regardless of who acts as an intermediary, the check collection process looks largely the same. For your reference, the basic process is diagramed below:[4]

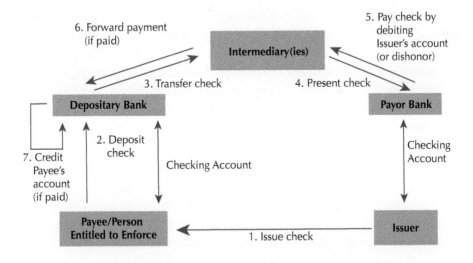

4   The black arrows depict the bank customer relationship. The numbered blue arrows depict the transaction flow.

I. The Rights and Responsibilities of Collecting Banks and the Payor Bank

In the check collection process described above, Collecting Banks and Payor Banks both play a central role in the process by which a customer obtains payment. We now turn to the respective rights and responsibilities of each.

1. Collecting Banks

a. The Duty to Exercise Due Care

READING THE CODE

> ### Maryland Commercial Law Code Section 4–201
>
> **(a)** Unless a contrary intent clearly appears and before the time that a settlement given by a collecting bank for an item is or becomes final, the bank, with respect to the item, is an agent or subagent of the owner of the item and any settlement given for the item is provisional . . .

Each Collecting Bank is an agent of the customer with respect to a deposited check. *See* section 4–201. Article 4's use of the term Collecting Bank is significant. It encompasses any bank that is involved in collecting on the check. This includes the Depositary Bank along with any Intermediary Banks and the Presenting Bank. All of them become agents of the customer in the collection process. As an agent, the Collecting Banks must exercise ordinary care throughout the collection process. *See* section 4–202(a).

READING THE CODE

> ### Maryland Commercial Law Code Section 4–202
>
> **(a)** A collecting bank must exercise ordinary care in:
>
> **(1)** Presenting an item or sending it for presentment;
>
> **(2)** Sending notice of dishonor or nonpayment or returning an item other than a documentary draft to the bank's transferor after learning that the item has not been paid or accepted, as the case may be;

(3) Settling for an item when the bank receives final settlement; and

(4) Notifying its transferor of any loss or delay in transit within a reasonable time after discovery thereof.

(b) A collecting bank exercises ordinary care under subsection (a) by taking proper action before its midnight deadline following receipt of an item, notice, or settlement. Taking proper action within a reasonably longer time may constitute the exercise of ordinary care, but the bank has the burden of establishing timeliness.

(c) Subject to subsection (a)(1), a bank is not liable for the insolvency, neglect, misconduct, mistake, or default of another bank or person or for loss or destruction of an item in the possession of others or in transit.

Section 4–402(a)(1) extends the duty to exercise ordinary care to presentment or sending checks for presentment. If the Collecting Bank is presenting the check, it must exercise ordinary care in the timing and manner of presentment. *See* section 4–202(a), comment 2. If the Collecting Bank is forwarding the check for presentment and collection, it must exercise ordinary care in selecting Intermediary Banks or agents.

The duty to exercise ordinary care does not end there. The standard applies regardless of the role of the Collecting Bank. This includes sending notice of dishonor or nonpayment, returning a check, settling for a check, and providing timely notice of any loss or delay in transit.

Collecting Banks, however, are only liable for their own failure to exercise ordinary care. *See* section 4–202(c). So if a Depositary Bank exercises ordinary care in selecting an Intermediary Bank, the Depositary Bank is not liable for misconduct, negligence, or mistake of the Intermediary Bank. However, the Intermediary Bank would be liable for its own actions.

b. Provisional Settlement and the Right to Chargeback

When a check is deposited, the Depositary Bank will typically issue a provisional credit to the customer's account for a check. This reflects an assumption that the check will be paid. Since the credit is provisional, the Depositary Bank may revoke the credit if the check is not paid. The Depositary Bank can then chargeback the customer's account or seek a refund from the customer. Sections 4–201(a) and 4–214(a) govern this process.

Section 4–201(a) creates a presumption that any settlement given by a Collecting Bank is provisional before the receipt of a final payment from the Payor Bank. Under section 4–214(a), Collecting Banks have the right to revoke their provisional settlement for any check if there is no final payment—for example, if the Payor Bank dishonors the check for insufficient funds or the check is subject to a stop-payment order.

After revoking a provisional settlement, the Collecting Bank has the right to a chargeback or refund. A chargeback is basically a reversal of the provisional credit. The Collecting Bank credited the customer's account for the check upon deposit so it simply debits the amount of the check. If the Collecting Bank has allowed the customer to draw on funds that have not been collected, the Collecting Bank has a claim for refund against the customer.

The requirements for obtaining a chargeback or refund are buried in section 4–214(a). The Collecting Bank can either return the check or send a notification of the facts. This must be done by the Collecting Bank's midnight deadline [midnight on the next banking day after receiving the check or notice (section 4–104(d)(2)] or within a longer reasonable time after learning the facts giving rise to the right of chargeback or refund.

Finally, there is one important difference between the right to chargeback and the right to refund. The Collecting Bank has the right to chargeback even if the Collecting Bank's failure to exercise ordinary care caused the nonpayment. *See* section 4–214(d)(2). The right to chargeback applies irrespective of the reason for nonpayment. But the Collecting Bank remains liable for any damages arising from its failure to exercise ordinary care.

2. The Payor Bank

a. Duty to Pay or Settle

When a check finally reaches the Payor Bank, there is a duty to act by the end of the day. The Payor Bank generally has three options. The Payor Bank can: (1) pay the check; (2) return the check unpaid or send a notice of nonpayment; or (3) settle. The Payor Bank becomes liable for the check if it fails to take one of these actions before midnight of the day that the check is received. *See* section 4–302(a).

By choosing to settle, the Payor Bank can buy a little more time to make a decision. As long as the settlement is provisional (most are), the Payor Bank can still revoke under section 4–301(a). Alternatively, the provisional settlement can become a final payment (discussed below).

Section 4–301(a) imposes two separate timing requirements on the Payor Bank's right to revoke. Settlement must occur by midnight on the day the check was received. In addition, revocation of settlement must occur by midnight of the day after the check was received. So if the Payor Bank receives a check on Thursday, it must settle by midnight that same day. By doing so, the Payor Bank has the right to revoke at any time before midnight on Friday.

If the timing requirements are met, the act of revocation itself is relatively simple. The Payor Bank revokes by returning the check (or an image of the check if agreed upon) to the Presenting Bank unpaid. If the check is not available, the Payor Bank can send the Presenting Bank a notice of dishonor or nonpayment.

b. Final Payment

READING THE CODE

Maryland Commercial Law Code Section 4–215

(a) An item is finally paid by a payor bank when the bank has done any of the following:

(1) Paid the item in cash;

(2) Settled for the item without having a right to revoke the settlement under statute, clearing-house rule, or agreement; or

(3) Made a provisional settlement for the item and failed to revoke the settlement in the time and manner permitted by statute, clearing-house rule, or agreement.

(b) If provisional settlement for an item does not become final, the item is not finally paid.

(c) If provisional settlement for an item between the presenting and payor banks is made through a clearing house or by debits or credits in an account between them, then to the extent that provisional debits or credits for the item are entered in accounts between the presenting and payor banks or between the presenting and successive prior collecting banks seriatim, they become final upon final payment of the item by the payor bank.

(d) If a collecting bank receives a settlement for an item which is or becomes final, the bank is accountable to its customer for the amount of the item and any provisional credit given for the item in an account with its customer becomes final.

(e) Subject to (i) applicable law stating a time for availability of funds and (ii) any right of the bank to apply the credit to an obligation of the customer, credit given by a bank for an item in a customer's account becomes available for withdrawal as of right:

(1) If the bank has received a provisional settlement for the item,—when the settlement becomes final and the bank has had a reasonable time to receive return of the item and the item has not been received within that time;

(2) If the bank is both the depositary bank and the payor bank, and the item is finally paid,—at the opening of the bank's second banking day following receipt of the item.

(f) Subject to applicable law stating a time for availability of funds and any right of a bank to apply a deposit to an obligation of the depositor, a deposit of money becomes available for withdrawal as of right at the opening of the bank's next banking day after receipt of the deposit.

Final Payment is a defining moment in the lifecycle of a check. It is the point in time where the Payor Bank completes payment and no longer has the right to revoke. Final Payment is important for a number of reasons, but mostly because it starts the flow of funds back from the Payor Bank through the Collecting Banks to the customer. Provisional settlements between the Collecting Banks and the Payor Bank become final. *See* section 4–215(c). Provisional credits to the customer's account also become final. *See* section 4–215(d). The Depositary Bank must make the funds available to the customer and the customer now has a legal right to them. *See* section 4–215(e).

The Payor Bank makes a final payment by doing one of three things. First, the Payor Bank makes a final payment if it pays the check in cash. Second, the Payor Bank makes a final payment if it settles a check without having a right to revoke. Third, the Payor Bank makes a final payment if it fails to revoke a provisional settlement by the midnight deadline in section 4–301(a) or any other agreed-upon deadline.

Test Your Knowledge

To assess your understanding of the material in this chapter, <u>click here</u> to take a quiz.

28

Risk of Alteration and Forgery in the Checking System

Key Concepts

- The role of presentment warranties and transfer warranties as the primary means of shifting losses among participants in the checking system
- Who gives and receives the presentment warranties in Article 3 (and Article 4)
- Who gives and receives the transfer warranties in Article 3 (and Article 4)
- The law applicable to conversion of personal property applies to negotiable instruments
- The effect of negligence on the allocation of losses in the checking system

A. Losses in the Checking System

The checking system works remarkably well in the vast majority of cases. A person authorized to draw on the checking account writes a check. The check is issued to the payee. The check may be negotiated to one or more holders with appropriate indorsements until someone wishes to collect. The check then makes its way through the various banks that facilitate the collection process. Ultimately, the payor bank debits the appropriate amount of money from the bank account and pays the person that is entitled to it.

The checking system, however, is not immune from suffering losses. The system's dependency on paper checks and signatures leaves it susceptible to bad actors who seek to take or use funds from the drawer's bank account. Unfortunately, check fraud occurs with regularity and results in significant losses. Check fraud can take many different forms, but typically falls into one of the following categories:

1. **Forged Checks.** A bad actor could forge the drawer's signature in connection with creating a check that appears to be legitimately written. The simplest scenario involves the theft of blank checks drawn on the drawer's account. With blank checks in hand, it is simply a matter of writing the checks and forging the drawer's signature. A more sophisticated method of forgery is counterfeiting. Instead of obtaining actual checks, the bad actor creates and prints duplicate checks drawn on the drawer's account. The bad actor can then write counterfeit checks by forging the drawer's signature.

   Forged checks allow the bad actor to misappropriate funds in different ways. If a forged check is made payable to the bad actor, they can attempt to collect from the Payor Bank or sell the forged check to an unsuspecting person. Of course, the bad actor could also use the forged checks to purchase goods or services.

2. **Altered Checks.** A bad actor could also start with a check that the drawer actually wrote. A check that is legitimately issued by the drawer could be altered to increase the amount that is payable or to make it payable to another person. Because the drawer actually wrote the check, there is no need to forge the drawer's signature. The bad actor simply changes the amount of the check or the name of the payee.

   Check alteration can arise in a variety of different circumstances. For example, the payee could alter the check to increase the amount that is payable and attempt to collect. Alternatively, a thief might steal a check and alter the check to make it payable to another person—for example, to the thief or the seller of a good or service. The thief could then collect on the check, sell the check or use the check to obtain a valuable good or service.

3. **Forged Indorsements.** Like an altered check, a forged indorsement begins with a check that the drawer actually wrote. Instead of changing the amount of the check or the name of the payee, the bad actor forges the payee's signature. As you know, the payee's signature (if real) acts as a blank indorsement, which makes the check payable to bearer. It now appears that the bad actor is entitled to enforce the check because they have possession of what is seemingly a check that is payable to whoever holds it. The bad actor can then attempt to collect payment or sell the check to an unsuspecting purchaser.

The question then is who—of all the parties that have touched a check from issuance to presentment—bears the risk of loss for forged or altered checks?

You may recall that we previously explored the issue of who is liable to pay on an instrument in Chapter 23. Since a check is a type of instrument, what you learned remains applicable in the context of liability in the checking context. In Chapter 23, we saw that a person must sign an instrument to incur liability—for example, liability as a drawer under section 3–414 or liability as an indorser under section 3–415. Because a signature is a threshold requirement for liability, a person who has had their signature forged on a check is not liable. This is true for both a forged drawer signature and a forged indorsement. In both cases, the victim of forgery has not signed the check.

Let's turn now to the bad actor who forges a signature or alters a check. As you might expect, this person is liable. Section 3–403(a) provides that an "unauthorized signature is ineffective except as the signature of the unauthorized signer in favor of a person who in good faith pays or takes it for value." Thus, a forged signature is generally ineffective because it is an unauthorized signature. However, the forged signature is effective as the signature of the unauthorized signer. Section 3–403(a), therefore, makes the person who forges a signature liable as if they had signed their own name on the check. In addition, the bad actor will be subject to criminal penalties, and may also be liable for conversion of the check under section 3–420.[1] But even if the bad actor is caught, there is no guarantee that they will have the financial capability to pay restitution. As a result, some other party will typically suffer the loss.

The process for determining who will ultimately bear that loss starts with either the Payor Bank or the party presenting the check for payment. If the Payor Bank pays the forged or altered check, it will not be able to charge the drawer's account for the loss. The check was not properly payable. *See* section 4–401(a). If the Payor Bank instead dishonors the forged or altered check, the party presenting the check for payment will be left with an uncollectible check.

Whether the Payor Bank or the presenting party is stuck with the loss depends on their ability to shift the loss back to other participants in the process. In general, the UCC seeks to allocate responsibility to the party that is in the best position to prevent the loss from occurring—the earliest to take the forged/altered check. The UCC accomplishes this via a set of implied warranties called transfer warran-

---

1   Section 3–420(a) makes it clear the law applicable to conversion of personal property applies to instruments. Conversion generally occurs when the rightful owner is wrongfully deprived of property or its value. By taking a check, the thief is wrongfully depriving the person entitled to enforce the check of its value. This is no different than conversion of any other type of personal property—like stealing a car, purse or watch. Under section 3–420(b), the person converting a check is generally liable for the amount payable on the instrument.

ties and presentment warranties. These warranties are given each time a check is transferred to another party, or presented for payment or acceptance. Generally speaking, a loss may be shifted back to a predecessor in the process if any of the things they warrant to be true about the check turn out to be false.

B. Presentment Warranties

READING THE CODE

> ### Maryland Commercial Law Code Section 3–417
>
> **(a)** If an unaccepted draft is presented to the drawee for payment or acceptance and the drawee pays or accepts the draft, (i) the person obtaining payment or acceptance, at the time of presentment, and (ii) a previous transferor of the draft, at the time of transfer, warrant to the drawee making payment or accepting the draft in good faith that:
>
> **(1)** The warrantor is, or was, at the time the warrantor transferred the draft, a person entitled to enforce the draft or authorized to obtain payment or acceptance of the draft on behalf of a person entitled to enforce the draft;
>
> **(2)** The draft has not been altered; and
>
> **(3)** The warrantor has no knowledge that the signature of the drawer of the draft is unauthorized.
>
> **(b)** A drawee making payment may recover from any warrantor damages for breach of warranty equal to the amount paid by the drawee less the amount the drawee received or is entitled to receive from the drawer because of the payment. In addition, the drawee is entitled to compensation for expenses and loss of interest resulting from the breach. The right of the drawee to recover damages under this subsection is not affected by any failure of the drawee to exercise ordinary care in making payment. If the drawee accepts the draft, breach of warranty is a defense to the obligation of the acceptor. If the acceptor makes payment with respect to the draft, the acceptor is entitled to recover from any warrantor for breach of warranty the amounts stated in this subsection.

The presentment warranties are located in sections 3–417 and 4–208 of the UCC. The two sections are essentially mirror images of one another. However, section 3–417 applies to all negotiable instruments. In contrast, section 4–208 applies after a negotiable instrument or other item is deposited with a bank for collection. For our purposes, it suffices to treat the two sections as substantively identical.[2] For your reference, an excerpt from section 3–417 appears above.

1. Which Parties Give and Receive Presentment Warranties

Before turning to the substance of the warranties, it is important to identify who gives presentment warranties and to whom the warranties run. As you might expect, the person presenting a check and obtaining payment gives the presentment warranties. *See* section 4–208(a). But, each person that previously transferred the check also gives the presentment warranties. *Id.* Take a second to think about what that means. Why aren't presentment warranties limited only to the person who actually presents the check for payment? Is it appropriate for prior transferors to give presentment warranties as well?

EXAMPLES AND EXPLANATIONS

Consider the following example (diagramed below). David issues a check (drawn on his account at Second Bank) to Paula who is identified as the payee. Paula negotiates the check to Kevin with an indorsement. Kevin deposits the check in his account at First Bank. First Bank facilitates collection by presenting the check to Second Bank for payment.

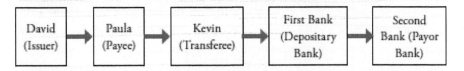

In this example First Bank, Kevin and Paula each give the presentment warranties. First Bank gives the presentment warranties as the party "obtaining payment or acceptance, at the time of presentment." *See* section

---

2   This approach is consistent with the Official Comments, which confirm that section 4–208 conforms to section 3–417 and is intended to extend section 3–417 to items other than negotiable instruments. *See* section 4–208, cmt. 1. Accordingly, the substance of section 4–208 is discussed in the Official Comments to section 3–417. *Id.*

> 4–208(a)(i). Kevin and Paula give the presentment warranties as "previous transferors" of the check. *See* sections 3–417(a)(ii); 4–208(a)(ii). David does not give the presentment warranties because the issuance of a check does not qualify as a transfer.

The next question is who receives the benefit of the presentment warranties. Presentment warranties only run to the Payor Bank (or drawee) that pays the check. *See* section 4–208(a). Note that the Payor Bank must actually pay the check. Presentment warranties do not arise if the Payor Bank dishonors the check. This should come as no surprise. The Payor Bank will only suffer a loss if it pays a forged or altered check. In these cases, the Payor Bank can attempt to recover from the presenting party or any prior transferor of the check if one of the presentment warranties proves to be false. As such, the Payor Bank may have multiple parties to pursue. Returning to the example above, Second Bank (as the Payor Bank) may be able to recover from First Bank, Kevin or Paula.

If the Payor Bank recovers for breach of a presentment warranty, it will have been successful in shifting the loss back to one of the predecessors in the process. Because presentment warranties only run to the Payor Bank, the predecessor that the Bank recovers from cannot recover from another party on that basis. Whether the loss can be shifted again (to another participant in the process) depends on the existence of some alternative basis for recovery.

To see how this plays out, let's return to the example above. Assume that Second Bank recovers from First Bank for breach of a presentment warranty. Kevin and Paula's presentment warranties run to the Payor Bank (here Second Bank). The presentment warranties do not run to anyone else. As a result, First Bank does not receive any presentment warranties. To shift the loss back to Kevin or Paula, First Bank must have a valid claim based on something other than breach of presentment warranty—for example breach of transfer warranty (discussed below).

2. What Is Being Warranted?

Now to the fun part—the substance of the warranties. Under sections 3–417(a) and 4–208(a), the presenter and any prior transferor give three warranties, which correspond to the types of check fraud discussed above.[3] The presenting party gives

---

3   The UCC also includes a fourth presentment warranty, which we will not concern ourselves with in this book. For those students with inquiring minds, the presentment warranty applies to a very specific type of check fraud involving remotely-created consumer items. *See* section 3–417(a)(4), section 4–208(a)(4). The term is defined in

each of the warranties at the time of presenting the check for payment. Each prior transferor gives the warranties at the time of transferring the check.

- **Forged Checks.** Under sections 3–417(a)(3) and 4–208(a)(3), the presenter and prior transferors warrant that they have no knowledge that the drawer's signature is unauthorized. Note that the warrantor's knowledge qualifies this warranty. Unless the warrantor has actual knowledge of a forged or unauthorized drawer signature, the Code allocates the risk of loss to the Payor Bank. This result is justified because the Payor Bank has a customer-bank relationship with the drawer. This relationship arguably puts the Payor Bank in the best position to identify a forged or unauthorized drawer signature.

- **Altered Checks.** Under sections 3–417(a)(2) and 4–208(a)(2), the presenter and prior transferors warrant that the check has not been altered. Note that this warranty (unlike the previous one) is unqualified by knowledge. Accordingly, in most cases, the warrantor is allocated the risk of loss for any alteration to the check. However, sections 3–407(c) and 4–401(d) affect this basic allocation of loss. These provisions supplement the presentment warranty as follows.

  First, if the payor bank pays a fraudulently altered check in good faith and without notice of the alteration, the payor bank can enforce the check "according to its original terms." *See* section 3–407(c)(i), section 4–401(d)(1). This typically arises when someone alters a check to increase the amount payable. In these cases, the payor bank can still charge the drawer's account for the original amount of the altered check. To recover the difference, the payor bank may pursue a breach of the no-alteration presentment warranty against the presenter or any prior transferor of the check.

  Second, different rules govern the allocation of loss if the drawer signs a check but does not complete it. If the incomplete check is altered by unauthorized completion (i.e., filling in the blanks), the drawer should bear more responsibility for the loss. The UCC reflects this. If the payor bank pays this type of altered check in good faith and without notice of

---

section 3–103(a)(6), but a practical example is probably a more useful illustration. Remotely-created consumer items most commonly arise when a customer makes a purchase over the phone or the Internet and authorizes the seller to obtain payment by creating and submitting a draft drawn on the customer's checking account. In these instances, the draft is not created by the payor bank and does not include the handwritten signature of the customer/drawer. It is created remotely.

alteration, the payor bank can enforce the check "according to its terms as completed." The payor bank can charge the drawer's account for the full amount of the completed check. The payor bank can do so even if someone stole the check from the issuer and completed it after the theft. *See* section 3–407, comment 2.

- **Forged Indorsements**. Under sections 3–417(a)(1) and 4–208(a)(1), the presenter and prior transferors warrant that they are the person entitled to enforce the check or authorized to obtain payment on behalf of the person entitled to enforce the check. The Official Comments explain that this is a warranty that there are no unauthorized or missing indorsements on the check. Note that this warranty is unqualified by knowledge. The Code effectively allocates the risk of loss for any forged or missing indorsements on the check to the warrantor. This result is justified because the party that first accepts a check with a missing or forged indorsement is in the best position to identify the problem and prevent the loss.

APPLYING THE CODE

Problem 28-1: Risk of Loss for Forged Checks

David has a checking account at First Bank. Two weeks ago David was working at a local coffee shop. Kevin, a petty thief, happened to be at the coffee shop looking for unsuspecting victims. While David stepped away from his belongings to purchase a latte, Kevin rifled through David's briefcase. Finding David's checkbook Kevin snatched a single blank check from the back. Kevin took off before David returned.

A) Assume that Kevin uses the stolen check to write a check out to himself in the amount of $1,000, signing David's name in the bottom right hand corner. Kevin then indorses the check by signing his own name on the back. Kevin takes the check directly to First Bank and presents it for payment. First Bank inspects the check. After determining that nothing is out of order, First Bank pays Kevin $1,000 in cash. A few days later, David is reviewing his checking transactions online when he finds that $1,000 was paid by First Bank for a check that he did not sign or authorize. If Kevin has skipped town and is nowhere to be found, who bears the $1,000 loss?

B) Instead of presenting the check directly to First Bank, Kevin deposits the $1,000 check in his own checking account at Second Bank. Second Bank does not have an existing check-collection relationship with First Bank, so it transfers the check to Third Bank. Third Bank presents the check to First Bank for payment. First Bank charges David's account and $1,000 is eventually deposited in Kevin's account at Second Bank. Kevin immediately withdraws the money and skips town. Assume that each bank processed the check through its electronic systems and no red flags were raised. Does First Bank have a valid claim for breach of presentment warranty? If so, which warranty(ies) and against which party(ies)?

C) Kevin is scared of being caught, so he does not present the check directly or deposit it into his account at Second Bank. After writing the check out to himself for $1,000, Kevin offers to sell it to his shady friend Wayne. Kevin says that he will take $100 for it because he needs to get out of town before the cops come for him. Kevin assures Wayne that he should have no problem depositing the stolen check and reminds Wayne that he will make $900 on the deal. Wayne agrees and Kevin indorses the check by signing his name on the back. Wayne then indorses the check by signing his own name before depositing the check in his account at First Bank. First Bank ultimately charges David's account and credits Wayne's account for $1,000. Does First Bank have a valid claim for breach of presentment warranty? If so, which warranty(ies) and against which party(ies)?

Problem 28-2: Risk of Loss for Forged Indorsements

Paula has a checking account with First Bank. Paula writes a rent check for $800 dollars that is payable to her landlord David. David gives the check to Wayne to satisfy an existing debt. Before handing the check over, David writes, "Pay to the order of Wayne" and signs his name. Wayne is on his way to deposit the check when he drops it on the sidewalk. Kevin (who is not a Good Samaritan) picks the check up off the ground. Kevin signs Wayne's name on the back of the check. Kevin deposits the check into his account at Second Bank. Second Bank sends the check to Third Bank, who presents the check to First Bank for payment. First Bank charges Paula's account for $800. After the $800 makes its way to Kevin's account at Second Bank, Kevin immediately withdraws it and disappears into the night. Does First Bank have a valid claim for breach of presentment warranty? If so, which warranty(ies) and against which party(ies)?

Problem 28-3: Risk of Loss and Alteration of Complete Checks

Paula writes David another rent check for $800 drawn on her account at First Bank. When David receives the check, he is in need of cash to make some unexpected repairs to the plumbing at the apartment building. David adds the numeral 1 and the words "one thousand" to make the amount of the check $1,800. David indorses the check and deposits it in his account at Third Bank. Third Bank presents the check to First Bank who pays it and deducts $1,800 from Paula's account. When Paula gets her bank statement, she immediately contacts First Bank to demand that it credit her account for the amount of the altered check. Can First Bank charge Paula's account for any of the $1,800? Can First Bank recover from Third Bank for breach of presentment warranty?

Problem 28-4: Risk of Loss and Alteration of Incomplete Check

Paula has contracted with Kevin to clean her house once a week. A few days ago, Kevin arrived to clean Paula's house while she was in the process of writing a check to pay her electrical bill. Paula had only dated and signed the check. Paula left the check on her desk when she went to let Kevin in. While Kevin was dusting in Paula's office, he spotted the check. Kevin (usually a nice guy) was in desperate need of cash to pay his rent. Kevin took the check as he left Paula's house. Kevin filled in the check with his own name as the payee and $1,000 as the amount payable. Kevin took the check to a gas station that cashed it for a small fee. At the end of the day, the gas station deposited the check at First Bank, who presented the check to Second Bank (Paula's bank) for payment. Before Paula noticed that the check was missing, Second Bank had debited her account and Kevin had spent the cash. If Paula calls Second Bank to complain, will she be successful in obtaining a credit of $1,000 to her account?

3. The Measure of Damages for Breach of Presentment Warranty

If a presentment warranty is breached, the Payor Bank can recover the damages caused by the breach from the warranting party. The basic measure of damages is the amount paid by the Payor Bank less any amount that the Payor Bank receives (or is entitled to receive) from the drawer of the check. The Payor Bank can also recover for any expenses (which may include attorney's fees) and loss of interest.

C. Transfer Warranties

READING THE CODE

> **Maryland Commercial Law Code Section 3–416**
>
> **(a)** A person who transfers an instrument for consideration warrants to the transferee and, if the transfer is by indorsement, to any subsequent transferee that:
>
> **(1)** The warrantor is a person entitled to enforce the instrument;
>
> **(2)** All signatures on the instrument are authentic and authorized;
>
> **(3)** The instrument has not been altered;
>
> **(4)** The instrument is not subject to a defense or claim in recoupment of any party which can be asserted against the warrantor; and
>
> **(5)** The warrantor has no knowledge of any insolvency proceeding commenced with respect to the maker or acceptor or, in the case of an unaccepted draft, the drawer.
>
> **(b)** A person to whom the warranties under subsection (a) are made and who took the instrument in good faith may recover from the warrantor as damages for breach of warranty an amount equal to the loss suffered as a result of the breach, but not more than the amount of the instrument plus expenses and loss of interest incurred as a result of the breach.

Like the UCC's provisions on presentment warranties, the transfer warranties are found in both Article 3 (section 3–416) and Article 4 (section 4–207). Once again, the two sections are essentially mirror images of one another. The primary distinction is that section 3–416 provides transfer warranties applicable to negotiable instruments generally, while section 4–207 extends those warranties to transfers specifically in the check-collection process. As a result, we will again treat the two provisions as substantively identical. For your reference, an excerpt of section 3–416 appears above.

1. Which Parties Give and Receive Transfer Warranties

Each person who transfers a check for consideration gives transfer warranties. See section 3–416(a). During the check-collection process, the customer and any collecting bank[4] also give transfer warranties. *See* section 4–207(a).

Unlike the presentment warranties, which only run to one party (the payor bank), many parties may receive transfer warranties. As you might expect, transfer warranties run directly from the warrantor to the immediate transferee of the check. *See* section 3–416(a), section 4–207(a). But transfer warranties also run to: (1) each subsequent transferee but only if the check is transferred by indorsement, and (2) any subsequent collecting bank. *Id.*

EXAMPLES AND EXPLANATIONS

Consider the following example (diagramed below). David issues a check (drawn on his account at Third Bank) to Paula (the identified payee). Paula negotiates the check to Kevin with an indorsement. Kevin deposits the check in his account at First Bank. First Bank sends the check to Second Bank, who presents the check to Third Bank for payment. Assume that Paula negotiates the check to Kevin for consideration.

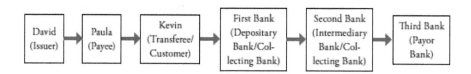

In this example, David does not give any transfer warranties because issuing the check does not qualify as a transfer. Paula gives the transfer warranties to Kevin (as the direct transferee of the check). *See* section 3–416(a). Since Paula indorsed the check to Kevin, Paula's transfer warranties also

---

4   Recall that a collecting bank is defined as any bank that handles a check for collection other than the payor bank. See section 4–105(5).

> run to First Bank and Second Bank as subsequent transferees. *Id.* If Paula
> had not indorsed the check, her transfer warranties would not run to any
> subsequent transferees. *Id.* Kevin (as a customer) gives transfer warranties
> to First Bank (as the direct transferee of the check) and Second Bank (as a
> subsequent collecting bank). *See* section 4–207(a). First Bank (as a collect-
> ing bank) gives the transfer warranties to Second Bank (as the direct trans-
> feree of the check). *Id.* Second Bank does not give any transfer warranties
> because presenting the check does not qualify as a transfer. In addition,
> Third Bank does not qualify as a subsequent collecting bank because payor
> banks are excluded from that definition.

You should now see how transfer warranties work in tandem with presentment warranties to allocate checking losses. As discussed above, if the payor bank honors a forged or altered check, it may be able to shift the loss to a party that breached a presentment warranty. The party that pays damages to the payor bank now bears the loss unless they can shift the loss to an earlier party that breached a transfer warranty, who will in turn attempt to shift the loss to yet another earlier party who breached a transfer warranty. If all the parties are financially capable of paying, the loss should ultimately land with the earliest party who breaches a transfer warranty.

In the example above, assume that Third Bank pays a forged or altered check and recovers from Second Bank for breach of presentment warranty. Second Bank will now suffer a loss unless it can recover from a prior party for breach of a transfer warranty. First Bank, Kevin and Paula each give transfer warranties to Second Bank. Therefore, Second Bank can seek to recover from any of them. Assume that Second Bank is successful in recovering from First Bank for breach of transfer warranty. First Bank will now attempt to recover from Kevin or Paula for breach of the same transfer warranty. If First Bank recovers from Kevin, he will sue Paula for breach of the same transfer warranty. If solvent, Paula (as the earliest party in the chain to give the transfer warranties) will bear the loss.

The same process of shifting the loss back based on breach of transfer warranties takes place even if the payor bank dishonors the forged or altered check. In these instances, the presenting party will be left with an uncollectible check. The presenting party will then start the process of shifting losses back by seeking to recover from any earlier party for breach of a transfer warranty. Once again, the loss will continue to shift back until it lands with the earliest solvent party who breached a transfer warranty.

2. What Is Being Warranted?

The transfer warranties in sections 3–416(a) and 4–207(a) include three warranties that are comparable to each of the presentment warranties discussed above.[5] Each of these transfer warranties (like the presentment warranties) may provide a basis for shifting losses incurred from the different types of check fraud discussed above.

- **Forged Checks.** Each party that gives transfer warranties warrants that all signatures on the check are authentic *and* authorized. *See* section 3–416(a)(2); section 4–207(a)(2). Because the transfer warranty covers all signatures, it is broader than the comparable presentment warranty (which only covers the drawer's signature). Note that the warrantor's knowledge does not qualify this transfer warranty (unlike the corresponding presentment warranty). As a result, the UCC allocates the risk of the loss to the earliest party to make the transfer warranty. This result is justified because the first party to take the forged check is in the best position to identify the forgery and prevent the loss.

- **Altered Checks.** Each party that gives transfer warranties warrants that the check has not been altered. *See* section 3–416(a)(3); section 4–207(a)(3). Like the comparable presentment warranty, the transfer warranty regarding alterations is unqualified. Accordingly, in most cases, the earliest warrantor is allocated the risk of loss for alteration.

  But like the comparable presentment warranty, this basic allocation of loss is also supplemented by sections 3–407(c) and 4–401(d) (examined above), which allow for some or all of the loss to be shifted to the drawer of the check.

  If the payor bank is able to enforce the check according to its original terms, the payor bank's claim for breach of presentment warranty will be for the difference between the original amount of the check (which is charged to the drawer) and the altered amount. In turn, any claim for breach of transfer warranty will be for the difference (not the full amount of the altered check).

  If the payor bank is able to enforce the check according to its terms as completed, the drawer will be charged with the full amount of the altered

---

5   The UCC also includes a transfer warranty that corresponds with the presentment warranty relating to remotely-created consumer items. *See* sections 3–416(a) and 4–207(a)(6).

check. Since the payor bank will not suffer a loss, there is no need to shift the loss back to a prior party via presentment warranties and transfer warranties.

- **Forged Indorsements.** Each party that gives transfer warranties warrants that they are a person entitled to enforce the check. *See* section 3–416(a)(1); section 4–207(a)(1). Like the comparable presentment warranty, this transfer warranty is effectively a warranty that there are no unauthorized or missing indorsements. *See* section 3–416, cmt. 2. In addition, the transfer warranty that all signatures on the check are authentic and authorized also covers forged indorsements. *See* section 3–416(a)(2); section 4–207(a)(2). Because these warranties are unqualified, the risk of loss from forged indorsements is allocated to the earliest party giving the transfer warranties. Again, this result is justified on the basis that this party has the best opportunity to identify the forged indorsement and prevent the loss.

The transfer warranties, however, go beyond check fraud, forgery and alteration. Those that give transfer warranties under the UCC also warrant that: (1) the check is not subject to a defense or claim in recoupment of any party that can be asserted against the warrantor; and (2) the warrantor has no knowledge of any insolvency proceeding against the drawer of the check. *See* sections 3–416(a)(1), (4) and (5).

The purpose of the additional transfer warranties is relatively straightforward. The first gives transferees the option of proceeding against the transferor of the check if the check is unenforceable, in whole or in part because the person obligated to pay the check has a defense or claim of offset against the warrantor. Even if the transferee qualifies as a holder in due course (that takes free from defenses and claims in recoupment), the transferee may want to recover from the transferor for breach of warranty instead of litigating holder in due course status against the person who wrote the check. The second is not a warranty against difficulties in collection or even insolvency. Instead, it is a limited warranty that the warrantor does not know of any insolvency proceedings instituted against the person obligated to pay the check.

APPLYING THE CODE

Problem 28-5: Who Gives and Receives Transfer Warranties?

Kevin writes a check for $100 that is payable to David. The check is drawn on Kevin's account at National Bank. David gifts the check to Paula writing "pay to Paula" on the back and signing his name below. Paula goes to Wayne's corner store and asks him to cash the check. After checking Paula's driver's license, Wayne agrees to take the check for $50 cash and a bottle of wine. Paula signs her name on the back of the check before leaving. Wayne deposits the check in his account at First Bank. In turn, First Bank sends the check to Second Bank, which presents the check to National Bank. For each participant in the process, determine whether that person gives transfer warranties. If you determine that any participant gives transfer warranties, identify who receives the benefit of those warranties.

Problem 28-6: Forged Indorsements

A few days before the end of the month, Wayne wrote a rent check in the amount of $800 drawn on his account at National Bank. After completing the check, Wayne mailed it to his landlord David. Two weeks later, David called to inform Wayne that his rent was past due. David swears that he never received the check. Wayne called National Bank to find out what was going on. Wayne learned that the check was cashed at Fast Fuel, a gas station. Fast Fuel deposited the check in its account with First Bank. The check was then forwarded to Second Bank, which presented the check for payment. National Bank paid the check and debited Wayne's account. It turns out that the check was intercepted by Kevin, who brought the check to Fast Fuel and indorsed it with the name "David."

A) Can Wayne require National Bank to credit his account with $800? Why or why not?

B) If National Bank does credit Wayne's account, can the bank recover for breach of presentment warranty? For breach of transfer warranty?

C) Assuming that all parties are solvent, who will ultimately bear the loss if Kevin is judgment proof?

Problem 28-7: Forged Checks

Paula is the chief financial officer of TechSense, a large corporation. As the chief financial officer, Paula is authorized to sign checks on behalf of the corporation. When TechSense first started, Paula would sign checks by hand. Things have changed. TechSense has grown significantly since that time. TechSense now issues thousands of payroll checks to its employees each month. In addition, TechSense pays most of its vendors and suppliers by check as well. Given the sheer numbers, TechSense now prints Paula's signature on its checks.

Kevin recently completed some consulting work for TechSense. TechSense paid Kevin for his work with a $1,000 check drawn on TechSense's account at National Bank. Kevin's childhood friend, Wayne, was visiting for a few days. Wayne saw the check on Kevin's kitchen table. Using sophisticated software and printing techniques, Wayne created a replica of the check (including Paula's digital signature) with Wayne's name printed on the payee line. Wayne indorses the check and cashes it at The Corner Store, a nearby grocery. The Corner Store deposited the check in its account at First Bank. The check was then sent to Second Bank, which presented the check to National Bank. If each party enforces its rights to the fullest, who will bear the loss if National Bank dishonors the check? Assume that Wayne is nowhere to be found. Does your answer change if National Bank honors the check?

---

3. The Measure of Damages for Breach of Transfer Warranty

If a transfer warranty is breached, the recipient of the warranty can recover damages from the warrantor so long as he or she took the check in good faith. The basic measure of damages for breach of transfer warranty is the amount of the loss suffered as a result of the breach. Damages, however, are capped at the amount of the check plus expenses (including attorney's fees) and loss of interest resulting from the breach. *See* section 3–416(b), section 3–207(c).

D. Conversion

Common law conversion is the final piece of Article 3's basic system for allocating the risk of checking losses. You likely encountered conversion in your study of

Property or Torts. If so, you will recall that conversion occurs when a person acts in a way that is inconsistent with another's property rights. Commonly, this happens when a person intentionally deprives another of the possession, use or value of their property. Conversion provides a civil cause of action for resulting damages.

The very first sentence of section 3–420(a) expressly states that, "the law applicable to conversion of personal property applies to [negotiable] instruments." Armed with only the rudimentary description of conversion found above, it should still be clear that: (1) a check is personal property and (2) theft, forgery or alteration of a check is often inconsistent with the property rights of another. This is particularly true if the bad actor deprives another of possession of the check or the value of the check by improperly obtaining payment. Thus, conversion provides an alternative means of shifting checking losses to another participant in the process. It supplements the shifting of losses via presentment warranties and transfer warranties.

You should now be asking yourself three questions. First, who among all of the parties in the check collection process can bring an action for conversion? Second, in the context of check collection, who is liable for conversion? Finally, what is the measure of liability for conversion of a negotiable instrument? Each of these questions is discussed in turn below.

1. Who Can Bring an Action for Conversion?

READING THE CODE

> ### Maryland Commercial Law Code Section 3–420
>
> **(a)** The law applicable to conversion of personal property applies to instruments. An instrument is also converted if it is taken by transfer, other than a negotiation, from a person not entitled to enforce the instrument or a bank makes or obtains payment with respect to the instrument for a person not entitled to enforce the instrument or receive payment. An action for conversion of an instrument may not be brought by (i) the issuer or acceptor of the instrument or (ii) a payee or indorsee who did not receive delivery of the instrument either directly or through delivery to an agent or a co-payee.

Section 3–420(a) does not expressly specify who *can* bring an action for conversion in the context of negotiable instruments and the check-collection process. Instead, section 3–420(a) tells us who *cannot* bring an action for conversion.

Neither issuers nor acceptors of a negotiable instrument can bring an action for conversion. *See* section 3–420(a)(i). In the context of check collection, this translates to the drawer (typically the customer that writes a check drawn on their account) and the drawee (the payor bank that accepts the check for payment). While both are participants in the check-collection process, neither qualifies as a person entitled to enforce the check.

The Official Comments explain in greater detail the rationale for not allowing the drawer of the check to bring an action for conversion. A check represents an obligation of the drawer to pay. The check is not the property of the drawer, so conversion is not an appropriate remedy. In addition, the drawer already has an adequate remedy against the payor bank. If the drawer's account is debited for a stolen, forged or altered check, the drawer will suffer a loss. But since the check was not properly payable, the payor bank must credit the drawer's account.

In addition, payees and indorsees cannot bring an action for conversion unless they have received delivery of the negotiable instrument. *See* section 3–420(a)(ii). In the context of check collection, this translates to the payee of a check (either the original payee or the indorsee to whom a check is subsequently made payable). Where the payee has never received possession of the check, the payee does not qualify as a person entitled to enforce. The Official Comments explain that there is no conversion action because the payee does not obtain an interest in the check until it is delivered—when the check comes into the possession of the payee either directly or through an agent or co-payee.

To illustrate, imagine that David writes a check to Wayne in the comfort of his home office. If a burglar steals the check during a break-in or a mail thief intercepts the check during transit, the check has never been delivered to Wayne. The check may be payable to Wayne but in both cases the wrongdoer has stolen David's property (not Wayne's). Once the check has been delivered—say to Wayne's mailbox—the result is different. Now the wrongdoer has stolen Wayne's property, which gives Wayne an action for conversion.

Although section 3–420(a) only spells out who cannot bring an action for conversion, the implication is relatively clear. Section 3–420(a) gives the person entitled to enforce the check at the time of conversion the right to bring an action.

2. Who Is Liable in an Action for Conversion?

The question of who is liable for conversion requires an understanding of what qualifies as conversion in the check-collection process. The most obvious culprit is the thief who takes a check and improperly obtains money that is payable to another person. By taking the check, the thief is subject to criminal prosecution. Because the first sentence of section 3–420(a) expressly applies the law of conversion to negotiable instruments, the thief is also liable in an action for conversion. The thief has converted the check by depriving the rightful owner of the value of the check. It is no different from a thief stealing some other form of personal property like a bicycle or comic book collection.

Admittedly, having an action for conversion against the thief is often of little use. The thief may be difficult or impossible to locate. Even if the thief is caught, the money may be gone and the thief may be judgment proof. The true impact of section 3–420(a) then is in the second sentence, which extends liability for conversion to others involved in the transfer and collection of checks. This is accomplished by identifying specific actions that constitute conversion in the checking context.

First, a check is converted if it is "taken by transfer, other than a negotiation, from a person not entitled to enforce the [check]." *See* section 3–420(a). The focus is on transferees of a check. As we have seen, a check may change hands several times before it is presented for payment. A transferee of the check is liable for conversion if the check is transferred (but not properly negotiated) to the transferee by a person who is not entitled to enforce it.

Second, a check is converted if "a bank makes or obtains payments with respect to the [check] for a person not entitled to enforce the [check] or receive payment." *See* section 3–420(a). This extends liability for conversion to banks in the check-collection process—specifically the payor bank and the depositary bank. A payor bank is liable for conversion if it pays a person who is not entitled to enforce the check. A depositary bank is liable for conversion if it obtains payment for a person that is not entitled to enforce the check. Section 3–420(c) generally excludes intermediary banks in the check-collection process because they merely act as representatives of the depositary bank in facilitating collection. The only exception is where the intermediary bank still retains the money and has not yet paid it out.

3. What Is the Measure of Liability of Conversion?

READING THE CODE

Maryland Commercial Law Code Section 3–420

(b) In an action under subsection (a), the measure of liability is presumed to be the amount payable on the instrument, but recov-

> ery may not exceed the amount of the plaintiff's interest in the instrument.

In a successful conversion action, the liability is presumed to be the amount of the check. *See* section 3–420(b). But if the person bringing the action only has a limited interest in the proceeds of the check, then the recovery will be limited accordingly. This arises most commonly in the context of co-payees. If one of the payees brings an action, they should not be able to obtain a windfall by recovering the entire amount of the check.

Conversion, therefore, provides the person entitled to enforce the check with a means of shifting the loss to another participant in the process. Do not make the mistake of believing that the loss will always be borne by the person who is held liable for converting a check. Conversion works with presentment warranties and transfer warranties in allocating checking losses. They are alternative means of shifting the loss. Thus, a person who is held liable for conversion may still shift the loss if he or she has a valid basis for doing so—for example, by pursuing a claim for breach of presentment warranty or transfer warranty. In the end, the loss is borne by the earliest person in the chain who does not have a basis for shifting the loss. This of course assumes that such person is actually capable of paying.

APPLYING THE CODE

Problem 28-8: Shifting Losses via Conversion

Kevin runs an organic produce stand at the weekend Farmer's Market. Paula, one of Kevin's loyal customers, purchased some beautiful heirloom tomatoes and paid with a check. The check was payable to Kevin in the amount of $15 and drawn on Paula's account at Third Bank. While Kevin was helping another customer, Wayne reached into Kevin's lock box and swiped the check. After forging Kevin's signature on the back of the check and signing his own name, Wayne deposited the check into his account at First Bank. First Bank sent the check to Second Bank who presented the check to Third Bank for payment. Third Bank paid the check and debited Paula's account.

A)   Under section 3–420, can Paula pursue a claim for conversion against any of the others who handled the check? If so, who?

B) Under section 3–420, can Kevin pursue a claim for conversion against any of the others who handled the check? If so, who?

C) Assume that Kevin is successful in bringing a conversion action against Third Bank. Is Third Bank stuck bearing the loss? Why or why not?

E. The Role of Negligence in Allocating Risk of Checking Losses

READING THE CODE

Maryland Commercial Law Code Section 3–406

(a) A person whose failure to exercise ordinary care substantially contributes to an alteration of an instrument or to the making of a forged signature on an instrument is precluded from asserting the alteration or the forgery against a person who, in good faith, pays the instrument or takes it for value or for collection.

(b) Under subsection (a), if the person asserting the preclusion fails to exercise ordinary care in paying or taking the instrument and that failure substantially contributes to loss, the loss is allocated between the person precluded and the person asserting the preclusion according to the extent to which the failure of each to exercise ordinary care contributed to the loss.

(c) Under subsection (a), the burden of proving failure to exercise ordinary care is on the person asserting the preclusion. Under subsection (b), the burden of proving failure to exercise ordinary care is on the person precluded.

To this point, our exploration of the UCC's system for allocating checking losses has not accounted for negligence by any of the participants. When shifting losses via presentment warranties, transfer warranties and conversion actions, we have assumed that the participants have each acted with ordinary care and complied with reasonable commercial standards. In doing so, we have seen that the loss generally lands on the person who is in the best position to prevent the loss from occurring.

How then does negligence affect the allocation of risk? Section 3–406(a) sets forth the basic rule. If a person fails to "exercise ordinary care" and that failure "substantially contributes" to the alteration of a check or a forged signature, then they will be precluded from asserting it against any person who in good faith: (1) pays the check; (2) takes the check for value; or (3) takes the check for collection. This protects the person who pays or takes an altered or forged check because they can defend by raising the other's negligence.

"Ordinary care" is defined in section 3–103(a)(9) as the "observance of reasonable commercial standards prevailing in the area in which the person is located, with respect to the business in which the person is engaged." However, the UCC does not define the type of conduct that will constitute a failure to exercise ordinary *care that substantially contributes to an alteration or forged signature.* This is a factual question for determination by the court or jury in light of all the circumstances. *See* section 3–406, comment 1.

Luckily, Official Comment 3 to section 3–406 discusses the kind of conduct that can be the basis of preclusion. For example, the factfinder might determine that the failure to safeguard check forms or a signature stamp precludes the drawer from demanding that the drawee credit their account for a loss. Other examples include mistakenly sending a check to the wrong payee or leaving a large blank space in front of the check amount. In both cases, the factfinder could determine that the act substantially contributed to a forged signature of alteration. If so, the drawee that pays the check could raise preclusion as a defense.

Section 3–406(a) deals with the easiest case—where one person fails to exercise ordinary care. But what happens if more than one person in the chain acts negligently? Section 3–406(b) essentially adopts the concept of comparative negligence to resolve the question. As such, the loss is allocated between the negligent parties "to the extent to which the failure of each to exercise ordinary care contributed to the loss." So if the drawer's negligence substantially contributes to an alteration or forgery, the drawee can assert preclusion as a defense if they pay the check. In turn, the drawer can raise any failure of the drawee to exercise ordinary care in processing or paying the check. If both are negligent, the loss is split between the two.

Although section 3–406 sets forth the general rules for negligence in allocating checking losses, it should be noted that other sections of the UCC contain special rules that deal with negligence in specific circumstances. You actually encountered one of these rules in Chapter 26. Recall section 4–406, which precludes customers from asserting an alteration or unauthorized signature against a payor bank if they should have discovered the unauthorized payment. Of course, the customer can assert that the payor bank's own negligence also contributed to the loss. Thus, section 4–406 reflects the same concept of comparative negligence.

Other special rules are found in sections 3–404 and 3–405. Section 3–404 deals with two unique situations where the drawer is tricked into giving the check to: (1) someone impersonating the intended payee, or (2) a payee that does not actually exist. Section 3–405 sets forth employers' responsibility for fraudulent indorsements by their employees. In both cases, the concept of negligence is the basis for allocating any resulting loss. We bring these special rules to your attention only to provide context. A more in-depth exploration of these provisions is beyond the scope of the core commercial law concepts covered in this book.

Test Your Knowledge

To assess your understanding of the material in this chapter, click here to take a quiz.

ALMOST THE LAST WORD TO STUDENTS

This course has been in part an advanced Contracts course and in part and advanced Property course. In learning new Uniform Commercial Code concepts, you encountered concepts from your first year Contracts course and concepts from your first year Property course. Most of which you had forgotten. Some of which you were certain that you had never learned.

This time next year, you will have forgotten most of the Uniform Commercial Code concepts that you have learned in this course. But just as your Contracts course and Property course made it easier to relearn Contracts and Property concepts and learn new Contracts and Property concepts, this course will make it easier to relearn Uniform Commercial Code concepts we have covered such as "risk of loss", the shelter principle" and "purchase money priority" and to learn the specific rules not covered in this survey course.

This page is entitled "Almost the Last Word" because, of course, your professor has the last word. Your professor might have some different idea from ours as to what is important, might even have some different ideas from ours as to what "the law" is.

Clearly, we are right. And, clearly that is not important to you. What is important to you is that your professor grades your examination. So your professor has the last word.

Subject Matter Index